Predictive Analytics and Data Mining

Predictive Analytics and Data Mining

Concepts and Practice with RapidMiner

Vijay Kotu

Bala Deshpande, PhD

Amsterdam • Boston • Heidelberg • London
New York • Oxford • Paris • San Diego
San Francisco • Singapore • Sydney • Tokyo
Morgan Kaufmann is an imprint of Elsevier

Executive Editor: Steven Elliot
Editorial Project Manager: Kaitlin Herbert
Project Manager: Punithavathy Govindaradjane
Designer: Greg Harris

Morgan Kaufmann is an imprint of Elsevier
225 Wyman Street, Waltham, MA 02451, USA

ISBN: 978-0-12-801460-8

British Library Cataloguing-in-Publication Data
A catalogue record for this book is available from the British Library.

Library of Congress Cataloging-in-Publication Data
A catalogue record for this book is available from the Library of Congress.

For information on all MK publications visit
our website at www.mkp.com.

Printed in the United States of America.
16 17 18 19 20   10 9 8 7 6 5 4 3 2

Working together
to grow libraries in
developing countries

www.elsevier.com • www.bookaid.org

Dedication

To the contributors to the Open Source Software movement

We dedicate this book to all those talented and generous developers around the world who continue to add enormous value to open source software tools, without whom this book would have never seen light of day.

Contents

Foreword

Everybody can be a data scientist. And everybody should be. This book shows you why everyone should be a data scientist and how you can get there. In today's world, it should be embarrassing to make any complex decision without understanding the available data first. Being a "data-driven organization" is the state of the art and often the best way to improve a business outcome significantly. Consequently we have seen a dramatic change with respect to the tools supporting us to get to this success quickly. It has only been a few years that building a data warehouse and creating reports or dashboards on top of the data warehouse has become the norm in larger organizations. Technological advances have made this process easier than ever and in fact, the existence of data discovery tools have allowed business users to build dashboards themselves without the need for an army of Information Technology consultants supporting them in this endeavor. But now, after we have managed to effectively answer questions based on our data from the past, a new paradigm shift is underway: Wouldn't it be better to answer what is going to happen instead? This is the realm of advanced analytics and data science: moving your interest from the past to the future and optimizing the outcomes of your business proactively.

Here are some examples of this paradigm shift:

- Traditional Business Intelligence (BI) system and program answers: *How many customers did we lose last year?* Although certainly interesting, the answer comes too late: the customers are already gone and there is not much we can do about it. Predictive analytics will show you *who will most likely churn within the next 10 days and what you can do best for each customer to keep them.*
- Traditional BI answers: *What campaign was the most successful in the past?* Although certainly interesting, the answer will only provide limited value to determine what is the best campaign for your upcoming product. Predictive analytics will show you *what will be the next best action to trigger a purchase action for each of your prospects individually.*

- Traditional BI answers: *How often did my production stand still in the past and why?* Although certainly interesting, the answer will not change the fact that profit was decreased due to suboptimal utilization. Predictive analytics will show you exactly *when and why a part of a machine will break and when you should replace the parts instead of backlogging production without control.*

Those are all high-value questions and knowing the answers has the potential to positively impact your business processes like nothing else. And the good news is that this is not science fiction; predicting the future based on data from the past and the inherent patterns living in the data is absolutely possible today. So why isn't every company in the world exploiting this potential all day long? The answer is the data science skills gap.

Performing advanced analytics (predictive analytics, data mining, text analytics, and the necessary data preparation) requires, well, advanced skills. In fact, a data scientist is seen as a superstar programmer with a PhD in statistics who just happens to understand every business problem in the world. Of course people with such a rare skill mix are very rare; in fact McKinsey has predicted a shortage of 1.8 million data scientists by the year 2018 only in the United States. This is a classical dilemma: we have identified the value of future-oriented questions and solving them with data science methods, but at the same time we can't find the answers to those questions since we don't have the people able to do so. *The only way out of this dilemma is a democratization of advanced analytics.* We need to empower more people to do create predictive models: business analysts, Excel power users, data-savvy business managers. We can't transform this group of people magically into data scientists, but we can give them the tools and show them how to use them *to act like a data scientist.* This book can guide you in this direction.

We are in a time of modern analytics with "big data" fueling the explosion for the need of answers. It is important to understand that big data is not just about volume but also about complexity. More data means new and more complex infrastructures. Unstructured data requires new ways of storage and retrieval. And sometimes the data is generated so fast it should not be stored at all, but analyzed directly at the source and the findings stored instead. Real-time analytics, stream mining, and the Internet of Things become a reality now. At the same time, it is also clear that we are in the midst of a sea change: data alone has no value, but the hidden patterns and insights in the data are an extremely valuable asset. Accessing this asset should no longer be an option for experts only but should be given into the hands of analytical practitioners and business managers of all kinds. This democratization of advanced analytics removes the bottleneck of data science and unleashes new business value in an instant.

This transformation comes with a huge advantage for those who are actually data scientists. If business analysts, Excel power users, and data-savvy business managers are empowered to solve 95% of their current advanced analytics problems on their own, it also frees up the scarce data scientist resources. This transition moves what has become analytical table stakes from data scientists to business analytics and leads to better results faster for the business. At the same time it allows data scientists to focus on new challenging tasks where the development of new algorithms is a must instead of reinventing the wheel over and over again.

We created RapidMiner with exactly this purpose in mind: empower nonexperts to get to the same findings as data scientists. Allow users to get to results and value much faster. And make deployment of those findings as easy as a single click. RapidMiner empowers the business analyst as well as the data scientist to discover the hidden patterns and unleash new business value much faster. This unlocks the huge business value potential in the marketplace. I hope that Vijay's and Bala's book will be an important contribution to this change, supporting you to remove the data science bottleneck in your organization, and, last but not least, discovering a complete new field for you that delivers success and a bit of fun while discovering the unexpected.

Ingo Mierswa
CEO and Co-Founder, RapidMiner

Preface

According to the technology consulting group Gartner, most emerging technologies go through what they term the "hype cycle." This is a way of contrasting the amount of hyperbole or hype versus the productivity that is engendered by the emerging technology. The hype cycle has three main phases: *peak of inflated expectation, trough of disillusionment,* and *plateau of productivity.* The third phase refers to the mature and value-generating phase of any technology. The hype cycle for predictive analytics (at the time of this writing) indicates that it is in this mature phase.

Does this imply that the field has stopped growing or has reached a saturation point? Not at all. On the contrary, this discipline has grown beyond the scope of its initial applications in marketing and has advanced to applications in technology, Internet-based fields, health care, government, finance, and manufacturing. Therefore, whereas many early books on data mining and predictive analytics may have focused on either the theory of data mining or marketing-related applications, this book will aim to demonstrate a much wider set of use cases for this exciting area and introduce the reader to a host of different applications and implementations.

We have run out of adjectives and superlatives to describe the growth trends of data. Simply put, the technology revolution has brought about the need to process, store, analyze, and comprehend large volumes of diverse data in meaningful ways. The scale of data volume and variety places new demands on organizations to quickly uncover hidden trends and patterns. This is where data mining techniques have become essential. They are increasingly finding their way into the everyday activities of many business and government functions, whether in identifying which customers are likely to take their business elsewhere, or mapping flu pandemic using social media signals.

Data mining is a class of techniques that traces its roots to applied statistics and computer science. The process of data mining includes many steps: framing the problem, understanding the data, preparing data, applying the right techniques to build models, interpreting the results, and building processes to deploy the models. This book aims to provide a comprehensive overview of data mining techniques to uncover patterns and predict outcomes.

So what exactly does the book cover? Very broadly, it covers many important techniques that focus on predictive analytics, which is the science of converting future uncertainties to meaningful probabilities, and the much broader area of data mining (a slightly well-worn term). Data mining also includes what is called descriptive analytics. A little more than a third of this book focuses on the descriptive side of data mining and the rest focuses on the predictive side of data mining. The most common data mining tasks employed today are covered: classification, regression, association, and cluster analysis along with few allied techniques such as anomaly detection, text mining, and time series forecasting. This book is meant to introduce an interested reader to these exciting areas and provides a motivated reader enough technical depth to implement these technologies in their own business.

WHY THIS BOOK?

The objective of this book is twofold: to help clarify the basic concepts behind many data mining techniques in an easy-to-follow manner, and to prepare anyone with a basic grasp of mathematics to implement these techniques in their business without the need to write any lines of programming code. While there are many commercial data mining tools available to implement algorithms and develop applications, the approach to solving a data mining problem is similar. We wanted to pick a fully functional, open source, graphical user interface (GUI)-based data mining tool so readers can follow the concepts and in parallel implement data mining algorithms. RapidMiner, a leading data mining and predictive analytics platform, fit the bill and thus we use it as a companion tool to implement the data mining algorithms introduced in every chapter. The best part of this tool is that it is also open source, which means *learning* data mining with this tool is virtually free of cost other than the time you invest.

WHO CAN USE THIS BOOK?

The content and practical use cases described in this book are geared towards business and analytics professionals who use data in everyday work settings. The reader of the book will get a comprehensive understanding of different data mining techniques that can be used for prediction and for discovering patterns, be prepared to select the right technique for a given data problem, and will be able to create a general purpose analytics process.

We have tried to follow a logical process to describe this body of knowledge. Our focus has been on introducing about 20 or so key algorithms that are in widespread use today. We present these algorithms in following framework:

1. A high-level practical use case for each algorithm.
2. An explanation of how the algorithm works in plain language. Many algorithms have a strong foundation in statistics and/or computer science. In our descriptions, we have tried to strike a balance between being academically rigorous and being accessible to a wider audience who don't necessarily have a mathematics background.
3. A detailed review of using RapidMiner to implement the algorithm, by describing the commonly used setup options. If possible, we expand the use case introduced at the beginning of the section to demonstrate the process by following a set format: we describe a problem, outline the objectives, apply the algorithm described in the chapter, interpret the results, and deploy the model. Finally, this book is neither a RapidMiner user manual nor a simple cookbook, although a recipe format is adopted for applications.

Analysts, finance, marketing, and business professionals, or anyone who analyzes data, most likely will use these advanced analytics techniques in their job either now or in the near future. For business executives who are one step removed from the actual analysis of data, it is important to know what is possible and not possible with these advanced techniques so they can ask the right questions and set proper expectations. While basic spreadsheet analyses and traditional slicing and dicing of data through standard business intelligence tools will continue to form the foundations of data exploration in business, especially for past data, data mining and predictive analytics are necessary to establish the full edifice of data analytics in business. Commercial data mining and predictive analytics software tools facilitate this by offering simple GUIs and by focusing on applications instead of on the inner workings of the algorithms. Our key motivation is to enable the spread of predictive analytics and data mining to a wider audience by providing both conceptual framework and a practical "how-to" guide in implementing essential algorithms. We hope that this book will help with this objective.

Vijay Kotu
Bala Deshpande

Acknowledgments

Writing a book is one of the most interesting and challenging endeavors one can take up. We grossly underestimated the effort it would take and the fulfillment it brings. This book would not have been possible without the support of our families, who granted us enough leeway in this time-consuming activity. We would like to thank the team at RapidMiner, who provided great help on everything, ranging from technical support to reviewing the chapters to answering questions on features of the product. Our special thanks to Ingo Mierswa for setting the stage for the book through the foreword. We greatly appreciate the thoughtful and insightful comments from our technical reviewers: Doug Schrimager from Slalom Consulting, Steven Reagan from L&L Products, and Tobias Malbrecht from RapidMiner. Thanks to Mike Skinner of Intel for providing expert inputs on the subject of Model Evaluation. We had great support and stewardship Morgan Kaufmann team: Steve Elliot, Kaitlin Herbert and Punithavathy Govindaradjane. Thanks to our colleagues and friends for all the productive discussions and suggestions regarding this project.

Vijay Kotu, California, USA
Bala Deshpande, PhD, Michigan, USA

CHAPTER 1

Introduction

Predictive analytics is an area that has been growing in popularity in recent years. However, data mining, of which predictive analytics is a subset, has already reached a steady state in its popularity. In spite of this recent growth and popularity, the underlying science is at least 40 to 50 years old. Engineers and scientists have been using predictive models since at least the first moon project. Humans have always been forward-looking creatures and predictive sciences are a reflection of this curious nature.

So who uses predictive analytics and data mining today? Who are the biggest consumers? A third of the applications are centered on marketing (Rexer, 2013). This involves activities such as customer segmentation and profiling, customer acquisition, customer churn, and customer lifetime value management. Another third of the applications are driven by the banking, financial services and insurance (BFSI) industry, which uses data mining and predictive analytics for activities such as fraud detection and risk analysis. Finally the remaining third of applications are spread among various industries ranging from manufacturing to technology/Internet, medical-pharmaceutical, government, and academia. The activities range from traditional sales forecasting to product recommendations to election sentiment modeling.

While scientific and engineering applications of predictive modeling are based on applying principles of physics or chemistry to develop models, the kind of predictive models we describe in this book are built on empirical knowledge, more specifically, historical data. As our ability to collect, store, and process data has increased in sync with Moore's Law, which implies that computing hardware capabilities double every two years, data mining has found increasing applications in many diverse fields. However, researchers in the area of marketing pioneered much of the early work. Olivia Parr Rud, in her *Data Mining Cookbook* (Parr Rud, 2001) describes an interesting anecdote on how back in the early 1990s building a logistic regression model took about 27 hours. More importantly, the process of predictive analytics had to be carefully orchestrated because a good chunk of model building work is data preparation. So she had to spend a whole week getting her data prepped, and finally submitted the model to run on her PC with a 600MB hard disk over the weekend (while praying that there would be no crashes)! Technology has come a long way in less than 20 years. Today we can run logistic regression models involving hundreds of predictors with hundreds of thousands of records (samples) in a matter of minutes on a laptop computer.

The process of data mining, however, has not changed since those early days and is not likely to change much in the foreseeable future. To get meaningful results from any data, we will still need to spend a majority of effort preparing, cleaning, scrubbing, or standardizing the data before our algorithms can begin to crunch them. But what may change is the automation available to do this. While today this process is iterative and requires analysts' awareness of best practices, very soon we may have smart algorithms doing this for us. This will allow us to focus on the most important aspect of predictive analytics: interpreting the results of the analysis to make decisions. This will also increase the reach of data mining to a broader cross section of analysts and business users.

So what constitutes data mining? Are there a core set of procedures and principles one must master? Finally, how are the two terms—predictive analytics and data mining—different? Before we provide more formal definitions in the next section, it is interesting to look into the experiences of today's data miners based on current surveys (Rexer, 2013). It turns out that a vast majority of data mining practitioners today use a handful of very powerful techniques to accomplish their objectives: decision trees (Chapter 4), regression models (Chapter 5), and clustering (Chapter 7). It turns out that even here an 80/20 rule applies: a majority of the data mining activity can be accomplished using relatively few techniques. However, as with all 80/20 rules, the long tail, which is made up of a large number of less-used techniques, is where the value lies, and for your needs, the best approach may be a relatively obscure technique or a combination of several not so commonly used procedures. Thus it will pay off to learn data mining and predictive analytics in a systematic way, and that is what this book will help you do.

1.1 WHAT DATA MINING IS

Data mining, in simple terms, is finding useful patterns in the data. Being a buzzword, there are a wide variety of definitions and criteria for data mining. Data mining is also referred to as knowledge discovery, machine learning, and predictive analytics. However, each term has a slightly different connotation depending upon the context. In this chapter, we attempt to provide a general overview of data mining and point out its important features, purpose, taxonomy, and common methods.

Data mining starts with *data*, which can range from a simple array of a few numeric observations to a complex matrix of millions of observations with thousands of variables. The act of data mining uses some specialized computational *methods* to discover meaningful and useful structures in the data. These computational methods have been derived from the fields of statistics, machine learning, and artificial intelligence. The discipline of data mining coexists and is closely associated with a number of related areas such as database systems, data cleansing, visualization, exploratory data analysis, and performance evaluation. We can further define data mining by investigating some its key features and motivation.

1.1.1 Extracting Meaningful Patterns

Knowledge discovery in databases is the nontrivial process of identifying valid, novel, potentially useful, and ultimately understandable patterns or relationships in the data to make important decisions (Fayyad et al., 1996) The term "nontrivial process" distinguishes data mining from straightforward statistical computations such as calculating the mean or standard deviation. Data mining involves inference and iteration of many different hypotheses. One of the key aspects of data mining is the process of *generalization* of patterns from the data set. The generalization should be valid not just for the data set used to observe the pattern, but also for the new unknown data. Data mining is also a process with defined steps, each with a set of tasks. The term "novel" indicates that data mining is usually involved in finding previously unknown patterns in the data. The ultimate objective of data mining is to find potentially useful conclusions that can be acted upon by the users of the analysis.

1.1.2 Building Representative Models

In statistics, a model is the representation of a relationship between variables in the data. It describes how one or more variables in the data are related to other variables. Modeling is a process in which a representative abstraction is built from the observed data set. For example, we can develop a model based on credit score, income level, and requested loan amount, to determine the interest rate of the loan. For this task, we need previously known observational data with the credit score, income level, loan amount, and interest rate. Figure 1.1 shows the inputs and output of the model. Once the representative model is created, we can use it to predict the value of the interest rate, based on all the input values (credit score, income level, and loan amount).

In the context of predictive analytics, data mining is the process of building the representative model that fits the observational data. This model serves two purposes: on the one hand it predicts the output (interest rate) based on the input variables (credit score, income level, and loan amount), and on the other hand we can use it to understand the relationship between the output variable and all the input variables. For example, does income level really matter in

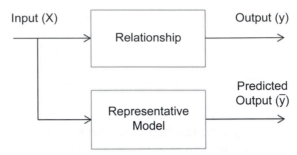

FIGURE 1.1
Representative model for Predictive Analytics.

determining the loan interest rate? Does income level matter more than credit score? What happens when income levels double or if credit score drops by 10 points? Model building in the context of data mining can be used in both predictive and explanatory applications.

1.1.3 Combination of Statistics, Machine Learning, and Computing

In the pursuit of extracting useful and relevant information from large data sets, data mining derives computational techniques from the disciplines of statistics, artificial intelligence, machine learning, database theories, and pattern recognition. Algorithms used in data mining originated from these disciplines, but have since evolved to adopt more diverse techniques such as parallel computing, evolutionary computing, linguistics, and behavioral studies. One of the key ingredients of successful data mining is substantial prior knowledge about the data and the business processes that generate the data, known as *subject matter expertise*. Like many quantitative frameworks, data mining is an iterative process in which the practitioner gains more information about the patterns and relationships from data in each cycle. The art of data mining combines the knowledge of statistics, subject matter expertise, database technologies, and machine learning techniques to extract meaningful and useful information from the data. Data mining also typically operates on large data sets that need to be stored, processed, and computed. This is where database techniques along with parallel and distributed computing techniques play an important role in data mining.

1.1.4 Algorithms

We can also define data mining as a process of discovering previously unknown patterns in the data using *automatic iterative methods*. Algorithms are iterative step-by-step procedure to transform inputs to output. The application of sophisticated algorithms for extracting useful patterns from the data differentiates data mining from traditional data analysis techniques. Most of these algorithms were developed in recent decades and have been borrowed from the fields of machine learning and artificial intelligence. However, some of the algorithms are based on the foundations of Bayesian probabilistic theories and regression analysis, originated hundreds of years ago. These iterative algorithms automate the process of searching for an optimal solution for a given data problem. Based on the data problem, data mining is classified into tasks such as classification, association analysis, clustering, and regression. Each data mining task uses specific algorithms like decision trees, neural networks, k-nearest neighbors, k-means clustering, among others. With increased research on data mining, the number of such algorithms is increasing, but a few classic algorithms remain foundational to many data mining applications.

1.2 WHAT DATA MINING IS *NOT*

While data mining covers a wide set of techniques, applications, and disciplines, not all analytical and discovery methods are considered data mining processes. Data mining is usually applied, though not limited to, large data sets. Data mining also goes through a defined process of exploration, preprocessing, modeling, evaluation, and knowledge extraction. Here are some commonly used data discovery techniques that are not considered data mining, even if they operate on large data sets:

- **Descriptive statistics:** Computing mean, standard deviation, and other descriptive statistics quantify the aggregate structure of a data set. This is essential information to understand any data set, but calculating these statistics is not considered a data mining technique. However, they are used in the exploration stage of the data mining process.
- **Exploratory visualization:** The process of expressing data in visual coordinates enables users to find patterns and relationships in the data and comprehend large data sets. Similar to descriptive statistics, they are integral in the preprocessing and postprocessing steps in data mining.
- **Dimensional slicing:** Business intelligence and online analytical processing (OLAP) applications, which are prevalent in business settings, mainly provide information on the data through dimensional slicing, filtering ,and pivoting. OLAP analysis is enabled by a unique database schema design where the data is organized as *dimensions* (e.g., Products, Region, Date) and quantitative facts or *measures* (e.g., Revenue, Quantity). With a well-defined database structure, it is easy to slice the yearly revenue by products or combination of region and products. While these techniques are extremely useful and may provide patterns in data (e.g., Candy sales decline after Halloween in the United States), this is considered information retrieval and not data mining.
- **Hypothesis testing:** In confirmatory data analysis, experimental data is collected to evaluate whether a hypothesis has enough evidence to support it or not. There are many types of statistical testing and

they have a wide variety of business applications (e.g., A/B testing in marketing). In general, data mining is a process where many hypotheses are generated and tested based on observational data. Since the data mining algorithms are iterative, we can refine the solution in each step.

■ **Queries:** Information retrieval systems, like web search engines, use data mining techniques like clustering to index vast repositories of data. But the act of querying and rendering of the result is not considered a data mining process. Query retrieval from databases and slicing and dicing of data are not generally considered data mining (Tan et al., 2005).

All of the above techniques are used in the steps of a data mining process and are used in conjunction with the term "data mining." It is important for the practitioner to know what makes up a complete data mining process. We will discuss the specific steps of a data mining process in the next chapter.

1.3 THE CASE FOR DATA MINING

In the past few decades, we have seen a massive accumulation of data with the advancement of information technology, connected networks and businesses it enables. This trend is also coupled with steep decline in the cost of data storage and data processing. The applications built on these advancements like online businesses, social networking, and mobile technologies unleash a large amount of complex, heterogeneous data that are waiting to be analyzed. Traditional analysis techniques like dimensional slicing, hypothesis testing, and descriptive statistics can only get us so far in information discovery. We need a paradigm to manage massive volume of data, explore the interrelationships of thousands of variables, and deploy machine learning algorithms to deduce optimal insights from the data set. We need a set of frameworks, tools, and techniques to intelligently assist humans to process all these data and extract valuable information (Piatetsky-Shapiro et al., 1996). Data Mining is one such paradigm that can handle large volumes with multiple attributes and deploy complex algorithms to search for patterns from the data. Let's explore each key motivation for using data mining techniques.

1.3.1 Volume

The sheer volume of data captured by organizations is exponentially increasing. The rapid decline in storage costs and advancements in capturing every transaction and event, combined with the business need to extract all possible leverage using data, creates a strong motivation to store more data than ever. A study by IDC Corporation in 2012 reported that the volume of recorded digital data by 2012 reached 2.8 zettabytes, and less than 1% of the data are currently analyzed (Reinsel, December 2012). As data becomes more granular, the need for using large volume data to extract information increases. A rapid increase in the volume of data exposes the limitations of current analysis methodologies. In a few implementations, the time to create generalization models is quite critical and data volume plays a major part in determining the time to development and deployment.

1.3.2 Dimensions

The three characteristics of the Big Data phenomenon are high volume, high velocity, and high variety. Variety of data relates to multiple types of values (numerical, categorical), formats of data (audio files, video files), and application of data (location coordinates, graph data). Every single record or data point contains multiple attributes or variables to provide context for the record. For example, every user record of an ecommerce site can contain attributes such as products viewed, products purchased, user demographics, frequency of purchase, click stream, etc. Determining what is the most effective offer an ecommerce user will respond to can involve computing information along all these attributes. Each attribute can be thought as a dimension in the data space. The user record has multiple attributes and can be visualized in multidimensional space. Addition of each dimension increases the complexity of analysis techniques.

A simple linear regression model that has one input dimension is relatively easier to build than multiple linear regression models with multiple dimensions. As the dimensional space of the data increases, we need an adaptable framework that can work well with multiple data types and multiple attributes. In the case of text mining, a document or article becomes a data point with each unique word as a dimension. Text mining yields a data set where the number of attributes ranges from a few hundred to hundreds of thousands of attributes.

1.3.3 Complex Questions

As more complex data are available for analysis, the complexity of information that needs to get extracted from the data is increasing as well. If we need to find the natural clusters in a data set with hundreds of dimensions, traditional analysis like hypothesis testing techniques cannot be used in a scalable fashion. We need to leverage machine-learning algorithms to automate searching in the vast search space.

Traditional statistical analysis approaches a data analysis problem by assuming a stochastic model to predict a response variable based on a set of input variables. Linear regression and logistic regression analysis are classic examples of this technique where the parameters of the model are estimated from the data. These hypothesis-driven techniques were highly successful in modeling simple relationships between response and input variables. However, there is a significant need to extract nuggets of information from large, complex data sets, where the use of traditional statistical data analysis techniques is limited (Breiman, 2001)

Machine learning approach the problem of modeling by trying to find an algorithmic model that can better predict the output from input variables. The algorithms are usually recursive and in each cycle estimate the output and "learn" from the predictive errors of previous steps. This route of modeling greatly assists in exploratory analysis since the approach here is not validating a hypothesis but generating a multitude of hypotheses for a given problem. In the context of the data problems we face today, we need to deploy both techniques. John Tuckey, in his article "We need both exploratory and confirmatory," stresses the importance of both exploratory and confirmatory analysis techniques (Tuckey, 1980). In this book, we discuss a range of data mining techniques, from traditional statistical modeling techniques like regressions to machine-learning algorithms.

1.4 TYPES OF DATA MINING

Data mining problems can be broadly categorized into *supervised* or *unsupervised* learning models. Supervised or directed data mining tries to infer a function or relationship based on labeled training data and uses this function to map new unlabeled data. Supervised techniques predict the value of the output variables based on a set of input variables. To do this, a model is developed from a *training* data set where the values of input and output are previously known. The model generalizes the relationship between the input and output variables and uses it to predict for the data set where only input variables are known. The output variable that is being predicted is also called a class label or target variable. Supervised data mining needs a sufficient number of labeled records to learn the model from the data. Unsupervised or undirected data mining uncovers hidden patterns in unlabeled data. In unsupervised data mining, there are no output variables to predict. The objective of this class of data mining techniques is to find patterns in data based on the relationship between data points themselves. An application can employ both supervised and unsupervised learners.

Data mining problems can also be grouped into classification, regression, association analysis, anomaly detection, time series, and text mining tasks (Figure 1.2). This book is organized around these data mining tasks. We present an overview of the types of data mining in this chapter and will provide an in-depth discussion of concepts and step-by-step implementations of many important techniques in the following chapters.

Classification and *regression* techniques predict a target variable based on input variables. The prediction is based on a generalized model built from a previously known data set. In regression tasks, the output variable is numeric (e.g., the mortgage interest rate on a loan). Classification tasks predict output variables, which are categorical or polynomial (e.g., the yes or no decision to approve a loan). *Clustering* is the process of identifying the natural groupings in the data set. For example, clustering is helpful in finding natural clusters in customer data sets, which can be used for market segmentation. Since this is unsupervised data mining, it is up to the end user to investigate why these clusters are formed in the data and generalize the uniqueness of each cluster. In retail analytics, it is common to identify pairs of items that are purchased together, so that specific items can be bundled or placed next to each other. This task is called market basket analysis or *association analysis*, which is commonly used in recommendation engines.

Anomaly or outlier detection identifies the data points that are significantly different from other data points in the data set. Credit card transaction fraud detection is one of the most prolific applications of anomaly detection. *Time series forecasting* can be either a special use of regression modeling (where models predict the future value of a variable based on the past value of the same variable) or a sophisticated averaging or smoothing technique (for example, daily weather prediction based on the past few years of daily data).

Text Mining is a data mining application where the input data is text, which can be in the form of documents, messages, emails, or web pages. To aid the

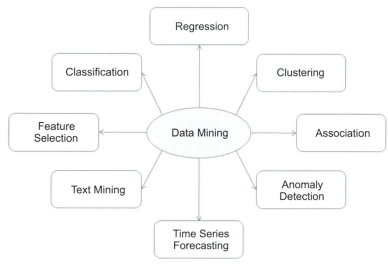

FIGURE 1.2
Data mining tasks.

data mining on text data, the text files are converted into document vectors where each unique word is considered an attribute. Once the text file is converted to document vectors, standard data mining tasks such as classification, clustering, etc. can be applied on text files. The *Feature selection* is a process in which attributes in a data set is reduced to a few attributes that really matter.

A complete data mining application can contain elements of both supervised and unsupervised techniques. Unsupervised techniques provide an increased understanding of the data set and hence are sometimes called descriptive data mining. As an example of how both unsupervised and supervised data mining can be combined in an application, consider the following scenario. In marketing analytics, clustering can be used to find the natural clusters in customer records. Each customer is assigned a cluster label at the end of the clustering process. A labeled customer data set can now be used to develop a model that assigns a cluster label for any new customer record with a supervised classification technique.

1.5 DATA MINING ALGORITHMS

An algorithm is a logical step-by-step procedure for solving a problem. In data mining, it is the blueprint for how a particular data problem is solved. Many of the algorithms are recursive, where a set of steps are repeated many times until a limiting condition is met. Some algorithms also contain a random variable as an input, and are aptly called *randomized algorithms*. A data mining classification task can be solved using many different approaches or algorithms such as decision trees, artificial neural networks, k-nearest neighbors (k-NN), and even some regression algorithms. The choice of which algorithm to use depends on the type of data set, objective of the data mining, structure of the data, presence of outliers, available computational power, number of records, number of attributes, and so on. It is up to the data mining practitioner to make a decision about what algorithm(s) to use by evaluating the performance of multiple algorithms. There have been hundreds of algorithms developed in the last few decades to solve data mining problems. In the next few chapters, we will discuss the inner workings of the most important and diverse data mining algorithms and their implementations.

Data mining algorithms can be implemented by custom-developed computer programs in almost any computer language. This obviously is a time-consuming task. In order for us to focus our time on data and algorithms, we can leverage data mining tools or statistical programing tools, like R, Rapid-Miner, SAS Enterprise Miner, IBM SPSS, etc., which can implement these algorithms with ease. These data mining tools offer a library of algorithms as functions, which can be interfaced through programming code or configuration through graphical user interfaces. Table 1.1 provides a summary of data mining tasks with commonly used algorithmic techniques and example use cases.

Table 1.1 Data Mining Tasks and Examples

Tasks	Description	Algorithms	Examples
Classification	Predict if a data point belongs to one of the predefined classes. The prediction will be based on learning from a known data set.	Decision trees, neural networks, Bayesian models, induction rules, k-nearest neighbors	Assigning voters into known buckets by political parties, e.g., soccer moms Bucketing new customers into one of the known customer groups
Regression	Predict the numeric target label of a data point. The prediction will be based on learning from a known data set.	Linear regression, logistic regression	Predicting unemployment rate for next year Estimating insurance premium
Anomaly detection	Predict if a data point is an outlier compared to other data points in the data set.	Distance based, density based, local outlier factor (LOF)	Fraud transaction detection in credit cards Network intrusion detection
Time series	Predict the value of the target variable for a future time frame based on historical values.	Exponential smoothing, autoregressive integrated moving average (ARIMA), regression	Sales forecasting, production forecasting, virtually any growth phenomenon that needs to be extrapolated
Clustering	Identify natural clusters within the data set based on inherit properties within the data set.	k-means, density-based clustering (e.g., density-based spatial clustering of applications with noise [DBSCAN])	Finding customer segments in a company based on transaction, web, and customer call data
Association analysis	Identify relationships within an item set based on transaction data.	Frequent Pattern Growth (FP-Growth) algorithm, Apriori algorithm	Find cross-selling opportunities for a retailer based on transaction purchase history

1.6 ROADMAP FOR UPCOMING CHAPTERS

It's time to explore data mining and predictive analytics techniques in more detail. In the next couple of chapters, we provide an overview of the data mining process and data exploration techniques. The following chapters present the main body of this book: the concepts behind each predictive analytics or descriptive data mining algorithm and a practical use case (or two) for each. You don't have to read the chapters in a sequence. We have organized this book in such a way that you can directly start reading about the data mining tasks and algorithms you are most interested in. Within each chapter focused on a technique (e.g., decision tree, k-means clustering), we start with a general overview, and then present the concepts and the logic of the algorithm and how it works in plain language. Later we show how the algorithm can be implemented using RapidMiner. RapidMiner is a widely known and used software tool for data mining and predictive analytics (Piatetsky, 2014) and we have chosen it particularly for ease of implementation using GUI and it is a open source data mining tool. We conclude each chapter with some closing thoughts and list further reading materials and references. Here is a roadmap of the book.

1.6.1 Getting Started with Data Mining

Successfully uncovering patterns in a data set is an iterative process. Chapter 2 Data Mining Process provides a framework to solve data mining problems. A five-step process outlined in this chapter provides guidelines on gathering subject matter expertise; exploring the data with statistics and visualization; building a model using data mining algorithms; testing the model and deploying in production environment; and finally reflecting on new knowledge gained in the cycle.

A simple data exploration either visually or with the help of basic statistical analysis can sometimes answer seemingly tough questions meant for data mining. Chapter 3 Data Exploration covers some of the basic tools used in knowledge discovery before deploying data mining techniques. These practical tools increase one's understanding of the data and are quite essential in understanding the results of data mining process.

1.6.2 An Interlude…

Before we dive into the key data mining techniques and algorithms, we want to point out two specific things regarding how you can implement Data Mining algorithms while reading this book. We believe learning the concepts and implementation immediately after enhances the learning experience. All of the predictive modeling and data mining algorithms explained in the following chapters are implemented in RapidMiner. First, we recommend that you download the free version of RapidMiner software from http://www.rapidminer.com (if you have not done so already) and second, review the first couple of sections of Chapter 13 Getting Started with RapidMiner to familiarize yourself with the features of the tool, its basic operations, and the user interface functionality. Acclimating with RapidMiner will be helpful while using the algorithms that are discussed in the following chapters. This chapter is set at the end of the book because some of the later sections in the chapter build upon the material presented in the chapters on algorithms; however the first few sections are a good starting point for someone who is not yet familiar with the tool.

Each chapter has a data set we use to describe the concept of a particular data mining task and in most cases the same data set is used for implementation. Step-by-step instructions on practicing data mining on the data set are covered in every algorithm that is discussed in the upcoming chapters. All the implementations discussed in the book are available at the companion website of the book at www.LearnPredictiveAnalytics.com.

Though not required, we encourage you to access these files to aid your learning. You can download the data set, complete RapidMiner processes (*.rmp files), and many more relevant electronic files from this website.

1.6.3 The Main Event: Predictive Analytics and Data Mining Algorithms

Classification is the most widely used data mining task in businesses. As a predictive analytics task, the objective of a classification model is to predict a target variable that is binary (e.g., a loan decision) or categorical (e.g., a customer type) when a set of input variables are given (e.g., credit score, income level, etc.). The model does this by learning the generalized relationship between the predicted target variable with all other input attributes from a known data set. There are several ways to skin this cat. Each algorithm differs by how the relationship is extracted from the known data, called a "training" data set. Chapter 4 on classification addresses several of these methods.

- *Decision trees* approach the classification problem by partitioning the data into "purer" subsets based on the values of the input attributes. The attributes that help achieve the cleanest levels of such separation are considered significant in their influence on the target variable and end up at the root and closer-to-root levels of the tree. The output model is a tree framework than can be used for the prediction of new unlabeled data.
- *Rule induction* is a data mining process of deducing IF-THEN rules from a dataset or from decision trees. These symbolic decision rules explain an inherent relationship between the attributes and labels in the data set that can be easily understood by everyone.
- *Naïve Bayesian* algorithms provide a probabilistic way of building a model. This approach calculates the probability for each value of the class variable for given values of input variables. With the help of conditional probabilities, for a given unknown record, the model calculates the outcome of all values of target classes and comes up with a predicted winner.
- Why go through the trouble of extracting complex relationships from the data when we can just memorize entire training data set and pretend we have generalized the relationship? This is exactly what the *k-nearest neighbor* algorithm does, and it is therefore called a "lazy" learner where the entire training data set is memorized as the model.
- Neurons are the nerve cells that connect with each other to form a biological neural network. The working of these interconnected nerve cells inspired the solution of some complex data problems by the creation of *artificial neural networks*. The neural networks section provides a conceptual background of how a simple neural network works and how to implement one for any general prediction problem.

- *Support vector machines (SVMs)* were developed to address optical character recognition problems: how can we train an algorithm to detect boundaries between different patterns and thus identify characters? SVMs can therefore identify if a given data sample belongs within a boundary (in a particular class) or outside it (not in the class).
- *Ensemble learners* are "meta" models where the model is a combination of several different individual models. If certain conditions are met, ensemble learners can gain from the wisdom of crowds and greatly reduce the generalization error in data mining.

The simple mathematical equation $y = ax + b$ is a linear regression model. Chapter 5 Regression Methods describes a class of predictive analytics techniques in which the target variable (e.g., interest rate or a target class) is *functionally* related to input variables.

- **Linear regression:** The simplest of all function fitting models is based on a linear equation, as mentioned above. Polynomial regression uses higher-order equations. No matter what type of equation is used, the goal is to represent the variable to be predicted in terms of other variables or attributes. Further, the predicted variable and the independent variables all have to be numeric for this to work. We explore the basics of building regression models and show how predictions can be made using such models.
- **Logistic regression:** It addresses the issue of predicting a target variable that may be binary or binomial (such as 1 or 0, yes or no) using predictors or attributes, which may be numeric.

Supervised data mining or predictive analytics predict the value of the target variables. In the next two chapters, we review two important *unsupervised* data mining tasks: Association analysis in Chapter 6 and Clustering in Chapter 7. Ever heard of the beer and diaper association in supermarkets? Apparently, a supermarket discovered that customers who buy diapers also tend to buy beer. While this may have been an urban legend, the observation has become a poster child for association analysis. Associating an item in a transaction with another item in the transaction to determine the most frequently occurring patterns is termed *association analysis*. This technique is about, for example, finding relationships between products in a supermarket based on purchase data, or finding related web pages in a website based on click stream data. This data mining application is widely used in retail, ecommerce, and media to creatively bundle products.

Clustering is the data mining task of identifying natural groups in the data. For an unsupervised data mining task, there is no target class variable to predict. After the clustering is performed, each record in the data set is associated with one or more cluster. Widely used in marketing segmentations and text mining, clustering can be performed by a wide range of algorithms. In Chapter 7, we will discuss three common algorithms with diverse identification approaches. The *k-means clustering* technique identifies a cluster based on a central prototype record. *DBSCAN* clustering partitions the data based on variation in the density of records in a data set. *Self-organizing maps (SOM)* create a two-dimensional grid where all the records related with each other are placed next to each other.

How do we determine which algorithms work best for a given data set? Or for that matter how do we objectively quantify the performance of any algorithm on a data set? These questions are addressed in Chapter 8 Model Evaluation, which covers performance evaluation. We describe the most commonly used tools for evaluating classification models such as a confusion matrix, ROC curves, and lift charts.

1.6.4 Special Applications

Chapter 9 Text Mining provides a detailed look into the emerging area of text mining and text analytics. It starts with a background on the origins of text mining and provides the motivation for this fascinating topic using the example of IBM's Watson, the Jeopardy!-winning computer program that was built almost entirely using concepts from text and data mining. The chapter introduces some key concepts important in the area of text analytics such as term frequency–inverse document frequency (TF-IDF) scores. Finally it describes two hands-on case studies in which the reader is shown how to use RapidMiner to address problems like document clustering and automatic gender classification based on text content.

Forecasting is a very common application of time series analysis. Companies use sales forecasts, budget forecasts, or production forecasts in their planning cycles. Chapter 10 on Time Series Forecasting starts by pointing out the clear distinction between standard supervised predictive models and time series forecasting models. It provides a basic introduction to the different time series methods ranging from data-driven moving averages to exponential smoothing, and model-driven forecasts including polynomial regression and lag-series based ARIMA methods.

Chapter 11 on Anomaly Detection describes how outliers in data can be detected by combining multiple data mining tasks like classification, regression, and clustering. The fraud alert received from credit card companies is the result of an anomaly detection algorithm. The target variable to be predicted is whether a transaction is an outlier or not. Since clustering tasks identify outliers as a cluster, distance-based and density-based clustering techniques can be used in anomaly detection tasks.

In predictive analytics, the objective is to develop a representative model to generalize the relationship between input attributes and target attributes, so that we can predict the value or class of the target variables. Chapter 12 introduces a preprocessing step that is often critical for a successful predictive modeling exercise: *feature selection*. Feature selection is known by several alternative terms such as attribute weighting, dimension reduction, and so on. There are two main styles of feature selection: filtering the key attributes before modeling (filter style) or selecting the attributes during the process of modeling (wrapper style). We discuss a few filter-based methods such as principal component analysis (PCA), information gain, and chi-square, and a couple of wrapper-type methods like forward selection and backward elimination. Even in just one data mining algorithm, there are many different ways to tweak the parameters and even the sampling for training data set.

If you are not familiar with RapidMiner, the first few sections of Chapter 13 Getting Started with RapidMiner should provide a good overview, while the latter sections of this chapter discuss some of the commonly used productivity tools and techniques such as data transformation, missing value handling, and process optimizations using RapidMiner. As mentioned earlier, while each chapter is more or less independent, some of the concepts in Chapters 8 Model Evaluation and later build on the material from earlier chapters and for beginners we recommend going in order. However, if you are familiar with the standard terminology and with RapidMiner, you are not constrained to move in any fashion.

REFERENCES

Breiman, L. (2001). Statistical Modeling: Two Cultures. *Statistical Science*, 6(3), 199–231.

Fayyad, U., Piatetsky-shapiro, G., & Smyth, P. (1996). From Data Mining to Knowledge Discovery in Databases. *AI Magazine*, 17(3), 37–54.

Parr Rud, O. (2001). *Data Mining Cookbook*. New York: John Wiley and Sons.

Piatetsky, G. (2014). KDnuggets 15th Annual Analytics, Data Mining, Data Science Software Poll: RapidMiner Continues To Lead. Retrieved August 01, 2014, from http://www.kdnuggets.com/2014/06/kdnuggets-annual-software-poll-rapidminer-continues-lead.html.

Piatetsky-Shapiro, G., Brachman, R., Khabaza, T., Kloesgen, W., & Simoudis, E. (1996). *An Overview of Issues in Developing Industrial Data Mining and Knowledge Discovery Applications*. KDD-96 Conference Proceedings.

Reinsel, J. G. (December 2012). *Big Data, Bigger Digital Shadows, and Biggest Growth in the Far East* Sponsored by EMC Corporation. IDC iView.

Rexer, K. (2013). *2013 Data Miner Survey Summary Report*. Winchester, MA: Rexer Analytics. www.rexeranalytics.com.

Tan, P.-N., Michael, S., & Kumar, V. (2005). *Introduction to Data Mining*. Boston, MA: Addison-Wesley.

Tuckey, J. (1980). We need exploratory and Confirmatory. *The American Statistician*, 34(1), 23–25.

CHAPTER 2

Data Mining Process

The methodological discovery of useful relationships and patterns in data is enabled by a set of iterative activities known as data mining process. The standard data mining process involves (1) understanding the problem, (2) preparing the data samples, (3) developing the model, (4) applying the model on a data set to see how the model may work in real world, and (5) production deployment. Over the years of evolution of data mining practices, different frameworks for the data mining process have been put forward by various academic and commercial bodies. In this chapter, we will discuss the key steps involved in building a successful data mining solution. The framework we put forward in this chapter is synthesized from a few data mining frameworks, and is explained using a simple example data set. This chapter serves as a high-level roadmap in building deployable data mining models, and discusses the challenges faced in each step, as well as important considerations and pitfalls to avoid. Most of the concepts discussed in this chapter are reviewed later in the book with detailed explanations and examples.

One of the most popular data mining process frameworks is CRISP-DM, which is an acronym for Cross Industry Standard Process for Data Mining. This framework was developed by a consortium of many companies involved in data mining (Chapman et al., 2000). The CRISP-DM process is the most widely adopted framework for developing data mining solutions. Figure 2.1 provides a visual overview of the CRISP-DM framework. Other data mining frameworks are SEMMA, which is an acronym for Sample, Explore, Modify, Model, and Assess, developed by the SAS Institute (*SAS Institute, 2013*); DMAIC, which is an acronym for Define, Measure, Analyze, Improve and Control, used in Six Sigma practice (Kubiak & Benbow, 2005); and the Selection, Preprocessing, Transformation, Data Mining, Interpretation, and Evaluation framework used in the knowledge discovery in databases (KDD) process (Fayyad et al., 1996). We feel all these frameworks exhibit common characteristics and hence we will be using a generic framework closely resembling the CRISP process. As with any process framework, a data mining process recommends the performance of a certain set of tasks to achieve optimal output. The process of extracting information from the data is iterative. The steps within the data mining process

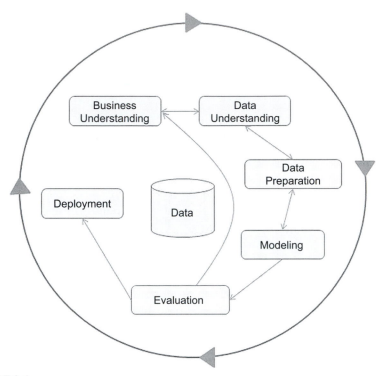

FIGURE 2.1
CRISP data mining framework.

are not linear and have many loops, going back and forth between steps and at times going back to the first step to redefine data mining problem statement.

The data mining process presented in Figure 2.2 is a generic set of steps that is business, algorithm, and, data mining tool agnostic. The fundamental objective of any process that involves data mining is to address the analysis question. The problem at hand could be segmentation of customers or predicting climate patterns or a simple data exploration. The algorithm used to solve the business question could be automated clustering or an artificial neural network. The software tools to develop and implement the data mining algorithm used could be custom coding, IBM SPSS, SAS, R, or RapidMiner, to mention a few.

Data mining, specifically in the context of big data, has gained a lot of importance in the last few years. Perhaps the most visible and discussed part of data mining is the third step: modeling. It involves building representative models that can be derived from the sample data set and can be used for either predictions (*predictive modeling*) or for describing the underlying pattern in the data (*descriptive or explanatory modeling*). Rightfully so, there is plenty of academic and business research in this step and we have dedicated most of the book to discussing various algorithms and quantitative foundations that go with it. We specifically wish to emphasize

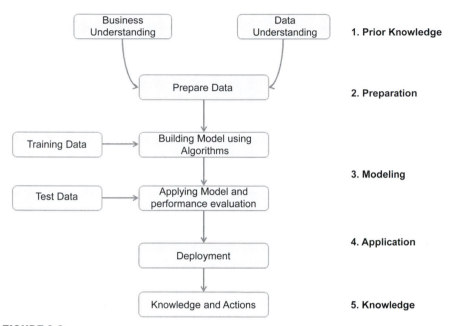

FIGURE 2.2
Data mining process.

considering data mining as an end-to-end, multistep, iterative process instead of just a model building step. Seasoned data mining practitioners can attest to the fact that the most time-consuming part of the overall data mining process is not the model building part, but the preparation of data, followed by data and business understanding. There are many data mining tools, both open source and commercial, available in the market that can automate the model building. The most commonly used tools are RapidMiner, R, Weka, SAS, SPSS, Oracle Data Miner, Salford, Statistica, etc. (Piatetsky, 2014). Asking the right business questions, gaining in-depth business understanding, sourcing and preparing the data for the data mining task, mitigating implementation considerations, and, most useful of all, gaining knowledge from the data mining process, remains crucial to the success of the data mining process. Lets get started with Step 1: Framing the data mining question and understanding the context.

2.1 PRIOR KNOWLEDGE

Prior knowledge refers to information that is already known about a subject. The objective of data mining doesn't emerge in isolation; it always develops on top of existing subject matter and contextual information that is already known. The prior knowledge step in the data mining process helps to define what problem we are solving, how it fits in the business context, and what data we need to solve the problem.

2.1.1 Objective

The data mining process starts with an analysis need, a question or a business objective. This is possibly the most important step in the data mining process (Shearer, 2000). Without a well-defined statement of the problem, it is impossible to come up with the right data set and pick the right data mining algorithm. Even though the data mining process is a sequential process and it is common to go back to previous steps and revise the assumptions, approach, and tactics. It is imperative to get the objective of the whole process right, even if it is exploratory data mining.

We are going to explain the data mining process using an hypothetical example. Let's assume we are in the consumer loan business, where a loan is provisioned for individuals with the collateral of assets like a home or car, i.e., a mortgage or an auto loan. As many home owners know, an important component of the loan, for the borrower and the lender, is the interest rate at which the borrower repays the loan on top of the principal. The interest rate on a loan depends on a gamut of variables like the current federal funds rate as determined by the central bank, borrower's credit score, income level, home value, initial deposit (down payment) amount, current assets and liabilities of the borrower, etc. The key factor here is whether the lender sees enough reward (interest on the loan) for the risk of losing the principal (borrower's default on the loan). In an individual case, the status of default of a loan is Boolean; either one defaults or not, during the period of the loan. But, in a group of tens of thousands of borrowers, we can find the default rate—a continuous numeric variable that indicates the percentage of borrowers who default on their loans. All the variables related to the borrower like credit score, income, current liabilities, etc. are used to assess the default risk in a related group; based on this, the interest rate is determined for a loan. The business objective of this hypothetical use case is: *If we know the interest rate of past borrowers with a range of credit scores, can we predict interest rate for a new borrower?*

2.1.2 Subject Area

The process of data mining uncovers hidden patterns in the data set by exposing relationships between attributes. But the issue is that it uncovers a lot of patterns. False signals are a major problem in the process. It is up to the data mining practitioner to filter through the patterns and accept the ones that are valid and relevant to answer the objective question. Hence, it is essential to know the subject matter, the context, and the business process generating the data.

The lending business is one of the oldest, most prevalent, and complex of all the businesses. If the data mining objective is to predict the interest rate, then it is important to know how the lending business works, why the prediction matters, what we do once we know the predicted interest rate, what data points can be collected from borrowers, what data points cannot be collected because of regulations, what other external factors can affect the interest rate, how we verify the validity of the outcome, and so forth. Understanding current models and business practices lays the foundation and establishes known knowledge. Analysis and mining the data provides the new knowledge that can be built on top of existing knowledge (Lidwell et al., 2003).

2.1.3 Data

Similar to prior knowledge in the subject area, there also exists prior knowledge in data. Data is usually collected as part of business processes in a typical enterprise. Understanding how the data is collected, stored, transformed, reported, and used is essential for the data mining process. This part of the step considers all the data available to answer the business question and if needed, what data needs to be sourced from the data sources. There are quite a range of factors to consider: quality of the data, quantity of data, availability of data, what happens when data is not available, does lack of data compel the practitioner to change the business question, etc. The objective of this step is to come up with a data set, the mining of which answers the business question(s). It is critical to recognize that a model is only as good as the data used to create it.

For the lending example, we have put together an artificial data set of ten data points with three attributes: identifier, credit score, and interest rate. First, let's look at some of the terminology used in the data mining process in relation to describing the data.

- A *data set* (*example set*) is a collection of data with a defined structure. Table 2.1 shows a data set. It has a well-defined structure with 10 rows and 3 columns along with the column headers.
- A *data point* (*record* or *data object* or *example*) is a single instance in the data set. Each row in Table 2.1 is a data point. Each instance contains the same structure as the data set.

Table 2.1 Data Set

Borrower ID	Credit Score	Interest Rate
01	500	7.31%
02	600	6.70%
03	700	5.95%
04	700	6.40%
05	800	5.40%
06	800	5.70%
07	750	5.90%
08	550	7.00%
09	650	6.50%
10	825	5.70%

- An *attribute* (*feature* or *input* or *dimension* or *variable* or *predictor*) is a single property of the data set. Each column in Table 2.1 is an attribute. Attributes can be numeric, categorical, date-time, text, or Boolean *data types*. In this example, credit score and interest rate are numeric attribute.
- A *label* (*class label* or *output* or *prediction* or *target* or *response*) is the special attribute that needs to be predicted based on all input attributes. In Table 2.1, interest rate is the output variable.
- *Identifiers* are special attributes that are used for locating or providing context to individual records. For example, common attributes like Names, account numbers, employee ID are identifier attributes. Identifiers are often used as lookup keys to combine multiple data sets. They bear no information that is suitable for building data mining models and should thus be excluded for the actual modeling step. In Table 2.1, the ID is the identifier.

2.1.4 Causation vs. Correlation

Let's invert our prediction objective: *Based on the data in Table 2.1, can we predict the credit score of the borrower based on interest rate?* The answer is yes—but it doesn't make business sense. From existing domain expertise, we know credit score *influences* the loan interest rate. Predicting credit score based on interest rate inverses that causation relationship. This question also exposes one of the key aspects of model building. The correlation between the input and output attributes doesn't guarantee causation. Hence, it is very important to frame the data mining question correctly using the existing domain and data knowledge. In this data mining example, we are going to predict the interest rate of the new borrower with unknown interest rate (Table 2.2) based on the pattern learned from known data in Table 2.1.

2.2 DATA PREPARATION

Preparing the data set to suit a data mining task is the most time-consuming part of the process. Very rarely data are available in the form required by the data mining algorithms. Most of the data mining algorithms would require data to be structured in a tabular format with records in rows and attributes in columns. If the data is in any other format, then we would need to transform the data by applying pivot or transpose functions, for example, to condition the data into required structure. What if there are incorrect data? Or missing values? For example, in hospital health records, if the height field of a patient is shown as 1.7 centimeters, then the data is

Table 2.2 New Data with Unknown Interest Rate		
Borrower ID	**Credit Score**	**Interest Rate**
11	625	?

obviously wrong. For some records height may not be captured in the first place and left blank. Following are some of the activities performed in Data Preparation stage, along with common challenges and mitigation strategies.

2.2.1 Data Exploration

Data preparation starts with an in-depth exploration of the data and gaining more understanding of the data set. Data exploration, also known as *Exploratory Data Analysis (EDA)*, provides a set of simple tools to achieve basic understanding of the data. Basic exploration approaches involve computing descriptive statistics and visualization of data. Basic exploration can expose the structure of the data, the distribution of the values, the presence of extreme values and highlights the interrelationships within the data set. Descriptive statistics like mean, median, mode, standard deviation, and range for each attribute provide an easily readable summary of the key characteristics of the distribution of the data. On the other hand, a visual plot of data points provides an instant grasp of all the data points condensed into one chart. Figure 2.3 shows the scatterplot of credit score vs. loan interest rate and we can observe that as credit score increases, interest rate decreases. We will review more data exploration techniques in Chapter 3. In general, a data set sourced to answer a business question has to be analyzed, prepared, and transformed before applying algorithms and creating models.

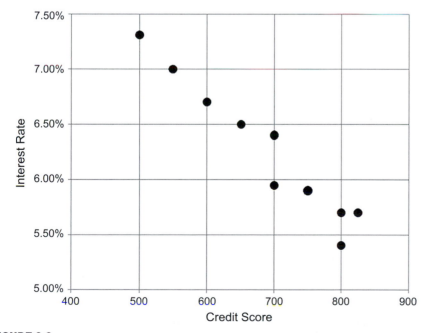

FIGURE 2.3
Scatterplot for interest rate data set.

2.2.2 Data Quality

Data quality is an ongoing concern wherever data is collected, processed, and stored. In the data set used as an example (Table 2.1), how do we know if the credit score and interest rate data are accurate? What if a credit score has a recorded value of 900 (beyond the theoretical limit) or if there was a data entry error? These errors in data will impact the representativeness of the model. Organizations use data cleansing and transformation techniques to improve and manage the quality of data and store them in companywide repositories called *Data Warehouses*. Data sourced from well-maintained data warehouses have higher quality, as there are proper controls in place to ensure a level of data accuracy for new and existing data. The data cleansing practices include elimination of duplicate records, quarantining outlier records that exceed the bounds, standardization of attribute values, substitution of missing values, etc. Regardless, it is critical to check the data using data exploration techniques in addition to using prior knowledge of the data and business before building models to ensure a certain degree of data quality.

2.2.3 Missing Values

One of the most common data quality issues is that some records having missing attribute values. For example, a credit score may be missing in one of the records. There are several different mitigation methods to deal with this problem, but each method has pros and cons. The first step in managing missing values is to understand the reason behind why the values are missing. Tracking the data lineage of the data source can lead to identifying systemic issues in data capture, errors in data transformation, or there may be a phenomenon that is not understood to the user yet. Knowing the source of a missing value will often guide what mitigation methodology to use. We can substitute the missing value with a range of artificial data so that we can manage the issue with marginal impact on the later steps in data mining. Missing credit score values can be replaced with a credit score derived from the data set (mean or minimum or maximum value, depending on the characteristics of the attribute). This method is useful if the missing values occur completely randomly and the frequency of occurrence is quite rare. If not, the distribution of the attribute that has missing data will be distorted. Alternatively, to build the representative model, we can ignore all the data records with missing value or records with poor data quality. This method reduces the size of the data set. Some data mining algorithms are good at handling records with missing values, while others expect the data preparation step to handle it before model is built and applied. For example, k-nearest neighbor (k-NN) algorithm for classification tasks are often robust with missing values. Neural network models for classification tasks do not perform well with missing attributes and thus the data preparation step is essential for developing neural network models.

2.2.4 Data Types and Conversion

The attributes in a data set can be of different types, such as continuous numeric (interest rate), integer numeric (credit score), or categorical. In some data sets, credit score is expressed as ordinal or categorical (poor, good, excellent). Different data mining algorithms impose different restrictions on what data types they accept as inputs. If the model we are about to build is a simple linear regression model, the input attributes need to be numeric. If the data that is available is categorical, then it needs to be converted to continuous numeric attribute. There are several methods available for conversion of categorical types to numeric attributes. For instance, we can encode a specific numeric score for each category value, such as poor = 400, good = 600, excellent = 700, etc. Similarly, numeric values can be converted to categorical data types by a technique called binning, where a range of values are specified for each category, e.g, low = [400–500] and so on.

2.2.5 Transformation

In some data mining algorithms like k-NN, the input attributes are expected to be numeric and normalized, because the algorithm compares the values of different attributes and calculates distance between the data points. It is important to make sure one particular attribute doesn't dominate the distance results because of large values or because it is denominated in smaller units. For example, consider income (expressed in USD, in thousands) and credit score (in hundreds). The distance calculation will always be dominated by slight variation in income. One solution is to convert the range of income and credit score to a more uniform scale from 0 to 1 by standardization or normalization. This way, we can make a consistent comparison between the two different attributes with different units. However, the presence of outliers may potentially skew the results of normalization.

In a few data mining tasks, it is necessary to reduce the number of attributes. Statistical techniques like principal component analysis (PCA) reduce attributes into a few key or principal attributes. PCA is discussed in Chapter 12 Feature Selection. The presence of multiple attributes that are highly correlated may be undesirable for few algorithms. For example, having both annual income and taxes paid are highly correlated and hence we may need to remove one of the attributes. This is explained in a little more detail in Chapter 5 Regression Methods, where we discuss regression.

2.2.6 Outliers

Outliers by definition are anomalies in the data set. Outliers may occur legitimately (income in billions) or erroneously (human height 1.73 centimeters). Regardless, the presence of outliers needs to be understood and will require special treatment. The purpose of creating a representative model is to generalize a pattern or a relationship in the data and the presence of outliers skews the model. The techniques for detecting outliers will be discussed in detail in Chapter 11 Anomaly Detection on anomaly detection. Detecting outliers may be the primary purpose of some data mining applications, like fraud detection and intrusion detection.

2.2.7 Feature Selection

The example data set shown in Table 2.1 has one *attribute* or *feature*—credit score—and one *label*—interest rate. In practice, many data mining problems involve a data set with hundreds to thousands of attributes. In text mining applications (see Chapter 9 Text Mining), every distinct word in a document is considered an attribute in the data set. Thus the data set used in this application contains thousands of attributes. Not all the attributes are equally important or useful in predicting the desired target value. Some of the attributes may be highly correlated with each other, like annual income and taxes paid. The presence of a high number of attributes in the data set significantly increases the complexity of a model and may degrade the performance of the model due to the *curse of dimensionality*. In general, the presence of more detailed information is desired in data mining because discovering nuggets of a pattern in the data is one of the attractions of using data mining techniques. But, as the number of dimensions in the data increases, data becomes sparse in high-dimensional space. This condition degrades the reliability of the models, especially in the case of clustering and classification (Tan et al., 2005).

Reducing the number of attributes, without significant loss in the performance of the model, is called feature selection. Chapter 12 provides details on different techniques available for feature selection and its implementation considerations. Reducing the number of attributes in the data set leads to a more simplified model and helps to synthesize a more effective explanation of the model.

2.2.8 Data Sampling

Sampling is a process of selecting a subset as a representation of the original data set for use in data analysis or modeling. Sample data serves as a representative of the original data set with similar properties, such as a similar mean. Sampling reduces the amount of data that needs to be processed for analysis and modeling. In most cases, to gain insights, extract the information and build representative predictive models from the data it is sufficient to work with samples. Sampling speeds up the build process of the modeling. Theoretically, the error introduced by sampling impacts the relevancy of the model but their benefits far outweighs the risks.

In the build process for Predictive Analytics applications, it is necessary to segment the data sets to training and test samples. Depending on the application, the training data set is sampled from the original data set using simple sampling or class label specific sampling. Let us consider the use cases for predicting anomalies in a data. Depending on the application, the training data set is sampled from the original data set using simple sampling or class label specific sampling. Let us consider the use cases for predicting anomalies in a data set (e.g., predicting fraudulent credit card transactions).

The objective of anomaly detection is to classify outliers in the data. These are rare events and often the example data does not have many examples of the outlier class. *Stratified sampling* is a process of sampling where each class is equally represented in the sample; this allows the model to focus on the difference between the patterns of each class. In classification applications, sampling is used create multiple base models, each developed using a different set of sampled training data sets. These base models are using to build one meta model, called the *ensemble model*, where the error rate is improved when compared to that of the base models.

2.3 MODELING

A model is the abstract representation of the data and its relationships in a given data set. A simple statement like "mortgage interest rate reduces with increase in credit score" is a model; although there is not enough quantitative information to use in a production scenario, it provides directional information to abstract a relationship between credit score and interest rate.

There are a few hundred data mining algorithms in use today, derived from statistics, machine learning, pattern recognition, and computer science body of knowledge. Fortunately, there are many viable commercial and open source predictive analytics and data mining tools in the market that implement these algorithms. As a data mining practitioner, all we need to be concerned with is having an overview of the algorithm. We want to know how it works and determine what parameters need to be configured based on our understanding of the business and data. Data mining models can be classified into the following categories: classification, regression, association analysis, clustering, and outlier or anomaly detection. Each category has a few dozen different algorithms; each takes a slightly different approach to solve the problem at hand. Classification and regression tasks are predictive techniques because they predict an outcome variable based on one or more input variables. Predictive algorithms need a known prior data set to "learn" the model. Figure 2.4 shows the steps in the modeling phase of predictive data mining. Association analysis and clustering are descriptive data mining techniques where there is no target variable to predict; hence there is no test data set. However, both predictive and descriptive models have an evaluation step. Anomaly detection can be predictive if known data is available or use unsupervised techniques if the known training data is not available.

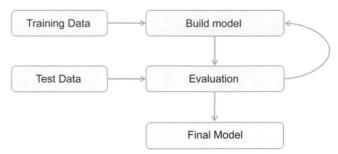

FIGURE 2.4
Modeling steps.

2.3.1 Training and Testing Data Sets

To develop a stable model, we need to make use of a previously prepared data set where we know all the attributes, including the target class attribute. This is called the *training data set* and it is used to create a model. We also need to check the validity of the created model with another known data set called the *test data set* or *validation data set*. To facilitate this process, the overall known data set can be split into a training data set and a test data set. A standard rule of thumb is for two-thirds of the data to go to training and one-third to go to the test data set. There are more sophisticated approaches where training records are selected by random sampling with replacement, which we will discuss in Chapter 4 Classification. Tables 2.3 and 2.4 show the random split of training and test data, based on the example data set shown in Table 2.1. Figure 2.5 shows the scatterplot of the entire example data set with the training and test data sets marked.

2.3.2 Algorithm or Modeling Technique

The business question and data availability dictate what data mining category (association, classification, regression, etc.) needs to be used. The data mining practitioner determines the appropriate data mining algorithm within the chosen category. For example, within classification any of the following algorithms can be chosen: decision trees, rule induction, neural networks, Bayesian models, k-NN, etc. Likewise within decision tree techniques, there are quite a number of implementations like CART, RAID, etc. We will review all these algorithms in detail in later chapters. It is not uncommon to use multiple data mining categories and algorithms to solve a business question.

Interest rate prediction is considered a regression problem. We are going to use a simple linear regression technique to model the data set and generalize the relationship between credit score and interest rate. The data set with 10 records can be split into training and test sets. The training set of seven records will be used to create the model and the test set of three records will be used to evaluate the validity of the model.

Table 2.3 Training Data Set

Borrower	Credit Score (X)	Interest Rate (Y)
01	500	7.31%
02	600	6.70%
03	700	5.95%
05	800	5.40%
06	800	5.70%
08	550	7.00%
09	650	6.50%

Table 2.4 Test Data Set

Borrower	Credit Score (X)	Interest Rate (Y)
04	700	6.40%
07	750	5.90%
10	825	5.70%

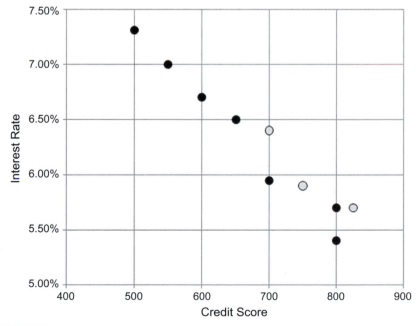

FIGURE 2.5
Scatterplot of training and test data.

The objective of simple linear regression can be visualized as fitting a straight line through the data points in a scatterplot (Figure 2.6). The line has to be built in such a way that the sum of the squared distance from the data points to the line is minimal. Generically, the line can be expressed as

$$y = a * x + b \qquad\qquad (2.1)$$

where y is the output or dependent variable, x is the input or independent variable, b is the y-intercept, and a is the coefficient of x. We can find the values of a and b in such a way so as to minimize the sum of the squared residuals of the line (Weisstein, 2013). We will review the concepts and steps in developing a linear regression model in greater detail in Chapter 5 Regression Methods.

The line shown in Equation 2.1 serves as a model to predict the outcome of new unlabeled data set. For the interest rate data set, we have calculated the simple linear regression for the interest rate (y):

$$y = 0.1 + \frac{6}{100,000} x$$

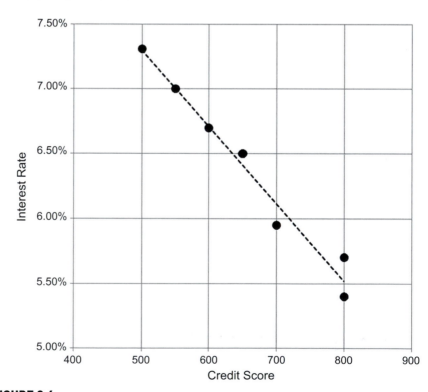

FIGURE 2.6
Regression model.

$$\text{Interest rate} = 10\,\% - \frac{6 * \text{Credit Score}}{1,000}\,\%$$

Using this model we can calculate the interest rate for a specified credit score of the borrower. Linear regression is one of the simplest models to get us started in model building and more complex models are discussed later in this book. In reality, the rate calculation involves a few dozen input variables and also takes into account the nonlinear relationship between variables.

2.3.3 Evaluation of the Model

The model generated in the form of an equation is generalized and synthesized from seven training records. We can substitute the credit score in the equation and see if the model estimates the interest rate for each of the seven training records. The estimation may not be exactly the same as the values in the training records. We do not want a model to memorize and output the same values that are in the training records. The phenomenon of a model memorizing the training data is called *overfitting*, which will be explored in Chapter 4 Classification. An overfitted model just memorizes the training records and will underperform on real production data. We want the model to generalize or *learn* the relationship between credit score and interest rate. To evaluate this relationship, the validation or test data set, which was not previously used in building the model, is used for evaluation, as shown in Table 2.5.

Table 2.5 provides the three testing records where the interest rate is known; these records were not used to build the model. The actual value of the interest rate can be compared against the predicted value using the model and thus the prediction error can be calculated. As long as the error is acceptable, this model can be used for deployment. The error rate can be used to compare this model with other models developed from different algorithms like neural networks or Bayesian models, etc.

2.3.4 Ensemble Modeling

Ensemble modeling is a process where multiple diverse models are created to predict an outcome, either by using many different modeling algorithms or using different training data sets. The ensemble model then aggregates the prediction

Table 2.5 Evaluation of Test Data Set

Borrower	Credit Score (X)	Interest Rate (Y)	Model Predicted (Y)	Model Error
04	700	6.40%	6.11%	-0.29%
07	750	5.90%	5.81%	-0.09%
10	825	5.70%	5.37%	-0.33%

of each base model and results in once final prediction for the unseen data. The motivation for using ensemble models is to reduce the generalization error of the prediction. As long as the base models are diverse and *independent*, the prediction error of the model decreases when the ensemble approach is used. The approach seeks the wisdom of crowds in making a prediction. Even though the ensemble model has multiple base models within the model, it acts and performs as a single model. Most of the practical data mining solutions utilize ensemble modeling techniques. Chapter 4 Classification covers the approaches of different ensemble modeling techniques and their implementation in detail.

At the end of the modeling stage of the data mining process, we have (1) analyzed the business question, (2) sourced the data relevant to answer the question, (3) picked a data mining technique to answer the question, (4) picked a data mining algorithm and prepared the data to suit the algorithm, (5) split the data into training and test data sets, (6) built a generalized model from the training data set, and (7) validated the model against the test data set. This model now can be used to predict the target variable based on an input variable of unseen data. This answers the business question on prediction. Now, the model needs to be deployed, for example by integrating the model in the production loan approval process of an enterprise.

2.4 APPLICATION

Deployment or application is the stage at which the model becomes production ready or "live." In business applications, the results of the data mining, either the model for predictive tasks or the learning framework for association rules or clustering, need to be assimilated into the business process—usually in software applications. The model deployment stage leads to some key considerations: assessing model readiness, technical integration, response time, model maintenance, and assimilation.

2.4.1 Production Readiness

The production readiness part of the deployment determines the critical qualities required for the deployment objective. Let's consider two distinct use cases: determining whether a consumer qualifies for a loan account with a commercial leading institution and determining the groupings of customers for an enterprise.

The consumer credit approval process is a real-time endeavor. Either through a consumer-facing website or through a specialized application for frontline agents, the credit decisions and terms need to be provided in real time as soon as prospective customers provide relevant information. It is seen as a competitive advantage to provide a quick decision while also providing accurate results in the interest of customer and the company. The decision-making model needs to collect data from the customer, integrate third-party data like credit history, and make a decision on the loan approval and terms in a matter of seconds. The critical quality in this model deployment is real-time prediction.

Segmenting customers based on their relationship with the company is a thoughtful process where signals from various interactions through a number of departments in a company are considered. Based on the patterns, similar customers are put in cohorts and treatment strategies are deviced to best engage the customer. For this application, batch processing, where data is collected overnight from various departments and sources, is integrated and the overall customer records are segmented. The critical quality in this application is the ability to find unique patterns amongst customers, not the response time of the model. The business application informs the choices that need to be made in data preparation and modeling steps, in terms of accessibility of the data and algorithms.

2.4.2 Technical Integration

Most likely some kind of data mining software tool (R, RapidMiner, SAS, SPSS, etc.) would have been used to create the data mining models. Data mining tools save time by not requiring the writing of custom codes to implement the algorithm. This allows the analyst to focus on the data, business logic, and exploring patterns from the data. The models created by data mining tools can be ported to production applications by utilizing the Predictive Model Markup Language (PMML) (Guazzelli et al., 2009) or by invoking data mining tools in the production application. PMML provides a portable and consistent format of model description which can be read by most Predictive Analytics and Data Mining tools. This allows the flexibility for practitioners to develop the model with one tool (e.g., RapidMiner) and deploy it in another tool (e.g., SAS). PMML standards are developed and maintained by the Data Mining Group, an industry-lead consortium. Models such as simple regression, decision trees, and induction rules for predictive analytics can be incorporated directly into business applications and business intelligence systems easily. Since these models are represented by simple equations and if-then rules, they can be ported easily to most programming languages.

2.4.3 Response Time

Some data mining algorithms, like k-NN, are easy to build but quite slow in predicting the target variables. Algorithms such as the decision tree take time to build but can be reduced to simple rules that can be coded into almost any application. The trade-offs between production responsiveness and build time need to be considered and if needed, the modeling phase needs to be revisited if the response time is not acceptable by business application. The quality of prediction, accessibility of input data and the response time of the prediction remains the most important quality factors in the business application.

2.4.4 Remodeling

The key criterion for the ongoing relevance of the model is the representativeness of the data set it is processing. It is quite normal that the conditions in which the model is built change after the model is sent to deployment. For example, the relationship between the credit score and interest rate change frequently based on the prevailing macroeconomic conditions. Hence the model needs to be updated frequently for this application. The validity of the model can be routinely tested by using the new known test data set and calculating the error rate. If the error rate exceeds a particular threshold, then we can rebuild the model and redo the deployment. Creating a maintence schedule is a key part of a deployment plan that will sustain a living model.

2.4.5 Assimilation

In descriptive data mining applications, deploying a model to live systems may not be the objective. The challenge is often to assimilate the knowledge gained from data mining to the organization or a specific application. For example, the objective may be finding logical clusters in the customer database so that separate treatment can be provided to each customer cluster. Then the next step may be a classification task for new customers to put them in one of known clusters. Association analysis provides a solution for the market basket problem, where the task is to find which two products are purchased together most often. The challenge for the data mining practitioner is to articulate these findings, relevance to the original business question, a quantification of risks in the model and expected business impact to the business users. Often, this is a challenging task for data mining practitioner. The business user community is an amalgamation of different point of views, different quantitative mind set and skill set. Not everyone is aware about process of Data Mining and what it can and cannot do. Some aspect of this challenge can be addressed by focusing on the end result and it's impact of knowing the information instead of technical process of extracting the information through data mining. Understanding and rationalizing the results for these tasks may lead to taking action through business processes.

2.5 KNOWLEDGE

The data mining process provides a framework to extract nontrivial information from data. With the advent of massive storage, increased data collection, and advanced computing paradigms, the data at our disposal are only increasing. To extract knowledge from these massive data assets, we need to employ advanced approaches like data mining algorithms, in addition to standard time series reporting or simple statistical processing. Though many of these algorithms can provide valuable knowledge extraction, it's up to the analytics professional to skillfully apply the right algorithms and transform a business problem to a data problem. Data mining, like any other technology, provides options in terms of algorithms and parameters within the algorithms. Using these options to extract the right information is a bit of art and can be developed with practice.

The data mining process starts with prior knowledge and ends with posterior knowledge, which is the incremental insight gained about the business via data through the process. As with any quantitative analysis, the data mining process can point out spurious irrelevant patterns from the data set. Not all discovered patterns leads to knowledge. Again, it is upon the practitioner to invalidate the irrelevant patterns and identify meaningful information. The impact of the information gained through data mining can be measured in an application. It's the difference between having the information through the data mining process and the insights from basic data analysis. Finally, the whole data mining process is a framework to invoke the right questions (Chapman et al., 2000) and guide us through the right approaches to solve a business problem. It is not meant to be used as a set of rigid rules, but as a set of iterative, distinct steps that aid in knowledge discovery.

WHAT'S NEXT?

In upcoming chapters, we will dive into the details of the concepts discussed in this chapter, along with the implementation details. Exploring data by using basic statistical and visual techniques are an important step in preparing the data for data mining. The next chapter on Data Exploration provides a practical tool kit to explore and understand the data. The techniques of data preparation are explained in the context of individual data mining techniques in the chapters on classification, association analysis, clustering, and anomaly detection. Chapter 13 Getting Started with RapidMiner covers the practical implementation of data preparation techniques using RapidMiner.

REFERENCES

Chapman, P., Clinton, J., Kerber, R., Khabaza, T., Reinartz, T., Shearer, C., & Wirth, R. (2000). CRISP-DM 1.0: Step-by-step Data Mining guide. *SPSS Inc*. Retrieved from ftp://ftp.software.ibm.com/software/analytics/spss/support/Modeler/Documentation/14/UserManual/CRISP-DM.pdf.

Fayyad, U., Piatetsky-Shapiro, G., & Smyth, P. (1996). From Data Mining to Knowledge Discovery in Databases. *AI MAGAZINE, 17*(3), 37–54.

Guazzelli, A., Zeller, M., Lin, W., & Williams, G. (2009). PMML: An Open Standard for Sharing Models. *The R Journal, 1*(1), 60–65.

Kubiak, T., & Benbow, D. W. (2005). *The Certified Six Sigma Black Belt Handbook*. Milwaukee, WI: ASQ, Quality Press.

Lidwell, W., Holden, K., & Butler, J. (2010). *Universal Principles of Design, Revised and Updated: 125 ways to Enhance Usability, Influence Perception, Increase Appeal, Make Better Design Decisions, and Teach Through Design*. Beverly, MA: Rockport Publishers.

Piatetsky, G. (2014). KDnuggets 15th Annual Analytics, Data Mining, Data Science Software Poll: RapidMiner Continues To Lead. Retrieved August 01, 2014, from http://www.kdnuggets.com/2014/06/kdnuggets-annual-software-poll-rapidminer-continues-lead.html.

SAS Institute (2013). *Getting Started with SAS Enterprise Miner 12.3*. (pp. 1–3).

Shearer, C. (2000). The CRISP-DM Model: The New Blueprint for Data Mining. *Journal of Data Warehousing, 5*(4), 13–22.

Tan, P.-N., Steinbach, M., & Kumar, V. (2005). Introduction to Data Mining. *Journal of School Psychology, 19*, 51–56. http://dx.doi.org/10.1016/0022-4405(81)90007-8.

Weisstein, E. W. (2013). Least Squares Fitting. MathWorld - Wolfram Research, Inc. Retrieved from http://mathworld.wolfram.com/LeastSquaresFitting.html.

CHAPTER 3

Data Exploration

The word "data" is derived from Latin word *dare*, which means "something given"—an observation or a fact about a subject. Data mining helps decipher the hidden relationships within the data. Before venturing into any advanced analysis of the data using statistical, machine learning, and algorithmic techniques, it is essential to perform basic data exploration to study the main characteristics of the data. Data exploration helps us to understand the data better, to prepare the data in a way that makes advanced analysis possible, and sometimes to get the necessary insights from the data faster than using advanced analytical techniques.

Data exploration, also known as exploratory data analysis (EDA), provides a set of simple tools to obtain some basic understanding of the data. The results of data exploration can be extremely powerful in grasping the structure of the data, the distribution of the values, and the presence of extreme values and interrelationships within the data set. Data exploration also provides guidance on applying the right kind of further statistical and data mining treatment to the data. Data exploration tools are a part of standard data analysis software packages from the ubiquitous Microsoft Excel® to advanced data mining software like R, RapidMiner, SAS, IBM SPSS etc. Simple pivot table functions, computing statistics like mean and deviation, and plotting data as a line, bar, and scatter charts are part of data exploration techniques that are used in everyday business setting.

Data exploration can be broadly classified into two types—descriptive statistics and data visualization. Descriptive statistics is the process of condensing key characteristics of the data set into simple numeric metrics. Some of the common metrics used are mean, standard deviation, and correlation. Visualization is the process of projecting the data, or parts of it, into multidimensional space or into abstract images. Data exploration in the context of data mining uses both descriptive statistics and visualization techniques. This chapter serves as a roadmap for exploring and analyzing a data set. The process of structured data exploration reveals much information about the data, which can be used to decide on the next steps for mining the data.

3.1 OBJECTIVES OF DATA EXPLORATION

In the data mining process, data exploration is leveraged in many different steps including preprocessing or data preparation, modeling, and interpretation of the modeling results.

1. **Data understanding:** With preliminary analysis, data exploration provides a high level overview of each attribute in the data set and interaction between the attributes. Data exploration helps answers the questions like what is the typical value of an attribute, how much the data points differ from the typical value, or are there any outliers in the data set, for example.

2. **Data preparation:** Before applying the data mining algorithm, we need to prepare the data set for handling of any anomalies that may be present in the data. But first, those anomalies need to be identified, which includes finding outliers, missing values, and removal of duplicate or highly correlated attributes. Some data mining algorithms do not work very well when input attributes are correlated with each other. Thus, correlated attributes need to be identified and removed.

3. **Data mining tasks:** Basic data exploration can sometime substitute for the entire data mining process. For example, scatterplots can identify clusters in low-dimensional data or can help develop regression or classification models with simple visual rules.

4. **Interpreting the results:** Finally, data exploration is used in understanding the prediction, classification, and clustering results of the data mining process. In low dimensional clustering, a scatterplot is an efficient way to visualize clusters. Histograms allow for comprehension of the distribution of the attribute and can also be useful for visualizing numeric prediction, error rate estimation, etc.

3.2 DATA SETS

Throughout the rest of the chapter and the book we will introduce a few classic data sets that are simple to understand, easy to explain, and can be used commonly across many different data mining techniques, which allows us to compare the performance of these techniques. The most popular of all data sets for data mining is probably the *Iris data set*, introduced by Ronald Fisher, in his seminal work on discriminant analysis, "The use of multiple measurements in taxonomic problems" (Fisher, 1936). Iris is a flowering plant that is widely found across the world. The genus of Iris contains more than 300 different species. Each species exhibits different physical characteristics like shape and size of the flowers and leaves. The Iris data set contains 150 observations of three different species, *Iris setosa*, *Iris virginica*, and *Iris versicolor*, with 50 observations each. Each observation

FIGURE 3.1

Iris versicolor. Photo by Danielle Langlois. July 2005 (Image modified from original by marking parts. "Iris versicolor 3." Licensed under Creative Commons Attribution-Share Alike 3.0 via Wikimedia Commons.[1])

[1]http://commons.wikimedia.org/wiki/File:Iris_versicolor_3.jpg#mediaviewer/File:Iris_versicolor_3.jpg

consists of four attributes: sepal length, sepal width, petal length, and petal width. The fifth attribute is the name of the species observed, which takes the values *Iris setosa*, *Iris virginica*, and *Iris versicolor*. Petals are the brightly colored inner part of the flowers and sepals form the outer part of the flower and are usually green in color. In an Iris however, both sepals and petals are purple in color, but can be distinguished from each other by differences in shape (Figure 3.1).

All four attributes in the Iris data set are numeric continuous values measured in centimeters. One of the species, *Iris setosa*, can be easily distinguished from the other two using linear regression or simple rules, but separating the *virginica* and *versicolor* classes requires more complex rules that involve more attributes. The data set is available in all standard data mining tools, such as RapidMiner, or can be downloaded from public websites such as the University of California Irvine – Machine Learning repository[2] (Bache & Lichman, 2013). This data set and other data sets used in this book can be downloaded from the companion website www.LearnPredictiveAnalytics.com.

The Iris data set is used for learning data mining mainly because it is simple to understand and explore and can be used to illustrate how different data mining algorithms perform on the same standard data set. The data set extends beyond two dimensions, with three class labels of which one class is easily separable (*Iris setosa*) by visual exploration, while classifying the

[2]http://archive.ics.uci.edu/ml

other two classes is slightly challenging. It helps to reaffirm the classification results that can be derived based on visual rules, and at the same time sets the stage for data mining to build new rules beyond the limits of visual exploration.

3.2.1 Types of Data

Data comes in different formats and types. Understanding the properties of each variable or features or attributes provides information about what kind of operations can be performed on that variable. For example, the temperature in weather data can be expressed as any of the following formats:

- Numeric centigrade (31ºC, 33.3ºC) or Fahrenheit (100ºF, 101.45ºF) or on the Kelvin scale
- Ordered label as in Hot, Mild, or Cold
- Number of days within a year below 0ºC (10 days in a year below freezing)

All of these attributes indicate temperature in a region, but each has different data type. A few of these data types can be converted from one to another.

Numeric or Continuous

Temperature expressed in centigrade or Fahrenheit is numeric and continuous because it can be denoted by numbers and take an infinite number of values between digits. Values are ordered and calculating the difference between values makes sense. Hence we can apply additive and subtractive mathematical operations and logical comparison operations like greater than, less than, and is equal operations.

An integer is a special form of the numeric data type that doesn't have decimals in the value or more precisely doesn't have infinite values between consecutive numbers. Usually, they denote a count of something like number of days with temperature less than 0ºC, number of orders, number of children in a family, etc.

If a zero point is defined, numeric becomes a *ratio* or *real* data type. Examples include temperature in Kelvin scale, bank account balance, and income. Along with additive and logical operations, ratio operations can be performed with this data type. Both integer and ratio data types are categorized as a *numeric* data type in most Data Mining tools.

Categorical or Nominal

Categorical data types are variables treated as distinct symbols or just names. The color of the human iris is a categorical data type because it takes a value like black, green, blue, grey, etc. There is no direct relationship among the data values and hence we cannot apply mathematical operators except the logical or "is equal" operator. They are also called a nominal or polynominal data type, derived from the Latin word for "name."

An ordered data type is a special case of a categorical data type where there is some kind of order among the values. An example of an ordered data type is credit score when expressed in categories such as poor, average, good, and excellent. People with a good score have a credit rating better than average and an excellent rating is a credit score better than the good rating.

Data types are relevant to understanding more about the data and how the data is sourced. Not all data mining tasks can be performed on all data types. For example, the neural network algorithm does not work with categorical data. However, we can convert data from one data type to another using a type conversion process, but this may be accompanied with possible loss of information. For example, credit scores expressed in poor, average, good, and excellent categories can be converted to either 1, 2, 3, and 4 or average underlying numerical scores like 400, 500, 600, and 700 (scores here are just an example). In this type conversion, there is no loss of information. However, conversion from numeric credit score to categories (poor, average, good, and excellent) does incur some loss of information.

3.3 DESCRIPTIVE STATISTICS

Descriptive statistics refers to the study of aggregate quantities such as mean, standard deviation or distributions quantification of the main characteristics of a data set. The descriptive measures increases the understanding of the data set; these measures are some of the commonly used notations in everyday life when we deal with data. Some examples of descriptive statistics include average annual income, median home price in a neighborhood, range of credit scores of a population, etc. In general, descriptive analysis covers the following characteristics of the sample or population data set (Kubiak & Benbow, 2006):

Characteristics of the Data Set	Measurement Technique
Center of the data set	Mean, median, and mode
Spread of the data set	Range, variance, and standard deviation
Shape of the distribution of the data set	Symmetry, skewness, and kurtosis

We will explore the definition of these metrics shortly. In a different context, descriptive statistics can be broadly classified into univariate and multivariate exploration depending on number of variables under analysis.

3.3.1 Univariate Exploration

Univariate data exploration denotes analysis of one variable or an attribute at a time. The example Iris data set for one species, *Iris setosa*, has 50 observations and 4 attributes, as shown in Table 3.1. Let's explore some of the descriptive statistics for Sepal length variable.

Measure of Central Tendency

The objective of finding the central location of a variable is to quantify the data set with one central or most common number.

- **Mean:** The mean is the arithmetic average of all observations in the data set. It is calculated by summing all the data points and dividing by the number of data points. The mean for sepal length in centimeters is 5.0060.
- **Median:** The median is the value of the central point in the distribution. The median is calculated by sorting all the observations from small to large and selecting the mid-point observation in the sorted list. If the number of data points is even, then the average of the middle two data points is used as the median. The median for sepal length is 5.0000.
- **Mode:** The mode is the most frequently occurring observation. In the data set, data points may be repetitive and the most repetitive data point is the mode of the data set. In this example, the mode is 5.1000.

In a variable, the mean, media, and mode may be different numbers and this indicates the shape of the distribution. If the data set has outliers, the mean will get affected while in most cases the median will not. The mode of the distribution can be different from the mean or median, if the underlying data set has more than one natural normal distribution.

Measure of Spread

In desert regions, it is common for the temperature to cross above 110ºF during the day and drop below 30ºF during the night while the average temperature for a

Table 3.1 Iris Data Set and Descriptive Statistics (Fisher, 1936)				
Observation	**Sepal Length**	**Sepal Width**	**Petal Length**	**Petal Width**
1	5.1	3.5	1.4	0.2
2	4.9	3.1	1.5	0.1
…	…	…	…	…
49	5	3.4	1.5	0.2
50	4.4	2.9	1.4	0.2
Statistics	**Sepal Length**	**Sepal Width**	**Petal Length**	**Petal Width**
Mean	5.006	3.418	1.464	0.244
Median	5.000	3.400	1.500	0.200
Mode	5.100	3.400	1.500	0.200
Range	1.500	2.100	0.900	0.500
Standard Deviation	0.352	0.381	0.174	0.107
Variance	0.124	0.145	0.030	0.011

24-hour period is around 70ºF. Obviously, the experience is not same as living in a tropical region with an average daily temperature around 70ºF, where the temperature is between a more narrow range from 60ºF to 80ºF. What matters here is not just central location of the temperature, but the spread of temperature. There are two common metrics to quantify spread.

- **Range:** The range is the difference between the maximum value and the minimum value of the variable. The range is simple to calculate and articulate but has shortcomings as it is severely impacted by the presence of outliers and fails to consider the distribution of all other data points in the attributes, especially the central point. In the above example, the range for the temperature in the desert is 80ºF and the range for the tropics is 20ºF. A desert experiences larger temperature swings as indicated by the range.
- **Deviation:** The variance and standard deviation measure the spread by considering the values of all the data points of the attribute. Deviation is simply measured as the difference between any given value and the mean of the sample $(x_i - \mu)$, where μ is the mean of the distribution and x_i is the individual data point. The variance is the sum of the squared deviations of all data points from the average data point divided by the number of data points. Standard deviation is the square root of the variance. For a data set with N observations, the variance is given by Equation 3.1:

$$\text{Variance} = s^2 = \frac{1}{N} \sum_{i=1}^{N} (x_i - \mu)^2 \tag{3.1}$$

Since the standard deviation is measured in the same units as the variable, it is easy to understand the magnitude of the metric. High standard deviation means the data points are in general spread widely around the central point. Low standard deviation means data points are closer to the central point. If the distribution of the data aligns with the *normal distribution*, then 63% of the data points lie within one standard deviation from the mean. Figure 3.2 provides the univariate summary of the Iris data set with all 150 observations, for each of the four numeric attributes.

				Min	Max	Average	Deviation
Sepal Length	Real	0		4.300	7.900	5.843	0.828
Sepal Width	Real	0		2	4.400	3.054	0.434
Petal Length	Real	0		1	6.900	3.759	1.764
Petal Width	Real	0		0.100	2.500	1.199	0.763

FIGURE 3.2
Descriptive statistics for the Iris data set.

3.3.2 Multivariate Exploration

Multivariate exploration is the study of more than one attribute in the data set at the same time. This technique is critical to understanding the relationship between the attributes, which is very central to the objectives of Data Mining problems. Like univariate explorations, we will discuss the measure of central tendency and variations in the data.

Central Data Point

In the Iris data set, we can express each data point as a set of all the four attributes:

observation i: {sepal length, sepal width, petal length, petal width}

For example, we have observation 1: {5.1, 3.5, 1.4, 0.2}. This observation point can also be expressed in four-dimensional Cartesian coordinates and can be plotted in a graph (although plotting more than three dimensions in a visual graph can be challenging). In this way, we can express all 150 observations in Cartesian coordinates. If our objective is to find the most "typical" observation point, it would be a data point made up of the mean of each attribute in the data set independently. For the Iris data set shown in Table 3.1, the central mean point is {5.006, 3.418, 1.464, 0.244}. Since we are calculating the mean, this data point may not be an actual observation. It will be a hypothetical data point with the most typical attribute values.

Correlation

Correlation measures the statistical relationship between two variables, particularly dependence of one variable with another variable. When two variables are highly correlated with each other, they both vary at the same rate with each other either in the same or in opposite directions. For example, consider average temperature in a day and ice cream sales. Statistically, the two variables that are correlated are dependent on each other and one may be used to predict the other. If we have sufficient data, we can predict future sales of ice cream if we know the temperature forecast. However, correlation between two variables does not imply causation, that is, one doesn't necessarily cause other. Ice cream sales and shark attacks are correlated, however there is no causation. Both ice cream sales and shark attacks are influenced by the third variable—the summer season. Generally, ice cream sales sees an increase as temperature rises and more people go to beaches, which cause an increase in encounters with sharks.

Correlation between two attributes is commonly measured by the Pearson correlation coefficient (r), which measures the strength of *linear* dependence (Figure 3.3). Correlation coefficients take a value from $-1 <= r >= 1$. A value

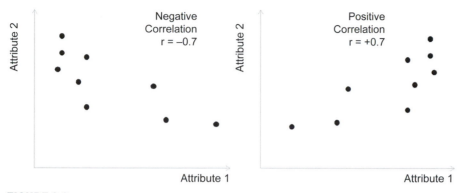

FIGURE 3.3

Correlation of variables.

closer to 1 or –1 indicates the two variables are highly correlated, with perfect correlation at 1 or –1. Perfect correlation exists when the variables are governed by laws of physics, for example, when we observe the values of gravitational force and mass of the object (Newton's second law) and the price of the product and total sales (price * volume). A correlation value of 0 means there is no *linear* relationship between two variables.

The Pearson correlation coefficient between two variables x and y is calculated by the following formula:

$$r_{xy} = \frac{\sum_{i=1}^{n} (x_i - \bar{x})(y_i - \bar{y})}{\sqrt{\sum_{i=1}^{n} (x_i - \bar{x})^2 \sum_{i=1}^{n} (y_i - \bar{y})^2}}$$

$$= \frac{\sum_{i=1}^{N} (x_i - \bar{x})(y_i - \bar{y})}{N * S_x * S_y}$$

(3.2)

where s_x and s_y are the standard deviations of random variables x and y, respectively. The correlation coefficient has some limitations in quantifying the strength of correlation. When data sets have more complex nonlinear relationships like quadratic functions, only the effects on linear relationships are considered and quantified using correlation coefficient. The presence of outliers can also skew the measure of correlation. Visually, correlation can be observed using scatterplots of variables in each Cartesian coordinate (Figure 3.3). In fact, visualization should be the first step in understanding correlation because it can identify nonlinear relationships and show any outliers clearly in the data set. *Anscombe's quartet* (Anscombe, 1973) clearly illustrates the limitations of relying only on the correlation coefficient (Figure 3.4). The quartet consists of four different data sets, with two variables (x, y). All four data sets have same mean, variance for x and y, and

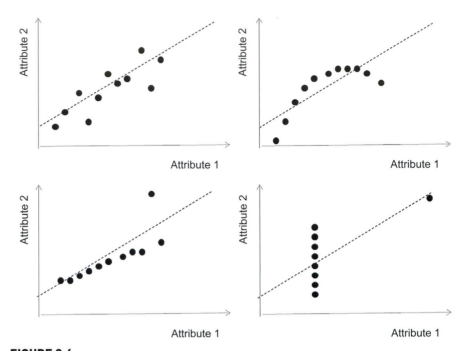

FIGURE 3.4

Anscombe's Quartet: descriptive statistics vs. visualization (Anscombe, F. J., 1973. Graphs in Statistical Analysis, *American Statistician 27* (1), pp. 19–20.)

correlation coefficient between x and y, but look drastically different when plotted in the chart. This evidence illustrates the necessity of visualizing the variables instead of just calculating statistical properties.

3.4 DATA VISUALIZATION

Visualizing data is one of the most important aspects of data discovery and exploration. Though visualization is not considered a data mining technique, terms like visual mining or pattern discovery based on visuals are increasingly used in the context of data mining, particularly in the business world. The discipline of data visualization encompasses the methods of expressing data in an abstract visual form. The visual representation of data provides easy comprehension of complex data with multiple variables and their underlying relationships. The motivation for data visualization includes:

- **Comprehension of dense information:** A simple visual chart can easily include thousands of data points. By using visuals, the user can see the big picture, as well as longer-term trends that are extremely difficult to interpret purely by expressing data in numbers.

- **Relationships:** Visualizing data in Cartesian coordinates enables exploration of the relationships between the variables. Although representing more than three variables on the x-, y-, and z-axes is not feasible in Cartesian coordinates, there are a few creative solutions available by changing properties like the size, color, and shape of data markers or using flow maps (Tufte, 2001), where more than two attributes are used in a two-dimensional medium.

Vision is the most powerful sense in the human body. As such, it is intimately connected with cognitive thinking (Few, 2006). Human vision is trained to discover patterns and anomalies even in the presence of a large set of data. However the effectiveness of the pattern detection depends on how effectively the information is visually presented. Hence, selecting suitable visuals to explore data is critically important in discovering and comprehending hidden patterns in the data (Ware, 2004). In this chapter, we are categorizing visualization techniques into: Univariate visualization, multi-variate visualization and visualization of large number of variables using parallel dimensions.

We will review some of the common data visualization techniques used to analyze data. Most of these visualization techniques are available in a commercial spreadsheet software like MS Excel (R). RapidMiner, like any other data mining tool, offers a wide range of visualization tools. To maintain consistency with rest of the book, all the following visualization is output from RapidMiner using the Iris data set. If you are new to RapidMiner, we suggest you review Chapter 13 Getting started with RapidMiner.

3.4.1 Visualizing the Frequency Distribution of Data in a Dimension

The visual exploration starts with investigating one attribute at a time using univariate charts. The techniques discussed in this section gives an idea of how the attribute values are distributed and shape of the distribution.

Histogram

A histogram is one of the most basic visual ways to understand the frequency of occurrence of a range of values for one variable. It approximately determines the distribution of the data by plotting the frequency of occurrence in a range. In a histogram, the continuous variable under inquiry takes the horizontal axis and the frequency of occurrence takes the vertical axis. For a continuous, numeric data type we need to specify the range or binning value to group a range of values; for example, in the case of human height in centimeters, all the occurrences between 152.00 and 152.99 are grouped under 152. There is no optimal number of bins or bin width that works for all distributions. In general, if the bin width is too small, the distribution becomes more precise but reveals the noise due to sampling. A general rule of thumb is to have a number of bins equal to the square root or cube root of the number of data points.

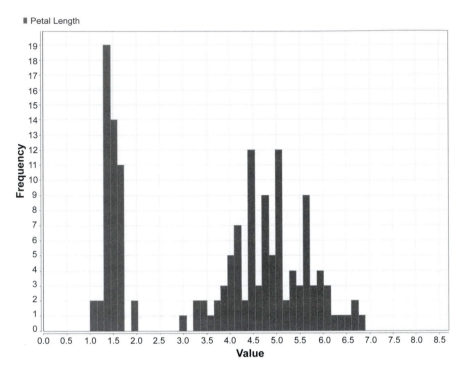

FIGURE 3.5
Histogram of petal length in Iris data set.

Histograms are used to find the central location, range, and shape of distribution. In the case of the petal length variable in the Iris data set, we see the data is multimodal (Figure 3.5), where the distribution does not follow the bell curve pattern. Instead, there are two peaks in the distribution. This is due to the fact that we have 150 observations of three different species in the data set. If we sum all the frequencies by ranges, it should sum to 150.

A histogram can be modified to include different classes, in this case species, in order to gain more insight. The enhanced histogram with class labels shows the data set is made of three different distributions (Figure 3.6). *Iris setosa's* distribution stands out with a mean around 1.25 and a range from 1 to 2 cm. *Iris versicolor* and *Iris virginica's* distributions overlap *Iris setosa's* slightly and have separate means.

Quartile
A *box whisker* plot is a simple visual way of showing the distribution of a continuous variable with information such as quartiles, median, and outliers, in some cases overlaid by mean and standard deviation. The main attraction of box whisker or quartile charts is that we can compare multiple distributions

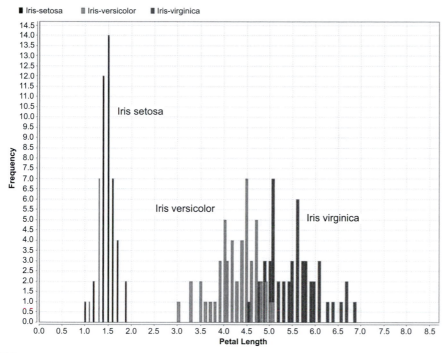

FIGURE 3.6

Class-stratified histogram of petal length in Iris data set.

side by side and deduce the overlap between them. Quartiles are denoted by Q1, Q2, and Q3 points, which indicate the data points with 25% bin size. In a distribution, 25% of the data points will be below Q1, 50% will be below Q2, and 75% will be below Q3.

The Q1 and Q3 points in a box whisker plot are denoted by the edges of the box. The Q2 point is indicated by a cross line within the box. Q2 is also the median of the distribution. Outliers are denoted by circles at the end of the whisker line. In some cases, the mean point is denoted by a solid dot overlay followed by standard deviation as a line overlay.

In Figure 3.7 quartile charts for all four variables of Iris data set are plotted side by side. We can observe petal length has the broadest distribution from the 150 observations and petal width is generally the smallest measurement out of all four variables.

We can also select one variable—petal length—and explore it further using quartile charts by introducing a class variable. In the plot in Figure 3.8, we can see the distribution of three species for the petal length measurement. Similar to the previous comparison, the distribution of multiple species can be compared.

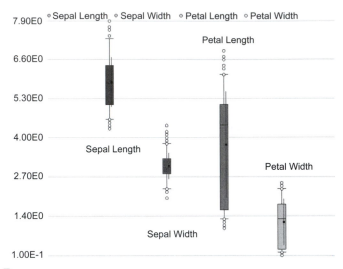

FIGURE 3.7
Quartile plot of Iris data set.

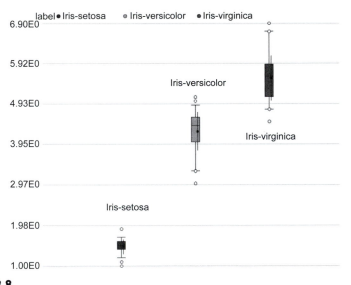

FIGURE 3.8
Class-stratified quartile plot of petal length in Iris data set.

Distribution Chart

For continuous numeric variables like petal length, instead of visualizing the actual data in the sample, we can instead visualize its normal distribution function. The normal distribution function of a continuous random variable is given by the formula

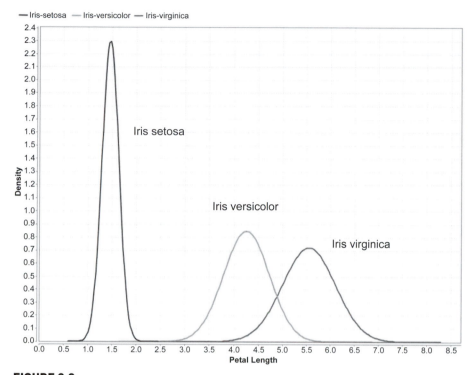

FIGURE 3.9
Distribution of petal length in Iris data set.

$$f(x) = \frac{1}{\sqrt{2\pi}\sigma} e^{\frac{(x-\mu)^2}{2\sigma^2}} \qquad (3.3)$$

where μ is the mean of the distribution and σ is the standard deviation of the distribution. Here we are making an inherent assumption that the measurements of petal length (or any continuous variable) follow the normal distribution and hence we can visualize its distribution instead of actual values. The normal distribution is also called the *Gaussian distribution* or "bell curve" for the attribute due to its bell shape. The normal distribution function tells the probability of occurrence of a data point within a range. If a data set exhibits normal distribution, then 68.2% of data points fall within one standard deviation from the mean. 95.4% of the points fall within 2σ and 99.7% within 3σ of the mean. When the normal distribution curves are stratified by class type, we can gain more insight into the data. Figure 3.9 shows the normal distribution curves for petal length measurement for each Iris species type. From the distribution chart, we can infer the petal length for *Iris setosa* sample is more distinct and cohesive than *Iris versicolor* and *Iris virginica*. If we get an unlabeled measurement with a petal length of 1.5 centimeter, we can predict that the species is *Iris setosa*; if the measurement is 5.0 centimeters, then there is no clear prediction based on petal length, as it could be either *Iris Versicolor* and *Iris virginica*.

3.4.2 Visualizing Multiple Variables in Cartesian Coordinates

The multivariate visual exploration considers more than one attribute in the same visual. The techniques discussed in this section focuses on the relationship of one attribute with another attribute. These visualizations examines two to four attributes simultaneously and becomes cumbersome when more than three attributes are studied.

Scatterplot

A scatterplot is one of the most powerful yet simple mathematical plots available. In a scatterplot, the data points are marked in Cartesian space with variables of the data set aligned in coordinates. The variables or dimensions are usually from a continuous data type. The data point itself can be colored to indicate one more variable from the data set. One of the key observations that can be concluded from a scatterplot is the existence of a relationship between two variables under inquiry. If the variables are correlated, then the data points align closer to an imaginary straight line; if they are not correlated, the data points are scattered. Apart from basic correlation, scatterplots can also indicate the existence of patterns or groups of clusters in the data and identify outliers in the data. This is particularly useful for low-dimensional data sets. Chapter 11 Anomaly Detection provides techniques for finding outliers in high-dimensional space, by calculating the distance between data points.

Figure 3.10 shows the scatterplot between petal length (x-axis) and petal width (y-axis). Generally, these two attributes are slightly correlated, because this is a measurement of the same part of the flower. When we color the data markers to indicate different species using class labels, we can observe more patterns. There is a cluster

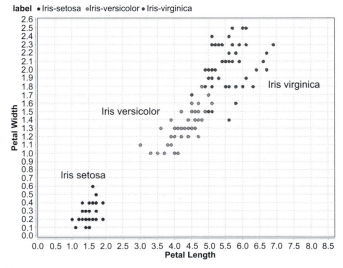

FIGURE 3.10

Scatterplot of Iris data set.

of data points, all belonging to species *Iris setosa*, on the lower left side of the plot. *Iris setosa* has much smaller petal length and width. This feature can be used as a rule to predict the species of unknown observations. One of the limitations of scatterplots is that only two variables can be used at a time, with additional variables possibly shown in the color of the data marker (usually reserved for class labels).

Scatter Multiple

A *scatter multiple* is an enhanced form of a simple scatterplot where more than two dimensions can be included in the chart and studied simultaneously. The primary variable is used for the x-axis coordinate. The secondary axis is shared with more variables or dimensions. In this example (Figure 3.11), the values on the y-axis are shared between sepal length, sepal width, and petal width. The variable information is conveyed by colors used in data markers. Here, sepal length is represented by data points occupying the topmost part of the chart, sepal width occupies the middle portion, and petal width is in the bottom portion. Note that the data points are *duplicated for each variable in the y-axis*. Data points are color-coded for each dimension in y-axis and the x-axis is anchored with one variable—petal length. Even though a scatter multiple plot allows for investigation of multiple dimensions, only two variables can be compared at a time, one of which one is on the primary axis.

Scatter Matrix

A scatter multiple enables comparison of more than two variables via scatterplot. But, the comparison is always with a primary variable and the relationship

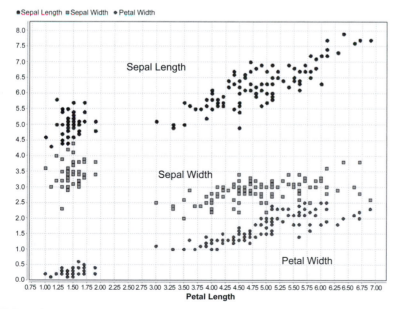

FIGURE 3.11
Scatter multiple plot of Iris data set.

between two variables used on the y-axis is not very visible. If the data set has more variables, it is important to look at combinations of all variables through a scatterplot. A *scatter matrix* solves this need by comparing all combinations of variables with individual scatterplots and arranging these plots in a matrix.

A scatter matrix for all four attributes in the Iris data set is shown in Figure 3.12. The color of the data point is used to indicate the species of the flower. Since there are four attributes, there are four rows and four columns, for a total of 16 scatter charts. Charts in the diagonal are a comparison of the variable with itself; hence they are eliminated. Also, the charts below the diagonal are mirror images of the charts above the diagonal. In effect, there are six

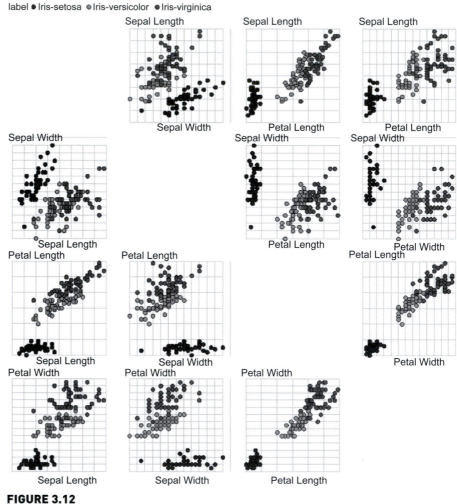

FIGURE 3.12

Scatter matrix plot of Iris data set.

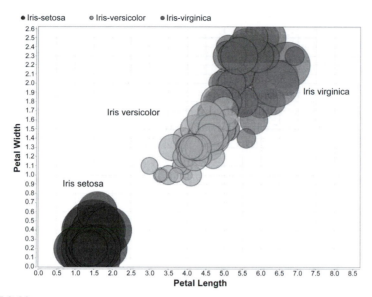

FIGURE 3.13
Bubble chart of Iris data set.

distinct comparisons in scatter multiples of four variables. Scatter matrices pro-vide an effective visualization of comparative, multivariate, and high-density data displayed in small multiples of the same scatterplots (Tufte, 2001).

Bubble Chart

A *bubble chart* is a variation of a simple scatterplot with the addition of one more variable, which is used to determine the size of the data point. In the Iris data set, petal length and petal width is used for x- and y-axes and sepal width is used for the size of the data point. The color of the data point is species class label (Figure 3.13).

Density Chart

Density charts are similar to scatterplots, with one more dimension included as background color. The data point can also be colored to visualize one dimen-sion and hence a total of four dimensions can be visualized in a density chart. In the example in Figure 3.14, petal length is used for the x-axis, sepal length for the y-axis, sepal width for the background color, and class label for the data point color.

3.4.3 Visualizing High-Dimensional Data by Projection

Visualizing more than three attributes on a two dimensional medium (like paper, screen) is challenging. We can overcome this limitation by using trans-formation techniques to project the data points in parallel axis space. In this approach, a Cartesian axis is shared by more than one attribute.

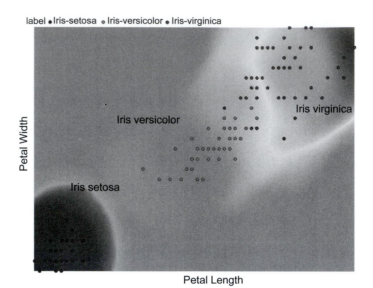

FIGURE 3.14
Density chart of a few variables in the Iris data set.

Parallel Chart

A *parallel chart* visualizes a data point quite innovatively by transforming or projecting multidimensional data into two-dimensional chart medium. In this chart, every attribute or dimension is linearly arranged in one coordinate (x-axis) and all the measures are arranged in the other coordinate (y-axis). Since the x-axis is multivariant, each data point is represented as a *line* in a parallel universe.

In the case of the Iris data set, all four attributes are arranged along the x-axis and each observation is represented as a data point. The y-axis represents generic distance and it is "shared" by all these attributes on the x-axis. Hence, parallel charts work only when attributes share a common unit of numerical measure. If there are different units, we can still use parallel charts by normalizing the attribute. This visualization is called a *parallel axis* because all four attributes are represented in four parallel axes, parallel to the y-axis.

In this chart, a class label is used to color each data *line* so that we introduce one more dimension into the picture. By observing this parallel chart in Figure 3.15, we notice that there is overlap between the three species on the sepal width attribute. So, sepal width cannot be the metric used to differentiate these three species. However, there is clear separation of species in petal length. No observation of *Iris setosa* species has a petal length below 2.5 cm and there is very little overlap between the *Iris virginica* and *Iris versicolor* species. Visually,

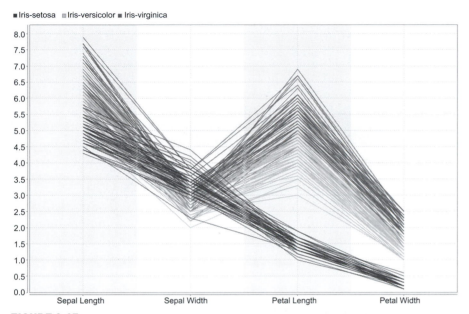

FIGURE 3.15
Parallel chart of Iris data set.

just by knowing the petal length of an unknown observation, we can predict the species of the Iris flower. We will check this hypothesis in later chapter on Classification.

Deviation Chart

A *deviation chart* is very similar to a *parallel chart* as it has parallel axes for all the attributes on the x-axis. Data points are extended across the dimensions as lines and there is one common y-axis. Instead of plotting all data points, deviation charts only show the mean and standard deviation statistics. For each class, deviation charts show the mean line connecting the mean of each attribute; the standard deviation is shown as the band above and below the mean line. The mean line doesn't correspond to a data point (line). In a way, information is elegantly displayed and the essence of a parallel chart is maintained.

In Figure 3.16, a deviation chart for the Iris data set is shown with species class label used for color and stratification. We can observe that the petal length is the key differentiator of the species class label because the mean line and the standard deviation bands for the species are well separated.

Andrews Curves

An *Andrews plot* belongs to a family of visualization techniques where the high-dimensional data is projected into a vector space so that each data point

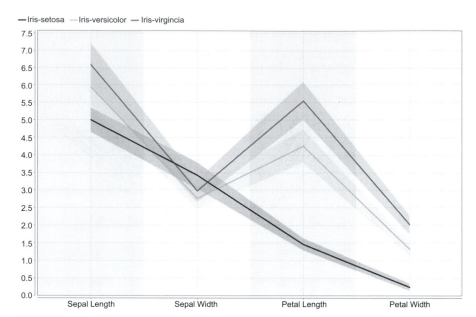

FIGURE 3.16
Deviation chart of Iris data set

takes the form of a line or curve. In an Andrews plot, each data point X with d dimensions, $X = (x_1, x_2, x_3, \ldots, x_d)$, takes the form of a Fourier series:

$$f_x(t) = \frac{x_1}{\sqrt{2}} + x_2 \sin(t) + x_3 \cos(t) + x_4 \sin(2t) + x_5 \cos(2t) + \cdots \qquad (3.4)$$

This function is plotted for $-\pi < t < \pi$ for each data point. Andrews plots are useful to determine if there are any outliers in the data and to identify potential patterns within the data points (Figure 3.17). If two data points are similar, then the curves for the data points are closer to each other. If curves are far apart and belong to different classes, then we can use the information to classify the data (Garcia-Osorio & Fyfe, 2005).

Many of the charts and visuals discussed in this chapter explore the multivariate relationships within the data set. They form the set of classic data visualizations used for data exploration, post-processing, and understanding data mining models. Some new developments in the area visualization deals with networks and connections within the data objects (Lima, 2011). To better analyze data extracted from graph data, social networks, and integrated applications, connectivity charts are often used. Interactive exploration of data using visualization software provides an essential tool to observe multiple attributes at the same time, but has limitations on the number of attributes used in visualizations. Hence, dimensional reduction using techniques

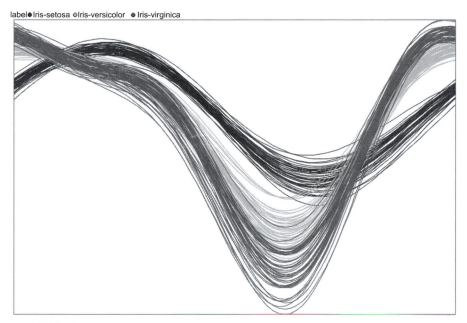

FIGURE 3.17
Andrews curves of Iris data set.

discussed in Chapter 12 Feature Selection can help in visualizing higher-dimensional data.

3.5 ROADMAP FOR DATA EXPLORATION

If we have a new data set that has not been investigated before, having a structured way to explore and analyze the data will be helpful. We present here a summary roadmap to inquire about a new data set. Not all steps may be relevant for every data set and the order may need to be adjusted for some sets, so readers are encouraged to view this roadmap as guideline.

1. **Organize the data set:** Structure the data set with standard rows and columns. Organizing the data set to have objects or instances in rows and dimensions or attributes in columns will be helpful for many data analysis tools. Identify the target or "class label" attribute, if applicable.

2. **Find the central point for each attribute:** Calculate *mean*, *median*, and *mode* for each attribute and the class label, if applicable. If all three values are very different, it may indicate the presence of an outlier, or a multimodal or non-normal distribution for an attribute.

3. **Understand the spread of the attributes:** Calculate the *standard deviation* and *range* for an attribute. Compare the standard deviation with the mean to understand the spread of the data, along with the max and min data points.

4. **Visualize the distribution of each attribute:** Develop the *histogram* and *distribution* plots for the attributes. Repeat the same for class-stratified histograms and distribution plots, where the plots are either repeated or color-coded for each class.

5. **Pivot the data:** Sometimes called dimensional slicing, a pivot is helpful to comprehend different values of the attributes. This technique can stratify by class and drill down to the details of any of the attributes. Microsoft Excel® popularized this technique of data analysis for general business users.

6. **Watch out for outliers:** Use scatter plot or Quartiles to find outliers. The presence of outliers skews some measures like mean, variance, and range. Based on the application, outliers can be excluded when rerunning data analysis. Notice if the results change. Identifying the outlier may be the objective in some applications.

7. **Understanding the relationship between attributes:** Measure the *correlation* between attributes and develop a correlation matrix. Notice what attributes are dependent with each other and investigate why they are dependent.

8. **Visualize the relationship between attributes:** Plot a quick scatter matrix to discover the relationship between multiple attributes at once. Zoom in on the attribute pairs with simple two-dimensional scatterplots stratified by class.

9. **Visualization high-dimensional data sets:** Create *parallel charts* and *Andrews curves* to observe the class differences exhibited by each attribute. *Deviation charts* provide a quick assessment of the spread of each class for each attribute.

REFERENCES

Anscombe, F. J. (1973). Graphs in Statistical Analysis. *American Statistician, 27*(1), 17–21.

Bache, K., & Lichman, M. (2013). *University of California, School of Information and Computer Science.* Retrieved from UCI Machine Learning Repository http://archive.ics.uci.edu/ml.

Few, S. (2006). *Information Dashboard Design: The Effective Visual Communication of Data.* O'Reilly Media.

Fisher, R. A. (1936). The use of multiple measurements in taxonomic problems. *Annals of Human Genetics, 7,* 179–188. http://dx.doi.org/10.1111/j.1469-1809.1936.tb02137.x.

Garcia-Osorio, C., & Fyfe, C. (2005). Visualization of High-Dimensional Data via Orthogonal Curves. *Journal of Universal Computer Science, 11*(11), 1806–1819.

Kubiak, T., & Benbow, D. W. (2006). *The Certified Six Sigma Black Belt Handbook*. Milwaukee, WI: ASQ Quality Press.

Lima, M. (2011). *Visual Complexity: Mapping Patterns of Information*. New York: Princeton Architectural Press.

Tufte, E. R. (2001). *The Visual Display of Quantitative Information*. Cheshire, CT: Graphics Press.

Ware, C. (2004). *Information Visualization: Perception for Design*. Waltham, MA: Morgan Kaufmann.

CHAPTER 4

Classification

We are entering the realm of predictive analytics—the process in which historical records are used to make a prediction about an uncertain future. At a very fundamental level, most predictive analytics problems can be categorized into either classification or numeric prediction problems. In classification or class prediction, we try to use the information from the predictors or independent variables to sort the data samples into two or more distinct *classes* or *buckets*. In the case of numeric prediction, we try to predict the numeric value of a dependent variable using the values assumed by the independent variables, as is done in a traditional regression modeling.

Let us describe the classification process with a simple, fun example. Most golfers enjoy playing if the weather and outlook conditions meet certain requirements: too hot or too humid conditions, even if the outlook is sunny, are not preferred. On the other hand, overcast skies are no problem for playing even if the temperatures are somewhat cool. Based on the historic records of these conditions and preferences, and information about a day's temperature, humidity level, and outlook, classification will allow us to predict if someone prefers to play golf or not. The outcome of classification is to categorize the weather conditions when golf is likely to be played or not, quite simply: Play or Not Play (two classes). The predictors can be continuous (temperature, humidity) or categorical (sunny, cloudy, windy, etc.). Those beginning to explore predictive analytics tools are confused by the dozens of techniques that are available to address these types of classification problems. In this chapter we will explore several commonly used data mining techniques where the idea is to develop rules, relationships, and models based on predictor information that can be applied to classify outcomes from new and unseen data.

We start out with fairly simple schemes and progress to more sophisticated techniques. Each section contains essential algorithmic details about the technique, describes how it is developed using simple examples, and finally closes out with implementation details using RapidMiner.

4.1 DECISION TREES

Decision trees (also known as classification trees) are probably one of the most intuitive and frequently used data mining techniques. From an analyst's point of view, they are easy to set up and from a business user's point of view they are easy to interpret. Classification trees, as the name implies, are used to separate a data set into classes belonging to the response variable. Usually the response variable has two classes: *Yes or No (1 or 0)*. If the response variable has *more* than two categories, then variants of the decision tree algorithm have been developed that may be applied (Quinlan, 1986). In either case, classification trees are used when the response or target variable is categorical in nature.

Regression trees (Brieman, 1984) are similar in function to classification trees and may be used for numeric prediction problems, when the response variable is numeric or continuous: for example, predicting the price of a consumer good based on several input factors. Thus regression trees are applicable for *prediction* type of problems as opposed to *classification*. Keep in mind that in either case, the predictors or independent variables may be either categorical or numeric. It is the *target variable* that determines the type of decision tree needed. (Collectively, the algorithm for classification and regression trees is referred to as CART.)

4.1.1 How it Works

A decision tree model takes a form of decision flowchart (or an inverted tree) where an attribute is tested in each node. At end of the decision tree path is a leaf node where a prediction is made about the target variable based on conditions set forth by the decision path. The nodes split the data set into subsets. In a decision tree, the idea is to *split* the data set based on homogeneity of data. Let us say for example we have two variables, age and weight, that predict if a person is likely to sign up for a gym membership or not. In our training data if it was seen that 90% of the people who are older than 40 signed up, we may split the data into two parts: one part consisting of people older than 40 and the other part consisting of people under 40. The first part is now "90% pure" from the standpoint of which class they belong to. However we need a rigorous measure of impurity, which meets certain criteria, based on computing a proportion of the data that belong to a class. These criteria are simple:

1. The measure of impurity of a data set must be at a maximum when all possible classes are equally represented. In our gym membership example, in the initial data set if 50% of samples belonged to "not signed up" and 50% of samples belonged to "signed up," then this nonpartitioned raw data would have maximum impurity.
2. The measure of impurity of a data set must be zero when only one class is represented. For example, if we form a group of only those people who signed up for the membership (only one class = members), then this subset has "100% purity" or "0% impurity."

Measures such as *entropy* or *Gini index* easily meet these criteria and are used to build decision trees as described in the following sections. Different criteria will build different trees through different biases, for example, *information gain* favors tree splits that contain many cases, while *information gain ratio* attempts to balance this.

HOW PREDICTIVE ANALYTICS CAN REDUCE UNCERTAINTY IN A BUSINESS CONTEXT: THE CONCEPT OF ENTROPY

Imagine a box that can contain one of three colored balls inside—red, yellow, and blue, see Figure 4.1. Without opening the box, if you had to "predict" which colored ball is inside, you are basically dealing with lack of information or uncertainty. Now what is the *highest* number of "yes/no" questions that can be asked to reduce this uncertainty and thus increase our information?

1. Is it red? No.
2. Is it yellow? No.

Then it must be blue.

That is *two* questions. If there were a fourth color, green, then the highest number of yes/no questions is *three*. By extending this reasoning, it can be mathematically shown that the maximum number of *binary* questions needed to reduce uncertainty is essentially log(T), where the log is taken to base 2 and T is the number of possible outcomes (Meagher, 2005) (e.g., if you have only one color, i.e., one outcome, then log(1) = 0, which means there is no uncertainty!)

Many real world business problems can be thought of as extensions to this "uncertainty reduction" example. For example, knowing only a handful of characteristics such as the length of a loan, borrower's occupation, annual income, and previous credit behavior, we can use several of the available predictive analytics techniques to rank the riskiness of a potential loan, and by extension, the interest rate of the loan. This is nothing but a more sophisticated uncertainty reduction exercise, similar in spirit to the ball-in-a-box problem. Decision trees embody this problem-solving technique by systematically examining the available attributes and their impact on the eventual class or category of a sample. We will examine in detail later in this section how to predict the credit ratings of a bank's customers using their demographic and other behavioral data and using the decision tree which is a practical implementation of the entropy principle for decision making under uncertainty.

FIGURE 4.1
Playing 20 questions with entropy.

Continuing with the example in the box, if there are T events with equal probability of occurrence P, then T = 1/P. Claude Shannon, who developed the mathematical underpinnings for information theory (Shannon, 1948), defined entropy as log(1/P) or –log P where P is the probability of an event occurring. If the probability for all events is not identical, we need a weighted expression and thus entropy, H, is adjusted as follows:

$$H = -\sum p_k \log_2 (p_k) \tag{4.1}$$

where k = 1, 2, 3, …, m represent the m classes of the target variable. The p_k represent the proportion of samples that belong to class k. For our gym membership example from earlier, there are two classes: member or nonmember. If our data set had 100 samples with 50% of each, then the entropy of the dataset is given by H = –[(0.5 $\log_2$ 0.5) + (0.5 $\log_2$ 0.5)] = –$\log_2$ 0.5 = –(–1) = 1. On the other hand, if we can partition the data into two sets of 50 samples each that contain all members and all nonmembers, the entropy of either of these two partitioned sets is given by H = –1 $\log_2$ 1 = 0. Any other proportion of samples within a data set will yield entropy values between 0 and 1.0 (which is the maximum). The Gini index (G) is similar to the entropy measure in its characteristics and is defined as

$$G = \sum \left(1 - p_k^2\right) \tag{4.2}$$

The value of G ranges between 0 and a maximum value of 0.5, but otherwise has properties identical to H, and either of these formulations can be used to create partitions in the data (Cover, 1991).

Let us go back to the example of the golf data set introduced earlier, to fully understand the application of entropy concepts for creating a decision tree. This was the same dataset used by J. Ross Quinlan to introduce one of the original decision tree algorithms, the *Iterative Dichotomizer 3*, or ID3 (Quinlan, 1986). The full data is shown in Table 4.1.

There are essentially two questions we need to answer at each step of the tree building process: *where to split the data* and *when to stop splitting*.

Classic Golf Example and How It Is Used to Build a Decision Tree
Where to split data?

There are 14 examples, with four attributes—Temperature, Humidity, Wind, and Outlook. The target attribute that needs to be predicted is Play with two classes: Yes and No. We want to understand how to build a decision tree using this simple data set.

Table 4.1 The Classic Golf Data Set

Outlook	Temperature	Humidity	Windy	Play
sunny	85	85	FALSE	no
sunny	80	90	TRUE	no
overcast	83	78	FALSE	yes
rain	70	96	FALSE	yes
rain	68	80	FALSE	yes
rain	65	70	TRUE	no
overcast	64	65	TRUE	yes
sunny	72	95	FALSE	no
sunny	69	70	FALSE	yes
rain	75	80	FALSE	yes
sunny	75	70	TRUE	yes
overcast	72	90	TRUE	yes
overcast	81	75	FALSE	yes
rain	71	80	TRUE	no

Start by partitioning the data on each of the four regular attributes. Let us start with Outlook. There are three categories for this variable: sunny, overcast, and rain. We see that when it is overcast, there are four examples where the outcome was Play = yes for all four cases (see Figure 4.2) and so the proportion of examples in this case is 100% or 1.0. Thus if we split the data set here, the resulting four sample partition will be 100% pure for Play = yes. Mathematically for this partition, the entropy can be calculated using Eq. 4.1 as

$$H_{outlook:overcast} = -(0/4)\log_2(0/4) - (4/4)\log_2(4/4) = 0.0$$

Similarly, we can calculate the entropy in the other two situations for Outlook:

$$H_{outlook:sunny} = -(2/5)\log_2(2/5) - (3/5)\log_2(3/5) = 0.971$$

$$H_{outlook:rain} = -(3/5)\log_2(3/5) - (2/5)\log_2(2/5) = 0.971$$

For the attribute on the whole, the total "information" is calculated as the weighted sum of these component entropies. There are four instances of Outlook = overcast, thus the proportion for overcast is given by $p_{outlook:overcast}$ = 4/14. The other proportions (for Outlook = sunny and rain) are 5/14 each:

$$I_{outlook} = p_{outlook:overcast} * H_{outlook:overcast} + p_{outlook:sunny} * H_{outlook:sunny} + p_{outlook:rain} * H_{outlook:rain}$$

Row No.	Play	Outlook △
3	yes	overcast
7	yes	overcast
12	yes	overcast
13	yes	overcast
4	yes	rain
5	yes	rain
6	no	rain
10	yes	rain
14	no	rain
1	no	sunny
2	no	sunny
8	no	sunny
9	yes	sunny
11	yes	sunny

FIGURE 4.2
Splitting the data on the Outlook attribute.

$$I_{outlook} = (4/14) * 0 + (5/14) * 0.971 + (5/14) * 0.971 = 0.693$$

Had we *not* partitioned the data along the three values for Outlook, the total information would have been simply the weighted average of the respective entropies for the two classes whose overall proportions were 5/14 (Play = no) and 9/14 (Play = yes):

$$I_{outlook, no\ partition} = -(5/14)\log_2(5/14) - (9/14)\log_2(9/14) = 0.940$$

By creating these splits or partitions, we have reduced some entropy (and thus gained some information). This is called, aptly enough, *information gain*. In the case of Outlook, this is given simply by

$$I_{outlook,\ no\ partition} - I_{outlook} = 0.940 - 0.693 = 0.247$$

We can now compute similar information gain values for the other three attributes, as shown in Table 4.2.

Table 4.2 Computing the Information Gain for All Attributes

Attribute	Information Gain
Temperature	0.029
Humidity	0.102
Wind	0.048
Outlook	0.247

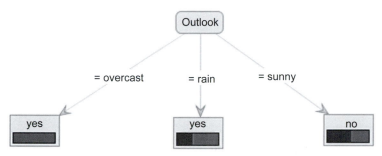

FIGURE 4.3

Splitting the golf data on the Outlook attribute yields three subsets or branches. The middle and right branches may be split further.

For numeric variables, possible split points to examine are essentially averages of available values. For example, the first potential split point for Humidity could be Average [65,70], which is 67.5, the next potential split point could be Average [70,75], which is 72.5, and so on. We use similar logic for the other numeric attribute, Temperature. The algorithm computes the information gain at each of these potential split points and chooses the one which maximizes it. Another way to approach this would be to discretize the numerical ranges, for example, Temperature >=80 could be considered "Hot," between 70 to 79 "Mild," and less than 70 "Cool."

From Table 4.2, it is clear that if we partition the data set into three sets along the three values of Outlook, we will experience the largest information gain. This gives the first node of the decision tree as shown in Figure 4.3. As noted earlier, the terminal node for the Outlook = overcast branch consists of four samples, all of which belong to the class Play = yes. The other two branches contain a mix of classes. The Outlook = rain branch has three yes results and the Outlook = sunny branch has three no results.

Thus not all the final partitions are 100% homogenous. This means that we could apply the same process for each of these subsets till we get "purer" results. So we revert back to the first question once again—where to split the data? Fortunately this was already answered for us when we computed the

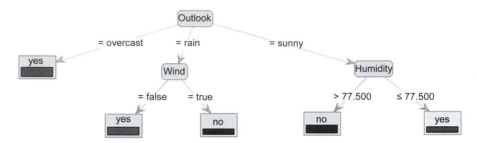

FIGURE 4.4
A final decision tree for the golf data.

information gain for all attributes. We simply use the other attributes that yielded the highest gains. Following the logic, we can next split the Outlook = sunny branch along Humidity (which yielded the second highest information gain) and split the Outlook = rain branch along Wind (which yielded the third highest gain). The fully grown tree shown in Figure 4.4 does precisely that.

Pruning a Decision Tree: When to Stop Splitting Data?

In real world data sets, it is very unlikely that we will get terminal nodes that are 100% homogeneous as we just saw for the golf data set. In this case, we will need to instruct the algorithm when to stop. There are several situations where we can terminate the process:

- No attribute satisfies a minimum information gain threshold (such as the one computed in Table 4.2).
- A maximal depth is reached: as the tree grows larger, not only does interpretation get harder, but we run into a situation called "overfitting."
- There are less than a certain number of examples in the current subtree: again a mechanism to prevent *overfitting*.

So what exactly is overfitting? Overfitting occurs when a model tries to memorize the training data instead of generalizing the relationship between inputs and output variables. Overfitting often has the effect of performing very well on the training data set, but performing poorly on any new data previously unseen by the model. As mentioned above, overfitting by a decision tree results not only in a difficult to interpret model, but also provides quite a useless model for unseen data. To prevent overfitting, we may need to restrict tree growth or reduce it, using a process called *pruning*. All of the three stopping techniques mentioned above constitute what is known as *pre-pruning* the decision tree, because the pruning occurs before or during the growth of the tree. There are also methods that will not restrict the number of branches and allow the tree to grow as deep as the data will allow, and *then* trim or prune those branches that do not effectively change the classification error rates. This is called *post-pruning*. Post-pruning may sometimes be a better option because we will not miss any small but potentially significant relationships between attribute values and classes if we allow the tree to reach its maximum depth. However, one drawback with post-pruning is that it requires additional computations, which may be wasted when the tree needs to be trimmed back.

We can now summarize the application of the decision tree algorithm as the following simple five-step process:

1. Using Shannon entropy, sort the data set into homogenous (by class) and nonhomogenous variables. Homogenous variables have low information entropy and nonhomogenous variables have high information entropy. This was done in the calculation of $I_{outlook,no\ partition}$.
2. Weight the influence of each independent variable on the target or dependent variable using the entropy weighted averages (sometimes called joint entropy). This was done during the calculation of $I_{outlook}$ in the above example.
3. Compute the information gain, which is essentially the reduction in the entropy of the target variable due to its relationship with each independent variable. This is simply the difference between the information entropy found in step 1 minus the joint entropy calculated in step 2. This was done during the calculation of $I_{outlook,no\ partition} - I_{outlook}$.
4. The independent variable with the highest information gain will become the "root" or the first node on which the data set is divided. This was done during the calculation of the information gain table.
5. Repeat this process for each variable for which the Shannon entropy is nonzero. If the entropy of a variable is zero, then that variable becomes a "leaf" node.

4.1.2 How to Implement

Before jumping into a business use case of decision trees, let us "implement" the decision tree model that was shown in Figure 4.4 on a small test sample using RapidMiner. Figure 4.5 shows the test data set, which is very much like our training data set but with small differences in attribute values.

We have built a decision tree model using training data set. The RapidMiner process of building a decision tree is shown in Figure 4.6. More over, the same process shows the application of the decision tree model to test data set. When this process is executed, and the connections are made as shown in

view ✕ | 🗒 ExampleSet (Retrieve Golf-Testset) ✕ | 🗒 ExampleSet (Retriev

ExampleSet (14 examples, 1 special attribute, 4 regular attributes)

Row No.	Play	Outlook	Temperature	Humidity	Wind
1	yes	sunny	85	85	false
2	no	overcast	80	90	true
3	yes	overcast	83	78	false
4	yes	rain	70	96	false
5	yes	rain	68	80	true
6	no	rain	65	70	true
7	yes	overcast	64	65	true
8	no	sunny	72	95	false
9	yes	sunny	69	70	false
10	no	sunny	75	80	false
11	yes	sunny	68	70	true
12	yes	overcast	72	90	true
13	no	overcast	81	75	true
14	yes	rain	71	80	true

FIGURE 4.5
Golf: Test data has a few minor differences in attribute values from the training data.

Figure 4.6, we get the table output shown in Figure 4.7. You can see that the model has been able to get 9 of the 14 class predictions correct and 5 of the 14 (in boxes) wrong, which translates to about 64% accuracy.

Let us examine a more involved business application to better understand how to apply decision trees for real world problems. Credit scoring is a fairly common predictive analytics problem. Some types of situations where credit scoring could be applied are:

1. **Prospect filtering**: Identify which prospects to extend credit to and determine how much credit would be an acceptable risk.
2. **Default risk detection**: Decide if a particular customer is likely to default on a loan.
3. **Bad debt collection**: Sort out those debtors who will yield a good cost (of collection) to benefit (of receiving payment) performance.

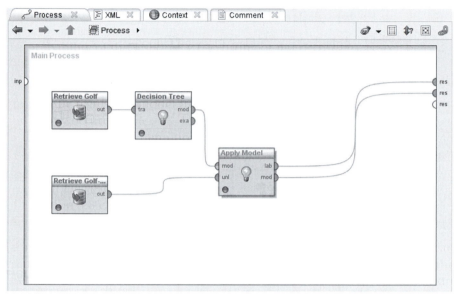

FIGURE 4.6
Applying the simple decision tree model on unseen golf test data.

We will use the well-known German Credit data set from the University of California-Irvine Machine Learning data repository[1] and describe how to use RapidMiner to build a decision tree for addressing a *prospect filtering problem*.

This is the first discussion of the implementation of a predictive analytics technique, so we will spend some extra effort in going into detail on many of the preliminary steps and also introduce several additional tools and concepts that will be required throughout the rest of this chapter and other chapters that focus on supervised learning methods. These are the concepts of *splitting data into testing and training samples*, and *applying the trained model* on testing (or validation data). It may also be useful to first review Sections 13.1 (Introduction to the GUI) and 13.2 (Data Import and Export) from Chapter 13 Getting Started with RapidMiner before working through the rest of this implementation. As a final note, we will not be discussing ways and means to improve the performance of a classification model using RapidMiner in this section, but will return to this very important part of predictive analytics in several later chapters, particularly in the section on using optimization in Chapter 13.

---

[1]http://archive.ics.uci.edu/ml/datasets/Statlog+%28German+Credit+Data%29. All data sets used in this book are available at the companion website.

ExampleSet (14 examples, 4 special attributes,		
Row No.	Play	prediction(Play)
1	yes	no
2	no	yes
3	yes	yes
4	yes	yes
5	yes	no
6	no	no
7	yes	yes
8	no	no
9	yes	yes
10	no	no
11	yes	yes
12	yes	yes
13	no	yes
14	yes	no

FIGURE 4.7
Results of applying the simple decision tree model.

There are four main steps in setting up any supervised learning algorithm for a predictive modeling exercise:

1. Read in the cleaned and prepared data (see Chapter 2 Data Mining Process), typically from a spreadsheet, but the data can be from any source.
2. Split data into training and testing samples.
3. Train the decision tree using the training portion of the data set.
4. Apply the model on the testing portion of the data set to evaluate the performance of the model.

Step 1 may seem rather elementary, but can confuse many beginners and thus we will spend some time explaining this in somewhat more detail. The next few parts will describe other steps also in detail.

Step 1: Data Preparation
The raw data is in the format shown in Table 4.3. It consists of 1,000 samples and a total of 20 attributes and 1 label or target attribute. There are seven numeric attributes and the rest are categorical or qualitative, including the

Table 4.3 A View of the Raw German Credit data.

Checking Account Status	Duration in Month	Credit History	Purpose	Credit Amount	Savings Account/ Bonds	Present Employment Since	Credit Rating
A11	6	A34	A43	1169	A65	A75	1
A12	48	A32	A43	5951	A61	A73	2
A14	12	A34	A46	2096	A61	A74	1
A11	42	A32	A42	7882	A61	A74	1
A11	24	A33	A40	4870	A61	A73	2
A14	36	A32	A46	9055	A65	A73	1
A14	24	A32	A42	2835	A63	A75	1
A12	36	A32	A41	6948	A61	A73	1
A14	12	A32	A43	3059	A64	A74	1
A12	30	A34	A40	5234	A61	A71	2
A12	12	A32	A40	1295	A61	A72	2
A11	48	A32	A49	4308	A61	A72	2

label, which is a binomial variable. The label attribute is called Credit Rating and can take the value of 1 (good) or 2 (bad). In the data 70% of the samples fall into the "good" credit rating class. The descriptions for the data are shown in Table 4.3. Most of the attributes are self-explanatory, but the raw data has encodings for the values of the qualitative variables. For example, attribute 4 is the *purpose of the loan* and can assume any of 10 values (A40 for new car, A41 for used car, and so on). The full details of these encodings are provided under the "Data Set Description" on the UCI-ML website.

RapidMiner's easy interface allows quick importing of spreadsheets. A useful feature of the interface is the panel on the left, called the "Operators." Simply typing in text in the box provided automatically pulls up all available Rapid-Miner operators that match the text. In this case, we need an operator to read an Excel spreadsheet, and so we simply type "excel" in the box. As you can see, the three Excel operators are immediately shown in Figure 4.8a: two for reading and one for exporting data.

Either double-click on the *Read Excel* operator or drag and drop it into the Main Process panel—the effect is the same, see Figure 4.8b. Once the *Read Excel* operator appears in the main process window, we need to configure the data import process. What this means is telling RapidMiner which columns to import, what is contained in the columns, and if any of the columns need special treatment.

This is probably the most "cumbersome" part about this step. RapidMiner has a feature to automatically detect the type of values in each attribute (Guess Value types). But it is a good exercise for the analyst to make sure that the right

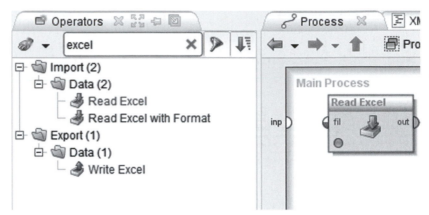

FIGURE 4.8a
Using the Read Excel operator.

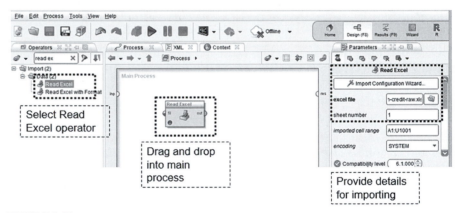

FIGURE 4.8b
Configuring the Read Excel operator.

columns are picked (or excluded) and the value types are correctly guessed. If not, as seen in Figure 4.9, we can change the value type to the correct setting by clicking on the button below the attribute name.

Once the data is imported, we must assign the target variable for analysis, also known as a "label." In this case, it is the Credit Rating, as shown in Figure 4.9. Finally it is a good idea to "run" RapidMiner and generate results to ensure that all columns are read correctly.

An optional step is to convert the values from A121, A143, etc. to more meaningful qualitative descriptions. This is accomplished by the use of another operator called *Replace (Dictionary)*, which will replace the values with bland encodings such as A121 and so on with more descriptive values. We need to create a dictionary and supply this to RapidMiner as a comma-separated value (csv) file to enable this. Such a dictionary is easy to create and is shown in

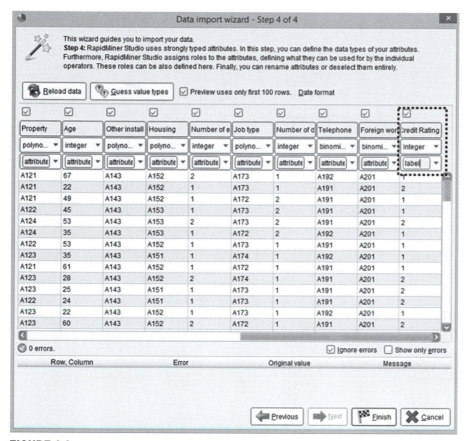

FIGURE 4.9
Verifying data read-in and adjusting attribute value types if necessary.

Figure 4.10a; the setup is shown in Figure 4.10b. Note that we need to let RapidMiner know which column in our dictionary contains old values and which contains new values.

The last preprocessing step we show here is converting the numeric label (see Figure 4.9) into a binomial one by connecting the "exa"mple output of *Replace (Dictionary)* to a *Numerical to Binominal* operator. To configure the *Numerical to Binominal* operator, follow the setup shown in Figure 4.10c.

Finally, let us change the name of the label variable from Credit Rating to Credit Rating = Good so that it makes more sense when the integer values get converted to true or false after passing through the *Numerical to Binominal* operator. This can be done using the *Rename* operator. When we run this setup, we will generate the data set shown in Figure 4.11. Comparing to Figure 4.9, we will see that the label attribute is the first one shown and the values are "true" or "false." We can examine the statistics tab of the results to get more information about the distributions of individual attributes and also to check for

```
File  Edit  Format  View  Help
OldValue,NewValue
A11,"Less than 0 DM"
A12,"0 to 200 DM"
A13,"Greater than 200 DM"
A14,"no checking account"
A30,"no credits taken all credits paid back duly"
A31,"all credits at this bank paid back duly"
A32,"existing credits paid back duly till now"
A33,"delay in paying off in the past"
A34,"critical account other credits existing (not at this bank)"
A40,"new car"
A41,"used car"
A42,"furniture equipment"
A43,"radio television"
A44,"domestic appliances"
A45,"repairs"
A46,"education"
A47,"vacation"
A48,"retraining"
A49,"business"
A410,"others"
A61,"Less than 100 DM"
A62,"100 to 500 DM"
A63,"500 to 1000 DM"
```

FIGURE 4.10a

Attribute value replacement using a dictionary.

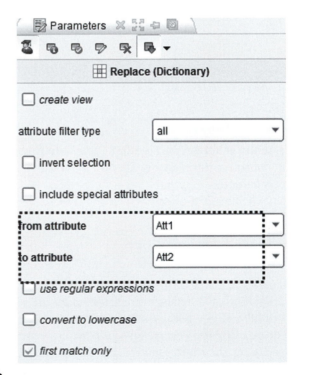

FIGURE 4.10b

Configuring the Replace (Dictionary) operator.

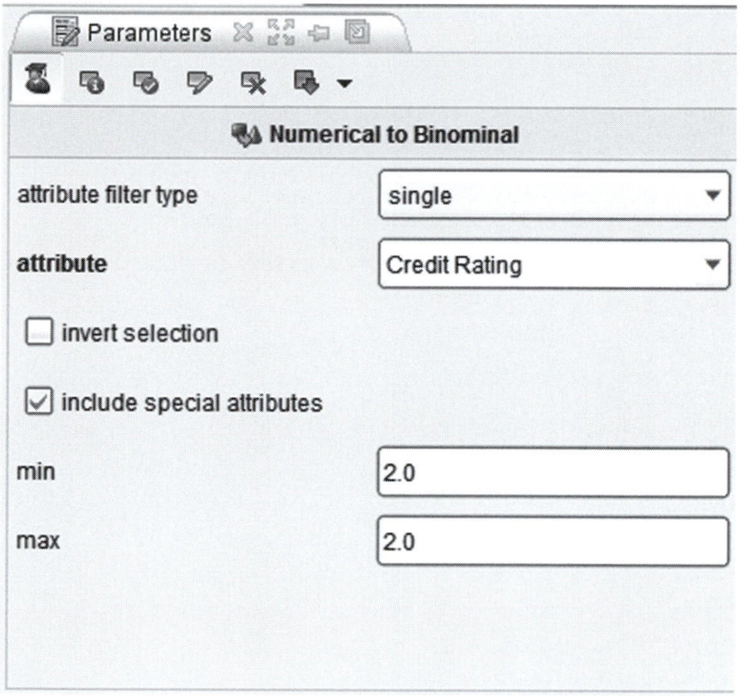

FIGURE 4.10c
Convert the integer Credit Rating label variable to a binomial (true or false) type.

missing values and outliers. In other words, we must make sure that the data preparation step (Section 2.2) is properly executed before proceeding. In this implementation, we will not worry about this because the data set is relatively "clean" (for instance, there are no missing values), and we can proceed directly to the model development phase.

Step 2: Divide Data Set into Training and Testing Samples

As with all supervised model building, data must be separated into two sets: one for "training" or developing an acceptable model, and the other for "validating" or ensuring that the model would work equally well on a different data set. The standard practice is to split the available data into a training set and a testing or validation set. Typically the training set contains 70% to 90% of the original data. The remainder is set aside for testing or validation.

Figure 4.12 shows how to do this in RapidMiner. The *Split Validation* tool sets up splitting, modeling, *and* the validation check in one operator. The utility of this will become very obvious as you develop experience in data mining, but as a beginner, this may be a bit confusing.

ExampleSet (1000 examples, 1 special attribute, 20 regular attributes)   Filter (1,000 / 1,000 examples): all

Row No.	Credit rating=Good	Checking A...	Duration in ...	Credit History	Purpose	Credit Amo...	Savings Acc...	Present Em...	Installment ...	Personal St...	Other debtors	Present res...	Property	Age	Other in
1	false	Less than 0	6	critical accou	radio televisi	1169	unknown no	Greater than	4	male single	none	4	0 to 200 DM:	67	no chec
2	true	0 to 200 DM	48	existing cred	radio televisi	5951	Less than 1(	1 to 4 years	2	female divor	none	2	0 to 200 DM:	22	no chec
3	false	no checking	12	critical accou	education	2096	Less than 1(	4 to 7 years	2	male single	none	3	0 to 200 DM:	49	no chec
4	false	Less than 0	42	existing cred	furniture equ	7882	Less than 1(	4 to 7 years	2	male single	guarantor	4	0 to 200 DM:	45	no chec
5	true	Less than 0	24	delay in payi	new car	4870	Less than 1(	1 to 4 years	3	male single	none	4	0 to 200 DM:	53	no chec
6	false	no checking	36	existing cred	education	9055	unknown no	1 to 4 years	2	male single	none	4	0 to 200 DM:	35	no chec
7	false	no checking	24	existing cred	furniture equ	2835	500 to 1000	Greater than	3	male single	none	4	0 to 200 DM:	53	no chec
8	false	0 to 200 DM	36	existing cred	used car	6948	Less than 1(	1 to 4 years	2	male single	none	2	0 to 200 DM:	35	no chec
9	false	no checking	12	existing cred	radio televisi	3059	Greater than	4 to 7 years	2	male divorce	none	4	0 to 200 DM:	61	no chec
10	true	0 to 200 DM	30	critical accou	new car	5234	Less than 1(	unemployed	4	male marrie	none	2	0 to 200 DM:	28	no chec

FIGURE 4.11

Data transformed for decision tree analysis.

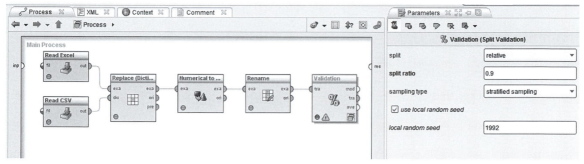

FIGURE 4.12
Using a *relative* split and a split ratio of 0.9 for training versus testing.

Choose *stratified sampling* with a split ratio of 0.9 (90% training). Stratified sampling will ensure that both training and testing samples have equal distributions of class values. (Although not necessary, it is sometimes useful to check the *use local random seed* option, so that it is possible to compare models between different iterations. Fixing the random seed ensures that the same examples are chosen for training (and testing) subsets each time the process is run.) The final sub step here is to connect the output from the *Numerical to Binominal* operator output to the *Split Validation* operator input.[2]

Step 3: Modeling Operator and Parameters
We will now see how to build a decision tree model on this data. As mentioned earlier, the *Validation* operator allows us to build a model and apply it on validation data in the same step. This means that two operations—model building and model evaluation—must be configured using the same operator. This is accomplished by double-clicking on the *Validation* operator, which is what is called a "nested" operator. All nested operators in RapidMiner have two little blue overlapping windows on the bottom right corner. When this operator is "opened," we can see that there are two parts inside (see Figure 4.13). The left box is where the *Decision Tree* operator has to be placed and the model will be built using the 90% of training data samples. The right box is for applying this trained model on the remaining 10% of the testing data samples using the *Apply Model* operator and evaluating the performance of the model using the *Performance* operator.

Configuring the Decision Tree Model
The main parameters to pay attention to are the Criterion pull-down menu and the minimal gain box. This is essentially a partitioning criterion and offers information gain, Gini index, and gain ratio as choices. We covered the first two criteria earlier, and the gain ratio will be briefly explained in the next section.

---

[2]This is just a basic sampling technique and the sampling itself can involve a lot of work to validate and produce the correct sampling.

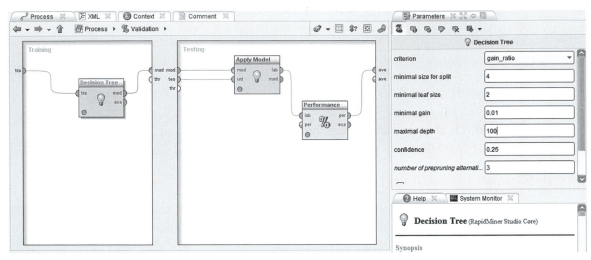

FIGURE 4.13
Setting up the split validation process.

As discussed earlier in this chapter, decision trees are built up in a simple five-step process by increasing the information contained in the reduced data set following each split. Data by its nature contains uncertainties. We may be able to systematically reduce uncertainties and thus increase information by activities like sorting or classifying. When we have sorted or classified to achieve the greatest reduction in uncertainty, we have basically achieved the greatest increase in information. We have seen how entropy is a good measure of uncertainty and how keeping track of it allows us to quantify information. So this brings us back to the options that are available within RapidMiner for splitting decision trees:

1. **Information gain:** Simply put, this is computed as the information before the split minus the information after the split. It works fine for most cases, unless you have a few variables that have a large number of values (or classes). Information gain is *biased* towards choosing attributes with a large number of values as root nodes. This is not a problem, except in extreme cases. For example, each customer ID is unique and thus the variable has too many values (each ID is a unique value). A tree that is split along these lines has no predictive value.

2. **Gain ratio (default):** This is a modification of information gain that reduces its bias and is usually the best option. Gain ratio overcomes the problem with information gain by taking into account the number of branches that would result before making the split. It corrects information gain by taking the *intrinsic information* of a split into account. Intrinsic information can be explained using our golf example.

Suppose each of the 14 examples had a unique ID attribute associated with them. Then the intrinsic information for the ID attribute is given by $14 * (-1/14 * \log(1/14)) = 3.807$. The gain ratio is obtained by dividing the information gain for an attribute by its intrinsic information. Clearly attributes that have very high intrinsic information (high uncertainty) tend to offer low gains upon splitting and hence will not be automatically selected.

3. **Gini index:** This is also used sometimes, but does not have too many advantages over gain ratio.
4. **Accuracy:** This is also used to improve performance. The best way to select values for these parameters is by using many of the optimizing operators. This is a topic that will be covered in detail in Chapter 13.

The other important parameter is the *minimal gain* value. Theoretically this can take any range from 0 upwards. In practice, a minimal gain of 0.2 to 0.3 is considered good. The default is 0.1.

The other parameters (*minimal size for a split, minimal leaf size, maximal depth*) are determined by the size of the data set. In this case, we proceed with the default values. The best way to set these parameters is by using an optimization routine (which will be briefly introduced in Chapter 13 Getting Started with RapidMiner.

The last step in training the decision tree is to connect the input ports ("tra"in-ing) and output ports ("mod"el) as shown in the left (training) box of Figure 4.9. The model is ready for training. Next we add two more operators, *Apply Model* and *Performance (Binominal Classification)*, and we are ready to run the analysis. Configure the *Performance (Binominal Classification)* operator by selecting the *accuracy, AUC, precision,* and *recall* options.[3]

Remember to connect the ports correctly as this can be a source of confusion:

- "mod"el port of the Testing window to "mod" on Apply Model
- "tes"ting port of the Testing window to "unl"abeled on Apply Model
- "lab"eled port of Apply Model to "lab"eled on Performance
- "per"formance port on the *Performance* operator to "ave"rageable port on the output side of the testing box

The final step before running the model is to go back to the main perspective by clicking on the blue up arrow on the top left (see Figure 4.13) and connect the output ports "mod"el and "ave" of the *Validation* operator to the main outputs.

Step 4: Process Execution and Interpretation
When the model is run as setup above, RapidMiner generates two tabs in the Results perspective (refer to Chapter 13 for the terminology).

---

[3]Performance criteria such as these are explained in Chapter 8 on evaluation.

The *PerformanceVector (Performance)* tab shows a confusion matrix that lists the model accuracy on the testing data, along with the other options selected above for the *Performance (Binominal Classification)* operator in step 3. The Tree (Decision Tree) tab shows a graphic of the tree that was built on the training data (see Figure 4.14). Several important points must be highlighted before we discuss the performance of this model:

1. The root node—Checking Account Status—manages to classify nearly 94% of the data set. This can be verified by hovering the mouse over each of the three terminal leaves for this node. The total occurrences (of Credit Rating = Good: *true* and *false*) for this node alone are 937 out of 1000. In particular, if someone has a *Checking Account Status = no checking account*, then the chances of them having a *"true"* score is 88% (= 348/394, see Figure 4.15).

2. However, the tree is unable to clearly pick out true or false cases for Credit Rating = Good if *Checking Account Status is Less than 0 DM*

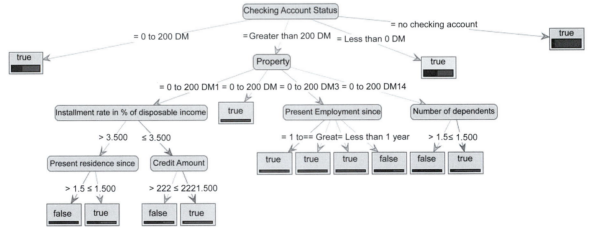

FIGURE 4.14
A decision tree model for the prospect scoring data.

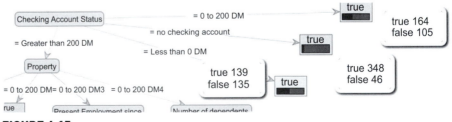

FIGURE 4.15
Predictive power of the root node of the decision tree model.

(or Deutsche mark) (only a 51% chance of correct identification). A similar conclusion results if someone has *0 to 200 DM*.

3. If the *Checking Account Status* is greater than 200 DM, then the other parameters come into effect and play an increasingly important role in deciding if someone is likely to have a *"good"* or *"bad"* credit rating.
4. However, the fact that there are numerous terminal leaves with frequencies of occurrence as low as 2 (for example, "Present Employment since"), it implies that the tree suffers from overfitting. As described earlier, overfitting refers to the process of building a model very specific to the training data that achieves close to full accuracy on the training data. However when this model is applied on new data or if the training data changes somewhat, then there is a significant degradation in its performance. Overfitting is a potential issue with all supervised models, not just decision trees. One way we could have avoided this situation is by changing the decision tree criterion *"Minimal leaf size"* to something like 10 (instead of the default, 2). But doing so, we would also lose the classification influence of all the other parameters, except the root node [try it!]

Now let us look at the Performance result. As seen in Figure 4.16, the model's overall accuracy on the testing data is 72%. The model has a class recall of 100% for the "true" class implying that it is able to pick out customers with good credit rating with 100% accuracy. However, its class recall for the "false" class is an abysmal 6.67%! That is, the model can only pick out a potential defaulter in 1 out of 15 cases!

One way to improve this performance is by penalizing false negatives by applying a cost for every such instance. This is handled by another operator called *MetaCost*, which is described in detail in Chapter 5 in the section on logistic regression. When we perform a parameter search optimization by iterating through three of the decision tree parameters, splitting criterion, minimum gain ratio, and maximal tree depth, we hit upon significantly improved performance as seen in Figure 4.17 below. More details on how to set this type of optimization are provided in Chapter 13.

When we run the best model (described by the parameters on the top row of the table in Figure 4.17), we obtain the confusion matrix shown in Figure 4.18.

accuracy: 72.00%			
	true false	true true	class precision
pred. false	2	0	100.00%
pred. true	28	70	71.43%
class recall	6.67%	100.00%	

FIGURE 4.16
Baseline model performance measures.

criterion	gain	tree depth	accuracy ▽	recall
gain_ratio	0.010	12	0.780	0.914
gini_index	0.010	5	0.760	0.871
gini_index	0.039	5	0.760	0.871
gini_index	0.068	5	0.760	0.871
gini_index	0.097	5	0.760	0.871
gini_index	0.126	5	0.760	0.871
gini_index	0.155	5	0.760	0.871
gini_index	0.184	5	0.760	0.871
gini_index	0.213	5	0.760	0.871
gini_index	0.242	5	0.760	0.871
gini_index	0.271	5	0.760	0.871
gini_index	0.300	5	0.760	0.871
gini_index	0.010	18	0.760	0.857
gini_index	0.039	18	0.760	0.857

FIGURE 4.17
Optimizing the decision tree parameters to improve accuracy and class recall.

accuracy: 78.00%			
	true false	true true	class precision
pred. false	64	16	80.00%
pred. true	6	14	70.00%
class recall	91.43%	46.67%	

FIGURE 4.18
Optimizing class recall for the credit default identification process.

Comparing this to Figure 4.16 we see that the recall for the more critical class (correctly identifying cases with a bad credit rating), has increased from about 7% to 91% whereas the recall for identifying a good credit rating has fallen below 50%. This may be acceptable in this particular situation if the costs of issuing a loan to a potential defaulter are significantly higher than the costs of losing revenue by denying credit to a creditworthy customer. The overall accuracy of the model is also higher than before.

In addition to assessing the model's performance by aggregate measures such as accuracy, we can also use gain/lift charts, receiver operator characteristic (ROC) charts, and area under ROC curve (AUC) charts. An explanation of how these charts are constructed and interpreted is given in Chapter 8 on model evaluation.

The RapidMiner process for a decision tree covered in the implementation section can be accessed from the companion site of the book at www.LearnPredictiveAnalytics.com. The RapidMiner process (*.rmp files) can be downloaded to the computer and imported to RapidMiner through File → Import Process. Additionally, all the data sets used in this book can be downloaded from www.LearnPredictiveAnalytics.com

4.1.3 Conclusions

Decision trees are one of the most commonly used predictive modeling algorithms in practice. The reasons for this are many. Some of the distinct advantages of using decision trees in many classification and prediction applications are explained below along with some common pitfalls.

- Easy to interpret and explain to nontechnical users

As we have seen in the few examples discussed so far, decision trees are very intuitive and easy to explain to nontechnical people, who are typically the consumers of analytics.

- Decision trees require relatively little effort from users for data preparation

There are several points that add to the overall advantages of using decision trees. If we have a data set consisting of widely ranging attributes, for example, revenues recorded in millions and loan age recorded in years, many algorithms require scale normalization before model building and application. Such variable transformations are not required with decision trees because the tree structure will remain the same with or without the transformation.

Another feature that saves data preparation time: missing values in training data will not impede partitioning the data for building trees. Decision trees are also not sensitive to outliers since the partitioning happens based on the proportion of samples within the split ranges and not on absolute values.

- Nonlinear relationships between parameters do not affect tree performance

As we describe in Chapter 5 on linear regression, highly nonlinear relationships between variables will result in failing checks for simple regression models and thus make such models invalid. However, decision trees do not require any assumptions of linearity in the data. Thus, we can use them in scenarios where we know the parameters are nonlinearly related.

- Decision trees implicitly perform variable screening or feature selection

We will discuss in Chapter 12 why feature selection is important in predictive modeling and data mining. We will introduce a few common techniques for performing feature selection or variable screening in that chapter. But when we fit a decision tree to a training data set, the top few nodes on which the tree is split are essentially the most important variables within the data set and feature selection is completed automatically. In fact, RapidMiner has an operator for performing variable screening or feature selection using the information gain ratio.

However, all these advantages need to be tempered with one key disadvantage of decision trees: without proper pruning or limiting tree growth, they tend to overfit the training data, making them somewhat poor predictors.

4.2 RULE INDUCTION

Rule induction is a data mining process of deducing if-then rules from a data set. These symbolic decision rules explain an inherent relationship between the attributes and class labels in the data set. Many real-life experiences are based on intuitive rule induction. For example, we can proclaim a rule that states "if it is 8 a.m. on a weekday, then highway traffic will be heavy" and "if it is 8 p.m. on a Sunday, then the traffic will be light." These rules are not necessarily right all the time. 8 a.m. weekday traffic may be light during a holiday season. But, in general, these rules hold true and are deduced from real-life experience based on our every day observations. Rule induction provides a powerful classification approach that can be easily understood by the general audience. Apart from its use in Predictive Analytics by classification of unknown data, rule induction is also used to describe the patterns in the data. The description is in the form of simple if-then rules that can be easily understood by general users.

The easiest way to extract rules from a data set is from a decision tree that is developed on the same data set. A decision tree splits data on every node and leads to the leaf where the class is identified. If we trace back from the leaf to the root node, we can combine all the split conditions to form a distinct rule. For example, in the Golf data set (Table 4.1), based on four weather conditions, we can generalize a rule set to determine when a player prefers to play golf or not. As discussed in the decision tree section, a decision tree from Golf data set can be developed. Figure 4.19 shows the decision tree developed from the Golf data with five leaf nodes and two levels. If we trace back the first leaf from the left, we can extract a rule: *If Outlook is overcast, then Play = yes*. Similarly, rules can be extracted from all the five leaves:

Rule 1: if (Outlook = overcast) then Play = yes
Rule 2: if (Outlook = rain) and (Wind = false) then Play = yes
Rule 3: if (Outlook = rain) and (Wind = true) then Play = no

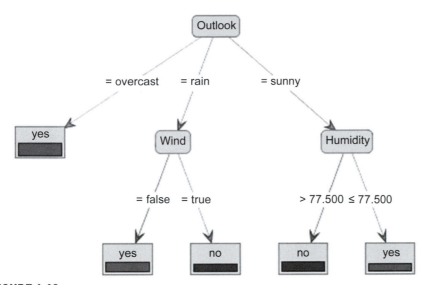

FIGURE 4.19

Approaches to rule generation.

Rule 4: if (Outlook = sunny) and (Humidity > 77.5) then Play = no
Rule 5: if (Outlook = sunny) and (Humidity ≤ 77.5) then Play = yes

The set of all the five rules is called a *rule set*. Each individual rule r_i is called a *disjunct* or classification rule. The entire rule set can be represented as

$$R = \{r_1 \cap r_2 \cap r_3 \cap .. \ r_k\}$$

where k is the number of disjuncts in a rule set. Individual disjuncts can be represented as

$r_i =$ (antecedent or condition) then (consequent)

For example, rule r_2: if (Outlook = rain) and (Wind = false) then Play = yes.

In the above example rule, (Outlook = rain) and (Wind = false) is the *antecedent* or *condition* of the rule. The condition of the rule can have many attributes and values each separated by a logical AND operator. Each attribute and value test is called the *conjunct* of the rule. An example of a conjunct is (Outlook = rain). The antecedent is a group of conjuncts with the AND operator. Each conjunct is a node in the equivalent decision tree.

In the Golf data set, we can observe a couple of properties of the rule set in relation with the data set. First, the rule set is mutually exclusive. This means that no example record will trigger more than one rule and hence the outcome of the prediction is definite. However, there can be rule sets that are not mutually exclusive. If a record activates more than one rule in a rule set and all the class predictions are the same, then there is no problem. If the class predictions differ, ambiguity exists on which class is the prediction of the induction rule model. There are a couple of techniques used to resolve conflicting class prediction by more than one rule. One technique is to develop an ordered list of rules where if a record activates many rules, the first rule in the order will take precedence. A second technique is where each active rule can "vote" for a prediction class. The predicted class with highest vote is the prediction of the rule set. The rule set discussed is also exhaustive. This means the rule set is activated for all the combinations of the attribute values in the record set, not just limited to training records. If the rule set is not exhaustive, then a final catch all bucket rule *"else Class = Default Class Value"* can be introduced to make the rule set exhaustive.

4.2.1 Approaches to Developing a Rule Set

Rules can be directly extracted from the data set or derived from the previously built decision trees from the same data set. Figure 4.20 shows the approaches to generate rules from the data set. The former approach is called the *direct* method, which is built on leveraging the relationship between the attribute and class label in the data set. Deriving a rule set from a previously built classifier decision tree model is a passive or *indirect* approach. Since building a decision tree is covered in previous section and the derivation of rules from the decision tree model is straightforward, we will focus the rest of the discussion on direct rule generation based on the relationship from the data. Specifically, we will focus on the *sequential covering* technique to build a rule set.

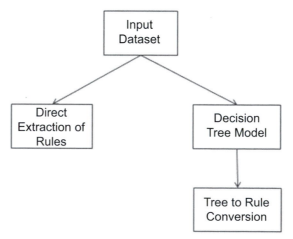

FIGURE 4.20
Decision tree model for Golf data set.

PREDICTING AND PREVENTING MACHINE BREAKDOWNS

A machine breakdown in the field almost always results in disruption of a manufacturing process. In a large-scale process like an oil refinery, chemical plants, etc., it causes serious financial damage to the company and manufacturers of the machines. Let's assume the machine under consideration is a motor. Rather than waiting for the machine to break down and react, it is much preferable to diagnose the problem and prevent the breakdown before a problem occurs. Large-scale machines track thousands of real-time readings from multiple parts of the machine (Such machines connected to networks that can gather readings and act based on smart logic are called Internet of Things (IoT).). One of the solutions is to leverage how these readings are trending and develop a rule base which says, for example, *if the cylinder temperature continues to report more than 852ºC, then the machine will break down in the near future.* These types of the rules are simple to interpret, don't require an expert to be around to take further action, and can be deployed by automated systems.

Developing learned rules requires historical analysis of all the readings that lead up to a machine failure (Langley & Simon, 1995). These learned rules are different and in many cases supersede the rule of thumb assumed by the machine expert. Based on the historic readings of a failure event and nonfailure events, the learned rule set can predict the failure of the machine and hence can alert the operator of imminent future breakdowns. Since these rules are very simple to understand, these preventive measures can be easily deployed to line workers. This use case demonstrates the need of not only a predictive data model, but also a descriptive model where the inner working of the model can be easily understood by the users. A similar approach can be developed to prevent customer churn, or loan default, for example.

4.2.2 How it Works

Sequential covering is an iterative procedure of extracting rules from the data set. The sequential covering approach attempts to find all the rules in the data set class by class. One specific implementation of the sequential covering approach is called the RIPPER, which stands for Repeated Incremental Pruning to Produce Error Reduction (Cohen, 1995). Consider the data set shown in Figure 4.21, which has two dimensions on the X and Y axis and two class labels marked by "+" and "−". Following are the steps in sequential covering rules generation approach (Tan et al. 2005).

Step 1: Class Selection

The algorithm starts with selection of class labels one by one. The rule set is class-ordered where all the rules for a class are developed before moving on to next class. The first class is usually the least-frequent class label. From Figure 4.21, the least frequent class is "+" and the algorithm focuses on generating all the rules for "+" class.

Step 2: Rule Development

The objective in this step is to cover all "+" data points using classification rules with none or as few "−" as possible. For example, in Figure 4.22, rule r_1 identifies the area of four "+" in the top left corner. Since this rule is based on simple logic operators in conjuncts, the boundary is rectilinear.

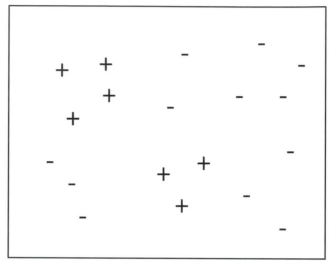

FIGURE 4.21
Data set with two classes and two dimensions.

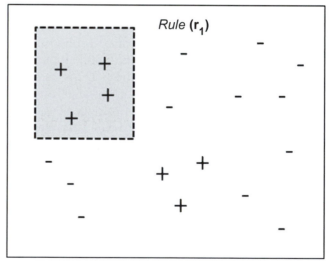

FIGURE 4.22
Generation of rule r_1.

Once rule r_1 is formed, the entire data points covered by r_1 are eliminated and the next best rule is found from data sets. The algorithm grows in a greedy fashion using a technique called Learn-One-Rule which is described in the next section. One of the outcomes of greedy algorithms that start with initial configuration is that they yield *local optima* instead of a *global optimum*. A local optimum is a solution that is optimal in the neighborhood of potential solutions, but worse than the global optimum.

Step 3: Learn-One-Rule

Each rule r_i is grown by the learn-one-rule approach. Each rule starts with an empty rule set and conjuncts are added one by one to increase the rule accuracy. Rule accuracy is the ratio of amount of + covered by the rule to all records covered by the rule:

$$\text{Rule accuracy } A(r_i) = \frac{\text{Correct records covered by rule}}{\text{All records covered by the rule}}$$

Learn-one-rule starts with an empty rule set: if {} then class = "+". Obviously the accuracy of this rule is the same as the proportion of + data points in the data set. Then the algorithm greedily adds conjuncts until the accuracy reaches 100%. If the addition of a conjunct decreases the accuracy, then the algorithm looks for other conjuncts or stops and starts the iteration of the next rule.

Step 4: Next Rule

After a rule is developed, then all the data points covered by the rule are eliminated from the data set. The above steps are repeated for the next rule to cover the rest of the "+" data points. In Figure 4.23, rule r_2 is developed after the data points covered by r_1 are eliminated.

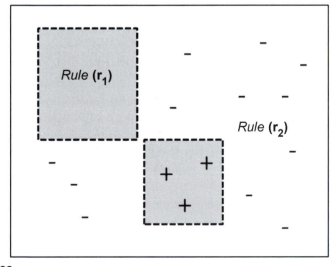

FIGURE 4.23
Elimination of r_1 data points and next rule.

Step 5: Development of Rule Set

After the rule set is developed to identify all "+" data points, the rule model is evaluated with a data set used for pruning to reduce generalization errors. The metric used to evaluate the need for pruning is (p − n)/(p + n), where p is the number of positive records covered by the rule and n is the number of negative records covered by the rule. The conjunct is iteratively removed if it improves the metric. All rules to identify "+" data points are aggregated to form a rule group. In multi-class problem, the previous steps are repeated with for next class label. Since this is a two class problem, any data points not covered by the rule set for identifying "+" are predicted to be "−". The outcome of the sequential covering or RIPPER algorithm is a set of optimized rules that can describe the relationship between attributes and the class label, which is also the predictive classification model (Saian & Ku-Mahamud, 2011).

4.2.3 How to Implement

Rules remain the most common expression to communicate the inherent relationship in the data. There are a few different ways to generate rules from the data using RapidMiner. The modeling operators for *rule induction* are available in the *Modeling> Classification and Regression > Rule Induction* folder. The following modeling operators available:

- **Rule Induction:** Commonly used generic rule induction modeler based on the RIPPER algorithm.
- **Single Rule Induction (Attribute):** Uses only one attribute in antecedent, usually the attribute with most predictive power.
- **Single Rule Induction:** Generates only one rule with if/else statement.
- **Tree to Rule:** Indirect method of rule generation that is based on underlying decision tree.

Single rule induction is used for quick discovery of the most dominant rule. Because of its simplicity, single rule modeling operators are used to establish a baseline performance for other classification models. We will review the implementation using the *Rule Induction* and *Tree to Rule* modeling operators in RapidMiner.

Step 1: Data Preparation

The data set we use in the implementation is the standard Iris data set (See Table 3.1 and Figure 3.1) with four attributes, sepal length, sepal width, petal length, and petal width, and a class label to identify the species of flower viz. *Iris setosa, Iris versicolor* and *Iris virginica*. The Iris data set is available in the Rapid-Miner repository under Sample > Data. Since the original data set refers to the four attributes as a1 to a4, we use the *Rename* operator to change the name of

the attributes (not values) so they can be more descriptive. The *Rename* operator is available in Data Transformation > Name and Role modification. Like a
decision tree, rule induction can accept both numeric and polynominal data
types. The Iris data set is split into two equal sets for training and testing, using
the *Split Data* operator (Data Transformation > Filtering > Sampling). The split
ratio used in this implementation is 50%-50% for training and test data.

Step 2: Modeling Operator and Parameters

The Rule Induction modeling operator accepts the training data and provides
the rule set as the model output. The rule set is the text output of if-then rules,
along with the accuracy and coverage statistics. The following parameters are
available in the model operator and can be configured for desired modeling
behavior.

- **Criterion:** Since the algorithm takes the greedy strategy, it needs
  an evaluation criterion to indicate whether adding a new conjunct
  helps in a rule. Information gain is commonly used for RIPPER and
  is similar to information gain for decision trees. Another easy-to-use
  criterion is accuracy, which was discussed in the sequential covering
  algorithm.
- **Sample ratio:** This is the ratio of data used for training in the example
  set. The rest of the data is used for pruning. This sample ratio is different
  from the training/test split ratio that is used in the data preparation
  stage.
- **Pureness:** This is the minimal ratio of accuracy desired in the
  classification rule.
- **Minimal prune benefit:** This is the percentage increase in the prune
  metric required at the minimum.

The output of the model is connected to the *Apply Model* operator to apply
the developed rule base against the test data set. The test data set from the
Split Data operator is connected to the *Apply Model* operator. The *Performance*
operator for classification is then used to create the performance vector from
the labeled data set generated from the *Apply Model* operator. The process can
be saved and executed after the output ports are connected to the result ports.
Figure 4.24 shows the complete RapidMiner process for rule induction. The
completed process and the data set can be downloaded from the companion
website of the book at www.LearnPredictiveAnalytics.com.

Step 3: Results Interpretation

The results screen consists of the Rule Model window, the labeled test data set,
and the performance vector. The performance vector is similar to the decision
tree performance vector. The Rule Model window, shown in Figure 4.25, consists of a sequence of if-then rules along with antecedents and consequents.

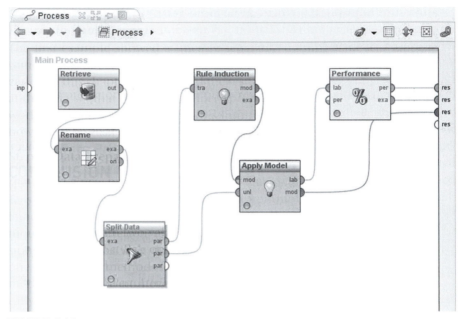

FIGURE 4.24
RapidMiner process for rule induction.

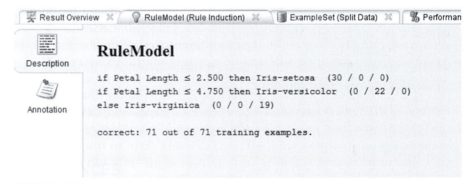

FIGURE 4.25
Rule output for rule induction.

The parentheses next to each classification rule indicate the class distribution of the rule covered from the training data set. Note that these statistics are based on the training data set, not the test dataset.

The Performance Vector window provides the accuracy statistics of the prediction based on the rules model for the test data set. For the Iris data set and the RapidMiner process shown in this example, the accuracy of prediction is 92%.

Sixty-nine out of 75 test records are predicted accurately based on simple rules developed by the rule induction model. Not bad for a quick, easy-to-use and easy-to-understand model!

Alternative Approach: Tree-to-Rules

An indirect but easy way to generate a mutually exclusive and exhaustive rule set is to convert a decision tree to an induction rule set. Each classification rule can be traced from the leaf node to the root node, where each node becomes a conjunct and the class label of the leaf becomes the consequent. Even though tree-to-rules may be simple to implement, the resulting rule set may not be the most optimal to understand, as there are many repetitive nodes in the rule path.

In the data mining process developed in RapidMiner, we can just replace the previous Rule Induction operator with the *Tree to Rules* operator. This modeling operator does not have any parameters as it simply converts the tree to rules. However, we have to specify the decision tree in the inner subprocess of the *Tree to Rules* operator. On double-clicking the *Tree to Rules* operator, we can see the inner process where a *Decision Tree* modeling operator has to be inserted as shown in Figures 4.26 and 4.27.

The parameters for a decision tree are the same and reviewed in Section 4.1 of this chapter. The RapidMiner process can be saved and executed. The result set consists of set of rule models, usually with repetitive conjuncts in

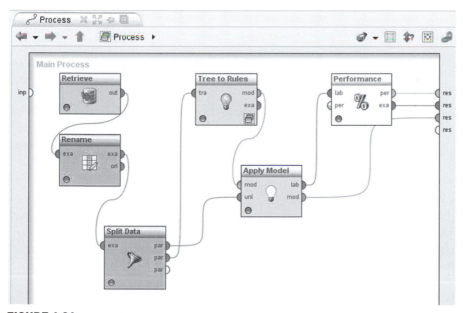

FIGURE 4.26
RapidMiner process for Tree to Rules operator.

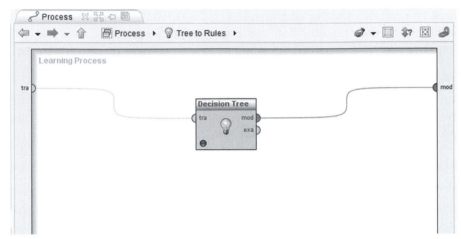

FIGURE 4.27
Decision Tree operator inside the subprocess for Tree to Rules.

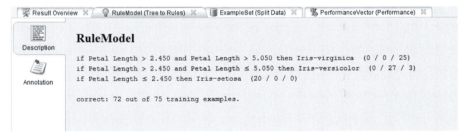

FIGURE 4.28
Rules based on decision tree.

antecedents, a fingerprint of rules derived from trees. Note the difference between the rules that are developed for the Rule Induction operator and the rules developed from *Tree to Rules* operator. The rules generated from Tree to Rules are shown in Figure 4.28.

4.2.4 Conclusion

Classification using rules provides a simple framework to identify a relationship between factors and the class label that is not only used as a predictive model, but a descriptive model. Rules are closely associated to decision trees. They split the data space in rectilinear fashion and generate mutually exclusive and exhaustive data sets. When the rule set is not mutually exclusive, then the data space can be divided by complex and curved decision boundaries. Single rule learners are the simplest form of data mining model and indicate the most powerful predictor in the given set of attributes. Since rule induction is a greedy algorithm, the result may not be the most globally optimal solution and like decision trees, rules can overlearn the example set. This scenario can be mitigated by pruning. Given the wide reachability of rules, rule induction is commonly used as a tool to express the results of data mining, even if other data mining algorithms are used.

4.3 k-NEAREST NEIGHBORS

The predictive data mining using decision trees and rule induction techniques were built by generalizing the relationship within the data set and using it to predict the outcome of new unseen data. If we need to predict the loan interest rate based on credit score, income level, and loan amount, one approach is to develop a mathematical relationship such as an equation $y = f(X)$ based on the known data and then using the equation to predict interest rate for new data points. These approaches are called *eager learners* because they attempt to find a best approximation of the actual relationship between the input and target variables. But there is also a simple alternative approach. We can "predict" the interest rate for a given credit score, income level and loan amount by *looking up* the interest rate of other customer loan records with similar credit score, closely matching income level and loan amount from the training data set. This alternative class of learners adopts a blunt approach, where no "learning" is performed from the training data set; rather the training data set is used as a *lookup* table to match the input variables and find the outcome. These approaches are called *lazy learners*.

The underlying idea here is somewhat similar to the old adage, "birds of a feather flock together." Similar records congregate in a neighborhood in n-dimensional space, with the same target class labels. This is the central logic behind the approach used by the k-nearest neighbor algorithm, or simply k-NN. The entire training data set is "memorized" and when unlabeled example records need to be classified, the input attributes of the new unlabeled records are compared against the entire training set to find a closest match. The class label of the closest training record is the predicted class label for the unseen test record. This is a nonparametric method, where no generalization or attempt to find the distribution of the data set is made (Altman, 1992). Once the training records are in memory, the classification of the test record is very straightforward. We need to find the closest training record for each test record. Even though no mathematical generalization or rule generation is involved, finding the closet training record for a new unlabeled record can be a tricky problem to solve, particularly when there is no exact match of training data available for a given test data record.

PREDICTING THE TYPE OF FOREST

Satellite imaging and digital image processing have provided a wealth of data about almost every part of the earth's landscape. There is strong motivation for forestry departments, government agencies, universities, and research bodies to understand the makeup of forests, species of trees and their health, biodiversity, density, and forest condition. Field studies for developing forest databases and classification project are quite a tedious task and expensive. However, we can aid this process by leveraging satellite imagery, limited field data, elevation models, aerial photographs, and survey data (McInerney, 2005). The objective is to classify whether the landscape is a forest or not and further predict the type of trees and species.

The approach to classifying the landscape involves dividing the area into land units (e.g., a pixel in a satellite image) and creating a vector of all the measurements for the land unit, by combining all the available data sets. Each unit's measurements are then compared against the measurements of known pre-classified units. For a given pixel, we can find a pixel in the pre-classified catalog, which has measurements very close to the measurement of the pixel to be predicted. Say the pre-classified pixel with the closest measurement corresponds to birch trees. Thus, we can predict the pixel area to be a birch forest. Every pixel's measurement is compared to measurements of the pre-classified data set to determine the like pixels and hence same forest types. This is the core concept of the k-nearest neighbor algorithm that is used to classify the landscape areas. (Haapanen et al., 2001)

4.3.1 How it Works

Any record in a data set can be visualized as a point in an n-dimensional space, where n is the number of attributes. While it is hard for humans to visualize in more than three dimensions, mathematical functions are scalable to any dimension and hence we can perform all the operations that can be done in two-dimensional spaces in the n-dimensional space. Let's consider the standard Iris data set (150 examples, four attributes, one class label. See Figure 3.1 and Table 3.1) and focus on two attributes, petal length and petal width. The scatterplot of these two dimensions is shown in Figure 4.29. The colors indicate the species of Iris, the target class variable. For an unseen test data point A with (petal length, petal width) values (2.1, 0.5), we can deduce visually that the predicted species for the values of data point A would be *Iris setosa*. This is based on the fact that test data point A is in the neighborhood of other data points that belong to species *Iris setosa*. Similarly, unseen test data point B has values (5.7, 1.9) and is in the neighborhood of *Iris versicolor*, hence the test data point can be classified as *Iris versicolor*. However, if the data points are in between the boundaries of two species, for data points such as (5.0, 1.8), then the classification can be tricky because the neighborhood has more than one species in the vicinity. We need an efficient algorithm to resolve these corner cases and measure nearness of data points with more than two dimensions. One technique is to find the nearest training data point from an unseen test data point in multidimensional space, and use the target class value of the nearest training data point as the predicted target class for the test data point. This is similar to how the k-NN algorithm works.

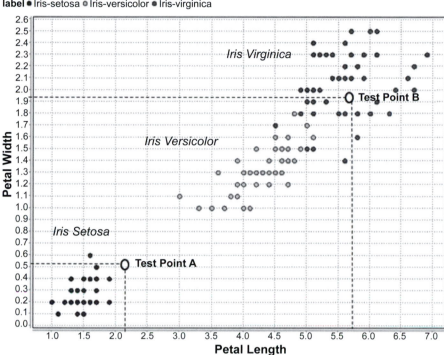

label ● Iris-setosa ○ Iris-versicolor ● Iris-virginica

FIGURE 4.29

Two-dimensional plot of Iris data set: sepal length and sepal width. Classes are stratified with colors.

The k in the k-NN algorithm indicates the number of close training record(s) that need to be considered when making the prediction for an unlabeled test record. When k = 1, the model tries to find the *first* nearest record and adopts the class label of the first nearest training record as the predicted target class value. Figure 4.30 provides an example training set with two dimensions and the target class values as circles and triangles. The unlabeled test record is the dark square in the center of the scatterplot. With k = 1, the predicted target class value of an unlabeled test record is *triangle* because the closest training record is a triangle. But, what if the closest training record is an outlier with the incorrect class in the training set? Then, all the unlabeled test records near the outlier will get wrongly classified. To prevent this misclassification, we can increase the value of k to, say, 3. When k = 3, we consider the nearest *three* training records instead of one. From Figure 4.30, based on the major-ity class of the nearest three training records, we can conclude the predicted class of the test record is *circle*. Since the class of the target record is evalu-ated by voting, k is usually assigned an odd number for a two-class problem (Peterson, 2009).

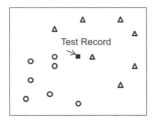 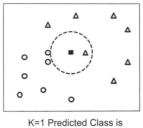 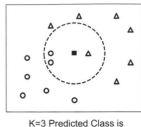

K=1 Predicted Class is
triangle

K=3 Predicted Class is
circle

FIGURE 4.30

(a) Data set with a record of unknown class. (b) Decision boundary with k = 1 around unknown class record. (c) Decision boundary with k = 3 around unknown test record.

The key task in the k-NN algorithm is determination of the nearest training record from the unlabeled test record using a measure of proximity. Once the nearest training record(s) are determined, the subsequent voting of the nearest training records is straightforward. Let's discuss the various techniques used to measure proximity.

Measure of Proximity

The effectiveness of the k-NN algorithm hinges on the determination of how similar or dissimilar a test record is when compared with the memorized training record. A measure of proximity between two records is measure of proximity of its attributes. To quantify similarity between two records, there is a range of techniques available such as calculating distance, correlation, Jaccard similarity, and cosine similarity (Tan, Michael, & Kumar, 2005).

A. Distance

The distance between two points X (x_1, x_2) and Y (y_1, y_2) in two-dimensional space can be calculated by Equation 4.3:

$$\text{Distance d} = \sqrt{(x_1 - y_1)^2 + (x_2 - y_2)^2} \tag{4.3}$$

We can generalize the two-dimensional distance formula shown in Equation 4.3 for n-dimensional space, where X is $(x_1, x_2, ..., x_n)$ and Y is $(y_1, y_2, ..., y_n)$, as

$$\text{Distance d} = \sqrt{(x_1 - y_1)^2 + (x_2 - y_2)^2 + \bullet \bullet \bullet + (x_n - y_n)^2} \tag{4.4}$$

For example, the first two records of a four-dimensional Iris data set (Fisher, 1936) is X = (4.9, 3.0, 1.4, 0.2) and Y = (4.6, 3.1, 1.5, 0.2). The distance between X and Y is d = $\sqrt{(0.3)^2 + (0.1)^2 + (0.1)^2 + (0)^2}$ = 0.33 centimeters. All the attributes in the Iris data set are homogenous in terms of measurements (length of flower parts) and units (centimeters). However in a typical practical data set, it is common to see attributes in different measures (e.g., credit score, income) and varied units. One problem with the distance approach is that it depends on the scale and units of the attributes. For example, the variance in credit score between two records could be a few hundred points, which is minor in magnitude compared to the variance in income, which could on the order of thousands. Consider two pairs of data points with credit score and annual income in USD. Pair A is (500, $40,000) and (600, $40,000). Pair B is (500, $40,000) and (500, $39,800). The first data point in both the pairs is same. The second data point is different than the first data point, with only one attribute changed. In Pair A, credit score is 600, which is significantly different than 500, while the income is the same. In Pair B, income is down by $200 when compared to the first data point, which is only a 0.5% change. One can rightfully conclude that the data points in Pair B are more similar than the data points in Pair A. However, the distance (Equation 4.4) between data points in Pair A is 100 and the distance between Pair B is 200! The variation in income overpowers the variation in credit score. The same phenomenon can be observed when attributes are measured in different units, scales, etc. To mitigate the problem caused by different measures and units, all the inputs of k-NN are usually normalized, where the data values are rescaled to fit a particular range. Normalizing all the attributes provides a fair comparison between them.

Normalization can be performed by a few different methods. Range transformation rescales values of all the attributes to specified min and max values, usually 0 to 1. Z-transformation attempts to rescale all the values by subtracting the mean from each value and dividing the result by the standard deviation, resulting in a transformed set of values that has a mean of 0 and standard deviation of 1. For example, when the Iris data set is normalized using Z-transformation, sepal length, which takes values between 4.3 and 7.9 centimeters, and has a standard deviation of 0.828, is transformed to values between −1.86 and 2.84, with standard deviation 1. The distance measurement discussed so far is also called *Euclidean distance*, which is the most common distance measure for numeric attributes. In addition to the Euclidean, *Manhattan*, and *Chebyshev* distance measures are sometimes used to calculate the distance between two numeric data points. Let's consider two data points X (1,2) and Y (3,1), as shown in Figure 4.31. The Euclidean distance between X and Y is the straight-line distance between X and Y, which is 2.7. Manhattan distance is the sum of the difference between individual attributes, rather than the root difference square. The Manhattan distance between X and Y is (3 − 1) + (2 − 1) = 3. Manhattan distance is also called the taxi cab distance, due to similarities of the visual path traversed by a vehicle around city blocks (In Figure 4.31, the total distance that is covered by

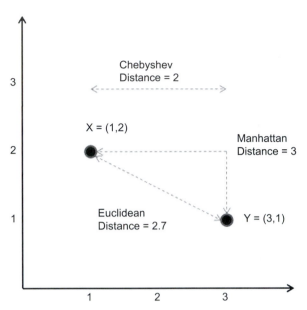

FIGURE 4.31
Distance measures.

a cab that has to travel from X to Y in terms of city blocks is two blocks to the right and one block down). Chebyshev distance is the maximum difference between all attributes in the data set. In this example, the Chebyshev distance is the max of [(3 – 1), (1 – 2)] = 2. If Figure 4.31 were a chess board, Chebyshev distance would be the minimum number of moves required by the king to go from one position to another and Manhattan distance is the minimum number of squares covered by the move of a rook from one position to another.

All three aforementioned distance measures can be further generalized by one formula, the **Minkowski** distance measure. The distance between two points X $(x_1, x_2,..., x_n)$ and Y $(y_1, y_2,..., y_n)$ in n-dimensional space is given by Equation 4.5:

$$d = \left(\sum_{i=1}^{n} |x_i - y_i|^p \right)^{\frac{1}{p}} \tag{4.5}$$

When $p = 1$, the distance measure is the Manhattan distance, when $p = 2$ the distance measure is the Euclidean distance, and when p = ∞ the distance measure is the Chebyshev distance. p is also called the *norm* and Equation 4.5 is called the *p*-norm distance. The choice of distance measure depends on the data (Grabusts, 2011). The Euclidean measure is the most commonly used distance measure for numeric data. Manhattan distance (or Hamming distance) is used for binary attributes. For an unknown (no prior knowledge) data set, there is no rule-of-thumb distance measure. Euclidean distance would be a good start and the model can be tested with a selection of other distance measures and the corresponding performance. Once the nearest k neighbors are determined, the process of determining the predicted target class is straightforward. The predicted target class is the majority class of the nearest k neighbors. Equation 4.6 provides the prediction of the k-NN algorithm:

$$y' = \text{maximum class } (y_1, y_2, \cdots, y_k) \qquad (4.6)$$

where y' is the predicted target class of the test data point and y_i is the class of ith neighbor n_i.

Weights

The premise of the k-NN algorithm is that data points closer to each other are similar and hence they have the same target class labels. When k is more than one, it can be argued that the closest neighbors should have more say in the outcome of the predicted target class than the farther neighbors (Hill & Lewicki, 2007). The far away neighbors have less influence in determining the final class outcome. This can be accomplished by assigned weights for all the neighbors, with the weights increasing as the neighbors get closer to the data point. The weights are included in the final multivoting step, where the predicted class is calculated. Weights (w_i) should satisfy two conditions: they should be proportional to the distance of the data point from the neighbor and the sum of all weights should be equal to one. One of the calculations for weights shown in Equation 4.7 follows an exponential decay based on distance:

$$w_i = \frac{e^{-d(x, n_i)}}{\sum_{i=1}^{k} e^{-d(x, n_i)}} \qquad (4.7)$$

where w_i is the weight of ith neighbor n_i, k the is total number of neighbors, and x is the test data point. The weight is used in predicting target class y':

$$y' = \text{maximum class } (w_1 * y_1, w_2 * y_2, \cdots, w_k * y_k) \qquad (4.8)$$

where y_i is the class outcome of neighbor n_i.

The distance measure works well for numeric attributes. However, if the attribute is categorical (nominal), the distance between two points is either 0 or 1. If the attribute values are the same, the distance is 0 and if the attribute values are different, the distance is 1. An example distance (overcast, sunny) = 1 and distance (sunny, sunny) = 0. If the attribute is ordinal with more than two values, then the ordinal values can be converted to the integer data type with values 0, 1, 2, ..., n – 1 and the converted attribute can be treated as a numeric attribute for distance calculation. Obviously, converting ordinal into numeric retains more information than using it as a categorical data type, where the distance value is either 0 or 1.

B. Correlation similarity

Correlation between two data points X and Y is the measure of the linear relationship between the attributes X and Y. Pearson correlation takes the value from −1 (perfect negative correlation) to +1 (perfect positive correlation) with the value of zero being no correlation between X and Y. Since correlation is a measure of "linear" relationship, a zero value doesn't mean there is no relationship. It just means that there is no linear relationship, but there may be a quadratic or any other higher degree relationship between the data points. Also, we are now exploring correlation between one data point and another. *This is quite different from correlation between variables.* Pearson correlation between two data points X and Y is given by

$$\text{Correlation }(X,Y) = \frac{s_{xy}}{s_x * s_y} \tag{4.9}$$

where s_{xy} is the covariance of X and Y, which is calculated as
$s_{xy} = \frac{1}{n-1}\sum_{i=1}^{n}(x_i - \bar{x})(y_i - \bar{y})$ and s_x and s_x are the standard deviation of X and Y, respectively. The Pearson correlation of two data points X

(1,2,3,4,5) and Y (10,15,35,40,55) is 0.98.

C. Simple matching coefficient

The simple matching coefficient (SMC) is used when data sets have binary attributes. For example, let X be (1,1,0,0,1,1,0) and Y be (1,0,0,1,1,0,0). We can measure the similarity between these two data points based on simultaneous occurrence of 0 or 1 with respect to total occurrences. The simple matching coefficient for X and Y can be calculated as follows:

$$\text{Simple matching coefficient }(SMC) = \frac{matching\ occurences}{total\ occurences}$$

$$= \frac{m_{00} + m_{11}}{m_{10} + m_{01} + m_{11} + m_{00}} \tag{4.10}$$

where
m_{11} = occurrences where X = is 1 and Y = is 1 = 2
m_{10} = occurrences where X = is 1 and Y = is 0 = 2
m_{01} = occurrences where X = is 0 and Y = is 1 = 1
m_{00} = occurrences where X = is 0 and Y = is 0 = 2

$$\text{Simple matching coefficient }(SMC) = \frac{matching\ occurences}{total\ occurences}$$

$$= \frac{m_{00} + m_{11}}{m_{10} + m_{01} + m_{11} + m_{00}} = \frac{4}{7}$$

D. Jaccard similarity

If X and Y represent two text documents, each word can be an attribute in a data set called a term document matrix or document vector. Each record in the document data set corresponds to a separate document or a text blob. This is explained in greater detail in Chapter 9 Text Mining. In this application, the number of attributes would be very large number, often in the thousands. When comparing two documents X and Y, most of the attribute values will be zero. This means that two documents do not contain the same rare words. In this instance, what is interesting is that the comparison of the *occurrence* of the same word and nonoccurrence of the same word doesn't convey any information and we can ignore it. The Jaccard similarity measure is similar to the simple matching similarity but the nonoccurrence frequency is ignored from the calculation. For the same example X $(1,1,0,0,1,1,0)$ and Y $(1,0,0,1,1,0,0)$,

$$\text{Jaccard coefficient} = \frac{common\ occurences}{total\ occurences}$$

$$= \frac{m_{11}}{m_{10} + m_{01} + m_{11}} = \frac{2}{5} \tag{4.11}$$

E. Cosine similarity

We continue the example of the document vectors, where attributes represent either the presence or absence of a word, which takes a binary form of either 1 or 0. It is possible to construct a more informational vector with the number of occurrences in the document, instead of occurrences and nonoccurrences denoted by 1 and 0 respectively. Document data set are usually long vectors with thousands of variables or attributes. For simplicity, consider the example of the vectors with X $(1,2,0,0,3,4,0)$ and Y $(5,0,0,6,7,0,0)$. The cosine similarity measure for two data points is given by

$$\text{Cosine similarity} (|X, Y|) = \frac{x \cdot y}{\| x \| \| y \|} \tag{4.12}$$

where *x·y* is the dot product of the *x* and *y* vectors with $X \cdot Y = \sum_{i=1}^{n} x_i y_i$, and $\| x \| 1 = \sqrt{x \cdot x}$. For this example

$$x \cdot y = \sqrt{1*5 + 2*0 + 0*0 + 0*6 + 3*7 + 4*0 + 0*0} = 5.1$$
$$\| x \| = \sqrt{1*1 + 2*2 + 0*0 + 0*0 + 3*3 + 4*4 + 0*0} = 5.5$$
$$\| y \| = \sqrt{5*5 + 0*0 + 0*0 + 6*6 + 7*7 + 0*0 + 0*0} = 10.5$$

$$\text{Cosine similarity} (|x \cdot y|) = \frac{x \cdot y}{\| x \| \| y \|} = \frac{5.1}{5.5 * 10.5} = 0.08$$

As with distance measures, there are a few similarity measures available for a categorical attribute in a k-NN implementation. The cosine similarity measure is one of the most used similarity measures, but the determination of the optimal measure comes down to the data structures. The choice of distance or similarity measure can also be parameterized, where multiple models are created with each different measure. The model with a distance measure that best fits the data with the smallest generalization error can be the appropriate distance measure for the data.

4.3.2 How to Implement

Implementation of lazy learners is the most straightforward process amongst all the data mining methods. Since the key functionality here is referencing or looking up the training data set, we could implement the entire algorithm in spreadsheet software like MS Excel, using lookup functions. Of course, if the complexity of the distance calculation or number of attributes rises, then we may need to rely on data mining tools or programming languages. In Rapid-Miner, k-NN implementation is similar to other classification and regression process, with data preparation, modeling, and performance evaluation operators. The modeling step memorizes all the training records and accepts input in the form of real and nominal values. The output of this modeling step is just the data set of all the training records.

Step 1: Data Preparation

The data set used in this example is the standard Iris data set with 150 examples and four numeric attributes. First we need to normalize all attributes using the *Normalize* operator, from the Data Transformation > Value Modification > Numerical Value Modification folder. The *Normalize* operator accepts numeric attributes and outputs transformed numeric attributes. The user can specify one of four normalization methods in the parameter configurations: Z-transformation (most commonly used), range transformation, proportion transformation, and interquartile range. In this example, Z-transformation is used because we are standardizing all attributes to same standard deviation.

The data set is then split into two equal exclusive data sets using the *Split Data* operator. Split Data (from Data Transformation > Filtering > Sampling) is used to partition one data set into multiple data sets. The proportion of the partition and the sampling method can be specified in the parameter configuration of the split operator. For this example, the data is split equally between the training and test sets using shuffled sampling. One half of the data set is used as training data for developing the k-NN model and the other half of the data set is used to test the validity of the model.

Step 2: Modeling Operator and Parameters

The k-NN modeling operator is available in Modeling > Classification > Lazy Modeling. The following parameters can be configured in the operator settings:

- **k:** The value of k in k-NN can be configured. This defaults to one nearest neighbor. This example uses k = 3.
- **Weighted Vote:** In the case of k > 1, this setting determines if the algorithm needs to take into consideration the distance value while predicting the class value of the test record.

- **Measure Types:** There are more than two dozen distance measures available in RapidMiner. These measures are grouped in Measure Types. The selection of Measure Types drives the options for the next parameter (Measure).
- **Measure:** This parameter selects the actual measure like Euclidean distance, Manhattan distance, and so on. The selection of the measure will put restrictions on the type of input the model receives. Depending on the weighting measure, the input data type choices will be limited and hence the data type conversion is required if the input data contains attributes that are not compatible with that measure.

Step 3: Evaluation

Similar to other classification model implementations, we need to apply the model to test the data set, so the effectiveness of the model can be evaluated. Figure 4.32 shows the RapidMiner process where the initial Iris data set is split using a split operator. A random 75 of the initial 150 records are used to build the k-NN model and the rest of the data is the test data set. The *Apply Model* operator takes the test data and applies the k-NN model to predict the class type of the species. The *Performance* operator is then used to compare the predicted class with the labeled class for all of the test records. The complete RapidMiner process can be downloaded from the companion website www.LearnPredictiveAnalytics.com.

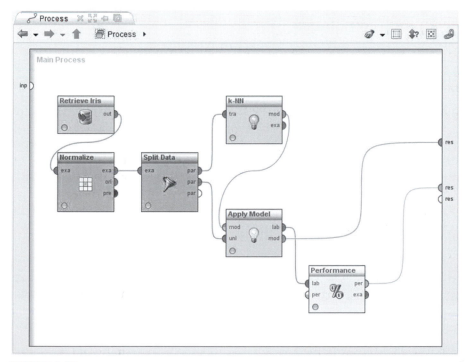

FIGURE 4.32

Data mining process for k-NN algorithm.

Step 4: Execution and Interpretation

After the output from the *Performance* operator has been connected to the result ports, as shown in Figure 4.32, the model can be executed. The following result output is observed.

1. **k-NN model:** The model for k-NN is just the set of training records. Hence no additional information is provided in this view, apart from the statistics of training records. Figure 4.33 shows the output model.
2. **Performance vector:** The output of the *Performance* operator provides the confusion matrix with correct and incorrect predictions for all of the test data set. The test set had 75 records. Figure 4.34 shows the accurate prediction of 71 records (sum of diagonal cells in the matrix) and 4 incorrect predictions.

4.3.3 Conclusion

The k-NN model requires normalization to avoid any bias by any attribute that has large or small units in the scale. The model is quite robust when there is any missing attribute value in the test record. If the value in the test record is missing, the entire attribute is ignored in the model, and still the model

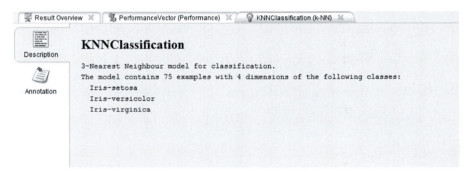

FIGURE 4.33

k-NN model output.

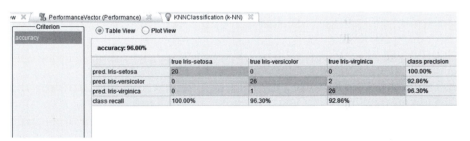

FIGURE 4.34

Performance vector for k-NN model.

can function with reasonable accuracy. In the implementation example, if the sepal length of a test record is not known, then the sepal length is ignored in the model. When an attribute value is missing, k-NN becomes a three-dimensional model instead of the regular four dimensions.

As a lazy learner, the relationship between input and output cannot be explained, as the model is just a memorized set of all training records. There is no generalization or abstraction of the relationship. Eager learners are better at explaining the relationship and providing a description of the model.

Model building in k-NN is just memorizing and doesn't require much time. But, when a new unlabeled record is to be classified, the algorithm needs to find the distance between the test record and *all* training records. This process can get very expensive, depending on the size of training set and the number of attributes. A few sophisticated k-NN implementations index the records so that it is easy to search and calculate the distance. We can also convert the actual "real" numbers to ranges so as to make it easy to index and compare it against the test record. However, k-NN is difficult to use in time-sensitive applications like serving an online advertisement or real-time fraud detection.

k-NN models can handle categorical inputs, but the distance between categorical attribute values is either 1, when the attribute values are different or 0, when the attribute values are same. Ordinal values can be converted to integers so that we can better leverage the distance function. Although the k-NN model is not good at generalizing the input-output relationship, it is still quite an effective model for leveraging existing relationships in the training records. For good quality outcomes, it requires a significant number of training records with the maximum possible permutations of input attributes.

4.4 NAÏVE BAYESIAN

The data mining algorithms used for classification tasks are quite diverse. The objective of these algorithms is the same—prediction of a target variable. But, the method of predicting is drawn from a range of multidisciplinary techniques. The naïve Bayes algorithm finds its roots in statistics and probability theory. In general, classification techniques try to predict class labels based on attributes by best approximating the relationship between input and output variables. Every day, we mentally estimate a myriad of outcomes based on past evidence. Consider the process of guessing commuting time to work. First, commute time depends heavily on when you are traveling. If you are traveling during peak hours, most likely the commute is going to be longer. Weather conditions like rain, snow, or dense fog will slow down the commute. If the day is a school holiday, like summer break, then the commute will be lighter than on school days. If there is any planned road work ahead, the commute usually takes longer. When more than one adverse factor is at play, then the commute will be even longer than if it is just one isolated factor. All this if-then knowledge is based on previous experience of commuting when one or more factors come into play. Our experience creates a model in our brain and we mentally run the model before pulling out of the driveway!

Let's take the case of defaults in home mortgages and assume the average overall default rate is 2%. The likelihood of an average person defaulting on their mortgage loan is 2%. However, if a given individual's credit history is above average (or excellent), then the likelihood of their default would be less than average. Furthermore, if we know that the person's annual salary is above average with respect to loan value, then the likelihood of default falls further. As we obtain more evidence on the factors that impact the outcome, we can make improved guesses about the outcome using probability theory. The naïve Bayesian algorithm basically leverages the probabilistic relationship between the factors (attributes) and the class label (outcome). The algorithm makes a strong and sometimes naïve assumption of independence between the attributes, thus its name. The independence assumption between attributes may not always hold true. In some cases, we can assume annual income and credit score are independent of each other. However, in many cases we just don't know. If one of the factors for the default rate is home value, then we have a scenario where both the annual income and home value factors are correlated and thus not independent. Homeowners with high income tend to buy more expensive houses. The independence assumption doesn't hold true always, but the simplicity and robustness of the algorithm offsets the limitation introduced by the independence assumption.

PREDICTING AND FILTERING SPAM EMAIL

Spam is unsolicited bulk email sent to a wide number of email users. At best it is an annoyance to recipients but many of the spam emails hide a malicious intent by hosting false advertisements or redirecting clicks to phishing sites. Filtering spam email is one of the essential features provided by email service providers and administrators. The key challenge is balance between incorrectly flagging a legitimate email as spam (false positive) versus not catching all the spam messages. There is no perfect spam filtering solution and spam detecting is a catch-up game. The spammers always try to deceive and outsmart the spam filters and email administrators fortify the filters for various new spam scenarios. Automated spam filtering based on algorithms provides a promising solution in containing spam and a learning framework to update the filtering solutions (Prosess Software, 2013).

Some words occur in spam emails more often than in legitimate email messages. For example, the probability of occurrence for words like free, mortgage, credit, sale, Viagra, etc. is higher in spam mails than in normal emails. We can calculate the exact probabilities if we have a sample of previously known spam emails and regular emails. Based on the known word probabilities, we can compute the overall probability of an email being spam based on all the words in the email and the probability of each word being in spam versus regular emails. This is the foundation of Bayesian spam filtering systems (Zdziarski, 2005). Any wrongly classified spam messages that are subsequently reclassified by the user is an opportunity to refine the model, making spam filtering adaptive to new spam techniques. Though recent spam reduction uses a combination of different algorithms, Bayesian-based spam filtering remains one of the foundational elements of spam prediction systems (Sahami et al., 1998).

4.4.1 How it Works

The naïve Bayesian algorithm is built on Bayes' theorem, named after Reverend Thomas Bayes. Bayes' work is described in "Essay Towards Solving a Problem in the Doctrine of Chances" (1763), published posthumously in the *Philosophical Transactions of the Royal Society of London* by Richard Price. Bayes' theorem is one of the most influential and important concepts in statistics and probability theory. It provides a mathematical expression for how a degree of subjective belief changes to account for new evidence. First, let's discuss the terminology used in Bayes' theorem.

Assume **X** is the evidence (or factors or attribute set) and Y is the outcome (or target or label class). Here **X** is a set, not individual attributes, hence $\mathbf{X} = \{X_1, X_2, X_3, ..., X_n\}$, where X_i is an individual attribute, such as credit rating. The probability of outcome P(Y) is called *prior probability*, which can be calculated from the data set. Prior probability shows the likelihood of an outcome in a given data set. For example, in the mortgage case, P(Y) is the default rate of a home mortgage, which is 2%. P(Y|**X**) is called the *conditional probability*, which provides the probability of an outcome given the evidence when we know the value of **X**. Again, using the mortgage example, P(Y|**X**) is the average rate of default given that an individual's credit history is known. If the credit history is excellent, then the probability of default is likely to be less than 2%. P(Y|**X**) is also called *posterior probability*. Calculating posterior probability is the objective of predictive analytics using Bayes' theorem. This is the likelihood of an outcome as we learn the values of the input attributes.

Bayes' theorem states that

$$P(Y|\mathbf{X}) = \frac{P(Y) * P(\mathbf{X}|Y)}{P(\mathbf{X})} \tag{4.13}$$

P(**X**|Y) is another conditional probability, called the *class conditional probability*. P(**X**|Y) is the probability that an attribute assumes a particular value given the class label. Like P(Y), P(**X**|Y) can be calculated from the data set as well. If we know the training set of loan defaults, we can calculate the probability of an "excellent" credit rating given that the default is a "yes." As indicated in Bayes' theorem, class conditional probability is crucial in calculating posterior probability. P(**X**) is basically the probability of the evidence. In the mortgage example, this is simply the proportion of individuals with a given credit rating. To classify a new record, we can compute P(Y|**X**) for *each class of Y* and see which probability "wins." Class label Y with the highest value of P(Y|**X**) wins for a particular attribute value **X**. Since P(**X**) is the same for every class value of the outcome, we don't have to calculate this and assume it as a constant. More generally, in an example set with n attributes $\mathbf{X} = \{X_1, X_2, X_3 ... X_n\}$,

$$P(Y|\mathbf{X}) = \frac{P(Y) * \prod_{i=1}^{n} P(X_i|Y)}{P(\mathbf{X})} \tag{4.14}$$

If we know how to calculate class conditional probability P(X|Y) or $\prod_{i=1}^{n}P(X_i|Y)$, then it is easy to calculate posterior probability P(Y|X). Since P(X) is constant for every value of Y, it is enough to calculate the numerator of the equation $P(Y) * \prod_{i=1}^{n}P(X_i|Y)$ for every class value.

To further explain how the naïve Bayesian algorithm works, let's use the modified Golf data set shown in Table 4.4. The Golf table is an artificial data set with four attributes and one class label. Note that we are using the nominal data table for easier explanation (temperature and humidity have been converted from the numeric type). In Bayesian terms, weather condition is the evidence and decision to play or not play is the belief. Altogether there are 14 examples with 5 examples of Play = no and nine examples of Play = yes. The objective is to predict if the player will Play (yes or no), given the information about a few weather-related measures, based on learning from the data set in Table 4.4. Here is the step-by-step explanation of how the Bayesian model works.

Step 1: Calculating Prior Probability P(Y)
Prior probability P(Y) is the probability of an outcome. In this example set there are two possible outcomes: Play = yes and Play = no. From Table 4.4, out of 14 records there are 5 records with the "no" class and 9 records with the "Yes" class. The probability of outcome is

P(Y = no) = 5/14
P(Y = yes) = 9/14

Table 4.4 Golf Data Set with Modified Temperature and Humidity Attributes

No.	Temperature X_1	Humidity X_2	Outlook X_3	Wind X_4	Play (Class Label) Y
1	high	med	sunny	false	no
2	high	high	sunny	true	no
3	low	low	rain	true	no
4	med	high	sunny	false	no
5	low	med	rain	true	no
6	high	med	overcast	false	yes
7	low	high	rain	false	yes
8	low	med	rain	false	yes
9	low	low	overcast	true	yes
10	low	low	sunny	false	yes
11	med	med	rain	false	yes
12	med	low	sunny	true	yes
13	med	high	overcast	true	yes
14	high	low	overcast	false	yes

Since the probability of an outcome is calculated from the data set, it is important that the data set used for data mining is *representative* of the population, if sampling is used. A class-stratified sampling of data from the population will not be compatible for naïve Bayesian modeling.

Step 2: Calculating Class Conditional Probability $P(X_i | Y)$

Class conditional probability is the probability of *each* attribute value for an attribute, for each outcome value. This calculation is repeated for all the attributes: Temperature (X_1), Humidity (X_2), Outlook (X_3), and Wind(X_4), and for every distinct outcome value. Let's calculate the class conditional probability of Temperature (X_1). For each value of the Temperature attribute, we can calculate $P(X_1|Y = no)$ and $P(X_1|Y = yes)$ by constructing a probability table as shown in Table 4.5. From the data set there are five $Y = no$ records and nine $Y = yes$ records. Out of the five $Y = no$ records, we can also calculate the probability of occurrence when the temperature is high, medium, and low. The values will be 2/5, 1/5, and 2/5, respectively. We can repeat the same process when the outcome $Y = yes$.

Similarly, we can repeat the calculation to find the class conditional probability for the other three attributes: Humidity (X_2), Outlook (X_3), and Wind(X_4). This class conditional probability table is shown in Table 4.6.

Table 4.5 Class Conditional Probability of Temperature

Temperature (X_1)	$P(X_1|Y = no)$	$P(X_1|Y = yes)$
high	2/5	2/9
med	1/5	3/9
low	2/5	4/9

Table 4.6 Conditional Probability of Humidity, Outlook, and Wind

Humidity (X_2)	$P(X_1|Y = no)$	$P(X_1|Y = yes)$
high	2/5	2/9
low	1/5	4/9
med	2/5	3/9
Outlook (X_3)	**$P(X_1|Y = no)$**	**$P(X_1|Y = yes)$**
overcast	0/5	4/9
Rain	2/5	3/9
sunny	3/5	2/9
Wind (X_4)	**$P(X_1|Y = no)$**	**$P(X_1|Y = yes)$**
false	2/5	6/9
true	3/5	3/9

Table 4.7 Test Record

No.	Temperature X_1	Humidity X_2	Outlook X_3	Wind X_4	Play (Class Label) Y
Unlabeled Test	high	low	sunny	false	?

Step 3: Predicting the Outcome Using Bayes' Theorem

We are all set with preparing class conditional probability tables and now they can be used in the future prediction task. If a new, unlabeled test record (Table 4.7) has the attribute values Temperature= high, Humidity = low, Outlook = sunny, and Wind = false, what would be the class label prediction? Play = Yes or No? The outcome class can be predicted based on Bayes' theorem by calculating the posterior probability $P(Y|X)$ for both values of Y. Once $P(Y = yes|X)$ and $P(Y = no|X)$ are calculated, we can determine which outcome has higher probability and the predicted outcome is the one that has the highest probability. While calculating both class conditional probabilities using Equation 4.14, it is sufficient to just calculate $P(Y) * \prod_{i=1}^{n} P(Xi|Y)$ as $P(X)$ is going to be same for both the outcome classes.

$$P(Y = yes|X) = \frac{P(Y) * \prod_{i=1}^{n} P(Xi|Y)}{P(X)}$$

$= P(Y = yes) * \{P(Temp = high|Y = yes) * P(Humidity = low|Y = yes) *$
$P(Outlook = sunny| Y = yes) * P(Wind = false|Y = yes)\}/P(X)$
$= 9/14 * \{2/9 * 4/9 * 2/9 * 6/9\}/P(X)$
$= 0.0094/P(X)$
$P(Y = no|X) = 5/14 * \{2/5 * 4/5 * 3/5 * 2/5\}$
$= 0.0274/P(X)$

We normalize both the estimates by dividing both by (0.0094 + 0.027) to get

$$\text{Likelihood of (Play = yes)} = \frac{0.0094}{0.0274 + 0.0094} = 26\%$$

$$\text{Likelihood of (Play = no)} = \frac{0.0094}{0.0274 + 0.0094} = 74\%$$

In this case $P(Y = yes|X) < P(Y = no|X)$, hence the prediction for the unlabeled test record will be Play = no.

Bayesian modeling is relatively simple to understand once you get past the notation (for beginners) and easy to implement in practically any programing language. The computation for model building is quite simple and involves the creation of a lookup table of probabilities. Bayesian modeling is quite robust in handling missing values. If the test example set does not contain a value, let's suppose temperature is not calculated in the example set, the Bayesian model simply omits the corresponding class conditional probability for the outcomes. Having missing values in the test set would be difficult to handle in decision trees and regression algorithms, particularly when the missing attribute is used higher up in the node of the decision tree or has more weight in regression. Even though the naïve Bayes algorithm is quite robust to missing attributes, it does have a few limitations. Here are couple of the most significant limitations and methods of mitigation.

Issue 1: Incomplete Training Set

Problems arise when an attribute value in the testing record has no example in the training record. In the Golf dataset (Table 4.4), if a test example consists of the attribute value Outlook = overcast, the probability of P(Outlook = overcast| Y = no) is zero. Even if one of the attribute's class conditional probabilities is zero, by nature of the Bayesian equation, the entire posterior probability will be zero.

> P(Y = no|X) = P(Y = No) * {P(Temp = high|Y = no) * P(Humidity = low| Y = no) * P(Outlook = overcast|Y = no) * P(Wind = false|Y = no)}/P(X)
> = 5/14 * {2/5 * 1/5 * 0 * 2/5}/P(X)
> = 0

In this case P(Y = yes|X) > P(Y = no|X), and the test example will be classified as Play = yes. If there are no training records for any other attribute value, like Temperature = low for outcome *yes*, then probability of both outcomes, P(Y = no|X) and P(Y = yes|X), will also be zero and an arbitrary prediction shall be made because of the dilemma.

To mitigate this problem, we can assign small default probabilities for the missing records instead of zero. With this, the absence of an attribute value doesn't wipe out the value of P(X|Y), albeit it will reduce the probability to small number. This technique is called Laplace correction. Laplace correction adds a controlled error in all class conditional probabilities.

In the above data set, if the example set contains Outlook = overcast, then P(X|Y = no) = 0. The class conditional probability for all the three values for Outlook is 0/5, 2/5, and 3/5, Y = no. We can add controlled error by adding 1 to all numerators and 3 for all denominators, so the class conditional probabilities are 1/8, 3/8 and 4/8. The sum of all the class conditional probabilities is still 1. Generically, the Laplace correction is given by

$$\text{corrected probability P}(X_i|Y) = \frac{0+\mu p_3}{5+\mu}, \frac{2+\mu p_2}{5+\mu}, \frac{3+\mu p_2}{5+\mu}$$

(4.15)

where $p_1 + p_2 + p_3 = 1$ and μ is the correction.

Issue 2: Continuous Attributes

If an attribute has continuous numeric values instead of nominal values, the solution discussed above will not work. We can always convert the continuous values to nominal values by discretization and use the same approach as discussed. But discretization requires exercising subjective judgment on the bucketing range, leading to loss of information. Instead, we can preserve the continuous values as such and use the probability density function. We assume the probability distribution for a numerical attribute follows a normal or Gaussian distribution. If the attribute value is known to follow some other distribution, such as Poisson, the equivalent probability density function can be used. The probability density function for a normal distribution is given by

$$f(x) = \frac{1}{\sqrt{2\pi}\sigma} e^{\frac{(x-\mu)^2}{2\sigma^2}}$$

(4.16)

where μ is the mean and σ is the standard deviation of the sample.

In the updated Golf data set shown in Table 4.8, temperature and humidity are continuous attributes. In such a situation, we compute the mean and standard deviation for both class labels (Play = yes and Play = no) for temperature and humidity (Table 4.9).

If an unlabeled test record has a Humidity value of 78, we can compute the probability density using the Equation 4.16, for both outcomes. For outcome

Table 4.8 Golf Data Set with Continuous Attributes

No.	Outlook X_1	Humidity X_2	Temperature X_3	Wind X_4	Play Y
1	sunny	85	85	false	no
2	sunny	80	90	true	no
6	rain	65	70	true	no
8	sunny	72	95	false	no
14	rain	71	80	true	no
3	overcast	83	78	false	yes
4	rain	70	96	false	yes
5	rain	68	80	false	yes
7	overcast	64	65	true	yes
9	sunny	69	70	false	yes
10	rain	75	80	false	yes
11	sunny	75	70	true	yes
12	overcast	72	90	true	yes
13	overcast	81	75	false	yes

Table 4.9 Mean and Deviation for Continuous Attributes

Play Value		Humidity X_2	Temperature X_3
Y = no	Mean	74.60	84.00
	Deviation	7.89	9.62
Y = yes	Mean	73.00	78.22
	Deviation	6.16	9.88

Play = yes, if we plug in the values $x = 78$, $\mu = 73$, and $\sigma = 6.16$ to the probability density function, the equation renders the value 0.04. Similarly for outcome Play = no, we can plug in $x = 78$, $\mu = 74.6$, $\sigma = 7.89$ and compute the probability density to obtain 0.05:

P(temperature = 78|Y = yes) = 0.04
P(temperature = 78|Y = no) = 0.05

The above values are probability densities and *not* probabilities. In a continuous scale, the probability of temperature being exactly at a particular value is zero. Instead, the probability is computed for a range, such as temperatures from 77.5 to 78.5 units. Since the same range is used for computing the probability density for both the outcomes, Play = yes and Play = no, it is not necessary to compute the actual probability. Hence we can substitute the above values in the Bayesian equation 4.14 for calculating class conditional probability P(**X**|Y).

Issue 3: Attribute Independence

One of the fundamental assumptions in the naïve Bayesian model is *attribute independence*. Bayes' theorem is guaranteed only for independent attributes. In many real-life cases, this is quite a stringent condition to deal with. This is why the technique is called "naïve" Bayesian, because it assumes attributes independence. However, in practice the naïve Bayesian model works fine with slightly correlated features (Rish, 2001). We can handle this problem by pre-processing the data. Before applying the naïve Bayesian algorithm, it makes sense to remove strongly correlated attributes. In the case of all numeric attributes, this can be achieved by computing a weighted correlation matrix. An advanced application of Bayes' theorem, called a Bayesian belief network, is designed to handle data sets with attribute dependencies.

The independence of two categorical (nominal) attributes can be tested by the *chi-square* (χ^2) test for independence. The chi-square test can be calculated by creating a contingency table of observed frequency like the one shown in Table 4.10A. A contingency table is a simple cross tab of two attributes under consideration.

Table 4.10 Contingency Tables with **Observed Frequency** (A) and **Expected Frequency** (B)

Outlook	Wind			Outlook	Wind		
	False	True	Total		False	True	Total
overcast	2	2	4	overcast	2.29	1.71	4
rain	3	2	5	rain	2.86	2.14	5
sunny	3	2	5	sunny	2.86	2.14	5
Total	8	6	14	Total	8	6	14

A contingency table of expected frequency (Table 4.10b) can also be created based on the following equation:

$$E_{r,c} = \frac{(\text{row total} * \text{column total})}{(\text{table total})}$$

(4.17)

The chi-square statistic (χ^2) calculates the sum of the difference between these two tables. χ^2 is calculated by Equation 4.18. In this equation, O is observed frequency and E is expected frequency:

$$\chi^2 = \sum (O - E)^2 / E$$

(4.18)

If the chi-square statistic (χ^2) is less than the critical value calculated from the chi-square distribution for a given confidence level, then we can assume the two variables under consideration are independent, for practical purposes. This entire test can be performed in statistical tools or in Microsoft Excel.

4.4.2 How to Implement

The naïve Bayesian model is one of the few data mining techniques that can be easily implemented in almost any programing language. Since the conditional probability tables can be prepared in the model building phase, the execution of the model in runtime is very quick. Data mining tools have dedicated naïve Bayes classifier functions. In RapidMiner, *Naïve Bayes* is operator available under *Modeling > Classification*. The process of building a model and applying it to new data is similar to decision trees and other classifiers. The *naïve Bayesian* algorithm can accept both numeric and nominal attributes.

Step 1: Data Preparation

The Golf data set shown in Table 4.8 is available in RapidMiner under Sample > Data in the repository section. The Golf data set can just be clicked and dropped in the process area to source all 14 records of the data set. Within the same repository folder, there is also a Golf-Test data set with a set of 14 records used for testing. Both data sets need to be added in Main process area. Since the Bayes operator accepts numeric and nominal data types, no other data transformation process is necessary. Sampling is a common method to extract the training data set from a large data set. *It is especially important for naïve Bayesian modeling for the training data set to be representative and proportional to the underlining data set.* Hence, random sampling is recommended instead of class-stratified sampling techniques.

Step 2: Modeling Operator and Parameters

The *Naïve Bayes* operator (Modeling > Classification) can now be connected to the Golf training data set. The *Naïve Bayesian* operator has only one parameter option to set: whether or not to include Laplace correction. For smaller data sets, Laplace correction is strongly encouraged, as a data set may not have all combinations of attribute values for every class value. In fact, by default, Laplace correction is checked. Outputs of the *Naïve Bayes* operator are the model and original training data set. The model output should be connected to *Apply Model* (Model Application folder) to execute the model on the test data set. The output of the *Apply Model* operator is the labeled test data set and the model.

Step 3: Evaluation

The labeled data set that we have after using the *Apply Model* operator is then connected to the *Performance – Classification* operator to evaluate the performance of the classification model. The *Performance – Classification* operator can be found under Evaluation > Performance Measurement > Performance. Figure 4.35 shows the complete naïve Bayesian predictive classification process. The output ports can be connected to result ports and the process can be saved and executed. The RapidMiner process is also available for download from the companion website www.LearnPredictiveAnalytics.com.

Step 4: Execution and Interpretation

The process shown in Figure 4.35 will has three result outputs: a model description, performance vector, and labeled data set. The labeled data set contains the test data set with the predicted class as an added column. The labeled data set also contains the confidence for each label class, which indicates the likelihood of each label class value.

The model description result contains more information on class conditional probabilities of all the input attributes, derived from the training data set. The Charts tab in model description contains probability density functions for the attributes, as shown in Figure 4.36. In the case of continuous attributes, we can discern the decision boundaries across the different class labels for the Humidity attribute. We can see when Humidity exceeds 82, the likelihood of Play =

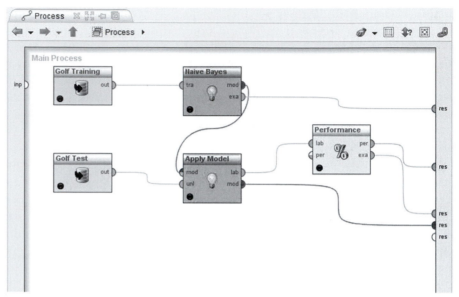

FIGURE 4.35

Data mining process for Naive Bayes algorithm.

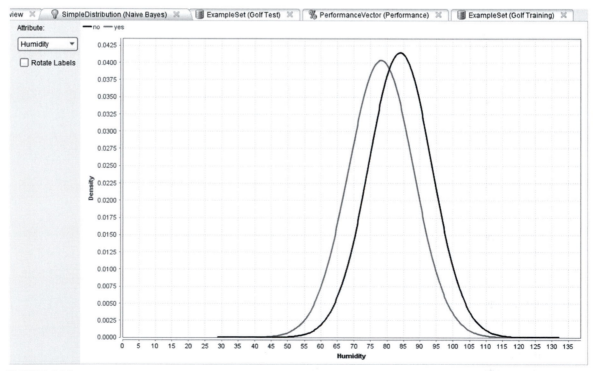

FIGURE 4.36

Naive Bayes model output: Probability density function for Humidity attribute.

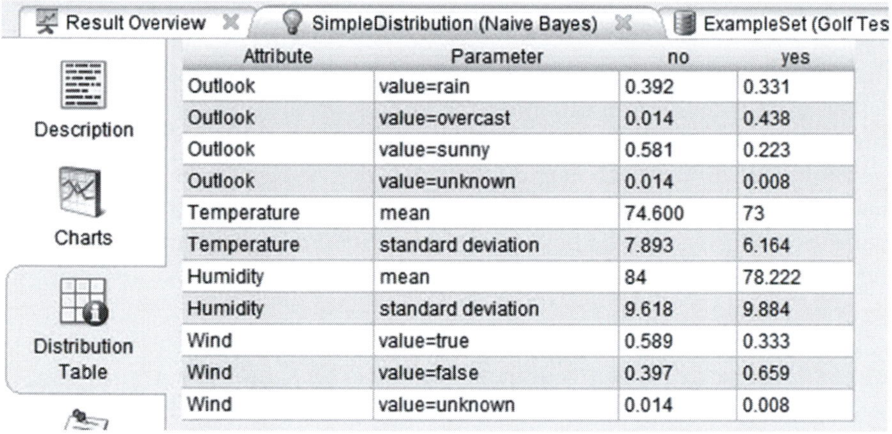

Attribute	Parameter	no	yes
Outlook	value=rain	0.392	0.331
Outlook	value=overcast	0.014	0.438
Outlook	value=sunny	0.581	0.223
Outlook	value=unknown	0.014	0.008
Temperature	mean	74.600	73
Temperature	standard deviation	7.893	6.164
Humidity	mean	84	78.222
Humidity	standard deviation	9.618	9.884
Wind	value=true	0.589	0.333
Wind	value=false	0.397	0.659
Wind	value=unknown	0.014	0.008

Result Overview — SimpleDistribution (Naive Bayes) — ExampleSet (Golf Tes

Description — Charts — Distribution Table

FIGURE 4.37
Naive Bayes distribution table output.

no increase. The distribution table is shown in Figure 4.37 with all attribute values and corresponding probability measures. The Distribution Table tab in the model description provides the familiar class conditional probability table similar to Table 4.5 and Table 4.6.

The performance vector output is similar to previously discussed classification algorithms. The performance vector provides the confusion matrix describing accuracy, precision, and recall metrics for the predicted test data set.

4.4.3 Conclusion

The Bayesian algorithm provides a probabilistic framework for a classification problem. It has a simple and sound foundation for modeling the data and is quite robust to outliers and missing values. This algorithm is deployed widely in text mining and document classification where the application has a large set of attributes and attribute values to compute. In our experience, the naïve Bayesian classifier is often a great place to start and is very workable as an initial model in the proof of concept (POC) stage for an analytics project. It also serves as a good benchmark for comparison to other models. Implementation of the Bayesian model in production systems is quite straightforward and the use of data mining tools is optional. One major limitation of the model is the assumption of independent attributes, which can be mitigated by advanced modeling or decreasing the dependence across the attributes through preprocessing. The uniqueness of the technique is that it leverages new information as it arrives and tries to make a best prediction considering new evidence. In this way, it is quite similar to how our mind works. Talking about the mind, the next algorithm mimics the biological process of human neurons!

4.5 ARTIFICIAL NEURAL NETWORKS

The objective of a predictive analytics algorithm is to model the relationship between input and output variables. The neural network technique approaches this problem by developing a mathematical explanation that closely resembles the biological process of a *neuron*. Although the developers of this technique have used many biological terms to explain the inner workings of neural network modeling process, it has a simple mathematical foundation. Consider the simple linear mathematical model:

$$Y = 1 + 2X_1 + 3X_2 + 4X_3$$

Where Y is the calculated output and $X_1, X_2,$ and X_3 are input attributes. 1 is the intercept and 2, 3, and 4 are the scaling factors or coefficients for the input attributes $X_1, X_2,$ and X_3, respectively. We can represent this simple linear model in a topological form as shown in Figure 4.38.

In this topology, X_1 is the input value and passes through a node, denoted by a circle. Then the value of X_1 is multiplied by its weight, which is 2, as noted in the connector. Similarly, all other attributes (X_2 and X_3) go through a node and scaling transformation. The last node is a special case with no input variable; it just has the intercept. Finally, values from all the connectors are summarized in an output node that yields predicted output Y. The topology shown in Figure 4.38 represents the simple linear model $Y = 1 + 2X_1 + 3X_2 + 4X_3$. The topology also represents a very simple *artificial neural network* (ANN). The neural networks model more complex nonlinear relationships of data and *learn* though adaptive adjustments of weights between the nodes. The ANN is a computational and mathematical model inspired by the biological nervous system. Hence, some of the terms used in an ANN are borrowed from biological counterparts.

In neural network terminology, nodes are called *units*. The first layer of nodes closest to the input is called the input layer or input nodes. The last layer of nodes is called the output layer or output nodes. The output layer performs

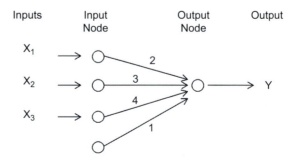

FIGURE 4.38
Model topology.

an *aggregation function* and also can have a *transfer function*. The transfer function scales the output into the desired range. Together with the aggregation and transfer function, the output layer performs an *activation function*. This simple two-layer topology, as shown in Figure 4.38, with one input and one output layer is called a *perceptron*, the most simplistic form of artificial neural network. A perceptron is a feed-forward neural network where the input moves in one direction and there are no loops in the topology.

BIOLOGICAL NEURONS

The functional unit of cells in the nervous system is the neuron. An artificial neural network of nodes and connectors has a close resemblance to a biological network of neurons and connections, with each node acting as a single neuron. There are close to 100 billion neurons in the human brain and they are all interconnected to form this very important organ of the human body (see Figure 4.39). Neuron cells are found in most animals; they transmit information through electrical and chemical signals. The interconnection between one neuron with another neuron happens through a *synapse*. A neuron consists of a cell body, a thin structure that forms from the cell body called dendrite, and a long linear cellular extension called an axon. Neurons are composed of a number of dendrites and one axon. The axon of one neuron is connected to the dendrite of another neuron through a synapse, and electrochemical signals are sent from one neuron to another. There are about 100 trillion synapses in a human brain.

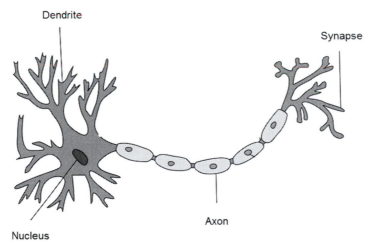

FIGURE 4.39

Anatomy of a neuron. (Modified from original "Neuron Hand-tuned." Original uploader: Quasar Jarosz at en.wikipedia.org. Transferred from en.wikipedia.org to Commons by user Faigl.ladislav using CommonsHelper. Licensed under Creative Commons Attribution-Share Alike 3.0 via Wikimedia Commons.[4])

[4]http://commons.wikimedia.org/wiki/File:Neuron_Hand-tuned.svg#mediaviewer/File:Neuron_Hand-tuned.svg

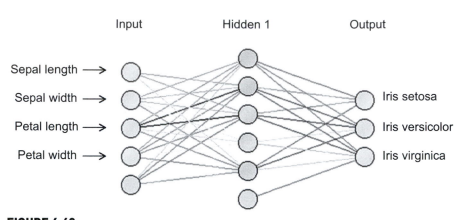

FIGURE 4.40
Topology of a neural network model.

A artificial neural network is typically used for modeling *nonlinear*, complicated relationships between input and output variables. This is made possible by the existence of more than one layer in the topology, apart from the input and output layers, called *hidden layers*. A hidden layer contains a layer of nodes that connects input from previous layers and applies an activation function. The output is now calculated by a more complex combination of input values, as shown in Figure 4.40.

Consider the example of the Iris data set. It has four input variables, sepal length, sepal width, petal length, and petal width, with three classes (*Iris setosa, Iris versicolor, Iris virginica*) in the label. An ANN based on the Iris data set yields a three-layer structure (the number of layers can be specified by the user) with three output nodes, one for each class variable. For a categorical label problem, as in predicting species for Iris, the ANN provides output for each class type. A winner class type is picked based on the maximum value of the output class label. The topology in Figure 4.40 is a feed-forward artificial neural network with one hidden layer. Of course, depending on the problem to be solved, we can use a topology with multiple hidden layers and even with looping where the output of one layer is used as input for preceding layers. Specifying what topology to use is a challenge in neural network modeling and it takes time to build a good approximating model.

The *activation function* used in the output node consists of a combination of an aggregation function, usually summarization, and a *transfer function*. Transfer functions can be anything from sigmoid to normal bell curve, logistic, hyperbolic, or linear functions. The purpose of sigmoid and bell curves is to provide a linear transformation for a particular range of values and a nonlinear transformation for the rest of the values. Because of the transformation function and the presence of multiple hidden layers, we can model or closely approximate almost any mathematical continuous relationship between input variables and output variables. Hence, a multilayer artificial neural network is called a *universal approximator*. However, the presence of multiple user options such as topology, transfer function, and number of hidden layers makes the search for an optimal solution quite time consuming.

OPTICAL CHARACTER RECOGNITION

Character recognition is the process of interpreting handwritten text and converting it into digitized characters. It has a multitude of practical applications in our everyday life, including converting handwritten notes to standardized text, automated sorting of postal mail by looking at the zip codes (postal area codes), automated data entry from forms and applications, digitizing classic books, license plate recognition, etc. How does it work?

In its most basic form, character recognition has two steps: digitization and development of the learning model. In the digitization step, every individual character is converted to a digital matrix, say 12x12 pixels, where each cell takes a value of either 0 or 1 based on the handwritten character overlay. The input vector now has 144 binary attributes (12x12) indicating the information of the handwritten characters. Let's assume the objective is to decipher a numeric handwritten zip code (Matan &

Kiang, 1990). We can develop an artificial neural network model which accepts 144 inputs and has 10 outputs, each indicating a digit from 0 to 9. The model has to be learned in such a way that when the input matrix is fed, one of the outputs shows the highest signal indicating the prediction for the character. Since a neural network is adaptable and relatively easy to deploy, it is increasingly getting used in character recognition, image processing, and related applications (Li, 1994). This specific use case is also an example where the explanatory aspect of the model is less important—maybe because no one knows exactly how the human brain does it. So there is less expectation that the model should be understandable as long as it works with acceptable performance. This also means ANN models are not easy to explain and in many situations this alone will remove them from consideration of the data mining techniques to use. We wish this wasn't the case!

4.5.1 How It Works

An artificial neural network learns the relationship between input attributes and the output class label through a technique called *back propagation*. For a given network topology and activation function, the key training task is to find the weights of the links. The process is rather intuitive and closely resembles the signal transmission in biological neurons. The model uses every training record to estimate the error of the predicted output as compared against the actual output. Then the model uses the error to adjust the weights to minimize the error for the next training record and this step is repeated until the error falls within the acceptable range (Laine, 2003). The rate of correction from one step to other should be managed properly, so that the model does not over-correct. Following are the key steps in developing an artificial neural network from a training data set.

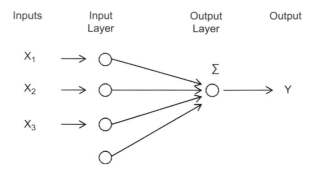

FIGURE 4.41

Two-layer topology with summary aggregation.

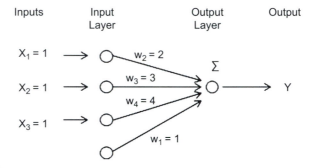

FIGURE 4.42

Initiation and first training record.

Step 1: Determine the Topology and Activation Function

For this example, let's assume a data set with three numeric input attributes (X_1, X_2, X_3) and one numeric output (Y). To model the relationship, we are using a topology with two layers and a simple aggregation activation function, as shown in Figure 4.41. There is no transfer function used in this example.

Step 2: Initiation

Let's assume the initial weights for the four links are 1, 2, 3, and 4. Let's take an example model and a test record with all the inputs as 1 and the known output as 15. So, $X_1 = X_2 = X_3 = 1$ and output Y = 15. Figure 4.42 shows initiation of first training record.

Step 3: Calculating Error

We can calculate the predicted output of the record from Figure 4.42. This is simple feed forward process of passing through the input attributes and calculating the predicted output. The predicted output $\overline{Y}$ according to current

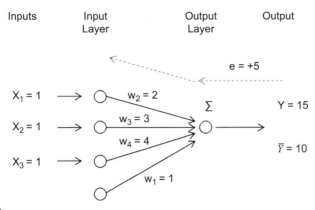

FIGURE 4.43
Neural network error back propagation.

model is $1 + 1 * 2 + 1 * 3 + 1 * 4 = 10$. The difference between the actual output from training record and predicted output is the error:

$$e = Y - \overline{Y}$$

The error for this example training record is $15 - 10 = 5$.

Step 4: Weight Adjustment

Weight adjustment is the most important part of learning in an artificial neural network. The error calculated in the previous step is passed back from the output node to all other nodes in the reverse direction. The weights of the links are adjusted from their old value by a *fraction* of the error. The fraction λ applied to the error is called learning rate. λ takes values from 0 to 1. A value close to 1 results in a drastic change to the model for each training record and a value close to 0 results in smaller changes and less correction. New weight of the link (w) is the sum of old weight (w') and the product of learning rate and proportion of the error ($\lambda * e$).

$$w = w' + \lambda * e$$

The choice of λ can be tricky in the implementation of an ANN. Some model processes start with λ close to 1 and reduce the value of λ while training each cycle. By this approach any outlier records later in the training cycle will not degrade the relevance of the model. Figure 4.43 shows the error propagation in the topology.

The current weight of the first link is $w_2 = 2$. Let's assume the learning rate is 0.5. The new weight will be $w_2 = 2 + 0.5 * 5/3 = 2.83$. The error is divided by 3 because the error is back propagated to three links from the output node. Similarly, the weight will be adjusted for all the links. In the next cycle, a new error

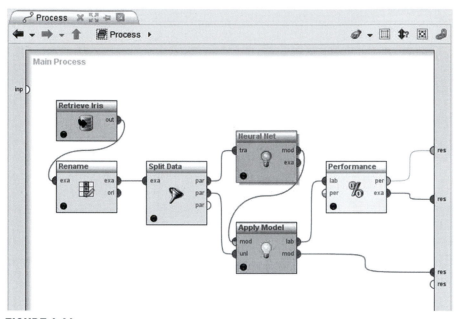

FIGURE 4.44
Data mining process for neural network.

will be computed for the next training record. This cycle goes on until all the training records are processed by iterative runs. The same training example can be repeated until the error rate is less than a threshold. We have reviewed a very simple case of an artificial neural network. In reality, there will be multiple hidden layers and multiple output links—one for each nominal class value. Because of the numeric calculation, an ANN model works well with numeric inputs and outputs. If the input contains a nominal attribute, a preprocessing step should be included to convert the nominal attribute into multiple numeric attributes—one for each attribute value, this process is similar to dummy variable introduction, which will be further explored in chapter 10 Time Series Forecasting. This specific preprocessing increases the number of input links for neural network in the case of nominal attributes and thus increases the necessary computing resources. Hence, an ANN is more suitable for attributes with a numeric data type.

4.5.2 How to Implement

An artificial neural network is one of the most popular algorithms available for data mining tools. In RapidMiner, the ANN model operators are available in the Classification folder. There are three types of models available: A simple perceptron with one input and one output layer, a flexible ANN model called *Neural Net* with all the parameters for complete model building, and advanced *AutoMLP* algorithm. AutoMLP (for Automatic Multilayer Perceptron) combines concepts from genetic and stochastic algorithms. It leverages an ensemble group of ANNs with different parameters like hidden layers and learning rates. It also optimizes by replacing the worst performing models with better ones and maintains an optimal solution. For the rest of the discussion, we will focus on the Neural Net model.

Step 1: Data Preparation

The Iris data set is used to demonstrate the implementation of an ANN. All four attributes for the Iris data set are numeric and the output has three classes. Hence the ANN model will have four input nodes and three output nodes. The ANN model will not work with categorical or nominal data types. If the input has nominal attributes, it should be converted to numeric using data transformation, see Chapter 13 Getting Started with RapidMiner. Nominal to binominal conversion operator can be used to convert each value of a nominal attribute to separate binominal attributes. In this example, we use the *Rename* operator to name the four attributes of the Iris data set and the *Split Data* operator to split 150 Iris records equally into the training and test data.

Step 2: Modeling Operator and Parameters

The training data set is connected to the *Neural Net* operator (Modeling > Classification and Regression > Neural Net Training). The *Neural Net* operator accepts real values and later converts them into the normalized range –1 to 1 and outputs a standard ANN model. The following parameters are available in ANN for users to change and customize in the model.

- **Hidden layer:** Determines the number of layers, size of each hidden layer, and names of each layer for easy identification in the output screen. The default size of the node is –1, which is actually calculated by (*number of attributes + number of classes*)/2 + 1. The default can be overwritten by specifying an integer of nodes, not including a no-input threshold node per layer.
- **Training cycles:** This number of times a training cycle is repeated; it defaults to 500. In a neural network, every time a training record is considered, the previous weights are quite different and hence it is necessary to repeat the cycle many times.
- **Learning rate:** The value of λ determines how sensitive the change in weight has to be in considering error for the previous cycle. It takes a value from 0 to 1. A value closer to 0 means the new weight would be more based on the previous weight and less on error correction. A value closer to 1 would be mainly based on error correction.
- **Momentum:** This value is used to prevent local maxima and seeks to obtain globally optimized results by adding a fraction of the previous weight to the current weight.

- **Decay:** During the neural network training, ideally the error would be minimal in the later portion of the record sequence. We don't want a large error due to any outlier records in the last few records, thereby impacting the performance of the model. Decay reduces the value of the learning rate and brings it closer to zero for the last training record.
- **Shuffle:** If the training record is sorted, we can randomize the sequence by shuffling it. The sequence has an impact in the model, particularly if the group of records exhibiting nonlinear characteristics are all clustered together in the last segment of the training set.
- **Normalize:** Nodes using a sigmoid transfer function expect input in the range of –1 to 1. Any real value of the input should be normalized in an ANN model.
- **Error epsilon:** The objective of the ANN model should be to minimize the error but not make it zero, at which the model memorizes the training set and degrades the performance. We can stop the model building process when the error is less than a threshold called the error epsilon.

The output of the *Neural Net* operator can be connected to the *Apply Model* operator, which is standard in every predictive analytics workflow. The *Apply Model* operator also gets an input data set from the *Split data* operator for the test data set. The output of the *Apply Model* operator is the labeled test data set and the ANN model.

Step 3: Evaluation
The labeled data set output after using the *Apply Model* operator is then connected to the *Performance – Classification* operator (Evaluation > Performance Measurement > Performance), to evaluate the performance of the classification model. Figure 4.44 shows the complete artificial neural network predictive classification process. The output connections can be connected to the result ports and the process can be saved and executed.

Step 4: Execution and Interpretation
The output results window for the model provides a visual on the topology of the ANN model. Figure 4.45 shows the model output topology. Upon a click on a node, we can get the weights of the incoming links to the node. The color of the link indicates relative weights. The description tab of the model window provides the actual values of the link weights.

The output performance vector can be examined to see the accuracy of the artificial neural network model built for the Iris data set. Figure 4.46 shows the performance vector for the model. A three-layer ANN model with the default parameter options and equal splitting of input data and training set yields 93% accuracy. Out of 75 examples, only 5 were misclassified.

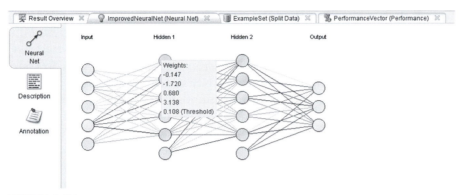

FIGURE 4.45
Neural network model output with three hidden layers and four attributes.

	true Iris-setosa	true Iris-versicolor	true Iris-virginica	class precision
pred. Iris-setosa	20	0	0	100.00%
pred. Iris-versicolor	0	25	3	89.29%
pred. Iris-virginica	0	2	25	92.59%
class recall	100.00%	92.59%	89.29%	

accuracy: 93.33%

FIGURE 4.46
Performance vector for artificial neural network.

4.5.3 Conclusion

Neural network models require strict preprocessing. If the test example has missing attribute values, the model cannot function, similar to regression or decision trees. The missing values can be replaced with average values or any default values to minimize the error. The relationship between input and output cannot be explained clearly by an artificial neutral network. Since there are hidden layers, it is quite complex to understand the model. In many data mining applications explanation of the model is as important as prediction itself. Decision trees, induction rules, and regression do a far better job at explaining the model.

Building a good ANN model with optimized parameters takes time. It depends on the number of training records and iterations. There are no consistent guidelines on the number of hidden layers and nodes within each hidden layer. Hence, we would need to try out many parameters to optimize the selection of parameters. However, once a model is built, it is straightforward to implement and an example record gets classified quite fast.

An ANN does not handle categorical input data. If the data has nominal values, it needs to be converted to binary or real values. This means one input attribute explodes to multiple input attributes and exponentially increases nodes, links, and complexity. Also, converting nonordinal categorical data, like zip code, to numeric provides an opportunity for ANN to make numeric calculations, which doesn't quite make sense. Having redundant correlated attributes is not going to be a problem in an ANN model. If the example set is large, having outliers will not degrade the performance of the model. However, outliers will impact the normalization of the signal, which most ANN models require for input attributes. Because model building is by incremental error correction, ANN can yield local optima as the final model. This risk can be mitigated by managing a momentum parameter to weigh the update.

Although model explanation is quite difficult with an ANN, the rapid classification of test examples makes an ANN quite useful for anomaly detection and classification problems. An ANN is commonly used in fraud detection, a scoring situation where the relationship between inputs and output is nonlinear. If there is a need for something that handles a highly nonlinear landscape along with fast real-time performance, then the artificial neural network is a good option.

4.6 SUPPORT VECTOR MACHINES

Support vector algorithms are a relatively recent concept, like so many other machine learning techniques. Cortes and Vapnik (Cortes, 1995) provided one of the first formal introductions to the concept while investigating algorithms for optical character recognition at the AT&T Bell Labs.

The term "support vector machine" is a confusing name for a predictive analytics *algorithm*. The fact is this term is very much a misnomer: there is really no specialized hardware. But it is a powerful algorithm that has been very successful in applications ranging from pattern recognition to text mining. A support vector machine (SVM) emphasizes the interdisciplinary nature of today's advanced analytics by drawing equally from three major areas: computer science, statistics, and mathematical optimization theory.

We start with essential terminology and definitions that are unique to SVMs. We will then conceptually explain the functioning of the algorithm for a simple "linear" data set and then a slightly more complex nonlinear dataset. We will provide a brief mathematical explanation of the workings of the algorithm before illustrating how to implement SVMs in practice with a case study. Finally we will highlight how SVMs perform better in some situations compared to other classification techniques and close out this section with a list of the advantages and disadvantages of SVMs in general.

4.6.1 Concept and Terminology

At a very basic level, a *support vector machine* is a classification method. It works on the principle of fitting a boundary to a region of points that are all alike (that is, belong to one class). Once a boundary is fitted (on the training sample), for any new points (test sample) that need to be classified, we must simply check whether they lie inside the boundary or not. The advantage of an SVM is that once a boundary is established, most of the training data is redundant. All it needs is a *core set of points* that can help identify and fix the boundary. These data points are called *support vectors* because they "support" the boundary. Why are they called vectors? Clearly because each data point (or observation) is a vector: that is, it is a row of data that contains values for a number of different attributes.

This boundary is traditionally called a *hyperplane*. In a simple example of two dimensions (two attributes), this boundary can be a straight line or a curve (as shown in Figure 4.47). In three dimensions it can be a plane or an irregular complex surface. Higher dimensions are obviously impossible to visualize and a hyperplane is thus a generic name for a boundary in more than three dimensions.

As seen in Figure 4.47, a number of such hyperplanes can be found for the same data set. Which one is the "correct" one? Clearly a boundary that separates the classes with minimal misclassification is the best one. In the above sequence of images shown in Figure 4.47, the algorithm applied to the third image appears to have zero misclassification and may be the best one. Additionally, a boundary line that ensures that the average geometric distance between the two regions (or classes) is maximized is even better. This (n-dimensional) distance is called a *margin*. An SVM algorithm therefore essentially runs an optimization scheme to maximize this margin. The points with the "X" through them are the support vectors.

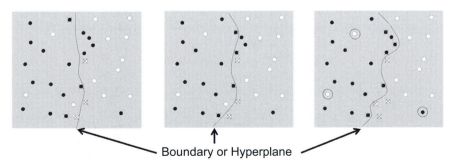

Boundary or Hyperplane

FIGURE 4.47

Three different hyperplanes for the same set of training data. There are two classes in this data set, which are shown as filled and open circles.

But it is not always possible to ensure that data can be cleanly separated. It may be rare to find that the data are *linearly separable*. When this happens, there may be many points within the margin. In this case the best hyperplane is the one that has a *minimum* number of such points within the margin. To ensure this, a *penalty* is charged for every "contaminant" inside the margin and the hyperplane that has a minimum aggregate penalty cost is chosen. In Figure 4.48, ξ represents the penalty that is applied for each error and the sum of all such errors is minimized to get the best separation.

What would happen if the data are not linearly separable (even without such contaminating errors)? For example, in Figure 4.49a, the data points belong to two main classes: an inner ring and an outer ring. We know that these two classes are not "linearly separable." In other words we cannot draw a straight line to split the two classes. However, it is intuitively clear that an elliptical or circular "hyperplane" can easily separate the two classes. In fact, if we were to run a simple "linear" SVM on this data, we would get a classification accuracy of around 46%.

How can we classify such complex feature spaces? In the above example, a simple trick would be to transform the two variables x and y into a new feature space involving x (or y) and a new variable z defined as $z = \sqrt{(x^2 + y^2)}$. The representation of z is nothing more than the equation for a circle. When the data is transformed in this way, the resulting feature space involving x and z will appear as shown in Figure 4.49b. The two clusters of data correspond to the two radii of the rings: the inner one with an average radius of around 5.5 and the outer cluster with an average radius of around 8.0. This problem is explored in greater detail in a case study later on in this chapter.

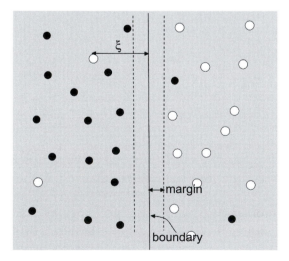

FIGURE 4.48
Key concepts in SVM construction: boundary, margin, and penalty, ξ.

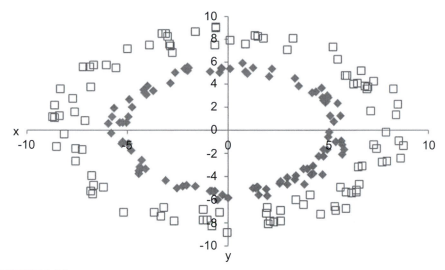

FIGURE 4.49a
Linearly nonseparable classes.

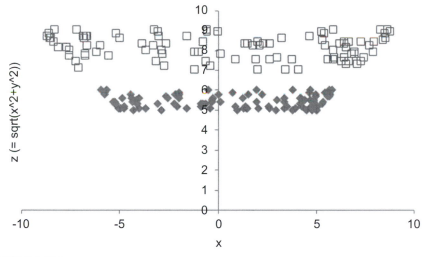

FIGURE 4.49b
Transformation to linearly separable.

Clearly this new problem in the x and z dimensions is now linearly separable and we can apply a standard SVM to do the classification. When we run a linear SVM on this transformed data, we get a classification accuracy of 100%. After classifying the transformed feature space, we can invert the transformation to get back our original feature space.

Kernel functions offer the user the option of transforming nonlinear spaces into linear ones. Most packages that include SVM will have several nonlinear kernels ranging from a simple polynomial basis functions to sigmoid functions. The user does not have to do the transformation beforehand, but simply has to select the appropriate kernel function; the software will take care of transforming the data, classifying it, and retransforming the results back into the original space.

Unfortunately with a large number of attributes in a data set it is difficult to know which kernel would work best. The most commonly used ones are polynomial and radial basis functions. From a practical standpoint, it is a good idea to start with a quadratic polynomial and work your way up into some of the more exotic kernel functions until we reach a desired accuracy level. This flexibility of support vector machines does come at the price of cost of computation.

Now that we have an intuitive understanding of how SVMs work, we can examine the working of the algorithm with a more formal mathematical explanation.

4.6.2 How it Works

Given a training data set, how do we go about determining the boundary and the hyperplane? Let us use the case of a simple linearly separable dataset consisting of two attributes, x_1 and x_2. We know that ultimately by using proper kernels any complex feature space can be mapped into a linear space, so this formulation will apply to any general data set. Furthermore, extending the algorithm to more than two attributes is conceptually straightforward.

There are three essential tasks involved here: the first step is to find the boundary of each class. Then the best hyperplane, **H**, is the one that maximizes the margin or the distance to each of the class boundaries (see Figure 4.48). Both of these steps use the training data. The final step is to determine on which side of this hyperplane a given test example lies in order to classify it.

Step 1: Finding the boundary. When we connect every point in one class of a data set to every other in that class, the outline that emerges defines the boundary of this class. This boundary is also known as the *convex hull*, as shown in Figure 4.50.

Each class will have its own convex hull and because the classes are (assumed to be) linearly separable, these hulls do not intersect each other.

Step 2: There are infinitely many available hyperplanes, two of which are shown in Figure 4.51. How do we know which hyperplane maximizes the margin? Intuitively we know that H_0 has a larger margin than H_1, but how can this be determined mathematically?

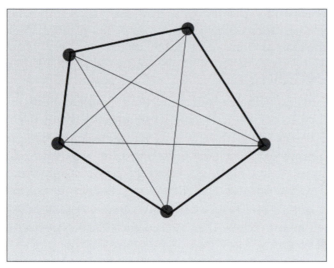

FIGURE 4.50
A convex hull for one class of data.

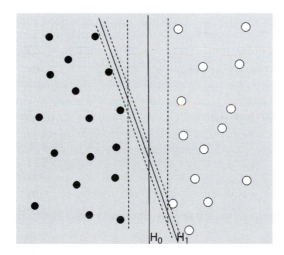

FIGURE 4.51
Both hyperplanes shown can separate data. It is intuitively clear that H_0 is better.

First of all, any hyperplane can be expressed in terms of the two attributes, x_1 and x_2, as follows:

$$H = b + w \cdot x = 0 \qquad (4.19)$$

where x is (x_1, x_2), the weight w is (w_1, w_2), and b_0 is an intercept-like term usually called the "bias." Note that this is similar to the standard form of the equation of a line. An optimal hyperplane, $\mathbf{H_0}$, is uniquely defined by $(b_0 + \mathbf{w_0} \bullet \mathbf{x} = 0)$. Once we define the hyperplane in this fashion, it can be shown that the margin is given by (Cortes, 1995)

$$\text{Margin} = 2/(\sqrt{w_0} \cdot w_0) \tag{4.20}$$

Maximizing this quantity requires quadratic programming, which is a well-established process in mathematical optimization theory (Fletcher, 1987). Furthermore, the $\mathbf{w_0}$ can be conveniently expressed in terms of only a few of the training examples, known as support vectors, as follows:

$$\left| \mathbf{w_0} = \sum y_{ii} \mathbf{x_i} \right| \tag{4.21}$$

where the y_i are the class labels (+1 or –1 for a binary classification), and the $\mathbf{x_i}$ are called the support vectors. The i's are coefficients that are nonzero only for these support vectors.

Step 3: Once we have defined the boundary and the hyperplane, any new test example can be classified by computing on which side of the hyperplane the example lies. This is easily found by substituting the test example, $\mathbf{x}$, into the equation for the hyperplane. If it computes to +1, then it belongs to the positive class and if it computes to –1 it belongs to the negative class. The interested reader is referred to Smola (2004) or Cortes (1995) for a full mathematical description of the formulation. Hsu (2003) provides a more practical demonstration of programming an SVM.

4.6.3 How to Implement

We will now show how RapidMiner determines the classes for two simple cases. *(Note: We have deliberately chosen a pair of simplistic datasets to illustrate how SVMs can be implemented. A more sophisticated case study will be used to demonstrate how to use SVMs for text mining in Chapter 9.)*

Example 1: Applying an SVM to a Simple Linearly Separable Example

The default SVM implementation in RapidMiner is based on the so-called "dot product" formulation shown in equations above. In this first example we will build an SVM using a two-dimensional data set that consists of two classes: A and B (Figure 4.52). A RapidMiner process reads in the training data set, applies the default SVM model, and then classifies new points based on the model trained.

The dataset consists of 17 rows of data for three attributes: x_1, x_2 and **class**. The attributes x_1 and x_2 are numeric and **class** is a binomial variable consisting of the two classes A and B. Table 4.11 shows the full data set and Figure 4.52

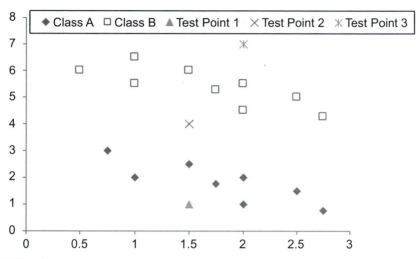

FIGURE 4.52
Two-class training data: class A (diamond) and class B (square). Points 1 to 3 are used to test the capability of the SVM.

Table 4.11 A Simple Data Set to demonstrate SVM

x_1	x_2	class
1.5	2.5	A
2	2	A
1	2	A
0.75	3	A
2	1	A
1.75	1.75	A
2.75	0.75	A
2.5	1.5	A
0.5	6	B
1.5	6	B
2	5.5	B
1	5.5	B
1	6.5	B
2	4.5	B
1.75	5.25	B
2.75	4.25	B
2.5	5	B
1.5	1	Test Point 1
1.5	4	Test Point 2
2	7	Test Point 3

shows the plot of the dataset. We will be using the model to classify the three test examples: $(1.5, 1), (1.5, 4)$, and $(2, 7)$.

Step 1: Data preparation

- Read simpleSVMdemo.csv into RapidMiner by either using the *Read csv* operator or import the data into your repository using Import csv file. The data set can be downloaded from the companion website www. LearnPredictiveAnalytics.com.
- Add a *Set Role* operator to indicate that *class* is a label attribute and connect it to the data retriever. See Figure 4.53a.

Step 2: Modeling operator and parameters

- In the Operators tab, type in **SVM**, drag and drop the operator into the main window, and connect it to Set Role. Leave the parameters of this operator in their default settings.
- Connect the "mod" output port of **SVM** to an *Apply Model* operator
- Insert a *Generate Data by User Specification* operator and click on the Edit List button of the attribute values parameter. When the dialog box opens up, click on Add Entry twice to create two test attribute names: x_1 and x_2. Set $x_1 = 2$ and $x_2 = 7$ under "attribute value." Note that you will need to change the attribute values for each new test point you want to classify.
- When this simple process is run, RapidMiner builds an SVM on the training data and applies the model to classify the test example, which was manually input using the Generate Data by User Specification operator.

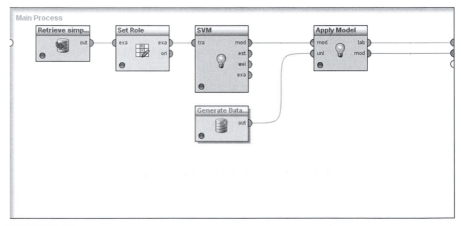

FIGURE 4.53a
A simple SVM setup for training and testing.

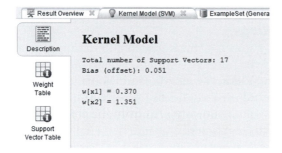

FIGURE 4.53b
The accompanying SVM model.

Row No.	prediction(c...	confidence(A)	confidence(...	x1	x2
1	B	0.074	0.926	2	7

ExampleSet (1 example, 3 special attributes, 2 regular attributes)   Filter (1 / 1 examples): all

FIGURE 4.54
Applying the simple SVM to classify test point 1 from Figure 4.52.

Step 3: Process execution and interpretation

For more practical applications, we may not be very interested in the Kernel Model output; we show it here (Figure 4.53b) to observe what the hyperplane for this simplistic example looks like. Note that this is essentially the same form as Equation 4.19 with bias $b_0 = 0.051$, $w_1 = 0.370$, and $w_2 = 1.351$.

- The more interesting result in this case is the output from the "lab" port of the Apply Model, which is the result of applying the SVM model on the test point $(2, 7)$.
- As you can see in Figure 4.54, the model has correctly classified this test point as belonging to class B (see the "prediction(class)" column). Furthermore, we are told that the confidence that this point belongs in class B is 92.6%. Looking at the chart, we see indeed that there is very little ambiguity about the classification of test point $(2, 7)$.
- If you change the test example input to the point $(1.5, 1)$, we see that this point would be classified under class A, with 88% confidence.
- However the same cannot be said of test point $(1.5, 4)$; you can run the process and test for yourself!

In actual practice the labeled test data with prediction confidences are the most useful results from an SVM application.

Example 2: Applying SVM for a Linearly Nonseparable Example (Two Rings)

The first example showed a linearly separable training data set. Suppose we want to now apply the same SVM (dot) kernel to the two ring problem we saw earlier in this chapter: what would the results look like? We know from looking at the data set that this is a nonlinear problem and the dot kernel should not work very well. We will confirm this intuitive understanding and demonstrate how it can be easily fixed in the steps described below.

Step 1: Data preparation

- Start a new process and read in the data set *nonlinearSVMdemodata. csv* using the same procedure as before. This dataset consists of 200 examples in four attributes: x_1, x_2, y, and ring. The ring is a binomial attribute with two values: inner and outer.
- Connect a *Set Role* operator to the data and select the "ring" variable to be the label.
- Connect a *Select Attributes* operator to this and select a subset of the attributes: x_1, x_2 and ring. Make sure that the *Include Special Attributes* checkbox is on.
- Connect a *Split Validation* operator. Set the "split" to relative, "split ratio" to 0.7, and "sampling type" to stratified.

Step 2: Modeling operator and parameters

- Double-click the *Split Validation* box and when you enter the nested layer, add an SVM operator in the training panel and *Apply Model* and *Performance (Classification)* operators in the testing panel.
- Once again, do not change the parameters for the SVM operator from its default values.
- Go back to the main level and add another *Apply Model* operator. Connect the "mod" output from the *Validation* box to the "mod" input port of *Apply Model (2)* and the "exa" output from the Validation box to the "unl" input port of *Apply Model (2)*. Also connect the "ave" output from the *Validation* box to the "res" port of the Main Process. Finally, connect the "lab" output from *Apply Model (2)* to the "res" port of the Main Process. Your final process should look like Figure 4.55.

Step 3: Execution and interpretation

- When you run this model, RapidMiner will generate two result tabs: *ExampleSet (Select Attributes)* and *PerformanceVector (Performance)*. Let's check the *performance* of the SVM classifier. Recall that 30% of the initial input examples are now going to be tested for classification accuracy (which is a total of 60 test samples).

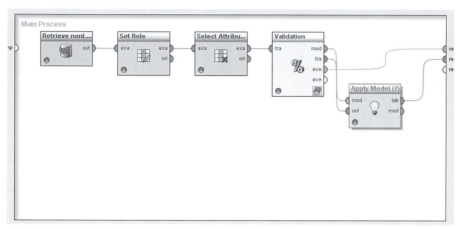

FIGURE 4.55

Setup for the nonlinear SVM demo model.

	true inner	true outer	class precision
pred. inner	12	17	41.38%
pred. outer	18	13	41.94%
class recall	40.00%	43.33%	

Table View ○ Plot View

accuracy: 41.67%

FIGURE 4.56

Prediction accuracy of a linear (dot) kernel SVM on nonlinear data.

- As you can see in Figure 4.56, the linear SVM can barely get 50% of the classes correct, which is to be expected considering we have linearly nonseparable data and we are using a linear (dot) kernel SVM.
- A better way to visualize this result is by means of the Scatter 3D Color plot. Click on the *ExampleSet (Select Attributes)* results tab and select Plot View and set up the Scatter 3D Color plot as shown in Figure 4.57.

The red-colored examples in the upper (outer) ring are correctly classified as belonging to the class "outer" while the cyan-colored examples have been incorrectly classified as belonging to class "inner." Similarly, the blue-colored examples in the lower (inner) ring have been correctly classified as belonging to class "inner" whereas the yellow-colored ones are not. As you can see, the classifier roughly gets about half the total number of test examples right.

To fix this situation, all we need to do is to go back to the SVM operator in the process and change the *kernel type* to *polynomial* (default degree 2.0) and rerun

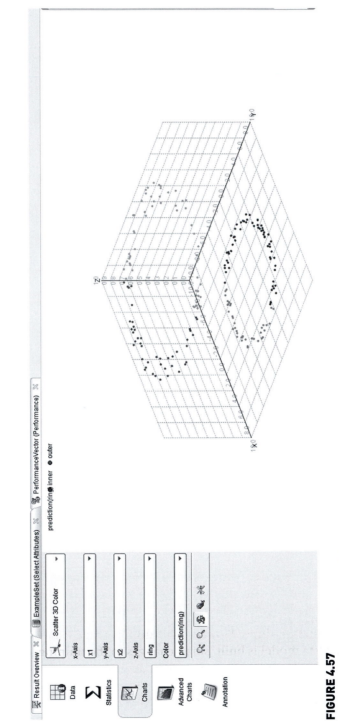

FIGURE 4.57

Visualizing the prediction from linear SVM.

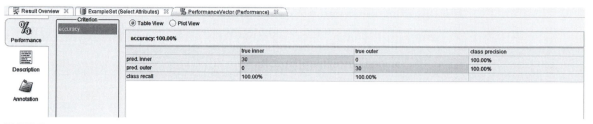

FIGURE 4.58
Classifying the two-ring nonlinear problem using a polynomial SVM kernel.

the analysis. This time we will be able to classify the points with 100% accuracy as seen in Figure 4.58. You will get the same result if you try a radial kernel as well.

The point of this exercise was to demonstrate the flexibility of SVMs and the ease of performing such trials using RapidMiner. Unfortunately with more realistic data sets, there is no way of knowing beforehand which kernel type would work best. The solution is to nest the SVM within an Optimization operator and explore a host of different kernel types and kernel parameters until we find one that performs reasonably well. (Optimization using RapidMiner is described in Chapter 13 Getting Started with RapidMiner.)

RapidMiner Parameter Settings

There are many different parameters that can be adjusted depending upon the type of kernel function that is chosen. There is, however, one parameter that is very critical in optimizing SVM performance: this is the SVM complexity constant, C, which sets the penalties for misclassification, as was described in an earlier section. Most real world data sets are not cleanly separable and therefore will require the use of this factor. For initial trials, however, it is best to go with the default settings. The help in RapidMiner provides more details on how C impacts the performance and we will not repeat that here.

4.6.4 Conclusion

A disadvantage with higher order SVMs is the computational cost. In general since SVMs have to compute the dot product for every classification (and during training), very high dimensions or a large number of attributes can result in very slow computation times. However this disadvantage is offset by the fact that once an SVM model is built, small changes to the training data will not result in significant changes to the model coefficients as long as the support vectors do not change. This overfitting resistance is one of the reasons why SVMs have emerged as the most versatile of machine learning algorithms.

In summary, the key advantages of SVM are

- **Flexibility in application:** SVMs have been applied for activities from image processing to fraud detection to text mining.
- **Robustness:** Small changes in data does not require expensive remodeling.
- **Overfitting resistance:** The boundary of classes within data sets can be adequately described usually by only a few support vectors.

These advantages have to be balanced with the somewhat high computational costs of SVMs.

4.7 ENSEMBLE LEARNERS

In supervised data mining, the objective is to build a model that can explain the relationship between inputs and output. The model can be considered a hypothesis that can map new input data to predicted output. For a given training set, multiple hypotheses can explain the relationship with varying degrees of accuracy. While it is difficult to find the exact hypothesis from an infinite hypothesis space, we would like the modeling process to find the hypothesis that can *best* explain the relationship with least error.

Ensemble methods or learners optimize the hypothesis-finding problem by employing an array of individual prediction models and then combining them to form an aggregate hypothesis or model. These methods provide a technique for generating a better hypothesis by combining multiple hypotheses into one. Since a single hypothesis can be locally optimal or overfit a particular training set, combining multiple models can improve the accuracy by forcing a meta-hypothesis solution. It can be shown that in certain conditions this combined predictive power is better than the predictive power of individual models. Since different methods often capture different features of the solution space as part of any one model, the ensembles of models have emerged as the most important technique for many practical classification problems.

4.7.1 Wisdom of the Crowd

Ensemble models have a set of base models that accept the same inputs and predict the outcome individually. Then the outputs from all of these base models are combined, usually by voting, to form an ensemble output. This approach is similar to decision making by a committee or a board. The method of improving accuracy by drawing together the prediction of multiple models is also called *meta learning*. We see this similar decision-making methodology in higher courts of justice, corporate boards, and

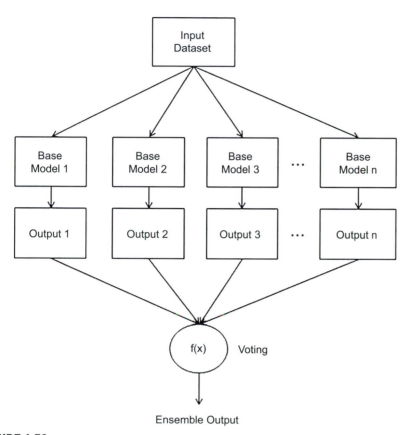

FIGURE 4.59
Ensemble model.

various committees in legislative bodies. While individual members have biases and options, the thinking here is collective decision making is better than one individual's assessment. Ensemble methods are used to improve the error rate and overcome the modeling bias of individual models. They can produce one strong learner by combining many weak learners. Figure 4.59 provides the framework of ensemble models.

The final step of aggregating the prediction is usually done by voting. The predicted class with more votes from the base learners is the output of the combined ensemble model. Base models predict the outcome with varied degrees of accuracy. Hence, we can also weight the vote by the accuracy rate of individual models, which causes base models with higher accuracy to have higher representation in the final aggregation than models with lower accuracy rate (Dietterich, 2007).

PREDICTING DROUGHT

Drought is a period of time where a region experiences far less than average water supply. With the onset of climate change, there has been an increase in frequency and duration of drought conditions in many parts of the world. Immediate drought is caused by the development of high-pressure regions, which inhibits the formation of clouds, which results in low precipitation and lower humidity. Predicting drought conditions in a region is a very challenging task. There is no clear start and end point for draught duration. There are too many variables that impact the climate patterns that lead to drought conditions. Hence, there is no strong model to predict drought well ahead of time (Predicting Drought, 2013). Predicting drought seasons in advance would provide time for regional administrations to mitigate the consequences of the drought.

Droughts involve a myriad factors including groundwater level, air stream flow, soil moisture, topology, and large-scale global weather patterns like El Nino and La Nina (Patel, 2012). With thousands of attributes and many unknown variables that influence the conditions for drought, there is no "silver bullet" massive model for predicting when drought is going to hit a region with a high degree of accuracy. What we have is many different "weak" models that use some of the thousands of attributes available, which make predictions marginally better than pure chance. These weak models may provide different drought predictions for the same region and time, based on the diverse input variables for each model. We can summarize the prediction by combining the predictions of individual models and take a vote. Ensemble models provide a systemic method to combine many weak models into one better model. Most of the data mining models deployed in production applications are ensemble models. Ensemble models greatly reduce generalization errors and improve the accuracy of the overall prediction, if certain conditions are met.

4.7.2 How it Works

Let's take an example of a hypothetical corporate boardroom with three board members. Assume that individually each board member makes wrong decisions about 20% of time. The board needs to make a yes/no decision for a major project proposal. If all board members make consistent unanimous decision every time, then the error rate of the board as a whole is 20%. But, if each board member's decisions are *independent* and if their outcomes are not correlated, the board makes an error only when more than *two board members make an error* at the same time. The board makes an error only when the majority of its members make an error. We can calculate the error rate of the board using the binomial distribution.

In binomial distribution, the probability of k successes in n independent trials each with a success rate of p is given by a probability mass function:

$$P(k) = \binom{n}{k} p^k (1-p)^{n-k}$$

(4.22)

P(Board wrong) = P(k ≥ 2) = P(2 members wrong) + P(3 members wrong)

$$P(\text{Board wrong}) = \binom{n}{3} p^k(1-p)^{n-k} + \binom{n}{2} p^k(1-p)^{n-k}$$

$$= \binom{3}{3} 0.2^3(1-0.2)^0 + \binom{3}{2} 0.2^2(1-0.2)^1$$

$$= 0.008 + 0.096$$

$$= 0.104$$

$$= 10.4\%$$

In this example, the error rate of the board (10.4%) is *less* than the error rate of the individuals (20%)! We therefore see the impact of collective decision making. A generic formula for calculating error rate for the ensemble is given by

$$P(\text{ensemble wrong}) = P(k \geq \text{round}(n/2)) = \sum_{k=0}^{n} \binom{n}{k} p^k(1-p)^{n-k}$$

However, some important criteria to note are:

- Each member of the ensemble should be independent.
- The individual model error rate should be less than 50% for binary classifiers.

If the error rate of the base classifier is more than 50%, its prediction power is worse than pure chance and hence, it is not a good model to begin with. Achieving the first criterion of independence amongst the base classifier is difficult. However there are a few techniques available to make base models as diverse as possible. In the board analogy, having a board with diverse and independent members makes statistical sense. Of course, they all have to make right decisions more than half the time.

Achieving the Conditions for Ensemble Modeling

We will be able to take advantage of combined decision-making power only if the base models are good to begin with. While meta learners can form a strong learner from several weak learners, those weak learners should be better than random guessing. Because all the models are developed based on the same training set, the diversity and independence condition of the model is difficult to accomplish. While complete independence of the base models cannot be achieved, we can take steps to promote independence by changing the training sets for each base model, varying the input attributes, building different classes of modeling techniques and algorithms, and changing the modeling parameters to build the base models. To achieve the diversity in the base models, we can alter the conditions in which the base model is built. The most commonly used conditions are:

- **Different model algorithms:** The same training set can be used to build different classifiers, such as decision trees using multiple algorithms, naïve Bayesian, k-nearest neighbors, artificial neural networks, etc. The inherent characteristics of these models will be different, which yields different error rates and a diverse base model set.
- **Parameters within the models:** Changing the parameters like depth of the tree, gain ratio, and maximum split for decision tree model can produce multiple decision trees. The same training set can be used to build all the base models.
- **Changing the training record set:** Since the training data is the key contributor to the error in a model, changing the training set to build the base model is one effective method for building multiple independent base models. A training set can be divided into multiple sets and each set can be used to build one base model. However, this technique requires a sufficiently large training set and is seldom used. Instead, we can sample training data with replacement from a data set and repeat the same process for other base models.
- **Changing the attribute set:** Similar to changing the training data where a sample of records are used for the building of each base model, we can sample the attributes for each base model. This technique works if the training data have a large number of attributes.

In the next few sections, we will be reviewing specific approaches to building ensemble models based on the above techniques on promoting independence among base models. There are some limitations in using ensemble models. If different algorithms are used for the base models, they impose different restrictions on the type of input data that can be used. Hence it could create a super-set of restrictions to inputs for an ensemble model.

4.7.3 How to Implement

In data mining tools, ensemble modeling operators can be found in meta learning or ensemble learning groupings. In RapidMiner, since ensemble modeling is used in the context of predicting, all the operators are located in Modeling > Classification and Regression > Meta Modeling. The process of building ensemble models is very similar to that of building any classification models like decision tress or neural networks. Please refer to previous classification algorithms for steps to develop individual classification processes and models in RapidMiner. There are a few options to choose for implementing meta modeling in RapidMiner. In the next few pages we will review the implementation of ensemble modeling with simple voting and a couple of other techniques to make the base models independent by altering examples for the training set.

Ensemble by Voting

Implementing an ensemble classifier starts with building a simple base classification process. For this example, we can build a decision tree process with the Iris data set as shown in Section 4.1 Decision Trees. The standard decision tree process involves data retrieval and a decision tree model, followed by applying the model to an unseen test data set sourced from the Iris data set and using a performance evaluation operator. To make it an ensemble model, the *Decision Tree* operator has to be replaced with the *Vote* operator from the meta learning folder. All other operators will remain the same. The ensemble process will look similar to the process shown in Figure 4.60.

The *Vote* operator is an ensemble learner that houses multiple base models inside the *inner subprocess* (Mierswa et al., 2006). The model output from the vote process behaves like any other classification model and it can be applied in any scenario where a decision tree can be used. In the apply model phase, the predicted classes are tallied up amongst all the base classifiers and the class with highest number of votes is the predicted class for the ensemble model.

On double-clicking the nested *Vote* meta modeling operator, we can add multiple base classification models inside the *Vote* operator. All these models accept the same training set and provide an individual base model as output. In this example we have added three models: decision tree, k-NN and naïve Bayes. Figure 4.61 shows the inner subprocess of the *Vote* meta modeling operator. The act of tallying

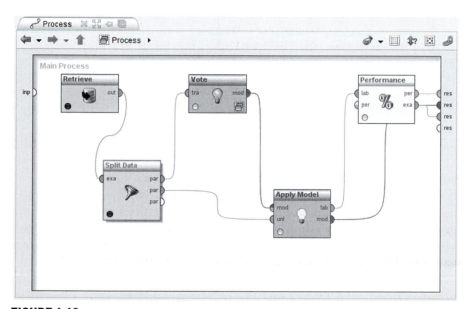

FIGURE 4.60
Data mining process using ensemble model.

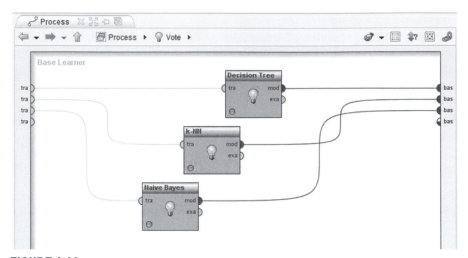

FIGURE 4.61
Subprocess inside the Vote operator.

all the predictions of these base learners and providing the majority prediction is the job of the meta model—the *Vote* modeling operator. This is the aggregation step in ensemble modeling and in RapidMiner it is called a stacking model. A stacking model is built into the *Vote* operator and is not visible on the screen.

The ensemble process with the *Vote* meta model can be saved and executed. Once the process is executed, the output panel of the performance vector is no different than a normal performance vector. Since this process has a meta model, the model panel in the results window exhibits new information, as shown in Figure 4.62. The model window shows all the individual base models and one stacking model, which is the combination of all the base models. The *Vote* meta model is simple to use wherever an individual base model could have been used independently. The limitation of the model is that all the base learners use the same training data set and different base models impose restrictions on what data types they can accept.

Bootstrap Aggregating or Bagging
Bagging is a technique where base models are developed by changing the training set for every base model. In a given training set T of n records, m training sets are developed each with n records, by sampling with replacement. Each training set $T_1, T_2, T_3, …, T_m$ will have the same record count of n as the original training set T. Because they are sampled with replacement, they can contain duplicate records. This is called *bootstrapping*. Each sampled training set is then used for a base model preparation. Through bootstrapping, we have a set of m base models and the prediction of each model is aggregated for an ensemble model. This combination of bootstrapping and aggregating is called *bagging*.

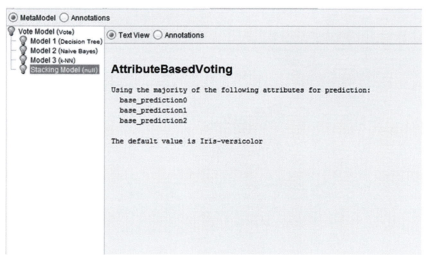

FIGURE 4.62
Output of ensemble model based on voting.

On average, each base training set T_i contains about 63% unique training records as compared to the original training set T. Sampling with replacement of n records contains $1 - (1 - 1/n)^n$ unique records. When n is sufficiently large we get $1 - 1/e = 63.2\%$ unique records on average. The rest of the data contains duplicates from already sampled data. The process of bagging improves the stability of unstable models. Unstable models like decision trees and neural network are highly dependent even on slight changes in the training data. Because a bagging ensemble combines multiple hypotheses of the same data, the new aggregate hypothesis helps neutralize these training data variations.

Implementation

The *Bagging* operator is available in the meta learning folder: Modeling > Classification and Regression > Meta modeling > Bagging. Like the *Vote* meta operator, *Bagging* is a nested operator with an inner subprocess. Unlike the vote process, bagging has only one model in the inner subprocess. Multiple base models are generated by changing the training data set. The *Bagging* operator has two parameters.

- **Sample ratio:** Indicates the fraction of records used for training.
- **Iterations (m):** Number of base modes that need to be generated.

Figure 4.63 shows the RapidMiner process for the *Bagging* operator. Figure 4.64 shows the inner subprocess for the *Bagging* operator with one model specification. Internally multiple base models are generated based on iterations (m) configured in the Bagging parameter. In this example, we are using a decision tree model for the inner subprocess.

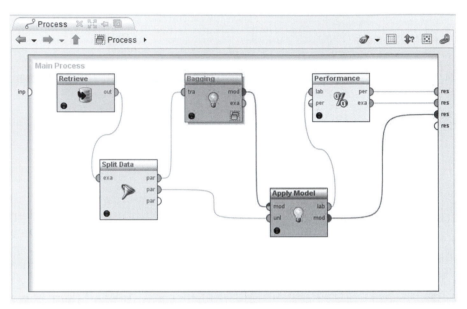

FIGURE 4.63
Ensemble process using bagging.

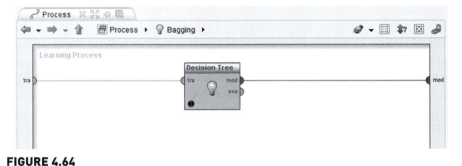

FIGURE 4.64
Bagging subprocess.

The RapidMiner process for bagging can be saved and executed. Similar to the *Vote* meta model, the *Bagging* meta model acts as one model with multiple base models inside. The results window shows the practiced example set, performance vector, and bagging model description. In the results window, we can examine all m (in this case 10) models that are developed based on m iterations of the training set. The base model results are aggregated using simple voting. Bagging is particularly useful when there is anomaly in the training data set that impacts the individual model significantly. Bagging provides a useful framework where the same data mining algorithm is used for all base

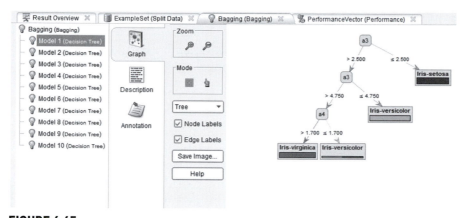

FIGURE 4.65
Output of bagging models.

learners. However, each base model differs because the training data used by the base learners are different. Since each base model explores a different solution space, the performance of the ensemble model would be better than that of base models. Figure 4.65 shows the model output of *Bagging* meta model with constituent decision trees.

Boosting

Boosting offers another approach to building an ensemble model by manipulating training data similar to bagging. As with bagging, it provides a solution to combine many weak learners into one strong learner, by minimizing bias or variance due to training records. Unlike bagging, boosting trains the base models in sequence one by one and assigns weights for all training records. The boosting process concentrates on the training records that are hard to classify and overrepresents them in the training set for the next iteration.

The boosting model is built by an iterative and sequential process where a base model is built and tested with all of the training data, and based on the outcome, the next base model is developed. To start with, all training records have equal weight. The weight of the record is used for the sampling distribution for selection with replacement. A training sample is selected based on the weights and used for model building. Then the model is used for testing with the whole training set. Incorrectly classified records are assigned a higher weight and correctly classified records are assigned a low weight, so hard-to-classify records have a higher propensity of selection for the next round. The training sample for the next round will be most likely filled with incorrectly classified records from the previous round. Hence the next model will focus on the hard-to-classify data space.

Boosting assigns the weight for each training record and has to adaptively change the weight based on difficulty of classification. This results in an ensemble of base learners specialized in classifying both easy-to-classify and hard-to-classify records. When applying the model, all base learners are combined through a simple voting aggregation.

AdaBoost

AdaBoost is one of the most popular implementations of the boosting ensemble approach. It is adaptive because it assigns weights for base models (α) based on the accuracy of the model, and changes weights of the training records (w) based on the accuracy of the prediction. Here is the framework of the AdaBoost ensemble model with m base classifiers and n training records $((x_1,y_1), (x_2,y_2), ..., (x_n,y_n))$. Following are the steps involved in AdaBoost:

1. Each training record is assigned an uniform weight $w_i = 1/n$.
2. Training records are sampled and the first base classifier $b_k(x)$ is built.
3. The error rate for the base classifier can be calculated by Equation 4.23:

$$e_k = \sum_{k=1}^{n} w_i * I\left(b_k\left(x_i\right) \neq y_i\right)$$

$$(4.23)$$

where $I(x) = 1$ when the prediction is right and 0 when the prediction is incorrect.

4. The weight of the classifier can be calculated as $\alpha_k = \ln\left(1 - e_k\right)/e_k$. If the model has a low error rate, then the weight of the classifier is high and vice versa.
5. Next, the weights of all training records are updated by

$$w_{k+1}\left(i+1\right) = w_k(i) * e^{\left(\alpha_k F(bk(xi) \neq yi)\right)}$$

where $F(x) = -1$ if the prediction is right and $F(x) = 1$ if the prediction is wrong.

Hence, the AdaBoost model updates the weights based on the prediction and the error rate of the base classifier. If the error rate is more than 50%, the record weight is not updated and reverted back to the next round.

AdaBoost Model in RapidMiner

The *AdaBoost* operator is available in the meta learning folder: Modeling > Classification and Regression > Meta modeling > AdaBoost. The operator functions similar to Bagging and has an inner subprocess. The number of iterations or base models is a configurable parameter for the *AdaBoost* operator. Figure 4.66 shows the AdaBoost data mining process. This example uses the Iris data set with the *Split Data* operator for generating training and test data sets. The output of the AdaBoost model is applied to the test set and the performance is evaluated by the *Performance* operator.

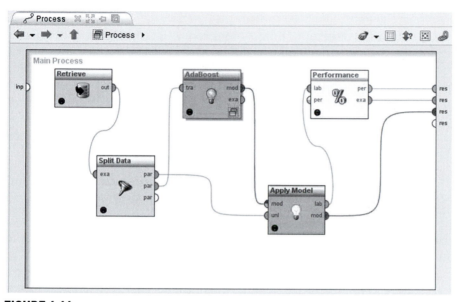

FIGURE 4.66
Data mining process using AdaBoost.

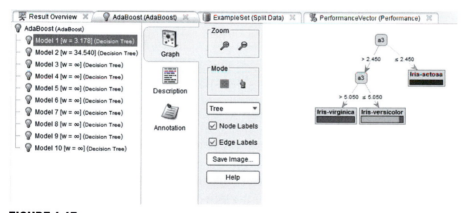

FIGURE 4.67
Output of AdaBoost model.

The number of iterations used in the AdaBoost is three, which is specified in the parameter. In the inner process, the model type can be specified. In this example the decision tree model is used. The completed RapidMiner process is saved and executed. The result window has the output ensemble model, base models, and the predicted records. The model window shows the decision trees for the base classifiers. Figure 4.67 shows the result output for the AdaBoost model.

Random Forest

Recall that in the bagging technique, for every iteration, a sample of training records is considered for building the model. The random forest technique uses a similar concept to the one used in bagging. When deciding on splitting each node in a decision tree, the random forest only considers a random subset of all the attributes in the training set. To reduce the generalization error, the algorithm is randomized in two levels, training record selection and attribute selection, in the inner working of each base classifier. The random forests concept was first put forward by Leo Breiman and Adele Cutler (Breiman, 2001).

In general, the model works using the following steps. If there are n training records with m attributes, and let k be the number of trees in the forest; then for each tree:

1. An n random sample is selected with replacement. This step is similar to bagging.
2. A number D is selected, where D << m. D determines the number of attributes to be considered for node splitting.
3. A decision tree is started. For each node, instead of considering all m attributes for the best split, a random number D attributes are considered. This step is repeated for every node.
4. As in any ensemble, the greater the diversity of the base trees, the lower the error of the ensemble.

Once all the trees in the forest are built, for every new record, all the trees predict a class and vote for the class with equal weights. The most predicted class by the base trees is the prediction of the forest (Gashler et al., 2008).

Implementation

The *Random Forest* operator is available in Modeling > Classification and Regression > Tree Induction > Random Forest. It works similarly to the other ensemble models where the user needs to specify the number of base trees to be built. Since the inner base model is always a decision tree, there is no explicit inner subprocess specification. Bagging or boosting ensemble models require explicit inner subprocess specification. All the tree-specific parameters like leaf size, depth, and split criterion can be specified in the *Random Forest* operator. The key parameter that specifies the number of base trees is *Number of Trees*. Figure 4.68 shows the RapidMiner process with the Iris data set, the *Random Forest* modeling operator, and the *Apply Model* operator. For this example, the number of base trees is specified as 10. The process looks and functions similarly to a simple decision tree classifier.

Once the process is executed, the results window shows the model, predicted output, and performance vector. Similar to other meta model output, the

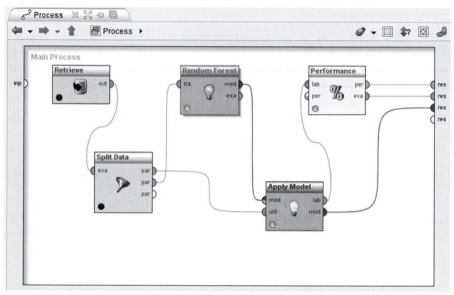

FIGURE 4.68
Data mining process using the Random Forest operator.

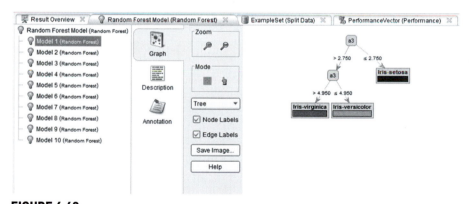

FIGURE 4.69
Output of Random Forest models.

Random Forest model shows the trees for all base classifiers. Figure 4.69 shows the model output for the *Random Forest* operator. Notice that the nodes are different in each tree. Since the attribute selection for each node is randomized, each base tree is different. Thus the Random Forest models strive to reduce the generalization error of the decision tree model. The Random Forest models are very useful as baseline ensemble models for comparative purposes.

4.7.4 Conclusion

Most of the data mining models developed for production applications are built on ensemble models. They are used in wide range of applications, including political forecasting (Montgomery et al., 2012), weather pattern modeling, media recommendation, web page ranking (Baradaran Hashemi et al., 2010), etc. Since many algorithms approach the problem of modeling the relationship between input and output differently, it makes sense to aggregate the prediction of a diverse set of approaches. Ensemble modeling reduces the generalization error that arises due to overfitting the training data set. The four ensemble techniques discussed provide fundamental methods of developing a cohort of base models by choosing different algorithms, changing parameters, changing training records, sampling, and changing attributes. All these techniques can be combined in one ensemble model. There is no one approach for ensemble modeling; all the techniques discussed in this chapter were proven to perform better than base models as long as they are diverse (Polikar, 2006). The wisdom of crowds makes sense in data mining as long as "group thinking" is controlled by promoting independence amongst base models.

REFERENCES

Altman, N. S. (1992). An Introduction to Kernel and Nearest-Neighbor Nonparametric Regression. *The American Statistician, 46*(3), 175–185.

Baradaran Hashemi, H., Yazdani, N., Shakery, A., & Pakdaman Naeini, M. (2010). Application of ensemble models in web ranking. *2010 5th International Symposium on Telecommunications,* 726–731. http://dx.doi.org/10.1109/ISTEL.2010.5734118.

Breiman, L. (2001). Random Forests. *Machine Learning, 45,* 5–32.

Brieman, L. F. (1984). *Classification and Regression Trees.* Chapman and Hall.

Cohen, W. W. (1995). Fast Effective Rule Induction. *Machine Learning: Proceedings of the Twelfth International Conference.*

Cortes, C. A. (1995). Support Vector Networks. *Machine Learning,* 273–297.

Cover, T. A. (1991). Entropy, Relative Information, and Mutual Information. In T. A. Cover (Ed.), *Elements of Information Theory* (pp. 12–49). John Wiley and Sons.

Dietterich, T. G. (2007). *Ensemble Methods in Machine Learning.* Retrieved from http://www.eecs.wsu.edu/~holder/courses/CptS570/fall07/papers/Dietterich00.pdf.

Fisher, R. A. (1936). The use of multiple measurements in taxonomic problems. *Annals of Human Genetics, 7,* 179–188. http://dx.doi.org/10.1111/j.1469-1809.1936.tb02137.x.

Fletcher, R. (1987). *Practical Methods of Optimization.* New York: John Wiley.

Gashler, M., Giraud-Carrier, C., & Martinez, T. (2008). Decision Tree Ensemble: Small Heterogeneous Is Better Than Large Homogeneous. *2008 Seventh International Conference on Machine Learning and Applications,* 900–905. http://dx.doi.org/10.1109/ICMLA.2008.154.

Grabusts, P. (2011). The Choice of Metrics for Clustering Algorithms. *Proceedings of the 8th International Scientific and Practical Conference, II*(1), 70–76.

Haapanen, R., Lehtinen, K., Miettinen, J., Bauer, M. E., & Ek, A. R. (2001). Progress in adapting k-NN methods for forest mapping and estimation using the new annual Forest Inventory and Analysis data. In Third Annual Forest Inventory and Analysis Symposium (p. 87).

Hill, T., & Lewicki, P. (2007). *Statistics: Methods and Applications* p. 815.

Hsu, C.-W. C.-C.-J. (2003). A practical guide to support vector classification. *Taipei: Department of Computer Science*, National Taiwan University.

Laine, A. (2003). *Neural Networks. In Encyclopedia of Computer Science 4th edition*. John Wiley and Sons Ltd. 1233–1239.

Langley, P., & Simon, H. a. (1995). Applications of machine learning and rule induction. *Communications of the ACM, 38*(11), 54–64. http://dx.doi.org/10.1145/219717.219768.

Peterson, L. (2009). K-Nearest Neighbors. *Scholarpedia*. Retrieved from http://www.scholarpedia. org/article/K-nearest_neighbor.

Li, E. Y. (1994). Artificial neural networks and their business applications. *Information & Management, 27*(5), 303–313. http://dx.doi.org/10.1016/0378-7206(94)90024-8.

Matan, O., et al. (1990). Handwritten Character Recognition Using Neural Network Architectures. *4th USPS Advanced Technology Conference*, 1003–1011.

McInerney, D. (2005). Remote Sensing Applications k-NN Classification. *Remote Sensing Workshop*. Retrieved April 27, 2014, from http://www.forestry.gov.uk/pdf/DanielMcInerneyworkshop. pdf/$FILE/DanielMcInerneyworkshop.pdf.

Meagher, P. (2005). *Calculating Entropy for Data Mining*. Retrieved from O'Reilly OnLamp.com PHP Dev Center. http://www.onlamp.com/pub/a/php/2005/01/06/entropy.html?page=1.

Mierswa, I., Wurst, M., Klinkenberg, R., Scholz, M., & Euler, T. (2006). YALE: Rapid prototyping for complex Data Mining tasks. *Proceedings of the ACM SIGKDD International Conference on Knowledge Discovery and Data Mining* (Vol. 2006). 935–940. http://dx.doi.org/10.1145/1150402.1150531.

Montgomery, J.M., Hollenbach, F.M., Ward. M.D. (2012). Improving predictions using ensemble Bayesian model averaging. *Political Analysis, 20*(3): 271–291.

Patel, P. (2012). Predicting the Future of Drought Prediction. *IEEE Spectrum*. Retrieved April 26, 2014, from http://spectrum.ieee.org/energy/environment/predicting-the-future-of-drought-prediction.

Polikar, R. (2006). Ensemble Based Systems in Decision Making. *IEEE CIRCUITS AND SYSTEMS MAGAZINE*, 21–45.

Predicting Drought (2013). National Drought Mitigation Center. Retrieved April 26, 2014, from http://drought.unl.edu/DroughtBasics/PredictingDrought.aspx.

Prosess Software (2013). Introduction to Bayseian Filtering. PreciseMail Whitepapers, 1–8. Retrieved from www.process.com.

Quinlan, J. (1986). Induction of Decision Trees. *Machine Learning*, 81–106.

Rish, I. (2001). An empirical study of the naive Bayes classifier. *IBM Research Report*.

Sahami, M., Dumais, S., Heckerman, D., & Horvitz, E. (1998). A Bayesian Approach to Filtering Junk E-Mail. Learning for Text Categorization. Papers from the 1998 Workshop. *AAAI Technical Report*.

Saian, R., & Ku-Mahamud, K. R. (2011). Hybrid Ant Colony Optimization and Simulated Annealing for Rule Induction. *2011 UKSim 5th European Symposium on Computer Modeling and Simulation*, 70–75. http://dx.doi.org/10.1109/EMS.2011.17.

Shannon, C. (1948). A Mathematical Theory of Communication. *Bell Systems Technical Journal*, 379–423.

Smola, A. A. (2004). A tutorial on support vector regression. *Statistics and Computing*, 199–222.

Tan, P.-N., Michael, S., & Kumar, V. (2005). Classfication and Classification: Alternative Techniques. In P.-N. Tan, S. Michael, & V. Kumar (Eds.), *Introduction to Data Mining* (pp. 145–315). Boston, MA: Addison-Wesley.

Zdziarski, J. A. (2005). *Ending spam: Bayesian content filtering and the art of statistical language classification*. No Starch Press.

CHAPTER 5

Regression Methods

In this chapter, we will explore one of the most commonly used predictive analytics techniques—fitting data with functions or *function fitting*. The basic idea behind function fitting is to predict the value (or class) of a dependent variable y, by combining the predictor variables $\mathbf{X}$ into a function, $y = f(\mathbf{X})$. Function fitting involves many different techniques and the most common ones are *linear regression* for numeric prediction *and logistic regression* for classification. These two form the majority of material in this chapter. According to an annual survey[1] on data mining, regression models continue to be one of the three most common analytics tools used today by practitioners (the others being decision trees and clustering).

Regression is a relatively "old" technique dating back to the Victorian era (1830s to early 1900s). Much of the pioneering work was done by Sir Francis Galton, a distant relative of Charles Darwin, who came up with the concept of *"regressing toward the mean"* while systematically comparing children's heights against their parents' heights. He observed there was a strong tendency for tall parents to have children slightly shorter than themselves, and for short parents to have children slightly taller than themselves. Even if the parents' heights were at the tail ends of a bell curve or normal distribution, their children's heights tended toward the mean of the distribution. Thus in the end, all the samples "regressed" toward a population mean. Therefore, this trend was called "regression" by Galton (Galton, 1888) and thus laid the foundations for linear regression

In the first section of this chapter we will provide the theoretical framework for the simplest of function-fitting methods: the *linear regression model*. Considering its widespread use and familiarity, we will not spend too much time discussing the theory behind it. Instead we will focus more on a case study and demonstrate how to build regression models. Due to the nature of the function fitting approach, a limitation that modelers have to deal with is the

---

[1] 2012 Rexer Analytics survey available from http://www.rexeranalytics.com .

"curse of dimensionality." As the number of predictors X, increases, not only will our ability to obtain a good model reduce, it also adds computational and interpretational complexity. We will introduce *feature selection* methods that can reduce the number of predictors or factors required to a minimum and still obtain a good model. We will explore the mechanics of using RapidMiner to do the data preparation, model building, and validation. Finally, in closing we will describe some checkpoints to ensure that linear regression is used correctly.

In the second section of this chapter we will discuss *logistic regression*. Strictly speaking, it is a classification technique, closer in its application to decision trees or Bayesian methods. But it shares an important characteristic with linear regression in its function-fitting methodology and thus merits inclusion in this chapter, rather than the previous one on classification.

We start by discussing how it is different from linear regression and when it makes sense to use it. We will then discuss logistic regression and its implementation using RapidMiner for a simple business analytics application. We will highlight the differences in the implementation of logistic regression in RapidMiner compared to other common tools. Finally, we will spend some time on explaining how to use a costing operator to selectively weight misclassifications while using logistic regression.

PREDICTING HOME PRICES VS. EXPLAINING WHAT FACTORS AFFECT HOME PRICES

What features would play a role in deciding the value of a home? For example, the number of rooms, its age, the quality of schools, its location with respect to major sources of employment, and its accessibility to major highways are some of the important considerations most potential home buyers would like to factor in. But which of these are the most significant influencers of the price? Is there a way to determine these? Once we know them, can we incorporate these factors in a model that can be used for predictions? The case study we discuss a little later in this chapter addresses this problem using multiple linear regression to predict the median home prices in an urban region given the characteristics of a home. A common goal that all businesses have to address in order to be successful is growth, in revenues and profits. Customers are what will enable this to happen. Understanding and increasing the likelihood that someone will buy again from the company is therefore critical. Another question that would help strategically, for example in customer segmentation, is being able to predict how much money a customer is likely to spend, given data about their previous purchase habits. Two very important distinctions need to be made here: understanding why someone purchased from the company will fall into the realm of *explanatory modeling* whereas predicting how much someone is likely to spend will fall into the realm of *predictive modeling*. Both these types of models fall under a broader category of "Surrogate" or empirical models that rely on historical data to develop rules of behavior as opposed to "System" models which use fundamental principles (such as laws of physics or chemistry) to develop rules. See Figure 1.2 for a taxonomy of Data Mining. In this chapter,

PREDICTING HOME PRICES VS. EXPLAINING WHAT FACTORS AFFECT HOME PRICES—CONT'D

we focus on the predictive capability of models as opposed to the explanatory capabilities. Much of applied linear regression history of statistics has been used for explanatory needs. We will show with an example, for the case of logistic regression, how *both* needs can be met with good analytical interpretation of models.

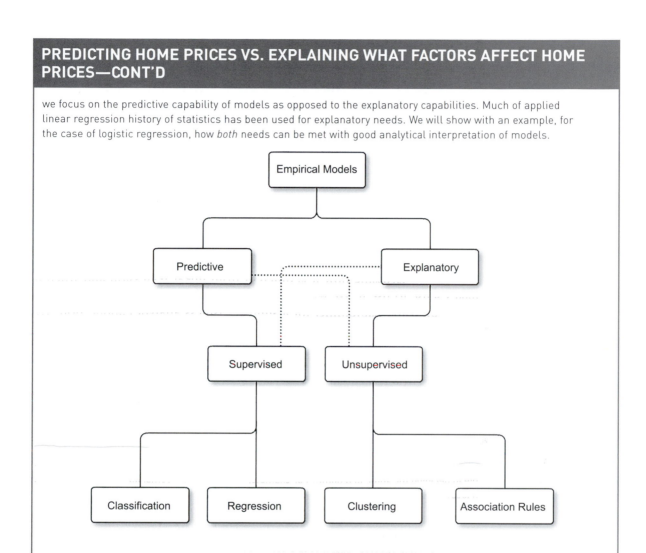

5.1 LINEAR REGRESSION

5.1.1 How it Works

Linear regression is not only one of the oldest predictive methodologies, but it also the most easily explained method for demonstrating function fitting. The basic idea is to come up with a function that explains and predicts the value of the target variable when given the values of the predictor variables. A simple example is shown in Figure 5.1: we would like to know the effect of the number of rooms in a house (predictor) on its median sale price (target). Each data point in the chart

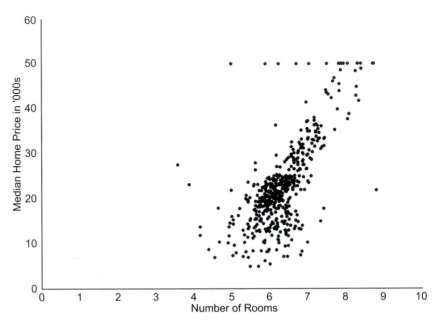

FIGURE 5.1

A simple regression model.

corresponds to a house (Harrison, 1978). We can see that on average, increasing the number of rooms tends to also increase median price. This general statement can be captured by drawing a straight line through the data. The problem in linear regression is therefore to find a line (or a curve) that best explains this tendency. If we have two predictors, then the problem is to find a surface (in a three-dimensional space). With more than two predictors, visualization becomes impossible and we have to revert to a general statement where we express the dependent (target) variable as a linear combination of independent (predictor) variable:

$$y = b_0 + b_1 x_1 + b_2 x_2 + ... + b_n x_n \tag{5.1}$$

Let's consider a problem with one predictor. Clearly we can fit an infinite number of straight lines through a given set of points such as the ones shown in Figure 5.1. How do we know which one is the best? We need a metric that helps to quantify the different straight line fits through the data. Once we find this metric, then selecting the best line becomes a matter of finding the optimum value for this quantity.

A commonly used metric is the concept of an error function. Let's suppose we fit a straight line through the data. In a single predictor case, the *predicted* value, $\hat{y}$, for a value of x that exists in the data set is then given by

$$\hat{y} = b_0 + b_1 x \tag{5.2}$$

Then, error is simply difference between the actual target value and predicted target value:

$$e = y - \hat{y} = y - (b_0 + b_1 x) \tag{5.3}$$

This equation defines the error at a single location (x, y) in the data set. We could easily compute the error for all existing points to come up with an aggregate error. Some errors will be positive and others will be negative. We could square the difference to eliminate the sign bias and calculate an average error for a given fit as follows:

$$\sum e^2 = 1/n * (y_i - \dot{y}_i)^2 = 1/n \sum (y_i - b_0 - b_i x_i)^2 \tag{5.4}$$

where n represents the number of points in the data set. For a given data set, we can then find the best combination of (b_0, b_1) that minimizes the error, e. This is a classical minimization problem, which is handled by methods of calculus. Stigler provides some interesting historical details on the origins of the method of least squares, as it is known (Stigler, 1999). It can be shown that b_1 is given by

$$b_1 = Cor(y, x) * sd(y) / sd(x) \tag{5.5a}$$

$$b_0 = y_{mean} - b_1 * x_{mean} \tag{5.5b}$$

where $Cor(x,y)$ is the correlation between x and y (or y and x) and $sd(y)$, $sd(x)$ are the standard deviations of y and x.

Finally, x_{mean} and y_{mean} are the respective mean values.

Practical linear regression algorithms use an optimization technique known as *gradient descent* (Marquardt, 1963; Fletcher, 1963) to identify the combination of b_0 and b_1 that will minimize the error function given in Equation 5.4. The advantage of using such methods is that even with several predictors, the optimization works fairly robustly. When we apply such a process to the simple example shown above, we get an equation of the form

Median Price = 9.1 * *Number of Rooms* – 34.7 $\tag{5.6}$

where b_1 is 9.1 and b_0 is –34.7. From this equation, we can calculate that for a house with six rooms, the value of the median price is about 20 (the prices are expressed in thousands of dollars). From Figure 5.1 we see that for a house with six rooms, the actual price can range between 10.5 and 25. We could have fit an infinite number of lines in this band, which would have all predicted a median price within this range—but the algorithm chooses the line that minimizes the average error over the full range of the independent variable and is therefore the best fit for the given dataset.

For some of the points (houses) shown in Figure 5.1 (at the top of the chart, where median price = 50) the median price appears to be independent of the number of rooms. This could be because there may be other factors that also influence the price. Thus we will need to model more than one predictor and will need to use *multiple linear regression (MLR)*, which is an extension of simple linear regression. The algorithm to find the coefficients of the regression equation 5.1 can be easily extended to more than one dimension.

MLR can be applied in any situation where a numeric prediction, for example "how much will something sell for," is required. This is in contrast to making categorical predictions such as "will someone buy/not buy" and "will fail/will not fail," where we use classification tools such as decision trees (Chapter 4) or logistic regression models (Section 5.4). In order to ensure regression models are not arbitrarily deployed, we must perform several checks on the model to ensure that the regression is accurate. This is discussed in more detail in Section 5.3.

5.1.2 Case Study in RapidMiner: Objectives and Data

Let us extend the housing example introduced earlier in this chapter to include additional variables. This comes from a study of urban environments conducted in the late 1970s (Harrison, 1978). The full data set and information are available in many public databases.[2] The objectives of this exercise are:

1. Identify which of the several attributes are required to accurately predict the median price of a house.
2. Build a multiple linear regression model to predict the median price using the most important attributes.

The original data consists of thirteen predictors and one response variable, which is the variable we are trying to predict. The predictors include physical characteristics of the house (such as number of rooms, age, tax, and location) and neighborhood features (school, industries, zoning) among others–refer to the original data source for full details. The response variable is of course the median value (MEDV) of the house in thousands of dollars. Table 5.1 shows a snapshot of the data set, which has altogether 506 examples. Table 5.2 describes the features or attributes of the data set.

---

[2]We use the data set described and presented here: http://archive.ics.uci.edu/ml/datasets/Housing. All data sets used in the book are available on our companion site.

Table 5.1 Sample view of the classic Boston Housing data set

CRIM	ZN	INDUS	CHAS	NOX	RM	AGE	DIS	RAD	TAX	PTRATIO	B	LSTAT	MEDV
0.00632	18	2.31	0	0.538	6.575	65.2	4.09	1	296	15.3	396.9	4.98	24
0.02731	0	7.07	0	0.469	6.421	78.9	4.9671	2	242	17.8	396.9	9.14	21.6
0.02729	0	7.07	0	0.469	7.185	61.1	4.9671	2	242	17.8	392.83	4.03	34.7
0.03237	0	2.18	0	0.458	6.998	45.8	6.0622	3	222	18.7	394.63	2.94	33.4
0.06905	0	2.18	0	0.458	7.147	54.2	6.0622	3	222	18.7	396.9	5.33	36.2
0.02985	0	2.18	0	0.458	6.43	58.7	6.0622	3	222	18.7	394.12	5.21	28.7
0.08829	12.5	7.87	0	0.524	6.012	66.6	5.5605	5	311	15.2	395.6	12.43	22.9
0.14455	12.5	7.87	0	0.524	6.172	96.1	5.9505	5	311	15.2	396.9	19.15	27.1

Table 5.2 Attributes of Boston Housing Data Set

1. CRIM per capita crime rate by town
2. ZN proportion of residential land zoned for lots over 25,000 sq.ft.
3. INDUS proportion of nonretail business acres per town
4. CHAS Charles River dummy variable (= 1 if tract bounds river; 0 otherwise)
5. NOX nitric oxides concentration (parts per 10 million)
6. RM average number of rooms per dwelling
7. AGE proportion of owner-occupied units built prior to 1940
8. DIS weighted distances to five Boston employment centers
9. RAD index of accessibility to radial highways
10. TAX full-value property-tax rate per $10,000
11. PTRATIO pupil-teacher ratio by town
12. B 1000(Bk − 0.63)^2 where Bk is the proportion of blacks by town
13. LSTAT % lower status of the population
14. MEDV Median value of owner-occupied homes in $1000's

5.1.3 How to Implement

In this section, we will show how to set up a RapidMiner process to build a multiple linear regression model for the Boston Housing dataset. We will describe the following:

1. Building a linear regression model
2. Measuring the performance of the model
3. Understanding the commonly used options for the *Linear Regression* operator
4. Applying the model to predict MEDV prices for unseen data

Step 1: Data Preparation

As a first step, let us separate the data into a training set and an "unseen" test set. The idea is to build the model with the training data and test its performance on the unseen data. With the help of the *Retrieve* operator, import the raw data into the RapidMiner process (refer to Chapter 13 for details on loading data). Apply the *Shuffle* operator to randomize the order of the data so that when we separate the two partitions, they are statistically similar. Next, using the *Filter Examples Range* operator, divide the data into two sets as shown in Figure 5.2. The raw data has 506 examples, which will be linearly split into a training set (from row 1 to 450) and a test set (row 451 to 506) using the two operators.

Insert the *Set Role* operator, change the role of MEDV to "label" and connect the output to a *Split Validation* operator's input *"tra"* or *training* port as shown in Figure 5.3. The training data is now going to be further split into a training set and a validation set (keep the default Split Validation options as is, i.e., *relative, 0.7*, and *shuffled*). This will be needed in order to measure the performance of the linear regression model. It is also a good

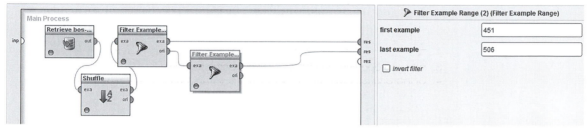

FIGURE 5.2
Separating the data into training and testing samples.

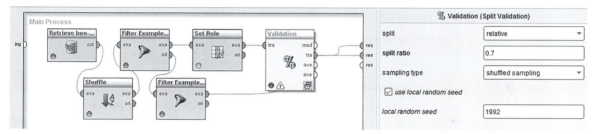

FIGURE 5.3
Using the split validation operator.

idea to set the local random seed (to default the value of 1992), which ensures that RapidMiner selects the same samples if we run this process at a later time.

After this step, double-click the *Validation* operator to enter the nested process. Inside this process insert the *Linear Regression* operator on the left window and *Apply Model* and *Performance (Regression)* in the right window as shown in Figure 5.4. Click on the *Performance* operator and check *"squared error,"* *"correlation,"* and *"squared correlation"* inside the *Parameters* options selector on the right.

Step 2: Model Building

Select the *Linear Regression* operator and change the *"feature selection"* option to "none." Keep the default "eliminate collinear features" checked, which will remove factors that are linearly correlated from the modeling process. When two or more attributes are correlated to one another, the resulting model will tend to have coefficients that cannot be intuitively interpreted and furthermore the statistical significance of the coefficients also tends to be quite low. Also keep the "use bias" checked to build a model with an intercept (the b_0 in Equation 5.2). Keep the other default options intact (Figure 5.5).

When we run this process we will generate the results shown in Figure 5.6 (assuming that the "mod" and "ave" output ports from the *Validation* operator

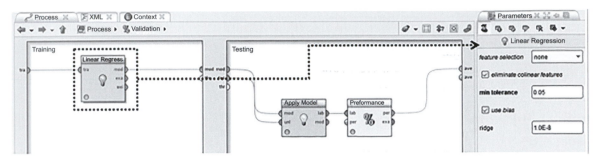

FIGURE 5.4
Applying the linear regression operator and measuring performance.

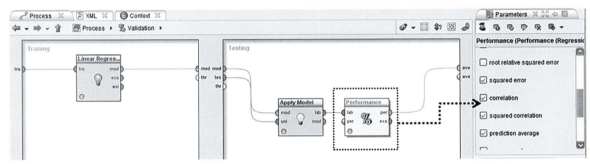

FIGURE 5.5
Do not choose any feature selection option.

are connected to the main output port): a *Linear Regression* model and an average *Performance Vector* output of the model on the validation set.

Step 3: Execution and Interpretation

There are two views that you can examine in the *Linear Regression* output tab: the Description view, which actually shows the function that is fitted (Figure 5.6a) and the more useful Data view, which not only shows the coefficients of the linear regression function, but also gives information about the significance of these coefficients (Figure 5.6b). The best way to read this table is to sort it by double-clicking on the column named "Code," which will sort the different factors according to their decreasing level of significance. RapidMiner assigns four stars (****) to any factor that is highly significant.

In this model we did not use any *feature selection* method (see Figure 5.5) and as a result all 13 factors are in the model, including AGE and INDUS, which have very low significance; see the Text view in Figure 5.7a. However, if we were to run the same model by selecting any of the options that are available in the drop-down menu of the *feature selection* parameter (see Figure 5.5),

(a)

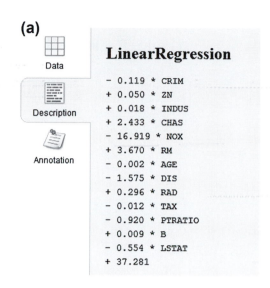

Data

Description

Annotation

LinearRegression

```
-  0.119 * CRIM
+  0.050 * ZN
+  0.018 * INDUS
+  2.433 * CHAS
- 16.919 * NOX
+  3.670 * RM
-  0.002 * AGE
-  1.575 * DIS
+  0.296 * RAD
-  0.012 * TAX
-  0.920 * PTRATIO
+  0.009 * B
-  0.554 * LSTAT
+ 37.281
```

FIGURE 5.6A

Description of the linear regression model.

(b)

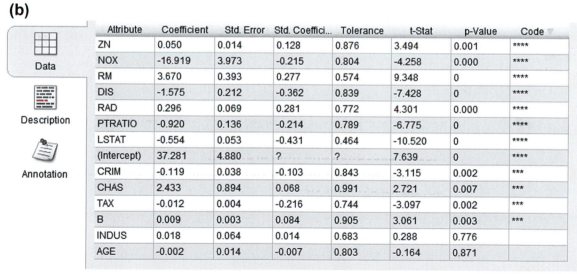

Attribute	Coefficient	Std. Error	Std. Coeffici...	Tolerance	t-Stat	p-Value	Code ▽
ZN	0.050	0.014	0.128	0.876	3.494	0.001	****
NOX	-16.919	3.973	-0.215	0.804	-4.258	0.000	****
RM	3.670	0.393	0.277	0.574	9.348	0	****
DIS	-1.575	0.212	-0.362	0.839	-7.428	0	****
RAD	0.296	0.069	0.281	0.772	4.301	0.000	****
PTRATIO	-0.920	0.136	-0.214	0.789	-6.775	0	****
LSTAT	-0.554	0.053	-0.431	0.464	-10.520	0	****
(Intercept)	37.281	4.880	?	?	7.639	0	****
CRIM	-0.119	0.038	-0.103	0.843	-3.115	0.002	***
CHAS	2.433	0.894	0.068	0.991	2.721	0.007	***
TAX	-0.012	0.004	-0.216	0.744	-3.097	0.002	***
B	0.009	0.003	0.084	0.905	3.061	0.003	***
INDUS	0.018	0.064	0.014	0.683	0.288	0.776	
AGE	-0.002	0.014	-0.007	0.803	-0.164	0.871	

Data

Description

Annotation

FIGURE 5.6B

Tabular view of the model. Sort the table according to significance by double-clicking on the "Code" column.

RapidMiner would have removed the least significant factors from the model. In the next iteration, we use the *greedy* feature selection and this has removed the least significant factors, INDUS and AGE, from the function as seen in Figure 5.7b. Notice that the intercept and coefficients are slightly different for the new model.

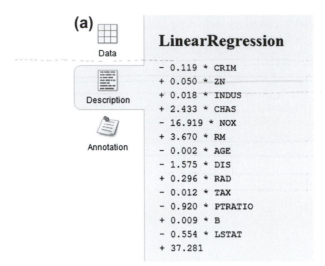

FIGURE 5.7A
Model without any feature selection.

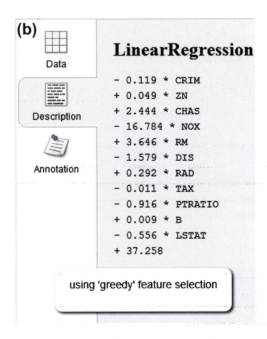

FIGURE 5.7B
Model with "greedy" feature selection.

Feature selection in RapidMiner can be done automatically within the *Linear Regression* operator as described above or by using external "wrapper" functions such as forward selection and backward elimination. These will be discussed separately in Chapter 12.

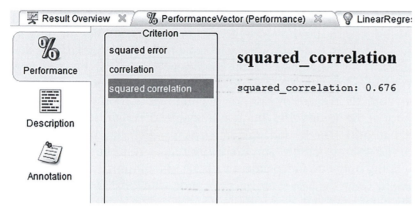

FIGURE 5.8
Generating the R² for the model.

Attribute	Coefficient	Std. Error	Std. Coeffici...	Tolerance	t-Stat	p-Value ▲	Code
RM	3.646	0.378	0.046	0.581	9.633	0	****
LSTAT	-0.556	0.049	-0.129	0.490	-11.408	0	****
DIS	-1.579	0.197	-0.119	0.823	-8.029	0	****
(Intercept)	37.258	4.785	?	?	7.787	0	****
PTRATIO	-0.916	0.132	-0.868	0.793	-6.935	0	****
NOX	-16.784	3.706	-0.469	0.812	-4.529	0.000	****
RAD	0.292	0.066	0.894	0.769	4.431	0.000	****
ZN	0.049	0.014	0.128	0.877	3.509	0.001	****
TAX	-0.011	0.003	-0.003	0.749	-3.329	0.001	***
CRIM	-0.119	0.038	-0.103	0.843	-3.128	0.002	***
B	0.009	0.003	0.161	0.905	3.059	0.003	***
CHAS	2.444	0.891	1.836	0.991	2.743	0.007	***

FIGURE 5.9
Ranking variables by their p-values.

The second output to pay attention to is the Performance: a handy check to test the goodness of fit in a regression model is the *squared correlation*. Conventionally this is the same as the adjusted R² for a model, which can take values between 0.0 and 1.0, with values closer to 1 indicating a better model. For either of the models shown above, we get a value around 0.67 (Figure 5.8). We also requested the squared error output: the raw value in itself may not tell us much, but this is useful in comparing two different models. In this case it was around 25.

One additional insight we can extract from the modeling process is ranking of the factors. The easiest way to check this is to rank by p-value. As seen in Figure 5.9, RM, LSTAT, and DIS seem to be the most significant factors. This is also reflected in their absolute t-stat values. The t-stat and p-values are the result of the hypothesis tests conducted on the regression coefficients. For the purposes of predictive analysis, the key takeaway is that a higher t-stat signals that the null hypothesis—which assumes that the coefficient is zero—can be safely rejected. The corresponding p-value indicates the probability of wrongly rejecting the null hypothesis. We already saw how the number of rooms (RM) was a good predictor of the home prices, but it was unable to explain all of the variations in median price. The R^2 and squared error for that one-variable model were 0.405 and 45, respectively. You can verify this by rerunning the model built so far using only one independent variable, the number of rooms, RM. This is done by using the *Select Attributes* operator, which has to be inserted in the process before the *Set Role* operator. When this model is run, we will obtain the equation shown earlier, Equation 5.6, in the model *Description*. By comparing the corresponding values from the MLR model (0.676 and 25) to the simple linear regression model, we see that both of these quantities have improved, thus affirming our decision to use multiple factors.

We now have a more comprehensive model that can account for much of the variability in the response variable, MEDV. Finally, a word about the sign of the coefficients: LSTAT refers to the percentage of low-income households in the neighborhood. A lower LSTAT is correlated with higher median home price, and this is the reason for the negative coefficient on LSTAT.

Step 4: Application to Unseen Test Data

We are now ready to deploy this model against the "unseen" data that was created at the beginning of this section using the second *Filter Examples* operator (Figure 5.2). We need to add a new *Set Role* operator, select MEDV under parameters and set it to target role "prediction" from the pull-down menu. Add another *Apply Model* operator and connect the output of *Set Role* to its "unl" or unlabeled port; additionally connect the output "mod" from the Validation process to the input "mod" or model port of the new *Apply Model*. What we have done is to change the attribute MEDV from the unseen set of 56 examples to a "prediction." When we apply the model to this example set, we will be able to compare the prediction (MEDV) values to the original MEDV values (which exist in our set) to test how well our model would behave on new data. The difference between prediction (MEDV) and MEDV is termed "residual." Figure 5.10 shows one way to quickly check the residuals for our model application. We would need a *Rename* operator to change the name of "prediction (MEDV)" to "predictedMEDV" to avoid confusing RapidMiner when we use the next operator, *Generate Attributes*, to calculate residuals (the reader must try without using the *Rename* operator to understand this issue as it can pop up in other instances where *Generate Attributes* is used). Figure 5.11 shows the

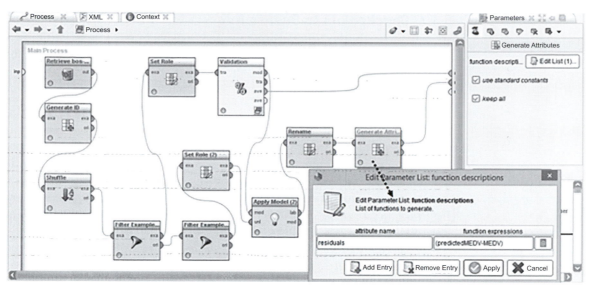

FIGURE 5.10

Setting up a process to do the comparison between the unseen data and the model predicted values.

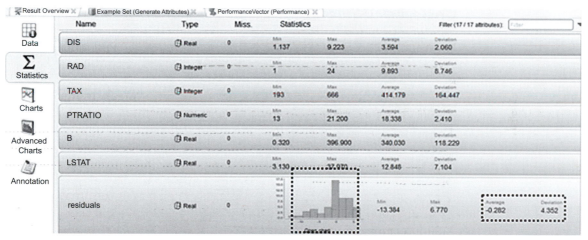

FIGURE 5.11

Statistics of the residuals for the unseen data show that some model optimization may be necessary.

statistics for this new attribute "residuals" which indicate that the mean is close to 0 (−0.275) but the standard deviation (and hence variance) at 4.350 is not quite small. The histogram also seems to indicate that the residuals are not quite normally distributed, which would be another motivation to continue to improve the model.

5.1.4 Checkpoints to Ensure Regression Model Validity

We will close this section on linear regression by briefly discussing several checkpoints to ensure that models are valid. This is a very critical step in the analytics process because all modeling follows the GIGO dictum of "garbage in, garbage out." It is incumbent upon the analyst to ensure these checks are completed.

Checkpoint 1: One of the first checkpoints to consider before accepting any regression model is to quantify the R^2, which is also known as the "coefficient of determination." R^2 effectively explains how much variability in the dependent variable is explained by the independent variables (Black, 2008). *In most cases of linear regression the R2 value lies between 0 and 1. The ideal range for r2 varies across applications; for example, in social and behavioral science models typically low values are acceptable. Generally, very low values (~ < 0.2) indicate that the variables in your model do not explain the outcome satisfactorily.* A word of caution about overemphasizing the value of R^2: When the intercept is set to zero (in RapidMiner, when you uncheck "use bias," Figure 5.5), R^2 values tend to be inflated because of the manner in which they are calculated. In such situations where you are required to have a zero intercept, it makes sense to use other checks such as the mean and variance of the residuals.

Checkpoint 2: This brings us to the next check, which is to ensure that all error terms in the model are normally distributed. To do this check in RapidMiner, we could have generated a new attribute called "error," which is the difference between the predicted MEDV and the actual MEDV in the test data set. This can be done using the *Generate Attributes* operator. This is what we did in step 5 in the last section. Passing checks 1 and 2 will ensure that the independent and dependent variable are related. However this does not imply that the independent variable is the cause and the dependent is the effect. Remember that *correlation is not causation*!

Checkpoint 3: Highly nonlinear relationships will result in simple regression models failing the above checks. However, this does not mean that the two variables are not related. In such cases it may become necessary to resort to somewhat more advanced analytical methods to test the relationship. This is best described and motivated by Anscombe's quartet, presented in Chapter 3 Data Exploration.

5.2 LOGISTIC REGRESSION

From a historical perspective, there are two main classes of predictive analytics techniques: those that evolved (Cramer, 2002) from statistics (such as regression) and those that emerged from a blend of statistics, computer science, and mathematics (such as classification trees). Logistic regression arose in the mid-twentieth century as a result of the simultaneous development of the concept of the *logit* in the field of biometrics and the advent of the digital computer, which made computations of such terms easy. So to understand logistic regression, we need to explore the logit concept first. The chart in Figure 5.12, adapted from data shown in Cramer (2002) shows the evolving trend from initial acceptance of the logit concept in the mid-1950s to the surge in references to this concept toward the latter half of the twentieh century. The chart is an indicator of how important logistic regression has become over the last few decades in a variety of scientific and business applications.

5.2.1 A Simple Explanation of Logistic Regression

To introduce the logit, we will consider a simple example. Recall that linear regression is the process of finding a function to fit the x's that vary linearly with y with the objective of being able to use the function as a model for prediction. The key assumptions here are that both the predictor

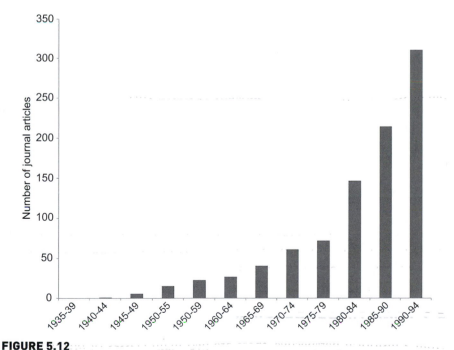

FIGURE 5.12
Growth of logistic regression applications in statistical research.

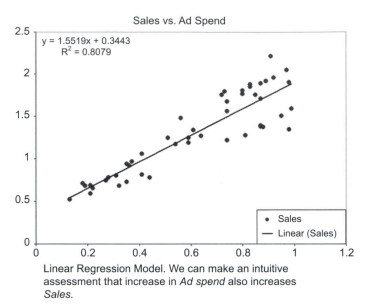

Linear Regression Model. We can make an intuitive assessment that increase in *Ad spend* also increases *Sales.*

FIGURE 5.13

Goal of linear regression.

and target variables are continuous, as seen in the chart in Figure 5.13. Intuitively, one can state that when x increases, y increases along the slope of the line.

What happens if the target variable is not continuous? Suppose our target variable is the response to advertisement campaigns—if more than a threshold number of customers buy for example, then we consider the response to be 1; if not the response is 0. In this case, the target (y) variable is discrete (as in Figure 5.14); the straight line is no longer a fit as seen in the chart. Although we can still estimate—approximately—that when x (advertising spend) increases, y (response or no response to a mailing campaign) also increases, there is no gradual transition; the y value abruptly jumps from one binary outcome to the other. Thus the straight line is a poor fit for this data.

On the other hand, take a look at the S-shaped curve in Figure 5.15. This is certainly a better fit for the data shown. If we then know the equation to this "sigmoid" curve, we can use it as effectively as we used the straight line in the case of linear regression.

Logistic regression is thus the process of obtaining an appropriate nonlinear curve to fit the data when the target variable is discrete. How is the sigmoid curve obtained? How does it relate to the predictors?

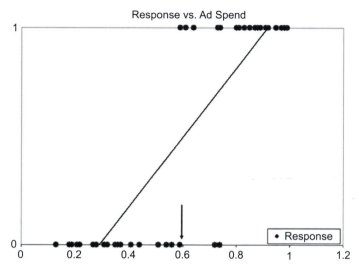

Linear Fit for a Binary outcome: Although we can
make an intuitive assessment that increase in *Ad spend*
increases *Response*, the switch is abrupt - around 0.6.
Using the straight line, we cannot really predict outcome.

FIGURE 5.14

Fitting a linear model to discrete data.

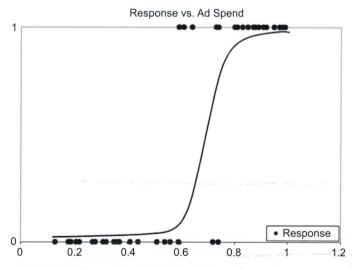

Logistic Regression Model. The S-shaped curve is
clearly a better fit for *most* of the data. we can state *Ad
spend* increases *Sales,* **and** we may also be able to predict
using this model.

FIGURE 5.15

Fitting a nonlinear curve to discrete data.

5.2.2 How It Works

Let us reexamine the dependent variable, y. If it is binomial, that is, it can take on only two values (yes/no, pass/fail, respond/does not respond, and so on), then we can encode y to assume only two values: 1 or 0. Our challenge is to find an equation that functionally connects the predictors, x, to the outcome y where y can only take on two values: 0 or 1. However ,the predictors themselves may have no restrictions: they could be continuous or categorical. Therefore, the functional range of these unrestricted predictors is likely to be also unrestricted (between −∞ to +∞). To overcome this problem, we must map the continuous function to a discrete function. This is what the logit helps us to achieve.

How Does Logistic Regression Find the Sigmoid Curve?

As we observed in Equation 5.1, a straight line can be depicted by only two parameters: the slope (b_1) and the intercept (b_0). The way in which x's and y are related to each other can be easily specified by b_0 and b_1. However an S-shaped curve is a much more complex shape and representing it parametrically is not as straightforward. So how does one find the mathematical parameters to relate the x's to the y?

It turns out that if we transform the target variable y to the *logarithm of the odds of y*, then the *transformed* target variable is *linearly* related to the predictors, x. In most cases where we need to use logistic regression, the y is usually a yes/no type of response. This is usually interpreted as the probability of an event happening (y = 1) or not happening (y = 0). Let us deconstruct this as follows:

- If y is an event (response, pass/fail, etc.),
- and p is the probability of the event happening (y = 1),
- then (1 − p) is the probability of the event *not* happening (y = 0),
- and p/(1 − p) are the *odds* of the event happening.

The logarithm of the odds, log (p/1 − p) is linear in the predictors, X, and log (p/1 − p) or the log of the odds is called the *logit function*.

We can express the logit as a linear function of the predictors X, similar to the linear regression model shown in Equation 5.1 as

$$logit = \log p/(1-p) = b_0 x + b_1 \tag{5.7}$$

For a more general case, involving multiple independent variables, x, we have

$$logit = b_0 + b_1 x_1 + b_2 x_2 + \ldots + b_n x_n \tag{5.8}$$

The logit can take any value from $-\infty$ to $+\infty$. For each row of predictors in a data set, we can now compute the logit. From the logit, it is easy to then compute the probability of the response y (occurring or not occurring) as seen below:

$$p = e^{logit}/(1 + e^{logit}) \tag{5.9}$$

The logistic regression model from Equation 5.8 ultimately delivers the probability of y occurring (i.e., y = 1), given specific value(s) of X via Equation 5.9. In that context, a good definition of logistic regression is that it is a *mathematical modeling approach in which a best-fitting, yet least-restrictive model is selected to describe the relationship between several independent explanatory variables and a dependent binomial response variable*. It is least restrictive because the right side of Equation 5.8 can assume any value from $-\infty$ to $+\infty$. Cramer (2002) provides more background on the history of the logit function.

From the data given we know the x's and using Equations 5.8 and 5.9 we can compute the p for any given x. But to do that, we first need to determine the coefficients, b, in Equation 5.8. How is this done? Let us assume that we start out with a trial of values for b. Given a training data sample, we can compute the following quantity:

$$p^y * (1 - p)^{(1 - y)}$$

where y is our original outcome variable (which can take on 0 or 1) and p is the probability estimated by the logit equation (Equation 5.9). For a specific training sample, if the actual outcome was y = 0 and our model estimate of p was high (say 0.9), i.e., the model was "wrong," then this quantity reduces to 0.1. If the model estimate of probability was low (say 0.1), i.e., the model was "good," then this quantity increases to 0.9. Therefore, this quantity, which is a simplified form of a *likelihood* function, is *maximized for good estimates* and *minimized for poor estimates*. If we compute a summation of the simplified likelihood function across *all* the training data samples, then a high value indicates a good model (or good fit) and vice versa.

In reality, nonlinear optimization techniques are used (methods such as a generalized reduced gradient search) to search for the coefficients, b, with the objective of maximizing the likelihood of correct estimation (or $p^y * (1 - p)^{(1 - y)}$, summed over all training samples). More sophisticated formulations of likelihood estimators are used in practice (Eliason, 1993). Assuming we have used a software package like RapidMiner to perform this optimization to generate a model, let us examine how to interpret and apply the model. In the next section, we will walk through a step-by-step process to build the model using RapidMiner.

A SIMPLE BUT TRAGIC EXAMPLE

In the 1912 shipwreck of the HMS Titanic, hundreds of people perished as the ship struck an iceberg in the North Atlantic (Hinde, 1998). When we dispassionately analyze the data, we see a couple of basic patterns emerge. 75% of the women and 63% of first class passengers survived. If a passenger was a woman and if she traveled first class, her probability of survival was 97%! The scatterplot in Figure 5.16 below depicts this in an easy to understand way (see the bottom right cluster).

A data mining competition used the information from this event and challenged analysts to develop an algorithm that could classify the passenger list into survivors and nonsurvivors (see http://www.kaggle.com/c/titanic-gettingStarted). We use the training data set provided there as an example[3] to demonstrate how logistic regression could be employed to make this prediction and also to interpret the coefficients from the model.

Table 5.3 shows part of a reduced data set consisting only of three variables: travel class of the passenger (pclass = 1st, 2nd, or 3rd), sex of the passenger (0 for male and 1 for female), and the label variable "survived" (true or false). When we fit a logistic regression model to this data consisting of 891 samples, we get the following equation for predicting the class "survived = false" (the details of a generic setup process will be described in the next section):

$$logit = -0.6503 - 2.6417 * sex + 0.9595 * pclass \qquad (5.10)$$

Comparing this to Equation 5.8, we see that b_0 = −0.6503, b_1 = −2.6417, and b_2 = 0.9595. How do we interpret these coefficients? In order to do this, we need to recall Equation 5.9,

$$p = e^{logit}/(1 + e^{logit})$$

which indicates that as logit increases to a large positive quantity, the probability that the passenger did not survive (survived = false) approaches 1. More specifically, when logit approaches −∞, p approaches 0 and when logit approaches +∞, p approaches 1. The negative coefficient

on variable "sex" indicates that this probability reduces for females (sex = 1) and the positive coefficient on variable p indicates that the probability of not surviving (survived = false) increases the higher the *number* of the travel class. This verifies the intuitive understanding that was provided by the scatterplot shown in Figure 5.16.

We can also examine the "odds" form of the logistic regression model, which is given below:

$$odds\ (survived = false)\ = e^{-0.6503} * 2.6103^{pclass} * 0.0712^{sex}$$
(5.11)

Recall that logit is simply given by log(odds) and we are essentially dealing with the same equation as Equation 5.10. A key fact to observe is that a positive coefficient in the logit model translates into a coefficient higher than 1 in the odds model (the number 2.6103 in the above equation is $e^{0.9595}$ and 0.0712 is $e^{-2.6417}$) and a negative coefficient in the logit model translates into coefficients smaller than 1 in the odds model. Again it is clear that odds of not surviving increases with travel class and reduces with gender = female.

An *odds ratio analysis* will reveal the value of computing the results in this format. Consider a female passenger (sex = 1). We can calculate the survivability for this passenger if she was in 1st class (pclass = 1) versus if she was in 2nd class as an odds ratio:

$$odds\ (survived = false\ 2nd\ class)\ /odds\ (survived = false\ 1st\ class)\ = 2.6103\hat{\ }2/2.6103\hat{\ }1 = 2.6103$$

Based on the Titanic data set, the odds that a female passenger would not survive if she was in 2nd class increases by a factor of 2.6 compared to her odds if she was in 1st class. Similarly the odds that a female passenger would not survive increases by nearly seven times if she was in 3rd class! In the next section, we discuss the mechanics of logistic regression and also the process of implementing a simple analysis using RapidMiner.

---

[3]All data sets are made available through the companion site for this book.

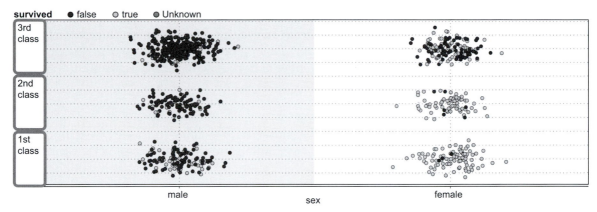

FIGURE 5.16

Probability of survival in the Titanic wreck based on gender and travel class.

Table 5.3 Portion of the Data Set from the Titanic Example

pclass	sex	survived?
3.0	male	0.0
1.0	female	1.0
3.0	female	1.0
1.0	female	1.0
3.0	male	0.0
3.0	male	0.0
1.0	male	0.0
3.0	male	0.0
3.0	female	1.0
2.0	female	1.0
3.0	female	1.0
1.0	female	1.0
3.0	male	0.0
3.0	male	0.0
3.0	female	0.0
2.0	female	1.0
3.0	male	0.0

5.2.3 How to Implement

The data we used comes from an example[4] for a credit scoring exercise. The objective is to predict DEFAULT (Y or N) based on two predictors: loan age (business age) and number of days of delinquency. There are 100 samples Table 5.4.

Step 1: Data Preparation

Load the spreadsheet into RapidMiner. Remember to set the DEFAULT column as "Label." Split the data into training and test samples using the *Split Validation* operator.

Step 2: Modeling Operator and Parameters

Add the *Logistic Regression* operator in the "training" subprocess of the *Split Validation* operator. Add the *Apply Model* operator in the "testing" subprocess of the *Split Validation* operator. Just use default parameter values. Add the *Performance (Binominal)* evaluation operator in the "testing" subprocess of *Split Validation* operator. Check the Accuracy, AUC, Precision, and Recall boxes in the parameter settings. Connect all ports as shown in Figure 5.17.

Step 3: Execution and Interpretation

Run the model and view results. In particular check for the kernel model, which shows the coefficients for the two predictors and the intercept. The bias (offset) is −1.820 and the coefficients are given by: w[BUSAGE]=0.592 and

Table 5.4 A Sample From the Loan Default Dataset

[BUSAGE]	[DAYSDELQ]	[DEFAULT]
87.0	2.0	N
89.0	2.0	N
90.0	2.0	N
90.0	2.0	N
101.0	2.0	N
110.0	2.0	N
115.0	2.0	N
115.0	2.0	N
115.0	2.0	N
117.0	2.0	N

---

[4]http://chem-eng.utoronto.ca/~datamining/dmc/datasets/credit_scoring.txt. All data sets are available at the companion site.

w[DAYSDELQ]=2.045. Also check the confusion matrix for Accuracy, Precision, and Recall and finally view the ROC curves and check the area under the curve or AUC. Chapter 8 Model Evaluation provides further details on these important performance measures.

The accuracy of the model based on the 30% testing sample is 83%. The ROC curves have an AUC of 0.863. The next step would be to review the kernel model and prepare for deploying this model. Are these numbers acceptable? In particular, pay attention to the class recall (bottom row of the confusion matrix in Figure 5.18). The model is quite accurate in predicting if someone is NOT a defaulter (91.3%), however its performance when it comes to identifying if someone IS a defaulter is questionable. For most predictive applications, the cost of wrong class predictions is not uniform. That is, a false positive (in the above case identifying someone as a defaulter, when they are

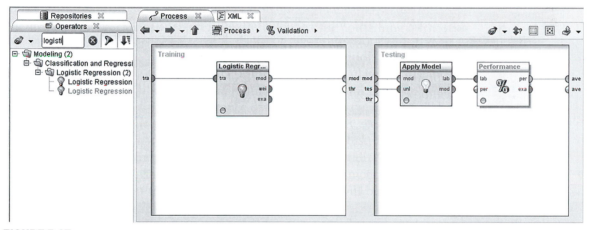

FIGURE 5.17
Setting up the RapidMiner process for a logistic regression model.

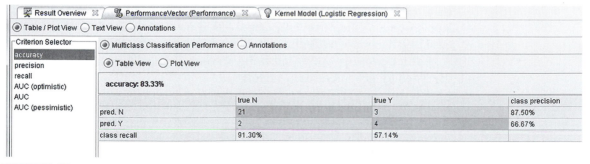

FIGURE 5.18
Confusion matrix for the testing sample.

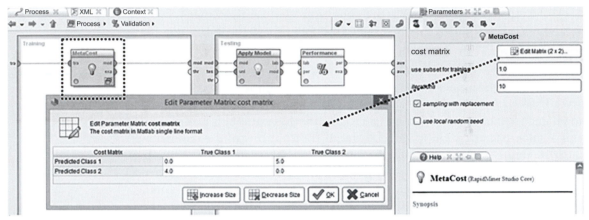

FIGURE 5.19
Configuring the MetaCost operator to improve class recall performance.

accuracy: 83.33%			
	true N	true Y	class precision
pred. N	20	2	90.91%
pred. Y	3	5	62.50%
class recall	86.96%	71.43%	

FIGURE 5.20
Improved classification performance with the usage of MetaCost operator.

not) may be less expensive than a false negative (in this above case identi-fying someone as a nondefaulter, when they actually are). There are ways to weight the cost of misclassification, and RapidMiner allows this thorugh use of the *MetaCost* operator.

Step 4: Using MetaCost

Nest the *Logistic Regression* operator inside a *MetaCost* operator to improve class recall. The *MetaCost* operator is now placed inside *Split Validation* oper-ator. Configure the *MetaCost* operator as shown in Figure 5.19. Notice that false negatives have twice the cost of false positives. The actual values of these costs can be further optimized using an optimization loop—optimization is discussed for general cases in Chapter 13.

When this process is run, the new confusion matrix that results is shown in Figure 5.20. The overall accuracy has not changed much. Note that while the class recall for the Default = Yes class has increased from 57% to 71%, but this has come at the price of reducing the class recall for Default = No from 91% to 87%. Is this acceptable? Again the answer to this comes from exam-ining the actual business costs. More details about interpreting the confusion

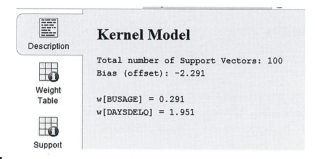

FIGURE 5.21
Default logistic regression model in RapidMiner is based on SVM.

matrix and evaluating the performance of classification models is provided in Chapter 8 Model Evaluation.

Step 5: Applying the Model to an Unseen Data Set

In RapidMiner, logistic regression is calculated by creating a support vector machine (SVM) with a modified loss function (Figure 5.21). SVMs were introduced in Chapter 4 on classification. That's the reason why you see support vectors at all (if you want a "standard" logistic regression, you may use the W-Logistic from the Weka extension to RapidMiner). Weka is another open source implementation of data mining algorithms (see http://www.cs.waikato.ac.nz/ml/weka/) and many of these implementations are available within RapidMiner. The Titanic example was analyzed using the *W-logistic* operator and it is highly recommended for applications where interpreting coefficients is valuable. Furthermore, the *Weka* operator may be faster for certain applications than the native SVM-based RapidMiner implementation. Refer to Chapter 4 for details on the mechanics and interpretation of an SVM model.

5.2.4 Summary Points for Logistic Regression Modeling

- Logistic regression can be considered equivalent to using linear regression for situations where when the target (or dependent) variable is discrete, i.e., not continuous. In principle, the response variable or label is binomial. A binomial response variable has two categories: Yes/No, Accept/Not Accept, Default/Not Default, and so on. Logistic regression is ideally suited for business analytics applications where the target variable is a binary decision (fail/pass, response/no response, etc). In RapidMiner, such variables are called "binominal."
- Logistic regression comes from the concept of the "logit." The logit is the logarithm of the odds of the response, y, expressed as a function of independent or predictor variables, x, and a constant term. That is, for example, $\log (\text{odds of } y = \text{Yes}) = b_1 x + b_0$.

- The above logit gives the odds of the "Yes" event, however if we want probabilities, we need to use the transformed equation below:

$$p\,(y = \text{"Yes"}) = 1/(1 + e^{(-b1_x - b_0)})$$

- The predictors can be either numerical or categorical for standard logistic regression. However in RapidMiner, the predictors can only be numerical, because it is based on the SVM formulation.

CONCLUSION

This chapter explored two of the most common function-fitting methods. Function-fitting methods are one of the earliest predictive modeling techniques based on the concept of supervised learning. The multiple linear regression model works with numeric predictors and a numeric label and is thus one of the go-to methods for numeric prediction tasks. The logistic regression model works with numeric or categorical predictors and a categorical (typically, binomial) label. We explained how a simple linear regression model is developed using the methods of calculus and discussed how feature selection impacts the coefficients of a model. We explained how to interpret the significance of the coefficients using the t-stat and p-values and finally laid down several checkpoints one must follow to build good quality models. We then introduced logistic regression by comparing the similar structural nature of the two function-fitting methods. We discussed how a sigmoid curve can better fit predictors to a binomial label and introduced the concept of logit, which enables us to transform a complex function into a more recognizable linear form. We discussed how the coefficients of logistic regression can be interpreted and how to measure and improve the classification performance of the model. We finally ended the section by pointing out the differences between the implementation of standard logistic regression and RapidMiner's version.

REFERENCES

Black, K. (2008). Multiple Regression Analysis. In K. Black (Ed.), *Business Statistics* (pp. 601–610). Hoboken: John Wiley and Sons.

Cramer, J. (2002). The origins of logistic regression. *Tinbergen Institute Discussion Paper*, 1–15.

Eliason, S. (1993). *Maximum Likelihood Estimation: Logic and Practice*. Newbury Park, CA: Sage Publishers.

Fletcher, R. A. (1963). A Rapidly Convergent Descent Method for Minimization. *The Computer Journal*, 163–168.

Galton, F. (1888). Co-relations and their measurement, chiefly from anthropometric data. *Proceedings of the Royal Society of London*, 135–145.

Germano, T. (n.d.). Retrieved from http://davis.wpi.edu/~matt/courses/soms/.

Harrison, D. A. (1978). Hedonic prices and the demand for clean air. *J. Environ. Economics & Management*, 81–102.

Hinde, P. (1998). Encyclopedia Titanica. Retrieved from http://www.encyclopedia-titanica.org/.

International Monetary Fund. (n.d.). Retrieved from http://www.imf.org/external/pubs/ft/weo/2012/02/weodata/index.aspx.

Marquardt, D. (1963). An Algorithm for Least-Squares Etimation of Nonlinear Parameters. *Journal of the Society for Industrial and Applied Mathematics*, 431–441.

Stigler, S. (1999). *Statistics on the Table: The History of Statistical Concepts and Methods.* Cambridge: Harvard University Press.

Telecom, F. (n.d.). Retrieved from http://perso.rd.francetelecom.fr/lemaire/cours/AnalyseExploratoireKohonen.pdf

CHAPTER 6

Association Analysis

The beer and diaper association story in Analytics circle is (urban) legendary (Power, 2002). There are many variations of this story, but the basic idea is that a supermarket company discovered that customers who buy diapers also tend to buy beer. The beer and diaper relationship heralded what unusual, unknown, and quirky nuggets can be learned from the purchase transaction data of a supermarket. How did the supermarket determine such a relationship between products existed? Answer: data mining. Specifically, association analysis.

Association analysis measures the strength of co-occurrence between one item and another. The objective of this class of data mining algorithms is not to predict an occurrence of an item, like classification or regression do, but to find usable patterns in the co-occurrences of the items. Association rules learning is a branch of an unsupervised learning process that discovers hidden patterns in data, in the form of easily recognizable *rules*.

Association algorithms are widely used in retail analysis of transactions, recommendation engines, and online clickstream analysis across web pages. One of the popular applications of this technique is called *market basket analysis*, which finds co-occurrences of one retail item with another item within the same retail purchase transaction (Agrawal et al., 1993). If patterns within data tell us that baby formula and diapers are usually purchased together in the same transaction, a retailer can take advantage of this association for bundle pricing, product placement, and even shelf space optimization within the store layout. Similarly, in an online business setting, this information can be leveraged for real-time cross selling, recommendations, cart offers and post purchase marketing strategies. In the case of retail business, many of the association rules results are commonly known, for example a burger with fries or baby formula with diapers; however, uncommon relationships are the prized discoveries, the ones businesses can take advantage of. The downside is association analysis may also yield spurious relationships between items. When dealing with data containing billions of transactions, we would find transactions with all kinds of possibilities with strange combinations of item sets (e.g., nicotine patch and cigarettes). It takes analytical skill and business knowledge to successfully apply the outcome of association

195

analysis. The model outcome of an association analysis can be represented as a set of rules, like the one below:

{Item A} -> {Item B}

This rule indicates that based on the history of all the transactions, if Item A is found in a transaction or a basket, there is a strong propensity of occurrence of Item B within the *same* transaction. Here, Item A is the *antecedent* or *premise* of the rule and Item B is *consequent* or *conclusion* of the rule. The antecedent and consequent of the rule can contain more than one item, like {Item A and Item C}. To mine these kinds of rules from the data, we would need to analyze all previous customer purchase transactions. In a retail business, there would be millions of transactions made in a day with thousands of Stock Keeping Units (SKU), which are unique identifiers for a product or an item sold and stocked. Hence, two of the key considerations of association analysis are computational time and resources. However, over the last two decades newer and more efficient algorithms have been developed to mitigate this problem.

CROSS SELLING: CUSTOMERS WHO BOUGHT THIS ALSO BOUGHT...

Consider an e-commerce website that sells a large selection of products online. One of the objectives in managing e-commerce business is to increase the average order value of the visit. Optimizing order size is even more critical when the businesses pay for acquisition traffic through search engine marketing, online advertisements, and affiliate marketing. Businesses attempt to increase average order value by cross-selling and up-selling relevant products to the customer, many times based on what they have purchased or are currently purchasing in the current transaction (a common fast-food equivalent: "Do you want fries with the burger?"). Businesses need to be careful by weighing the benefit of suggesting an extremely relevant product against the risk of irritating a customer who is already making a transaction. In a business where there are limited products (e.g., fast-food industry), cross-selling a product with another product is straightforward and is quite inherent in the business. But, when the number of unique products runs in thousands and millions, determining a set of *affinity products* when customers are looking at a product is quite a tricky problem.

To better learn about product affinity, we turn to purchase history data. The information on how one product creates affinity to another product relies on the fact that both the products appear in the same transaction. If two products are bought together, then we can speculate that the necessity of those products arise in the same time frame for the customer. If the two products are bought together many times, by a large number of customers, then there is definitely an affinity pattern within these products. In a new later transaction, if a customer picks one of those affinity products, then there is an increased likelihood that the other product will be picked by the customer, in the same transaction.

The key input for affinity analysis is a list of past transactions with product information. Based on the analysis of these transactions, we can determine what the most frequent product pairs are. We need to define a threshold for "frequent" because a few appearances of a product pair doesn't qualify as a pattern. The result of the affinity analysis is a rule set that says, "If product A is purchased, there is an increased likelihood that product B will be purchased in the same transaction." This rule set can be leveraged to provide cross sell recommendations on the product page of product A. Affinity analysis is the concept behind the web widgets which state, "Customers who bought this also bought..."

6.1 CONCEPTS OF MINING ASSOCIATION RULES

Basic association analysis just deals with the *occurrence* of one item with another. More complicated analysis can take into consideration the quantity of occurrence, price, and sequence of occurrence, etc. The method for finding association rules through data mining involves the following sequential steps:

Step 1: Prepare the data in transaction format. An association algorithm needs input data to be formatted in a particular format.

Step 2: Short-list frequently occurring *item sets*. Item sets are combination of items. An association algorithm limits the analysis to the most frequently occurring items, so the final rule set extracted in next step is more meaningful.

Step 3: Generate *relevant* association rules from item sets. Finally, the algorithm generates and filters the rules based on the interest measure.

To start with, let's consider a media website, like BBC or Yahoo News, with categories such as news, politics, finance, entertainment, sports, and arts. A session or transaction in this example is one visit for the website, where the same user accesses content from different categories, within a certain session period. A new session usually starts after 30 minutes of inactivity. Sessions are very much similar to transactions in a traditional brick and mortar model and the pages accessed can be related to items purchased. In online news sites, items are *visits* to the categories such as News, Finance, Entertainment, Sports, and Arts. We can collect the data as shown in Table 6.1, with a list of sessions and media categories accessed during a given session. Our objective in this data mining task is to find associations between media categories.

For association analysis of these media categories, we would need a data set in a particular transaction format. To get started with association analysis, it would be helpful to pivot the data in the format shown in Table 6.2.

This binary format indicates the presence or absence of article categories and ignores qualities such as minutes spent viewing or the sequence of access, which can be important in certain sequence analyses. For now, we are focusing on basic association analysis and we shall review the terminologies used in association rules.

Table 6.1

Session ID	List of media categories accessed
1	{News, Finance}
2	{News, Finance}
3	{Sports, Finance, News}
4	{Arts}
5	{Sports, News, Finance}
6	{News, Arts, Entertainment}

Table 6.2 Clickstream Data Set

Session ID	News	Finance	Entertainment	Sports	Arts
1	1	1	0	0	0
2	1	1	0	0	0
3	1	1	0	1	0
4	0	0	0	0	1
5	1	1	0	1	0
6	1	0	1	0	1

6.1.1 Item Sets

In the examples of association rules we discussed so far, the antecedent and consequent of the rules had only one item. But, as mentioned before, they can involve multiple items. For example a rule can be of the following sort:

{News, Finance} -> {Sports}

This rule implies, if users have accessed news and finance in the same session, there is a high likelihood that they would also access sports articles, based on historical transactions. The combination of news and finance item is called an *item set*. An item set can occur either in the antecedent or in the consequent portion of the rule; however, both sets should be disjointed, which means there should not be any common item on both sides of the rules. Obviously, there is no practical relevance for the rules like "News and Finance users are most likely to visit News and Sports page." Instead, rules like "If users visited Finance page they are more likely to visit News and Sports page" make more sense. Introduction of the item set with more than one item greatly increases the permutations of rules to be considered and tested for the strength of relationships.

The strength of an association rule is commonly quantified by the *support* and *confidence* measures of a rule. There are few more quantifications like *lift* and *conviction* measures that can be used in special cases. All these measures are based on the relative frequency of occurrences of a particular item set in the transactions data set used for training. Hence, it is important that the training set used for rule generation is unbiased and truly represents the universe of transactions. We will go through each of these frequency metrics in the following sections.

Support

The *support of an item* is simply the relative frequency of occurrence of an item set in the transaction set. In the data set shown in Table 6.2, support of {News} is five out of six transactions, 5/6 = 0.83. Similarly, support of an item set

{News, Finance} is the co-occurrence of both news and finance in a transaction with respect to all the transactions:

Support({News}) = 5/6 = 0.83
Support({News, Finance}) = 4/6 = 0.67
Support({Sports}) = 2/6 = 0.33

The *support of a rule* is a measure of how all the items in a rule are represented in overall transactions. For example, in the rule {News}->{Sports}, News and Sports occur in two of six transactions and hence support for the rule {News} -> {Sports} is 0.33. The support measure for a rule indicates whether a rule is worth considering. Since the support measure favors the items where there is high occurrence, it uncovers the patterns that are worth taking advantage of and investigating. This is particularly interesting for businesses because leveraging patterns in high volume items leads to more incremental revenue. Rules with low support have either infrequently occurring items or an item relationship occurs just by chance, which may yield spurious rules. In association analysis, a threshold of support is specified to filter out infrequent rules. Any rule that exceeds the support threshold is then considered for further analysis.

Confidence

The *confidence of a rule* measures the likelihood of occurrence of the consequent of the rule out of all the transactions that contain the antecedent of the rule. Confidence provides the reliability measure of the rule. Confidence of the rule (X -> Y) is calculated by

$$\text{Confidence } (X \to Y) = \frac{\text{Support}(X \cup Y)}{\text{Support } (X)} \tag{6.1}$$

In the case of the rule {News, Finance} -> {Sports}, the question that the confidence measure answers is, if an transaction has both News and Finance, what is the likelihood of seeing Sports in it?

$$\text{Confidence } (\{News, Finance\} \to \{Sports\}) = \frac{Support\ (\{News,\ Finance,\ Sports\})}{Support\ (\{News,\ Finance\})}$$
$$= \frac{2/6}{4/6}$$
$$= 0.5$$

Half of the transactions that contain News and Finance also contain Sports. This means 50% of users who visit the news and finance pages also visit sports pages.

Lift

Though confidence of the rule is widely used, the frequency of occurrence of a rule consequent (conclusion) is largely ignored. In some transaction item sets, this can provide spurious scrupulous rule sets because of the presence of infrequent items in the rule consequent. To solve this, we can have the support of a consequent in the denominator of a confidence calculation. This measure is called the *lift of the rule*. The lift of the rule can be calculated by

$$\text{Lift}(X\text{->}Y) = \frac{Support\,(X\cup Y)}{Support\,(X)*Support\,(Y)} \qquad (6.2)$$

In the case of our example:

$$\text{Lift}(\{\text{News, Finance}\}\text{->}\{\text{Sports}\}) = \frac{Support\,(X\cup Y)}{Support\,(X)*Support\,(Y)}$$

$$= \frac{0.333}{0.667*0.33} = 1.5$$

Lift is the ratio of the observed support of {News + Finance} and {Sports} with what is expected if {News + Finance} and {Sports} usage were completely independent. Lift values closer to 1 mean the antecedent and consequent of the rules are independent and the rule is not interesting. The higher the value of lift, the more interesting the rules are.

Conviction

The *conviction of the rule* X -> Y is the ratio of the expected frequency of X occurring in spite of Y and the observed frequency of incorrect predictions. Conviction takes into account the direction of the rule. The conviction of (X -> Y) is not the same as conviction of (Y -> X). Conviction of a rule (X -> Y) can be calculated by

$$\text{Conviction}(X\text{->}Y) = \frac{1 - Support\,(Y)}{1 - Confidence\,(X \rightarrow Y)} \qquad (6.3)$$

For our example,

$$\text{Conviction}(\{\text{news, finance}\}\text{->}\{\text{sports}\}) = \frac{1-0.33}{1-0.5} = 1.32$$

A conviction of 1.32 means that the rule ({News, Finance} -> {Sports}) would be incorrect 32% more often if the relationship between {News, Finance} and {Sports} is purely random.

6.1.2 The Process of Rule Generation

The process of generating meaningful association rules from the data set can be broken down into two basic tasks.

1. *Finding all frequent item sets.* For an association analysis of n items it is possible to find $2^n - 1$ item sets excluding the null item set. As the number of items increase, there is an exponential increase in the number of item sets. Hence it is critical to set a minimal support threshold to discard less frequently occurring item sets in the transaction

universe. All possible item sets can be expressed in a visual lattice form like the diagram shown in Figure 6.1. In this figure one item {Arts} is excluded from the item set generation. It is not uncommon to exclude items so that the association analysis can be focused on subset of important relevant items. In Supermarket example, some filler items like grocery bag can be excluded from the analysis. An item set tree (or lattice) helps demonstrate the methods to easily find frequent item sets.

2. *Extracting rules from frequent item sets.* For the data set with n items it is possible to find $3^n - 2^{n+1} + 1$ rules (Tan et al., 2005). This step extracts all the rules with a confidence higher than a minimum confidence threshold.

This two-step process generates hundreds of rules even for a small data set with dozens of items. Hence it is important to set a reasonable support and confidence threshold to filter out less frequent and less relevant rules in the search space. The generated rules can also be evaluated with support, confidence, lift,

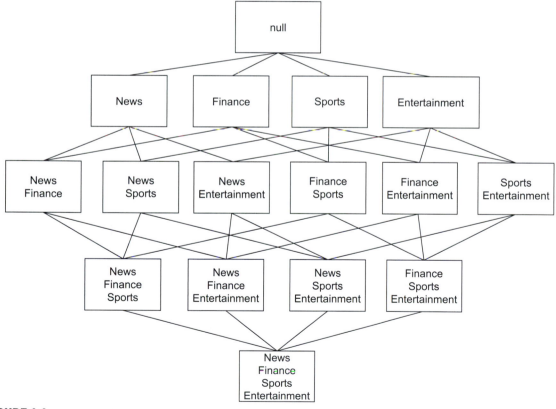

FIGURE 6.1

Item set tree.

and conviction measures. In terms of computational requirements, finding all the frequent item sets above a support threshold is more expensive than extracting the rules. Fortunately, there are some algorithmic approaches to efficiently find the frequent item sets. The Apriori and FP-Growth algorithms are two of the most popular association analysis algorithms.

6.2 APRIORI ALGORITHM

All association rule algorithms should efficiently find the frequent item sets from the universe of all the possible item sets. The Apriori algorithm leverages some simple logical principles on the lattice item sets to reduce the number of item sets to be tested for the support measure (Agrawal & Srikant, 1994). The Apriori principles states that "*If an item set is frequent, then all its subset items will be frequent.*" (Tan et al, 2005). The item set is "frequent" if the support for the item set is more that support threshold.

For example, if the item set {News, Finance, Sports} from the data set shown in Table 6.2 is a frequent item set, that is, its support measure (0.33) is higher

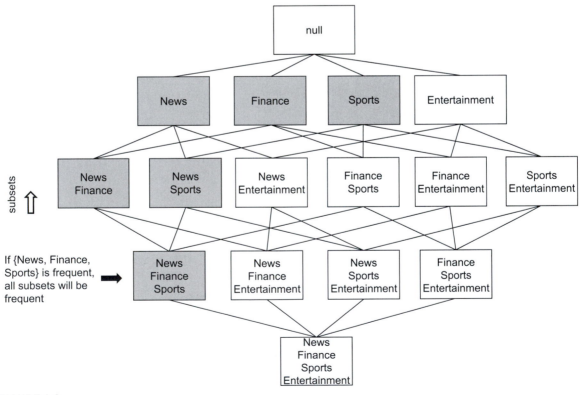

FIGURE 6.2

Frequent item sets using Apriori principle.

than the threshold support measure k (say, 0.25), then all of its subset items or item set will be frequent item sets. Subset item sets will have a support measure higher than or equal to the parent item set. Figure 6.2 shows the application of the Apriori principle in a lattice. The support measures of the subset item sets for {News, Finance, Sports} are

Support {News, Finance, Sports} = 0.33 (above threshold support)
Support {News, Finance} = 0.66
Support {News, Sports} = 0.33
Support {News} = 0.83
Support {Sports} = 0.33
Support {Finance} = 0.66

Conversely, if the item set is infrequent, then all its *supersets* will be infrequent. In this example, support of Entertainment is 0.16, and the support of all the supersets that contain Entertainment as an item will be less than or equal to 0.16, which is infrequent when considering the support threshold of 0.25. Superset exclusion of an infrequent item is shown in Figure 6.3.

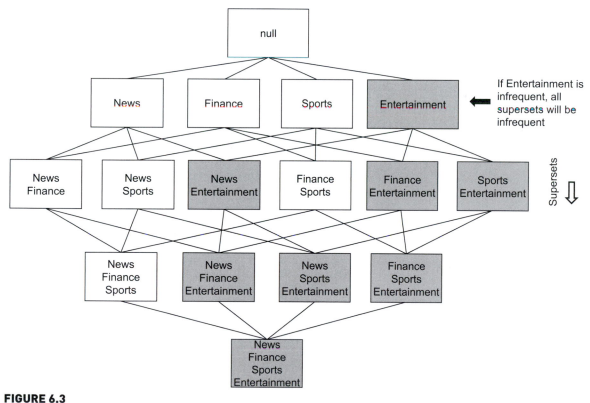

FIGURE 6.3
Frequent item sets using Apriori principle: Exclusion.

Table 6.3 Clickstream Data Set: Condensed Version

Session	News	Finance	Entertainment	Sports
1	1	1	0	0
2	1	1	0	0
3	1	1	0	1
4	0	0	0	0
5	1	1	0	1
6	1	0	1	0

The Apriori principle is helpful because not all item sets have to be considered for a support calculation and tested for the support threshold; hence generation of the frequent item sets can be handled efficiently by eliminating a bunch of item sets that have an infrequent item or item sets (Bodon, 2005).

6.2.1 Frequent Item Set Generation Using the Apriori Principle

Let's consider the data set shown in Table 6.3, which is the condensed version of the example set discussed above. In this data set there are six transactions. If the support threshold is assumed to be 0.25, then we expect all items should appear in at least two out of six transactions.

We can now calculate support count and support for all item set(s). *Support count* is the absolute count of the transactions and support is the ratio of support count to total transaction count. Any one item set below the threshold support count (which is 2 in this example) can be eliminated from further processing. Table 6.4 shows the support count and support calculation for each item. Since {Entertainment} has a support count less than the threshold, it can been eliminated for the next iteration of item set generation. The next step is generating possible two-item set generations for {News}, {Finance}, and {Sports}, which yield three two-item sets. If the {Entertainment} item set is not eliminated, we would obtain six two-item sets. Figure 6.4 shows the visual representation of the item sets with elimination of {Entertainment} item.

This process is continued until all n-item sets are considered from previous sets. At the end, there are seven frequent item sets passing the support threshold. The total possible number of item sets is 15 (= $2^4 - 1$). By eliminating {Entertainment} in the first step, we don't have to generate seven additional item sets that would not pass the support threshold anyway (Witten & Frank, 2005).

Table 6.4 Frequent Item Set Support Calculation

Item	Support Count	Support
{News}	5	0.83
{Finance}	4	0.67
{Entertainment}	1	0.17
{Sports}	2	0.33
Two-Item Sets	**Support Count**	**Support**
{News, Finance}	4	0.67
{News, Sports}	2	0.33
{Finance, Sports}	2	0.33
Three-Item Sets	**Support Count**	**Support**
{News, Finance, Sports}	2	0.33

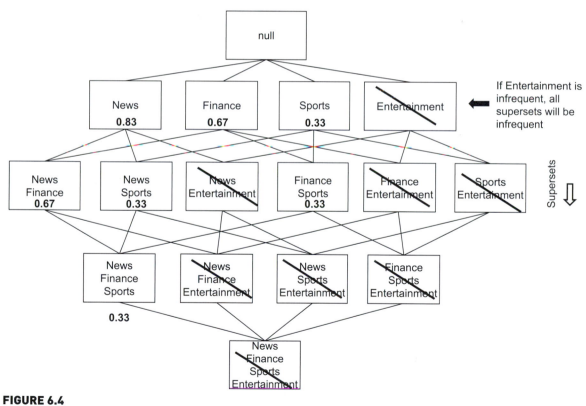

FIGURE 6.4

Frequent item set with support.

6.2.2 Rule Generation

Once the frequent item sets are generated, the next step in association analysis is generating useful rules which have a clear antecedent (premise) and consequent (conclusion), in the format of the following rule:

{Item A} -> {Item B}

The usefulness of the rule can be approximated by an objective measure of interest such as confidence, conviction, or lift. Confidence for the rule is calculated by the support scores of the individual items as given in Equation 6.1. Each frequent item set of n items can generate $2^n - 2$ rules. For example {News, Sports, Finance} can generate rules with the following confidence scores.

Rules and confidence scores

> {News, Sports}->{Finance} – 0.33 / 0.33 = 1.0
> {News, Finance}->{Sports} – 0.33 / 0.67 = 0.5
> {Sports, Finance}->{News} – 0.33 / 0.33 = 1.0
> {News}->{Sports, Finance} – 0.33 / 0.83 = 0.4
> {Sports}->{News, Finance} – 0.33 / 0.33 = 1.0
> {Finance}->{News, Sports} – 0.33 / 0.67 = 0.5

Since all the support scores have already been calculated in the item set generation step, there is no need for another set of computations for calculating confidence. However, it is possible to prune potentially low confidence rules using the same Apriori method. For a given frequent item set {News, Finance, Sports}, if the rule {News, Finance} -> {Sports} is a low confidence rule, then we can conclude any rules within the subset of the antecedent will be a low confidence rule. Hence we can discard all the rules like {News}->{Sports, Finance} and {Finance} -> {News, Sports}, which are in the subsets of the antecedent of the rule. The reason is that all three rules have the same numerator in the confidence score calculation (Equation 6.1), which is 0.33. The denominator calculation depends on the support of the antecedent. Since the support of a subset is always greater or equal to the set, we can conclude all further rules within a subset of an item set in the premises will be a low confidence rule, and hence can be ignored.

All the rules passing a particular confidence threshold are considered for output along with both support and confidence measures. These rules should be further evaluated for rational validity to determine if a useful relationship was uncovered, if there was an occurrence by chance, or if the rule confirms a known intuitive relationship.

6.3 FP-GROWTH ALGORITHM

The Frequent Pattern (FP)-Growth algorithm provides an alternative way of calculating a frequent item set by compressing the transaction records using a special graph data structure called *FP-Tree*. FP-Tree can be thought of as a transformation of the data set into graph format. Rather than the generate and test approach used in Apriori algorithm, FP-Growth first generates the FP-Tree and uses this compressed tree to generate the frequent item sets. The efficiency of the FP-Growth algorithm depends on how much compression can be achieved in generating the FP-Tree (Han, Pei, & Yin, 2000).

6.3.1 Generating the FP-Tree

Consider the data set shown in Table 6.5 containing six transactions of four items—news, finance, sports, and entrainment. To visually represent this data set in a tree diagram (Figure 6.6), we need to transform the list of transactions to a tree map, preserving all the information and representing the *frequent paths*. Let's build the FP-Tree for this data set step by step.

1. The first step is to sort all the items in each transaction in descending order of frequency (or support count). For example, News is the most frequent item and Sports is the least frequent item in the transaction, based on the data in Table 6.5. The third transaction of {Sports, News, Finance} has to be rearranged to {News, Finance, Sports}. This will help to simplify mapping frequent paths in later steps.

2. Once the items within a transaction are rearranged, we can now map the transaction to the FP-Tree. Starting with a null node, the first transaction {News, Finance} can be represented by Figure 6.5. The number within the parenthesis next to the item name is the number of transactions following the path.

3. Since the second transaction {News, Finance} is same as the first one, it follows the same path as first one. In this case, we can just increment the numbers.

4. The third transaction contains {News, Finance, Sports}. The tree is now extended to Sports and the item path count is incremented (Figure 6.6).

5. The fourth transaction only contains the {Sports} item. Since Sports is not preceded by News and Finance, a new path should be created from the null item and the item count should be noted. This node for Sports

Table 6.5 Transactions List: Session and Items

Session	Items
1	{News, Finance}
2	{News, Finance}
3	{News, Finance, Sports}
4	{Sports}
5	{News, Finance, Sports}
6	{News, Entertainment}

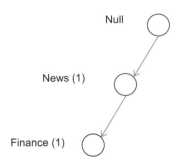

FIGURE 6.5

FP-Tree: Transaction 1.

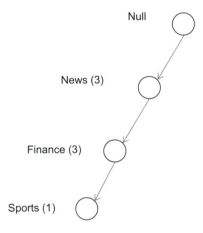

FIGURE 6.6

FP-Tree: Transactions 1, 2, and 3

is different from the Sports node next to Finance (the latter co-occurs with News and Finance). However, since both nodes indicate the same item, they should be linked by a dotted line.

6. This process is continued until all the transactions are scanned. All of the transaction records can be now represented by a compact FP-Tree (Figure 6.7).

The compression of the FP-Tree depends on how frequently a path occurs within a given transaction set. Since the key objective of association analysis is to identify these common paths, the data sets we use from this analysis contain many frequent paths. In the worst case, all transactions contain unique item set paths and there wouldn't be any compression. In that case the rule generation itself would be less meaningful for association analysis.

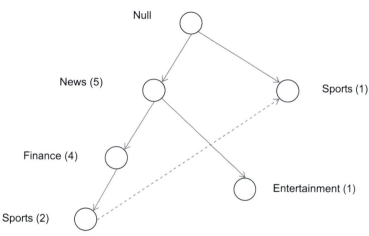

FIGURE 6.7
FP-Tree: Transactions 1 to 6.

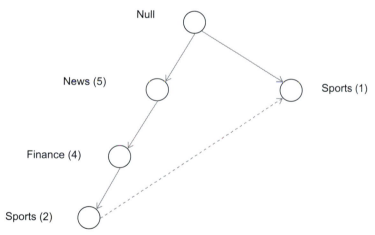

FIGURE 6.8
Trimmed FP-Tree.

6.3.2 Frequent Item Set Generation

Once the transaction set is expressed by a compact FP-Tree, the most frequent item set can be generated from the FP-Tree effectively. To generate the frequent item set, the FP-Growth algorithm adopts a bottoms-up approach of generating all the item sets starting with the least frequent items. Since the structure of the tree is ordered by the support count, the least frequent items can be found in leaves of tree. In Figure 6.8, the least frequent items are {Entertainment} and {Sports}, because the support count is just one transaction. If {Entertainment} is a frequent item

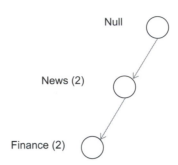

FIGURE 6.9
Conditional FP-Tree.

because the support exceeds the threshold, the algorithm finds all the item sets ending with entertainment, like {Entertainment} and {News, Entertainment}, by following the path from the bottom up. Since the support counts are mapped to the nodes, calculating the support for {News, Entertainment} will be instant. If {Entertainment} is not frequent, the algorithm skips the item and goes with the next item, {Sports}, and finds all possible item sets ending with sports: {Sports}, {Finance, Sports}, {News, Sports}, {News, Finance, Sports}.

Finding the entire item set ending with a particular item number is actually made possible by generating a prefix path and conditional FP-Tree for an item, as shown in Figure 6.9. The prefix path of an item is a subtree with only paths that contain the item of interest. A conditional FP-Tree for an item, say {Sports}, is the similar to the FP-Tree, but with the {Sports} item removed. Based on the conditional FP-Tree, the algorithm repeats the process of finding leaf nodes. Since leaf nodes of the sports conditional tree coexists with {Sports}, the algorithm finds the association with finance and generates {Finance, Sports}.

Rule generation in the FP-Growth algorithm is very similar to the Apriori algorithm. Since the intent is to find frequently occurring items, by definition, many of the transactions should have essentially the same path. Hence, in many practical applications the compaction ratio is very high. In those scenarios, the FP-Growth algorithm provides efficient results. Since the FP-Growth algorithm uses the graphs to map the relationship between frequent items, it has found applications beyond association analysis. It is now applied in research as a preprocessing phase for document clustering, text mining, and sentiment analysis (Akbar & Angryk, 2008). However, in spite of execution differences, both the FP-Growth and Apriori algorithms yield similar results. Rule generation from the frequent item sets is similar to the Apriori algorithm. Even though the concepts and explanation include analyzing graphs and subgraphs, FP-Growth algorithms can be easily ported to programming languages, particularly to SQL and PL/SQL programs on top of relational databases, where the transactions are usually stored (Shang et al., 2004).

6.3.3 How to Implement

The retrieval of association rules from a data set is implemented through the FP-Growth algorithm in RapidMiner. Since the modeling parameters and the result for most of the association algorithms are same, we will focus on the FP-Growth algorithm to observe the inputs, process, and the result of an association analysis implementation.

Step 1: Data Preparation

The Association analysis process expects transactions to be in a particular format. The input grid should have binominal (true or false) data with items in the columns and each transaction as a row. If the data set contains transaction IDs or session IDs, they can either be ignored or tagged as a special attribute in RapidMiner. Data sets in any other format have to be converted to this transactional format using data transformation operators. In this example, we have used the data shown in Table 6.3, with a session ID on each row and content accessed in the columns, indicated by 1 and 0. This integer format has to be converted to a binomial format by a *numerical to binominal* operator. The output of *Numerical to Binominal* is then connected to the *FP-Growth* operator to generate frequent item sets. The data set and RapidMiner process for association analysis can be accessed from the companion site of the book at www.LearnPredictiveAnalytics.com. Figure 6.10 shows the RapidMiner process of Association analysis with FP Growth algorithm.

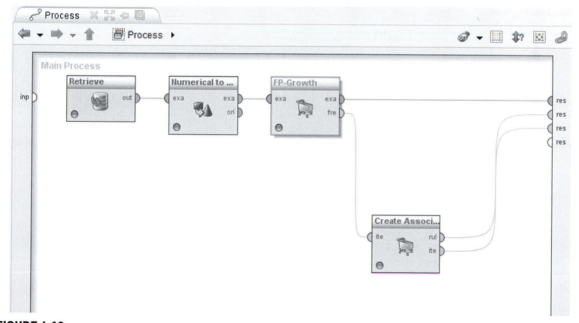

FIGURE 6.10
Data mining process for FP-Growth algorithm.

Step 2: Modeling Operator and Parameters

The *FP-Growth* operator in RapidMiner generates all the frequent item sets from the input data set meeting a certain parameter criterion. The modeling operator is available at Modeling > Association and Item Set Mining folder. This operator can work in two modes, one with a specified number of high support item sets (default) and the other with minimum support criteria. The following parameters can be set in this operator there by affecting the behavior of the model.

- **Min Support:** Threshold for support measure. All the frequent item sets passing this threshold will be provided in the output
- **Max Items:** Maximum number of items in an item set. Specifying this parameter limits too many items in an item set.
- **Must Contain:** Regular expression to filter item sets to contain specified items. Use this option to filter out items.
- **Find Minimum Number of Item Sets:** This option allows the *FP-Growth* operator to lower the support threshold, if fewer item sets are generated with the given threshold. The support threshold is decreased by 20% in each retry.
  - **Min Number of Item Sets:** Value of minimum number of item sets to be generated.
  - **Max number of Retries:** Number of retries allowed in achieving minimum item sets

In this example, we are setting *Min Support* to 0.25. The result of the *FP-Growth* operator is the set of item sets generated, which can be viewed in the results page. The reporting options include filtering based on the number of items and sorting based on the support threshold. Figure 6.11 shows the output of

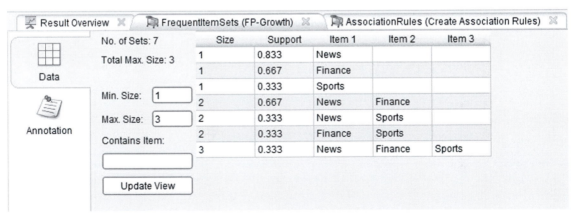

Size	Support	Item 1	Item 2	Item 3
1	0.833	News		
1	0.667	Finance		
1	0.333	Sports		
2	0.667	News	Finance	
2	0.333	News	Sports	
2	0.333	Finance	Sports	
3	0.333	News	Finance	Sports

No. of Sets: 7
Total Max. Size: 3
Min. Size: 1
Max. Size: 3
Contains Item:

Update View

FIGURE 6.11
Frequent item set output.

Frequent item sets operator where all possible item sets with support higher than the threshold can be seen.

Step 3: Create Association Rules

The next step in association analysis is generation of the most interesting rules from the frequent item sets created from the *FP-Growth* operator. The *Create Association Rules* operator generate relevant rules from frequent item sets. The interest measure of the rule can be specified by providing the correct interest criterion based on the data set under investigation. The input of the Create Association Rules operator is frequent item sets of *FP-Growth* operator and the output generates all the association rules meeting the interest criterion. The following parameters govern the functionality of this operator:

- **Criterion:** Used to select the interest measure to filter the association rule. All other parameters change based on the criterion selection. Confidence, lift, and conviction are commonly used interest criterion.
- **Min Criterion Value:** Specifies the threshold. Rules not meeting the thresholds are discarded.
- The **Gain theta** and **Laplace** parameters are the values specified when using gain and Laplace for the interest measure.

In this example process, we are using confidence as the criterion and a confidence value of 0.5. Figure 6.10 shows the completed RapidMiner process for association analysis. The process can be saved and executed.

Step 4: Interpreting the Results

The filtered association analysis rules extracted from the input transactions can be viewed in the results window (Figure 6.12). The listed association rules are in a table with columns including the premise and conclusion of the rule, as well as the

(FP-Growth) ✕　　AssociationRules (Create Association Rules) ✕　　ExampleSet (Numerical to Binominal) ✕

No.	Premises	Conclusion	Support	Confidence	LaPlace	Gain	p-s	Lift	Conviction
1	Finance	Sports	0.333	0.500	0.800	-1	0.111	1.500	1.333
2	Finance	News, Sports	0.333	0.500	0.800	-1	0.111	1.500	1.333
3	News, Finance	Sports	0.333	0.500	0.800	-1	0.111	1.500	1.333
4	News	Finance	0.667	0.800	0.909	-1	0.111	1.200	1.667
5	Finance	News	0.667	1	1	-0.667	0.111	1.200	∞
6	Sports	News	0.333	1	1	-0.333	0.056	1.200	∞
7	Sports	Finance	0.333	1	1	-0.333	0.111	1.500	∞
8	Sports	News, Finance	0.333	1	1	-0.333	0.111	1.500	∞
9	News, Sports	Finance	0.333	1	1	-0.333	0.111	1.500	∞
10	Finance, Sports	News	0.333	1	1	-0.333	0.056	1.200	∞

FIGURE 6.12
Association rules output.

(a)

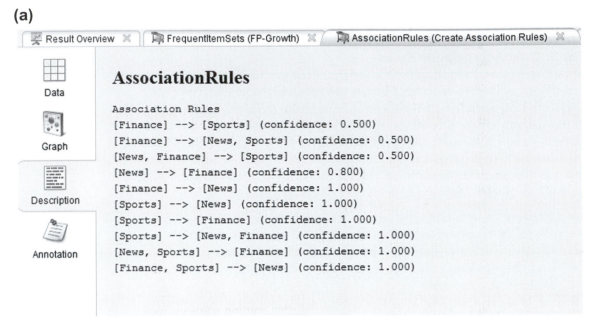

(b)

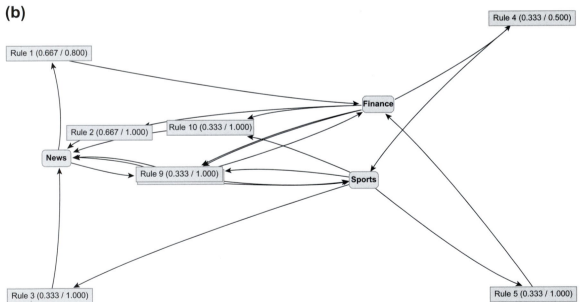

FIGURE 6.13

Association rules output (a) text view, (b) graph view.

support, confidence, gain, lift, and conviction of the rule. The interactive control window on the left-hand side of the screen allows the users to filter the processed rules to contain the selected item and ther is a slide bar to increase the confidence or criterion threshold, thereby showing fewer rules.

The main purpose of the association analysis is to understand the relationship between items. Since the items take the role of both premise and conclusion, a visual representation of relationships between all the items, through a rule, can help to comprehend the analysis. Figure 6.13 shows the rules in text format and by interconnected graph format through the results window, for selected items. Using the default option, the items selected are connected with the rules by arrows. The incoming item to a rule is the premise of the rule and the out-going item is the conclusion of the association rule.

CONCLUSION

Association rules analysis has gained popularity in the last two decades particularly in retail, online cross selling, recommendation engines, text analysis, document analysis, and web analysis. Typically, a commercial data mining software tool offers association analysis in its tool package. Though there may be a variation in how the algorithm is implemented in each commercial package, the framework of generating a frequent item set using a support threshold and generating rules from the item sets using an interest criterion is the same. Applications that involve very large amount of items and real-time decision making demand new approaches with efficient and scalable association analysis (Zaki, 2000). Association analysis is also one of the prevalent algorithms that is applied to information stored using big data technologies, data streams, and large databases (Tanbeer et al., 2008).

REFERENCES

Agrawal, R., Imieliński, T., & Swami, A. (1993). Mining association rules between sets of items in large databases. *SIGMOD '93 Proceedings of the 1993 ACM SIGMOD International Conference on Management of Data*, 207–216.

Agrawal, R., & Srikant, R. (1994). Fast Algorithms for Mining Association Rules. *The International Conference on Very Large Databases*, 487–499.

Akbar, M., & Angryk, R. (2008). Frequent pattern-growth approach for document organization. *Proceeding of the 2nd international workshop on Ontologies and information systems for the semantic web, ACM*, 77–82. Retrieved from http://dl.acm.org/citation.cfm?id=1458496.

Bodon, F. (2005). A trie-based APRIORI implementation for mining frequent item sequences. *Proceedings of the 1st International Workshop on Open Source Data Mining Frequent Pattern Mining Implementations - OSDM '05*, 56–65. http://dx.doi.org/10.1145/1133905.1133913.

Han, J., Pei, J., & Yin, Y. (2000). Mining frequent patterns without candidate generation. *SIGMOD '00 Proceedings of the 2000 ACM SIGMOD International Conference on Management of Data*, 1–12.

Power, D. J. (2002, Nov 10). *DSS News*. Retrieved Jan 21, 2014, from Desicion Support Systems (DSS) http://www.dssresources.com/newsletters/66.php.

Shang, X., Sattler, K. U., & Geist, I. (2004). *SQL Based Frequent Pattern Mining without Candidate Generation2004 ACM Symposium on Applied Computing - Poster Abstract.* 618–619.

Tan, P.-N., Steinbach, M., & Kumar, V. (2005). Association Analysis: Basic Concepts and Algorithms. In *Introduction to Data Mining* (pp. 327–404). Boston, MA: Addison Wesley.

Tanbeer, S. K., Ahmed, C. F., Jeong, B.-S., & Lee, Y.-K. (2008). Efficient frequent pattern mining over data streams. *Proceeding of the 17th ACM Conference on Information and Knowledge Mining - CIKM '08, 1,* 1447–1448. http://dx.doi.org/10.1145/1458082.1458326.

Witten, I. H., & Frank, E. (2005). Algorithms: The Basic Methods: Mining Assciation Rules. In *Data Mining: Practical Machine Learning Tools and Techniques* (pp. 112–118). San Francisco, CA: Morgan Kaufmann.

Zaki, M. J. (2000). Scalable algorithms for association mining. *IEEE Transactions on Knowledge and Data Engineering, 12*(3), 372–390. http://dx.doi.org/10.1109/69.846291.

CHAPTER 7

Clustering

Clustering is the process of finding meaningful groups in data. In clustering, the objective is not to predict a target class variable, but to simply capture the possible natural groupings in the data. For example, customers of a company can be grouped based on the purchase behavior. In recent years, clustering has even found its use in political elections (Pearson & Cooper, 2012). Prospective electoral voters can be clustered into different groups so that candidates can tailor messages to resonate within each group. Before we proceed, we should further clarify the difference between classification and clustering using a simple example. Categorizing a *given* voter as a soccer mom (a known user group) or not is a supervised learning task of classification task. Segregating a population of electorates into different groups, based on similar demographics is an unsupervised learning task of clustering. The process of identifying whether a data point belongs to a particular known group is classification. The process of dividing data into meaningful groups is clustering.

In many cases one would not know ahead of what groups to look for and thus the identified groups might be difficult to explain. These identified groups are referred to as clusters. The data mining task of clustering can be used in two different classes of applications: to describe a given data set and as a preprocessing step for other predictive algorithms.

CLUSTERING TO DESCRIBE THE DATA

The most common application of clustering is to explore the data and find all possible meaningful groups in the data. Clustering a company's customer records and attributes can yield a few groups in such a way that customers within a group are more like each other than customers belonging to a different group. Depending on the clustering technique used, the number of groups or clusters is either user defined or automatically determined by the algorithm. Since clustering is not about predicting the membership of a customer in a well-defined meaningful group (e.g., frequent high volume purchaser), we need to investigate carefully the similarities of customers within a group to make sense of the group as a whole. Some of the common applications of clustering to describe the underlying natural structure of the data are:

1. **Marketing:** Finding the common groups of customers based on all past customer behaviors, potential customers' attributes, and/or purchase patterns. This task is helpful to segment the customers, identify prototype customers (description of a typical customer of a group), and tailor a marketing message to the customers in a group.
2. **Document clustering:** One of the common text mining task is to automatically group the documents (or text blobs) into groups of similar topics. Document clustering provides a way of identifying key topics, comprehend and summarize these clustered groups than reading through whole documents. Document clustering is used for routing customer support incidents, online content sites, forensic investigations, etc.
3. **Session grouping:** In web analytics, clustering is helpful to understand clusters of clickstream patterns and discover different kinds of clickstream profiles. One clickstream profile may be that of customers who knows what they want and proceed straight to checkout. Another profile may be that of customers that research the products, read through customer reviews, and make a purchase during a later sessions. Clustering the web sessions by profile helps an ecommerce company to provide features fitting each customer profile.

CLUSTERING FOR PREPROCESSING

Since clustering processes consider all the attributes of the data set and "reduce" the information to a cluster, which is really another attribute (i.e. the ID of the cluster to which a record would belong to), clustering can be used as a data compression technique. The output of clustering is the cluster name for each record and can be used as an input variable for other predictive data mining tasks. Hence, clustering can be employed as a preprocessing technique for other data mining processes. In general, clustering can be used for two types of preprocessing:

1. **Clustering to reduce dimensionality:** In an n-dimensional data set (n number of attributes), the computational complexity is proportional to the number of dimensions or "n." With clustering, n-dimensional attributes can be converted or reduced to one categorical attribute— "Cluster ID". This reduces the complexity, although there will be some loss of information because of the dimensionality reduction to one single attribute. Chapter 12 Feature Selection provides an in-depth look at feature selection techniques.

2. **Clustering for object reduction:** Let's assume that the number of customers for a company is in the millions and the number of cluster groups is 100. For each of these 100 cluster groups, we can identify one "poster child" customer that represents the characteristics of all the customers in the cluster group. The poster child customer can be an actual customer or a fictional customer with typical characteristics of customers in the group. The prototype of a cluster is the most common representation of all the data objects and it may be a new object whose attribute values are the average values of all objects within the cluster for each attribute (the most frequently occurring value in the case of categorical attributes). Reducing millions of customer records to 100 prototype records provides an obvious benefit. For a few applications, instead of processing millions of records, we can just process the prototypes for further classification or regression tasks. This greatly reduces the record object count and can be used in algorithms like k-NN where computation complexity depends on the number of records.

7.1 TYPES OF CLUSTERING TECHNIQUES

Regardless of the types of clustering applications, the data mining task of clustering seeks to find the groupings in data, in such a way that data points within a cluster are more "similar" to each other than to data points in other clusters (Witten & Frank, 2005). One of the common ways of measuring similarity is the Euclidean distance measurement in n-dimensional space which is used in many clustering algorithms. In Figure 7.1 all data points in Cluster 2 are closer to other data points in Cluster 2 than other data points in Cluster 1.

Before we get into different ways to implement clustering, we need to define the different types of clusters. Based on a data point's membership to identified groups, clusters can be:

- **Exclusive or strict partitioning clusters:** Each data object belongs to one exclusive cluster, like the example shown in Figure 7.1. This is the most common type of cluster.
- **Overlapping clusters:** The cluster groups are not exclusive and each data object may belong to more than one cluster. These are also known as multiview clusters. For example, customers of a company can be grouped in a high-profit customer cluster and high-volume customer cluster at the same time.
- **Hierarchical clusters:** Each child cluster can be merged to form a parent cluster. For example, the most profitable customer cluster can be further divided into a long-term customer cluster and a cluster with new customers with high-value purchases.

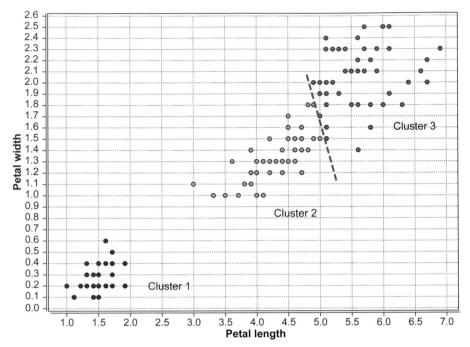

FIGURE 7.1
Example clustering of Iris data set without class labels.

- **Fuzzy or probabilistic clusters:** Each data point belongs to all cluster groups with varying degrees of membership from 0 to 1. For example, in a data set with clusters A, B, C, and D, a data point can be associated with all clusters with degree A = 0.5, B = 0.1, C = 0.4, and D = 0. Instead of a definite association of a data point with one cluster, fuzzy clustering associates a probability of membership to all the clusters.

Clustering techniques can also be classified based on the algorithmic approach used to find clusters in the data set. Each of these classes of clustering algorithms differ based on what relationship they leverage between the data objects.

- **Prototype-based clustering:** In prototype-based clustering, each cluster is represented by a central data object, also called a prototype. The prototype of each cluster is usually the center of the cluster, hence this clustering is also called centroid clustering or center-based clustering. For example, in clustering customer segments, each customer cluster will have a central prototype customer and customers with similar properties are associated with the prototype customer of a cluster.

- **Density clustering:** In Figure 7.1, we can observe that clusters occupy the area where there are more data points per unit space and are separated by sparse space. A cluster can also be defined as a dense region where data objects are concentrated surrounded by a low-density area where data objects are sparse. Each dense area can be assigned a cluster and the low-density area can be discarded as noise. In this form of clustering not all data objects are clustered since noise objects are unassigned to any clusters.
- **Hierarchical clustering:** Hierarchical clustering is a process where a cluster hierarchy is created based on the distance between data points. The output of a hierarchal clustering is a *dendrogam*: a tree diagram that shows different clusters at any point of precision which is specified by the user. There are two approaches to create a hierarchy of clusters. A bottom-up approach is where each data point is considered a cluster, and the clusters are merged to finally form one massive cluster. The top-down approach is where the data set is considered one cluster and they are recursively divided into different subclusters until individual data objects are defined as separate clusters. Hierarchical clustering is useful when the data size is limited. A level of interactive feedback is required to cut the dendrogam tree at a given level of precision.
- **Model-based clustering:** Model-based clustering gets its foundation from statistics and probability distribution models; this technique is also called distribution-based clustering. A cluster can be thought of as a grouping that has the data points belonging to the same probability distribution. Hence, each cluster can be represented by a distribution model (like Gaussian or Poisson), where the parameter of the distribution can be iteratively optimized between the cluster data and the model. With this approach, the entire data set can be represented by a mixture of distribution models. *Mixture of Gaussians* is one of the model-based clustering techniques used where a fixed number of distributions are initialized and parameters are optimized to fit the cluster data.

In the rest of the chapter, we will discuss common implementations of clustering. We will start with k-means clustering, which is a kind of prototype clustering technique. We will follow this with the Density-Based Spatial Clustering of Applications with Noise (DBSCAN) which provides a view into density clustering, and we finish off with a novel approach called self-organizing maps (SOM).

SEGMENTING CUSTOMER RECORDS

All business entities have customers and record most of the interaction with the customers, including but not limited to monetary transactions, customer service, customer location and details, online interactions, product usage, and warranty and service information. Let's take the telecommunication industry as an example. Telecommunications companies have now evolved to provide multiple services to different types of customers by packaging products like landlines, wireless voice, Internet Service Providers, data communications, corporate backbones, entertainment content, home security, etc. To better understand customers, whose numbers often range in the millions, it is necessary to combine multiple data sets about the customers and their interactions with each product. The vastness of the number and variety of attributes in the data set provides both an opportunity and challenge to better know customers (Berry & Linoff, 2000). One logical way to understand the customer beyond straightforward classifications like customer type (residential, corporate, government, etc) or revenue volume (high-, medium-, and low-revenue customers), is to segment the customer based on usage patterns, demographics, geography, and behavior patterns for product usage.

For a customer segmentation task, the data need to be prepared in such a way that each record (row) is associated with each customer and the columns contain all the attributes about the customer, including demographics, address, products used, revenue details, usage details of the product, call volume, type of calls, call duration, time of the call, etc. Table 7.1 shows an example structure of a denormalized customer data set. Preparing this data set is going to be time-consuming task. One of the obvious methods of segmentation is stratifying based on any of the existing attributes. For example, we can segment based on a customer's geographical location.

A clustering algorithm consumes this data and groups the customers with similar patterns into clusters based on all the attributes. Based on the data, clustering could be based on a combination of call usage, data patterns, and monthly bills. The resulting clusters could be a group of customers who have low data usage but with high bills at a location where there is weak cellular coverage, which may indicate dissatisfied customers.

The clustering algorithm doesn't explicitly provide the reason for clustering and doesn't intuitively label the cluster groups. While clustering can be performed using a large number of attributes, it is up to the data mining practitioner to carefully select the attributes that will be relevant for clustering. Automated feature selection methods (Chapter 12 Feature Selection) can reduce the dimensions for a clustering exercise. Clustering could be iteratively developed further by selecting or ignoring other attributes in the customer data set.

Table 7.1 Data Set for Customer Segmentation

Customer ID	Location	Demographics	Call Usage	Data Usage	Monthly Bill
01	San Jose, CA	Male	1400	200 MB	$75.23
02	Miami, FL	Female	2103	5,000 MB	$125.78
03	Los Angeles, CA	Male	292	2,000 MB	$89.90
04	San Jose, CA	Female	50	40 MB	$59.34

7.2 k-MEANS CLUSTERING

k-means clustering is a prototype-based clustering method where the data set is divided into k clusters. k-means clustering is one of the simplest and most commonly used clustering algorithms. In this technique, the user specifies the number of clusters (k) that need to be grouped in the data set. The objective of k-means clustering is to find a *prototype* data point for each cluster; all the data points are then assigned to the nearest prototype, which then forms a cluster. The prototype is called as the centroid, the center of the cluster. The center of the cluster can be the mean of all data objects in the cluster, as in k-means, or the most represented data object, as in k-medoid clustering. The cluster centroid or mean data object does not have to be a real data point in the data set and can be an imaginary data point that represents the characteristics of all data points within the cluster.

The k-means clustering algorithm is based on the works of Stuart Lloyd and E.W. Forgy (Lloyd, 1982) and is sometimes referred to as the Lloyd-Forgy algorithm or Lloyd's algorithm. Visually, the k-means algorithm divides the data space into k partitions or boundaries, where the centroid in each partition is the prototype of the clusters. The data objects inside a partition belong to the cluster. These partitions are also called *Voronoi partitions*, and each prototype is a seed in a Voronoi partition. A Voronoi partition is a process of segmenting a space into regions, around a set of points called seeds. All other points are then associated to the nearest seed and the points associated with the seed form a unique partition. Figure 7.2 shows a sample Voronoi partition around seeds marked as black dots.

FIGURE 7.2

Voronoi partition. ("Euclidean Voronoi Diagram" by Raincomplex – personal work. Licensed under Creative Commons Zero, Public Domain Dedication via Wikimedia Commons.[1])

---

[1]http://commons.wikimedia.org/wiki/File:Euclidean_Voronoi_Diagram.png#mediaviewer/
File:Euclidean_Voronoi_Diagram.png

k-means clustering creates k partitions in n-dimensional space, where n is the number of attributes in data sets. To partition the data set we would need to define a proximity measure. The most commonly used measure for a numeric attribute is the Euclidean distance. Figure 7.3 illustrates the clustering of the Iris data set with only the petal length and petal width attributes. This Iris data set is two dimensional, with numeric attributes and k specified as 3. The outcome of k-means clustering provides a clear partition space for Cluster 1 and a narrow space for the other two clusters, Cluster 2 and Cluster 3.

7.2.1 How it Works: Concepts

The logic of finding k-clusters with a given data set is rather simple and always converges to a solution. However, the final result in most cases will be locally optimal where the solution will not converge to the global best solution. The process of k-means clustering is very similar to Voronoi iteration, where the objective is to divide a space into cells around points. The difference is Voronoi iteration partitions space, whereas k-means clustering partitions data points in data space. Let's take the example of a two-dimensional data set (Figure 7.4) and walk through the step-by-step process of finding three clusters (Tan, Michael, & Kumar, 2005).

Step 1: Initiate Centroids

The first step in a k-means algorithm is to initiate k random centroids. The number of clusters k should be specified by the user. In this case we initiate three centroids in a given data space. In Figure 7.5, each initial centroid is given a shape (with a circle to differentiate centroids from other data points) so that data points assigned to a centroid can be indicated by same shape.

Step 2: Assign Data Points

Once centroids have been initiated, all the data points are now assigned to the nearest centroid to form a cluster. In this context the "nearest" is calculated by a proximity measure. Euclidean distance measurement is the most common proximity measure, though other measures like the Manhattan measure and Jaccard coefficient can be used. The Euclidean distance between two data points X $(x_1, x_2, ...x_n)$ and C $(c_1, c_2, ...c_n)$ with n attributes is given by

$$\text{Distance d} = \sqrt{(x_1 - c_1)^2 + (x_2 - c_2)^2 + ... + (x_n - c_n)^2} \tag{7.1}$$

All the data points associated to a centroid now have the same shape as their corresponding centroid as shown in Figure 7.6. This step also leads to partitioning of data space into Voronoi partitions, with lines shown as boundaries.

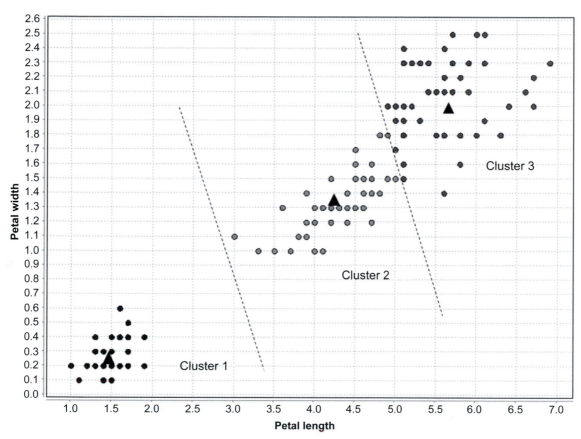

FIGURE 7.3
Prototype-based clustering and boundaries.

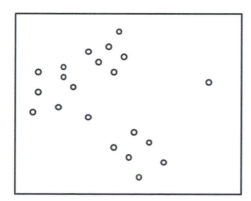

FIGURE 7.4
Data set with two dimensions.

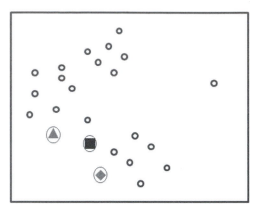

FIGURE 7.5
Initial random centroids.

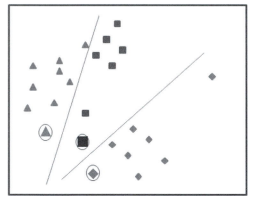

FIGURE 7.6
Assignment of data points to nearest centroids.

Step 3: Calculate New Centroids

For each cluster, we can now calculate a new centroid, which is also the pro-totype of each cluster group. This new centroid is the most representative data point of all data points in the cluster. Mathematically, this step can be expressed as minimizing the sum of squared errors (SSE) of all data points in a cluster to the centroid of the cluster. The overall objective of the step is to minimize the sum of squared errors of individual clusters. The SSE of a cluster can be calculated by Equation 7.2.

$$SSE = \sum_{i=1}^{k} \sum_{x_j \in C_i} ||x_j - \mu_i||2$$

$$(7.2)$$

where C_i is the ith cluster, j are the data points in a given cluster, μ_i is the cen-troid for ith cluster, and x_j is a specific data object. The centroid with minimal

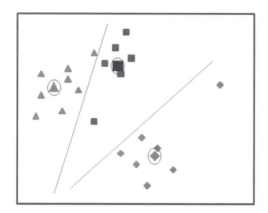

FIGURE 7.7
New centroids.

SSE for the given cluster i is the new mean of the cluster. The mean of the cluster can be calculated by

$$\mu_i = \frac{1}{j_i} \sum_{x \in c_i} X$$

(7.3)

where X is the data object vector $(x_1, x_2, \dots x_n)$. In the case of k-means clustering, the new centroid will be the mean of all the data points k-medoid clustering is a variation of k-means clustering, where the median is calculated instead of mean. Figure 7.7 shows the location of the new centroids.

Step 4: Repeat Assignment and Calculate New Centroids
Once the new centroids have been identified, assigning data points to the nearest centroid is repeated until all the data points are reassigned to new centroids. In Figure 7.8, note the change in assignment of two data points that belonged to different clusters in the previous step.

Step 5: Termination
Step 3, calculating new centroids, and step 4, assigning data points to new centroids, are iterative until no further change in assignment of data points happens or, in other words, no significant change in centroids are noted. The final centroids are declared the prototype data objects or vectors and they are used to describe the whole clustering model. Each data point in the data set is now tied with a new clustering ID attribute that identifies the cluster.

Special Cases
Even though k-means clustering is simple and easy to implement, one of the key drawbacks of k-means clustering is the algorithm seeks to find a *local optimum*, which may not yield globally optimal clustering. In this approach, the algorithm starts with an initial configuration (centroids) and continuously

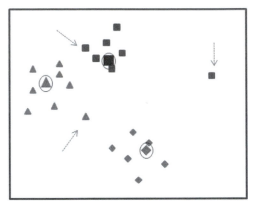

FIGURE 7.8
Assignment of data points to new centroids.

improves to find the best solution possible for that initial configuration. Since the solution is optimal to the initial configuration (locally optimal), there might be a better optimal solution if the initial configuration changes. The locally optimal solution may not be the most optimal solution (globally optimal) for the given clustering problem. Hence, the success of a k-means algorithm very much depends on the initiation of centroids. This limitation can be addressed by having multiple random initiations; in each run we can measure the cohesiveness of the clusters by a *performance criterion*. The clustering run with the best performance can be chosen as the final run. Evaluation of clustering is discussed in next section. Following are key issues to be considered in k-means clustering:

- **Initiation**: The final clustering grouping depends on the random initiator and the nature of the data set. When random initiation is used, we can run the entire clustering process (also called "runs") with a different set of random initiators and find the clustering process that has minimal total SSE. Another technique is hierarchical clustering, where each cluster is in turn split into multiple clusters and thereby minimal SSE is achieved. Hierarchical clustering is further divided into agglomerative or bottom-up clustering and divisive or top-down clustering, depending on how the clustering is initiated. Agglomerative clustering starts with each data point as an individual cluster and proceeds to combine data points into clusters. Divisive clustering starts with the whole data set as one big cluster and proceeds to split that into multiple clusters.
- **Empty clusters**: One of the possibilities in k-means clustering is the formation of empty clusters in which no data objects are associated. If empty clusters are formed, a new centroid can be introduced in

the cluster that has the highest SSE, thereby splitting the cluster that contributes to the highest SSE or selecting a new centroid that is at the farthest point away from any other centroid.

- **Outliers**: Since SSE is used as an objective function, k-means clustering is susceptible to outliers; they drift the centroid away from the representative data points in a cluster. Hence the prototype is no longer the best representative of the clusters it represents. While outliers can be eliminated by preprocessing techniques, in some applications finding outliers or a group of outliers is the objective of clustering, similar to identifying fraudulent transactions.
- **Postprocessing**: Since k-means clustering seeks to be locally optimal, we can introduce a few postprocessing techniques to force a new solution that has less SSE. We always can increase the number of clusters, k, and reduce SSE. But, this technique can start overfitting the data set and yields less useful information. There are a few approaches that can be deployed, such as bisecting the cluster that has highest SSE and merging two clusters into one even if SSE increases slightly.

Evaluation of Clusters

Evaluation of k-means clustering is different from regression and classification algorithms because in clustering there are no known external labels for comparison. We will have to develop the evaluation parameter from the very data set that is evaluated. This is called unsupervised or internal evaluation. Evaluation of clustering can be as simple as computing total SSE. Good models will have low SSE within the cluster and low overall SSE among all clusters. SSE can also be referred to as the average within-cluster distance and can be calculated for each cluster and then averaged for all the clusters.

Another commonly used evaluation measure is the Davies-Bouldin index (Davies & Bouldin, 1979). The Davies-Bouldin index is a measure of uniqueness of the clusters and takes into consideration both cohesiveness of the cluster (distance between the data points and center of the cluster) and separation between the clusters. It is the function of the ratio of within cluster separation to the separation between the clusters. The lower the value of the Davies-Bouldin index, the better the clustering. However, both SSE and the Davies-Bouldin index have the limitation of not guaranteeing better clustering when they have lower scores.

7.2.2 How to Implement

k-means clustering implementation in RapidMiner is simple and straightforward with one operator for modeling and one for unsupervised evaluation. In the modeling step, the parameter for the number of clusters, k, is specified as desired. The output model is a list of centroids for each cluster and a new attribute is attached to the original input data set with the cluster ID. The cluster label is appended to the original data set for each data point and can be visually evaluated after the clustering. A model evaluation step is required to calculate the average cluster distance and Davies-Bouldin index.

For this implementation, we are using the Iris data set with four attributes and 150 data objects (Fisher, 1936). Even though a class label is not needed for clustering, we choose to keep it for later explanation to see if identified clusters from an unlabeled data set are similar to natural clusters of species in the given data set.

Step 1: Data Preparation

k-means clustering accepts both numeric and polynominal data types; however, the distance measures are more effective with numeric data types. The number of attributes increases the dimension space for clustering. In this example we limit the number of attributes to two by selecting petal width (a3) and petal length (a4) using the *Select attribute* operator as shown in Figure 7.9. It is easy to visualize the mechanics of k-means algorithm by looking at two-dimensional plots for clustering. In practical implementations, clustering data sets will have more attributes.

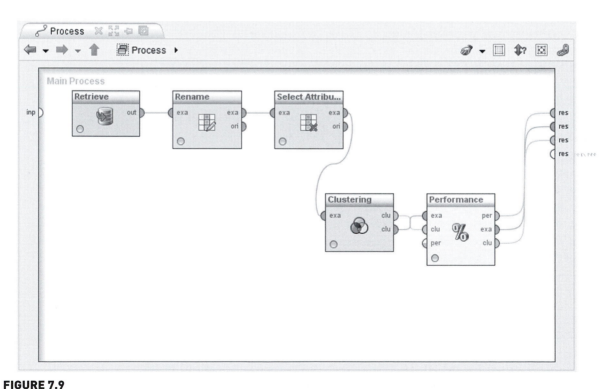

FIGURE 7.9
Data mining process for k-means clustering.

Step 2: Clustering Operator and Parameters

The k-means modeling operator is available in Modeling > Clustering and Segmentation folder of RapidMiner. The following parameters can be configured in the model operator:

- **k:** k is the desired number of clusters.
- **Add cluster as attribute:** Append cluster labels (IDs) into the original data set. Turning on this option is recommended for later analysis.
- **Max runs:** Since the effectiveness of k-means clustering is dependent on random initial centroids, multiple runs are required to select the clustering with the lowest SSE. The number of such runs can be specified here.
- **Measure type:** The proximity measure can be specified in this parameter. The default and most common measurement is Euclidean distance (L2). Other options here are Manhattan distance (L1), Jaccard coefficient, and cosine similarity for document data. Please refer to Chapter 4 Classification section k-NN for description on distance measures.
- **Max optimization steps:** This parameter specifies the number of iterations of assigning data objects to centroids and calculating new centroids.

The output of the modeling step includes the cluster model with k centroid data objects and the initial data set appended with cluster labels. Cluster labels are named generically such as cluster_0, cluster_1,…, cluster_k–1.

Step 3: Evaluation

Since the attributes used in the data set are numeric, we need to evaluate the effectiveness of clustering groups using SSE and the Davies-Bouldin index. In RapidMiner, the *Cluster Distance Performance* operator under Evaluation > Clustering is available for performance evaluation of cluster groups. *Performance* operator needs accepts both inputs from the modeling step: cluster centroid vector (model) and the labeled data set. The two measurement outputs of the evaluation are average cluster distance and the Davies-Bouldin index.

Step 4: Execution and Interpretation

After the outputs from the *performance* operator have been connected to the result ports, the data mining process can be executed. The following outputs can be observed from results window:

- **Cluster Model (Clustering):** The model output contains the centroid for each of the k clusters, along with their attribute values. As shown in Figure 7.10, in the text view and folder view sections, we can see all the data objects associated with the each cluster. The centroid plot view provides the parallel chart view (Chapter 3 Data Exploration) of centroids. A large separation between centroids is desirable, because well-separated clusters divide the data set cleanly.

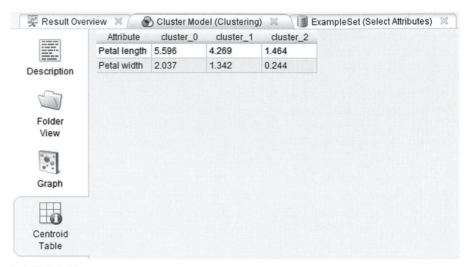

FIGURE 7.10

k-means clustering centroids output.

- **Labeled example set:** The appended data set has some of the most important information on clustering. The generic Iris data set of 150 observations is clustered in three groups. The cluster value is appended as a new special polynominal attribute and takes a generic label format. In the scatterplot view of this output data set, we can configure the x- and y-axes to be attributes of original data set, petal length and petal width. The Color Column can be configured for cluster labels. In the plot in Figure 7.11, we notice how the algorithm identified clusters. We can compare this output against the original label (Iris species) by swapping the Color Column to the species label. Here we can observe that only five data points in the border of versicolor and virginica are mis-clustered! The k-means clustering process identified the different species in the data set almost exactly.
- **Performance vector:** The output of the performance evaluation includes the average distance measured and the Davies-Bouldin index (Figure 7.12). This step can be used to compare multiple clustering processes with different parameters. In advanced implementations, it is possible to determine the value of k based on the clustering runs with the best performance vectors. Amongst multiple clustering runs, the low average-within-centroid distance and low Davies-Bouldin index yields better clusters, because they indicate the cohesiveness of the cluster.

The k-means clustering algorithm is simple, easy to implement, and easy to interpret. Although the algorithm can effectively handle an n-dimensional data set, the operation will be expensive with a higher number of iterations

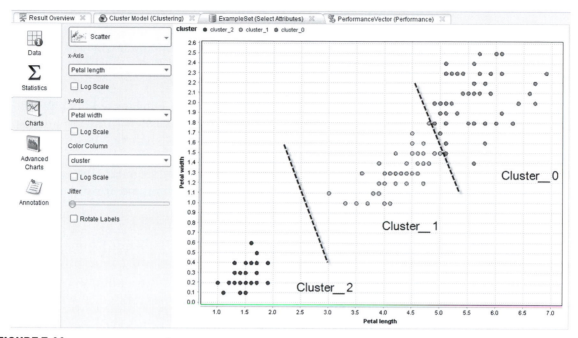

FIGURE 7.11
k-means clustering visual output.

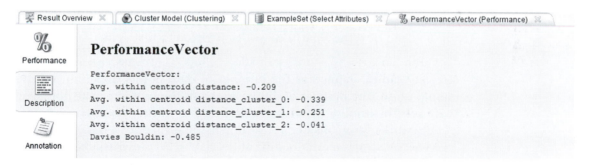

FIGURE 7.12
Performance measures of k-means clustering.

and runs. One of the key limitations of k-means is that it relies on the user to assign the value of k (Berry & Linoff, 2000). The number of clusters in the data set will be unknown to begin with and an arbitrary number can limit the ability to find the right number of natural clusters in the data set. There are a variety of methods to estimate the right number for k, ranging from the Bayesian Information Criterion (BIC) to hierarchical methods that increases the value of k until the data points assigned to the cluster are Gaussian (Hamerly & Elkan, 2003). For a start, we recommend a value of k in the low single digits and increasing it until it fits. Clustering using density methods will help provide an idea into the number of clusters and could be used as a value of k in k-means clustering.

Since the centroid prototype approach is used, k-means tends to find globular clusters in the data set. However, natural clusters can be of all shapes and sizes. The presence of outliers possesses a challenge in the modeling of k-means clustering. The simplicity of the k-means clustering technique makes it a great choice for quick evaluation of globular clusters and as a preprocessing technique for predictive modeling and for dimensionality reduction.

7.3 DBSCAN CLUSTERING

A cluster can also be defined as an area of high concentration (or density) of data objects surrounded by areas of low concentration (or density) of data objects. A density-clustering algorithm identifies clusters in the data based on measurement of the density distribution in n-dimensional space. Unlike centroid methods, specifying the number of the cluster parameter (k) is not necessary for density-based algorithms. Thus density-based clustering can serve as an important data exploration technique. DBSCAN (Density-Based Spatial Clustering of Applications with Noise) is one of the most commonly used density-clustering algorithms (Ester et al.,1996). To understand how the algorithm works, we need to first define the concept of density in a data space.

Density can be defined as the number of data points in a unit n-dimensional space. The number of dimensions n is the number of attributes in a data set. To simplify the visualization and to further understand how the model works, let's consider a two-dimensional space or a data set with two numeric attributes. From looking at the data set represented in Figure 7.13, we can visually conclude that density in the top-left section is higher than density in top-right, bottom-left, and bottom-right sections. Technically, density relates to the number of points in unit space, in this case a quadrant. Wherever there is high-density space amongst relatively low-density spaces, there is a cluster.

We can also measure density within a circular space around a point as in Figure 7.14. The number of points within a circular space with radius ε (epsilon) around a data point A is six. This measure is called center-based density since the space considered is globular with the center being the point that is considered.

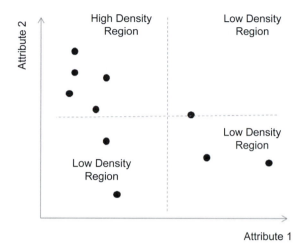

FIGURE 7.13
Data set with two attributes.

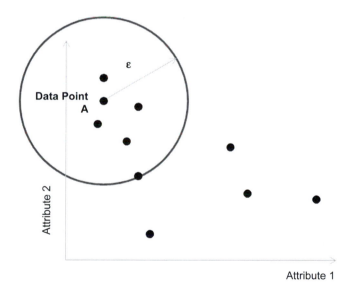

FIGURE 7.14
Density of a data point within radius ε.

7.3.1 How it Works

The DBSCAN algorithm creates clusters by identifying high-density and low-density space within the data set. Similar to k-means clustering, it is preferred that the attributes are numeric because distance calculation is still used. We can reduce the algorithm to three steps: defining threshold density, classification of data points, and clustering (Tan, Michael, & Kumar, 2005).

Step 1: Defining Epsilon and MinPoints

The DBSCAN algorithm starts with calculation of a density for all data points in a data set, with a given fixed radius ε (epsilon). To determine whether a neighborhood is high density or low density, we will have to define a threshold of data points (MinPoints) above which the neighborhood is considered high density. In Figure 7.14, the number of data points inside the space is defined by radius ε. If MinPoints is defined as 5, the space ε surrounding data point A is considered a high-density region. Both ε and MinPoints are user-defined parameters and can be altered for a data set.

Step 2: Classification of Data Points

In a data set, with a given ε and MinPoints, we can classify all data points into three buckets (Figure 7.15):

- **Core points:** All the data points inside the high-density region of at least one data point are considered a core point. A high-density region is a space where there are at least *MinPoints* data points within a radius of ε for any data points.
- **Border point:** Border points sit on the circumference of radius ε from a data point. A border point is the boundary between high-density and low-density space. Border points are counted within the high-density space calculation.
- **Noise point:** Any point that is neither a core point nor border point is called a noise point. They form a low-density region around the high-density region.

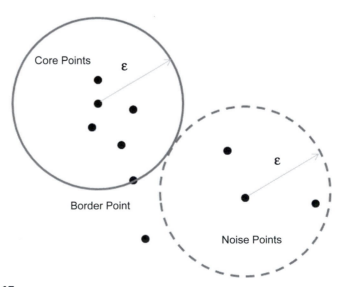

FIGURE 7.15
Core, border, and density points.

Step 3: Clustering

Once all data points in the data set are classified into density points, clustering is a straightforward task. Groups of core points form distinct clusters. If two core points are within ε of each other, then both core points are within the same cluster. All these clustered core points form a cluster, which is surrounded by low-density noise points. All noise points form low-density regions around the high-density cluster, and noise points are not classified in any cluster. Since DBSCAN is a partial clustering algorithm, a few data points are left unlabeled or associated to a default noise cluster.

Optimizing Parameters

One of the key advantages in using a density algorithm is that there is no need for specifying the number of clusters (k). Clusters are automatically found in the data set. However, there is an issue of selecting the distance parameter ε and a minimum threshold (MinPoints) to identify the dense region. One of the techniques used to estimate optimal parameters for the DBSCAN clustering algorithm relates to the k-nearest neighbor algorithm. We can estimate the initial values of the parameter by building a k-distribution graph. For a user-specified value of k (say, four data points), we can calculate the distance of the k-th nearest neighbor for a data point. If the data point is a core point in a high-density region, then the distance of the k-th nearest neighbor will be smaller. For a noise point, the distance will be larger. Similarly, we can calculate the k-distance for all data points in a data set. A k-distance distribution graph can be built by arranging all the k-distance values of individual data points in descending order, as shown in Figure 7.16. This arrangement is similar to Pareto charts. Points on the right-hand side of the chart will belong to data points inside a cluster, because the distance is smaller. In most data sets, the value of k-distance sharply rises after a particular value. The distance at which the chart rises will be the optimal value ε (epsilon) and the value of k can be used for MinPoints.

Special Cases: Varying Densities

The DBSCAN algorithm partitions data based on a certain threshold density. This approach creates an issue when a data set contains areas of varying data density. The data set in Figure 7.17 has four distinct regions numbered from 1 to 4. Region 1 is the high-density area A, regions 2 and 4 are of medium density B, and between them is region 3, which has very low density C. If the density threshold parameters are tuned in such a way to partition and identify region 1, then region 2 and 4 (with density B) will be considered noise, along with region 3. Even though region 4 with density B is next to a very-low-density area and clearly identifiable visually, the DBSCAN algorithm will classify regions 2 through 4 as noise. The k-means clustering algorithm is better at partitioning data sets with varying densities.

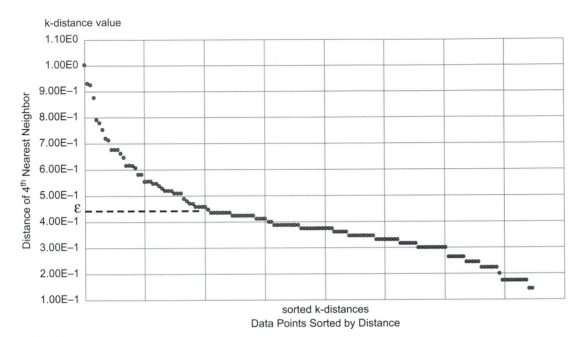

FIGURE 7.16
k-distribution chart for Iris data set with k = 4.

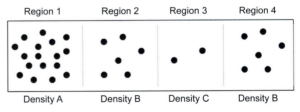

FIGURE 7.17
Data set with varying densities.

7.3.2 How to Implement

The implementation of the DBSCAN algorithm is supported in RapidMiner through the DBSCAN modeling operator. The DBSCAN operator accepts numeric and polynominal data set with provisions for user-specified ε (epsilon) and MinPoints parameters. Here are the implementation steps.

Step 1: Data Preparation

As with the k-means section, we will limit the number of attributes in the data set to A3 and A4 (petal length and petal width) using the *Select Attribute* operator, so that we can visualize the cluster and better understand the clustering process.

Step 2: Clustering Operator and Parameters

The modeling operator is available in the Modeling > Clustering and Segmentation folder, and is labeled DBSCAN. The ollowing parameters can be configured in the model operator:

- **Epsilon (ε):** Size of the high-density neighborhood. The default value is 1.
- **MinPoints:** Minimum number of data objects within the epsilon neighborhood to qualify as a cluster.
- **Distance measure:** The proximity measure can be specified in this parameter. The default and most common measurement is Euclidean distance. Other options here are Manhattan distance, Jaccard coefficient, and cosine similarity for document data. Please refer to Figure 4.32 for a summary of different distance measures.
- **Add cluster as attributes:** To append cluster labels into the original data set. Turing on this option is recommended for later analysis.

Step 3: Evaluation (Optimal)

Similar to k-means clustering implementation, we can evaluate the effectiveness of clustering groups using average within cluster distance. In RapidMiner, the *Cluster Density Performance* operator under Evaluation > Clustering is available for performance evaluation of cluster groups generated by Density algorithms. The clustering model and labeled data set is connected to *performance* operator for cluster evaluation. Additionally, to aid the calculation, *performance* operator expects Similarity Measure object. A similarity measure vector is a distance measure of every example data object with the other data object. The similarity measure can be calculated by using *Data to Similarity* Operator on the example data set.

Step 4: Execution and Interpretation

After the outputs from the *performance* operator have been connected to the result ports, as shown in Figure 7.18, the model can be executed. The following result output can be observed.

1. **Model:** The cluster model output contains information on the number or clusters found in the data set (Cluster 1, Cluster 2, …) and data objects identified as noise points (Cluster 0). If no noise points are found, then Cluster 0 is an empty cluster. As shown in Figure 7.19, the Folder view and Graph view from the output window provide the visualization of data points classified under different clusters.
2. **Clustered example set:** The example set now has a clustering label that can be used for further analysis and visualization. In the scatterplot view of this data set (Figure 7.20), we can configure the x- and y-axes to be attributes of the original data set, petal length and petal width. The Color Column can be configured to be the new cluster label. In the plot, we notice how the algorithm found two clusters within the example set.

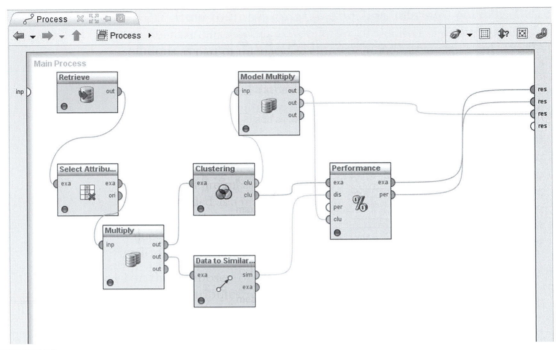

FIGURE 7.18
Data mining process with density clustering.

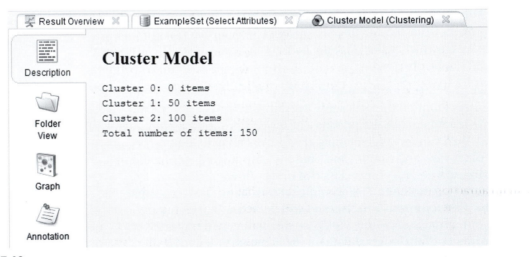

FIGURE 7.19
Density clustering model output.

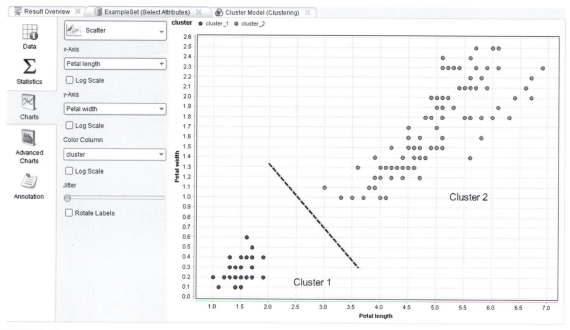

FIGURE 7.20
Density clustering visual output.

The *setosa* species data objects have clear high-density areas but there is a density bridge between the *verisicolor* and *virginica* species data points. There is no clear low-density area to partition these two species of data points. Hence *verisicolor* and *virginica* natural clusters are combined to one artificial predicted cluster. The epsilon and MinPoints parameters can be adjusted to find different results for the clustering.

3. **Performance vector:** The performance vector window shows average distance within each cluster and average of all clusters. The average distance is the distance between all the data points within the cluster divided by number of data points. These measures can be used to compare the performance of multiple model runs.

7.3.3 Conclusion

The main attraction of using DBSCAN clustering is that we do not have to specify the value of k, the number of clusters to be identified. In many practical applications, the number of clusters to be discovered will be unknown, like finding unique customers or electoral segments. DBSCAN uses variations in the density of the data distribution to find the concentration of structures in data. These clusters can be of any shape and they are not confined to globular structures as

(a)   **(b)**

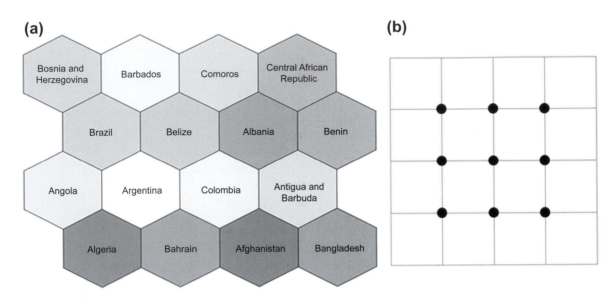

FIGURE 7.21
(a) SOM of countries by GDP data using a (a) hexagonal grid and (b) rectangular lattice.

in the k-means approach. But the density algorithms run into the risk of finding bridges between two natural clusters and merging them into one cluster.

Since the density clustering technique yields partial clustering, DBSCAN ignores noise and outlier data points and they are not clustered in final results. The inability to identify varying densities within a data set is one of the major limitations of DBSCAN clustering technique. Centroid methods are more successful at finding varying density patterns in the data set. A data set with a high number of attributes will have processing challenges with density clustering methods. Given the complementary pros and cons of the k-means and DBSCAN methods, it is advisable to cluster the data set by both methods and understand the patterns of both result sets.

7.4 SELF-ORGANIZING MAPS

A self-organizing map (SOM) is a powerful visual clustering technique that evolved from the combination of neural networks and prototype-based clustering. A SOM is a form of neural network where the output is an organized visual matrix, usually a two-dimensional grid with rows and columns. The objective of this neural network is to transfer all input data objects with n attributes (n dimensions) to the output lattice in such a way that objects next to each other are closely related to each other. Two example SOM layouts are provided in Figure 7.21. This two-dimensional matrix becomes an exploration tool in identifying the clusters of objects related to each other by visual examination. A key distinction in this neural network is the absence of an output target function to optimize or predict, hence it is an unsupervised learning algorithm. SOMs effectively arrange the data points in a lower dimensional space, thereby aids visualizing high-dimensional data through a low-dimensional space.

SOMs are relevant to clustering because the most common SOM output is a two-dimensional grid with data objects placed next to each other based on their similarity to one another. Objects related to each other are placed in close proximity. SOMs differ from other clustering techniques because there is no explicit clustering labels assigned to data objects. Data objects are arranged based on their attribute proximity and the task of clustering is left to visual analysis of the user. Hence, SOM is used as a *visual* clustering and data exploration technique (Germano, 1999).

Self-organizing maps were first proposed by Teuvo Kohonen (Kohonen, 1982) and hence this technique is also known as Kohonen networks; it is sometimes also referred to by a more specific name, self-organizing feature maps. SOM methodology is used to project data objects from *data space*, mostly in n dimensions, to *grid space*, usually resulting in two dimensions. Though other output formats are possible, most common output format for SOMs are (a) hexagonal lattice or a (b) rectangular grid as shown in Figure 7.21. Each data point from the data set occupies a cell or a node in the output lattice, with arrangement constraints depending on the similarity of data points. Each cell in the SOM grid corresponds to a group of data points, called a *neuron*. In a hexagonal grid, each neuron has six neighbors and a rectangular lattice has four neighbors.

SOMs are commonly used in comparing data points with a large number of numeric attributes. The objective of this kind of analysis is to compare the relative features of data objects in a simple two-dimensional setting where the placement of objects is related to each other. In Figure 7.21a, the SOM compares relative GDP data from different countries where countries with similar GDP profiles are placed either in same cells or next to each other. All similar countries around a particular cell can be considered a grouping. Although the individual data objects (countries) do not have a cluster membership, the placement of objects together aides in visual data analysis. This application is also called competitive self-organizing maps.

7.4.1 How it Works: Concepts

The algorithm for a SOM is similar to centroid-based clustering but with a neural network foundation. Since a SOM is essentially a neural network, the model accepts only numerical attributes. However, there is no target variable in SOM because it is an unsupervised learning model. The objective of the algorithm is to find a set of centroids (neurons) to represent the cluster but with topological constraints. The topology refers to an arrangement of centroids in the output grid. All the data objects from the data set are assigned to each centroid. Centroids closer to each other in the grid are more closely "related" to each other than to centroids further away in the grid. A SOM converts numbers from the data space to a grid space with additional inter-topology relationships.

Step 1: Topology Specification

The first step for a SOM is specifying the topology of the output. Even though multidimensional output is possible, two-dimensional rows and columns with either a rectangular lattice or hexagonal lattice are commonly used in SOMs to aid the visual discovery of clustering. One advantage in using a hexagonal lattice is that each node or centroid can have six neighbors, two more than in a rectangular lattice. Hence, in a hexagonal lattice, the association of a data point with another data point can be more precise than for a rectangular grid. The number of centroids can be specified by providing the number of rows and columns in the grid. The number of centroids is the product of the number of rows and columns in the grid. Figure 7.22 shows the hexagonal lattice SOM.

Step 2: Initialize Centroids

A SOM starts the process by initializing the centroids. The initial centroids are values of random data objects from the data set. This is similar to initializing centroids in k-means clustering.

Step 3: Assignment of Data Objects

After centroids are selected and placed on the grid in the intersection of rows and columns, data objects are selected one by one and assigned to the nearest centroid. The nearest centroid can be calculated using a distance function like Euclidean distance for numeric data or a cosine measure for document or binary data. Section 4.3.1 provides a summary of distance and similarity measures.

Step 4: Centroid Update

The centroid update is the most significant and distinct step in the SOM algorithm and is repeated for every data object. The centroid update has two related substeps.

The first substep is to update the closest centroid. The objective of the method is to update the data values of the nearest centroid of the data object, proportional to the difference between the centroid and the data object. This is similar to updating weights in the back propagation algorithm of neural networks. In the neural network section of Chapter 4 Classification, we discussed how the weights of neurons are updated based on the error difference between the predicted and actual value. Similarly, in the context of a SOM, the values of

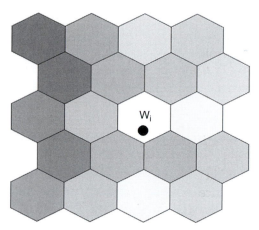

FIGURE 7.22
Weight of the centroid is updated.

centroids are updated. In fact, centroids are considered neurons in a SOM. Through this update, the closest centroid moves closer to the data object in the data space.

The centroid update step is repeated for number of iterations, usually in the thousands. Let's denote t as the tth iteration of the update where we pick the data point $d(t)$. Let w_1, w_2, w_3, ..., w_k represent all the centroids in the grid space. Figure 7.22 shows the lattice with centroid weight. Let r and c be the number of rows and columns in the grid. Then k will be equal to $r * c$. Let w_i be the nearest centroid for data object $d(t)$. During iteration t, the nearest centroid w_i is updated by Equation 7.4.

$$w_i(t + 1) = w_i(t) + f_i(t) * [d(t) - w_i(t)]$$
(7.4)

The effect of the update is determined by the difference between the centroid and data point in the data space and the neighborhood function $f_i(t)$. The neighborhood function decreases for every iteration so there are no drastic changes made in the final iteration. In addition to updating the nearest primary centroid, all other centroids in the grid space neighborhood of the primary centroid are updated as well. We will review this in more detail in the next substep.

The second substep is to update all centroids in the grid space neighborhood as shown in Figure 7.23. The neighborhood update step has to be proportional to the distance from the closest centroid to the centroid that is being updated. The update function has to be stronger when the distance is closer. Taking into account time decay and distance between neighborhood centroids, a Gaussian function is commonly used for $f_i(t)$:

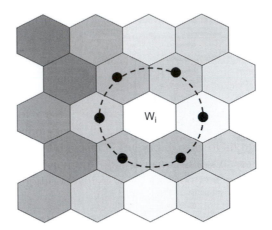

FIGURE 7.23
The weight of the neighborhood centroids are updated.

$$f_i(t) = \lambda_i(t)e^{\left(-\frac{(g_i - g_j)^2}{2\sigma^2}\right)}$$

(7.5)

Where $\lambda_i(t)$ is the learning rate function that takes a value between 0 and 1 and decays for every iteration. Usually it is either a linear rate function or an inverse of the time function. The variable in the exponential parameter $g_i - g_j$ is the distance between the centroid being updated and the nearest centroid of the data point in the grid space.

The variable σ determines the radius of the centroid update or the neighborhood effect. By updating the entire neighborhood of centroids in the grid, the SOM self-organizes the centroid lattice. Effectively, the SOM converts data from the data space to a location-constrained grid space.

Step 5: Termination
The entire algorithm is continued until no significant centroid updates take place in each run or until the specified number of the run counter is reached. The selection of the data object can be repeated if the data set size is small. Like with many data mining algorithms, a SOM tends to converge to a solution in most cases but doesn't guarantee an optimal solution. To tackle this problem, it is necessary to have multiple runs with various initiation measures and compare the results.

Step 6: Mapping a New Data Object
A SOM model itself is a valuable visualization tool that can describe the relationship between data objects and be used for visual clustering. After the grids with the desired number of centroids have been built, any new data object can

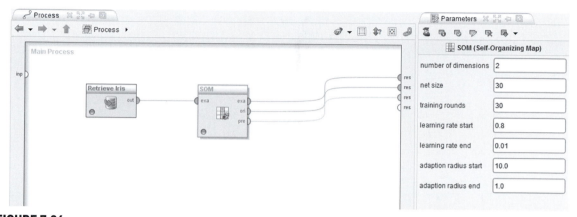

FIGURE 7.24
SOM in data transformation.

be quickly given a location on the grid space, based on its proximity to the centroids. The characteristics of new data objects can be further understood by studying the neighbors.

7.4.2 How to Implement

SOM can be implemented in a few different ways in RapidMiner, with varied functionality and resulting output.

- **Data exploration chart:** In Chapter 3 Data Exploration, we reviewed the SOM chart as one of the data exploration techniques. In RapidMiner, any data set connected to a result port has a SOM chart feature under the Chart tab. This is a quick and easy method where the number of rows and columns can be specified and a SOM chart can be rendered.

- **Data Transformation > Attribute set reduction > SOM Operator:** The *SOM* operator available under the Data Transformation folder is used to reduce the number of dimensions in the data set. It is similar to the application of principal component analysis (Chapter 12 Feature Selection) where the data set is reduced to a lower dimensionality. In theory, a SOM can help reduce the data to any number of dimensions below the dimension count of the data set. In this operator, the number of desired output dimensions can be specified in the parameters, as shown in Figure 7.24. The net size parameter indicates the unique values in each of the SOM dimensions. There is no visual output for this operator and in two dimensions, only a square topography can be achieved through the *SOM data transformation* operator.

- **RapidMiner Extension > SOM Modeling Operator:** The *SOM modeling* operator is available in the SOM extension (Motl, 2012) and offers

Row No.	Country	Current account balance	General government revenue	Gross national savings	Total investment
1	Afghanistan	3.877	21.977	30.398	26.521
2	Albania	-11.372	25.835	14.509	25.886
3	Algeria	7.489	36.458	48.947	41.428
4	Angola	9.024	43.479	21.692	12.668
5	Antigua and	-13.109	22.430	16.194	29.303
6	Argentina	0.658	37.199	22.595	24.451
7	Armenia	-14.653	20.970	16.660	31.313
8	Australia	-2.870	31.846	23.925	26.794
9	Austria	3.009	48.105	24.611	21.602
10	Azerbaijan	28.423	45.652	46.955	18.532
11	Bahrain	3.578	27.174	34.544	30.965

FIGURE 7.25
GDP by country data set.

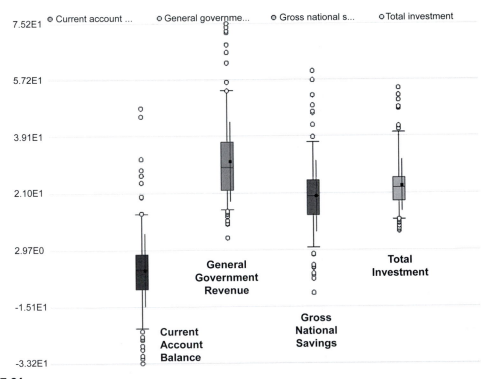

FIGURE 7.26
GDP by country: box-whisker (quartile) plot for all four attributes.

rich SOM visuals. We will be using SOM extensions for the rest of this implementation section, so readers are encouraged to install the SOM extension before proceeding further.

RapidMiner provides a marketplace platform called Extensions where third-party developers can develop new operators, data mining algorithms, data transformation operators, and visual exploration tools. Extensions are similar to add-ins in Microsoft Office programs. Extensions can be installed and uninstalled easily from Help → Updates and Extensions. SOM is one of the extensions, along with text mining, the R extension, Weka extensions, etc.

The data set we use in this section is the relative gross domestic product (GDP) information by country (IMF, 2012) from the *World Economic Outlook Database October 2012* by the International Monetary Fund. The data set has 186 records, one for each country, and four attributes in percentage of GDP: relative GDP invested, relative GDP saved, government revenue, and current account balance. Figure 7.25 shows the actual raw data for a few rows and Figure 7.26 shows the quartile plot for all the attributes.

The objective of the clustering is that we want to compare and contrast countries based on their percentage of GDP invested and saved, government revenue, and current account balance. Note that we are not comparing the size of the economy through absolute GDP but size of investment, national savings, current account, and size of government relative to the country's GDP. The goal of this modeling exercise is to arrange countries in a grid so that countries with similar characteristics of investing, savings, size of government, and current account are placed next to each other. We are compressing four-dimensional information to a two-dimensional map or grid. The data set and RapidMiner process can be accessed from the companion site of the book at www.LearnPredictiveAnalytics.com.

Step 1: Data Preparation

As a neural network, a SOM cannot accept polynominal or categorical attributes because centroid updates and distance calculations work only with numeric values. Polynominal data can be either ignored with information loss or converted to a numeric attribute using the *Nominal to Numerical* type conversion operator available in RapidMiner. In the Country-GDP data set, there are records (each record is a country) where there is no data. Neural networks cannot handle missing values and hence it needs to be replaced by either zero or the minimum or average value for the attribute using the *Replace Missing Value* operator. In this example we choose the average as the default missing value.

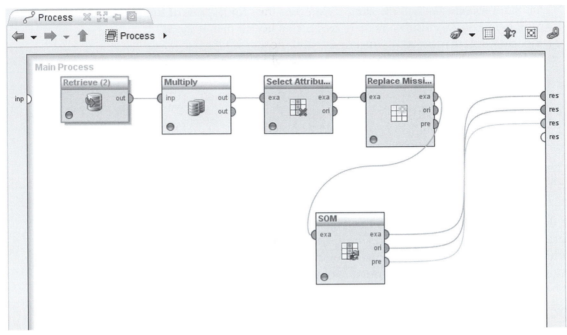

FIGURE 7.27
Clustering with SOM

Step 2: SOM Modeling Operator and Parameters

The *SOM modeling extension* operator is available in the Self-Organizing Map folder, labeled with the same name. Please note that SOM folder is visible only when SOM extension is installed. The following parameters can be configured in the model operator. The modeling operator accepts the example set with numeric data and a label attribute if applicable. In this example set, the country name is a label attribute. Figure 7.27 shows the RapidMiner process for developing a SOM model.

- **Training Rounds:** Defaults to 1000. This value indicates the number of training rounds for the data object selection process.
- **Net Size:** Indicates whether the grid size should be specified by the user or automatically approximated by the system. In this exercise we select user input for X and Y.
- **Net Size X:** Specifies the number of columns in the grid (horizontal direction). This is the same as the possible values for the SOM_0 attribute in the output. In this example we will set this value to 10.
- **Net Size Y:** Specifies the number of rows in the grid (vertical direction). This also indicates the values for the SOM_1 attribute in the output grid. In this example we will set this value to 10.

- **Learning Rate:** The neural network learning parameter (λ), which takes a value from 0 to 1. The value of λ determines how sensitive the change in weight is to the previous weights. A value closer to 0 means the new weight would be more based on previous weight and an λ closer to 1 means that weight would be mainly based on error correction. We are assigning the initial λ is 0.9 (see Chapter 4 Classification and Section 4.5 on Neural Networks).
- **Learning Rate function:** The learning rate function in a neural network is a time decay function of the learning process. The default and most commonly used time decay function is the inverse of time.

Step 3: Execution and Interpretation

The RapidMiner process can be saved and executed. The output of the *SOM modeling* operator consists of a visual model and a grid data set. The visual model is a lattice with centroids and mapped data points. The grid data set output is the example set labeled with location coordinates for each record in the grid lattice.

Visual Model

The visual model of the SOM displays the most recognizable form of SOM in a hexagonal grid format. The size of the grid is configured by the input parameters that set the net size of X and Y. There are several advanced visualization styles available in Visualization results window. The SOM visual output can be customized by the following parameters:

- **Visualization Style:** This selection controls the visual layout and background color of the SOM hexagons. The value of the selected measure is represented as a background gradient color. The default, U-Matrix, presents a background gradient color proportional to the distance of the central data points in adjacent hexagons. The P-Matrix option shows the number of example data points through the background gradient color. The selection of an individual attribute name for the visualization style renders the background gradient proportional to the value of the selected attribute. The visualization style selection does not rearrange the data points assigned to hexagons.
- **Label:** Selection shows the attribute value selected in the hexagons.
- **Color Schema:** Selection of monochrome or color scheme.

Figure 7.28 shows a SOM with the default selection of the label as Country and the visualization style as U-Matrix. We can observe how countries are placed on the grid based on their relationship with each other, as evaluated by the four economic metrics in relation with GDP. Countries with similar characteristics are placed closer to each other than others in the grid. If more than one country belongs to a centroid (hexagon), then the label of one country

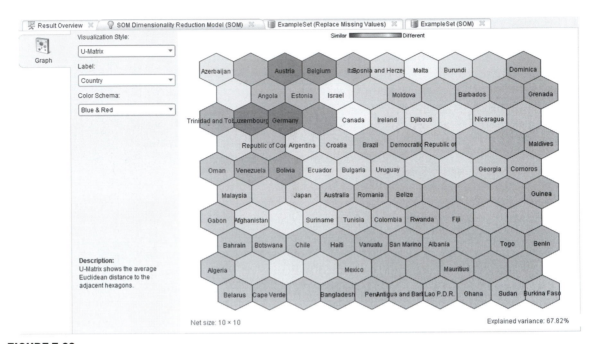

FIGURE 7.28
SOM output in the hexagonal grid.

closer to centroid is displayed on the grid. The grid locations of all the counties are listed in the location coordinates section of the results window.

A few interesting patterns in the data can be observed by changing the visualization style as a metric in the data set. In Figure 7.29, government revenue as percentage of GDP is used and visually, countries with high government revenue as a percentage of GDP is displayed on the top-left side of the grid (example: Belgium 48%) and countries with low government revenue are at bottom of the grid (Bangladesh 11%).

Figure 7.30 shows the national savings rate visualization to in the SOM; countries with a high savings rate (Algeria 49%) are concentrated on the left side and countries with a low savings rate (Maldives –2%) are concentrated on the right side of the SOM.

Location Coordinates

The second output of the *SOM* operator contains the location coordinates of the X- and Y-axes of grid with labels SOM_0 and SOM_1. The coordinate values of location range from 0 to net size – 1, as specified in the model parameters, since all data objects, in this case countries, are assigned to a specific location in the grid. This output, as shown in Figure 7.31, can be further used for postprocessing such as distance calculation of locations between countries in the grid space.

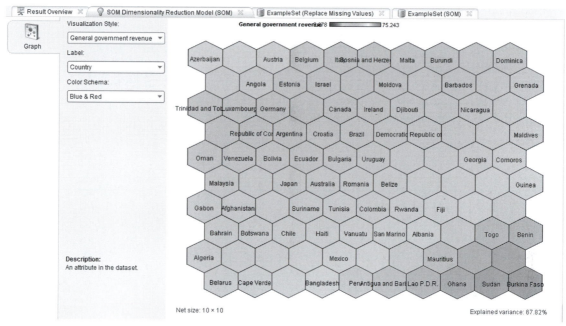

FIGURE 7.29

SOM output with color overlay related to government revenue.

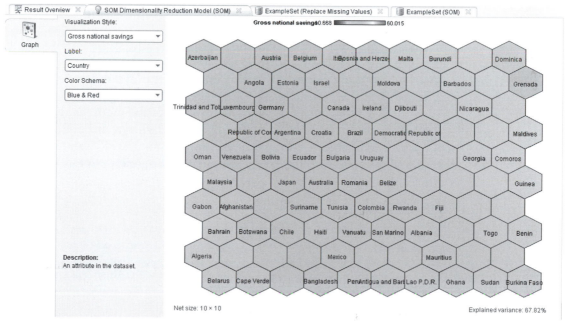

FIGURE 7.30

SOM output with color overlay related to national savings rate.

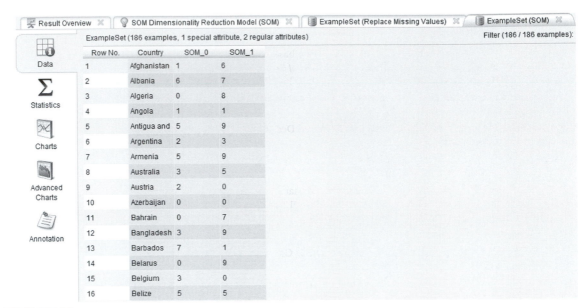

FIGURE 7.31
SOM output with location coordinates.

7.4.3 Conclusion

The methodology of self-organizing maps is derived from the foundations of both neural network and prototype-clustering approaches. Self-organizing maps are an effective visual clustering tool to understand numeric high-dimensional data. They reduce the features of the data set to two or three features, which is used to specify the topology of the layout. Hence, SOMs are predominantly used as a visual discovery and data exploration technique. Some of the recent applications of SOMs include the methods that are used in conjunction with other data mining and analytics techniques. SOMs are used in combination with graph mining (Resta, 2012), text mining (Liu et al., 2012), speech recognition (Kohonen, 1988), etc.

REFERENCES

Bache, K., & Lichman, M. (2013). *University of California, School of Information and Computer Science*. Retrieved from UCI Machine Learning Repository. http://archive.ics.uci.edu/ml.

Berry, M. J., & Linoff, G. (2000). Converging on the Customer: Understanding the Customer Behavior in the Telecommunications Industry. In M. J. Berry, & G. Linoff (Eds.), *Mastering Data Mining: The Art and Science of Customer Relationship Management* (pp. 357–394). John Wiley & Sons, Inc.

Berry, M. J., & Linoff, G. (2000). Data Mining Techniques and Algorithms. In M. J. Berry, & G. Linoff (Eds.), *Mastering Data Mining: The Art and Science of Customer Relationship Management* (pp. 103–107). John Wiley & Sons, Inc.

Davies, D. L., & Bouldin, D. W. (1979). A Cluster Separation Measure. *IEEE Transactions on Pattern Analysis and Machine Intelligence, 1*(2), 224–227.

Ester, M., Kriegel, H.-P., Sander, J., & Xu, X. (1996). A density-based algorithm for discovering clusters in large spatial databases with noise. In: *Proceedings of 2nd International Conference on Knowledge Discovery and Data Mining KDD-96.* (Vol. 96, pp. 226–231). AAAI Press.

Fisher, R. (1936). The use of multiple measurements in taxonomic problems. *Annual Eugenics,* 179–188.

Germano, T. (1999, March 23). *Self-Organizing Maps.* Retrieved Dec 10, 2013, from http://davis. wpi.edu/~matt/courses/soms/.

Hamerly, G., & Elkan, C. (2003). Learning the k in k-means. *Advances In Neural Information Processing Systems, 17,* 1–8 http://dx.doi.org/10.1.1.9.3574.

IMF (2012, Oct). *World Economic Outlook Database.* Retrieved Mar 15, 2013, from International Monetary Fund. http://www.imf.org/external/pubs/ft/weo/2012/02/weodata/index.aspx.

Kohonen, T. (1988). The "neural" phonetic typewriter. Computer,. *IEEE, 21*(3), 11–22. http://dx. doi.org/10.1109/2.28.

Kohonen, T. (1982). Self-Organized Formation of Topologically Correct Feature Maps. *Biological Cybernetics, 43,* 59–69.

Liu, Y., Liu, M., & Wang, X. (2012). Application of Self-Organizing Maps in Text Clustering: A Review. In M. Johnsson (Ed.), *Applications of Self-Organizing Maps* (pp. 205–220). InTech.

Lloyd, S. (1982). Least squares quantization in PCM. *IEEE Transactions on Information Theory, 28,* 129–137.

Motl, J. (2012). *SOM Extension for Rapid Miner.* Prague: Czech Technical University.

Pearson, P., & Cooper, C. (2012). Using Self Organizing Maps to Analyze Demographics and Swing State Voting in the 2008 U.S. Presidential Election. In N. Mana, F. Schwenker, & E. Trentin (Eds.), *Artificial Neural Networks in Pattern Recognition ANNPR'12 Proceedings of the 5th INNS IAPR TC 3 GIRPR conference* (pp. 201–212). Berlin: Heidelberg: Springer Berlin Heidelberg. http://dx.doi.org/10.1007/978-3-642-33212-8.

Resta, M. (2012). Graph Mining Based SOM: A Tool to Analyze Economic Stability. In M. Johnsson (Ed.), *Applications of Self-Organizing Maps* (pp. 1–26). InTech. Retrieved from http:// www.intechopen.com/books/applications-of-self-organizing-maps.

Tan, P.-N., Michael, S., & Kumar, V. (2005). Clustering Analysis: Basic Concepts and Algorithms. In P.-N. Tan, S. Michael, & V. Kumar (Eds.), *Introduction to Data Mining* (pp. 487–555). Boston, MA: Addison-Wesley.

Witten, I. H., & Frank, E. (2005). Algorithms: The Basic Methods. In *Data Mining: Practical Machine Learning Tools and Techniques* (pp. 136–139). San Francisco, CA: Morgan Kaufmann.

CHAPTER 8

Model Evaluation

In this chapter we will formally introduce the most commonly used methods for testing the quality of a predictive model. Throughout this book, we have used various "validation" techniques to split the available data into a training set and a testing set. We have used several different types of "performance" operators in RapidMiner in conjunction with validation without really explaining in detail how these operators function. We will now discuss several ways in which predictive models are evaluated for their performance.

There are three main tools that are available to test a classification model's quality: *confusion matricies* (or truth tables), *lift charts*, and *ROC* (receiver operator characteristic) curves. We will define and describe in detail how these tools are constructed and demonstrate how to implement performance evaluations using RapidMiner. To evaluate a numeric prediction from a regression model, there are many conventional statistical tests that may be applied (Black, 2008) which was discussed in Chapter 5 Regression Methods.

FROM EVALUATING PROSPECTS TO PREDICTIVE MODEL FACE-OFF

Direct marketing (DM) companies, which send out postal mail (or in the days before do-not-call lists, called prospects) were one of the early pioneers in applying predictive analytics techniques (Berry, 1999). A key performance indicator for their marketing activities is of course the improvement in their bottom line as a result of their utilization of predictive models.

Let us assume that a typical average response rate for direct mail campaign is 10%. Let us further make the following simple assumptions: cost per mail sent = $1 and potential revenue per response = $20. If they have 10,000 people to send out their mailers to, then they can expect to receive potential revenues of 10,000 x 10% x $20 = $20,000, with a net profit of $10,000. Typically, the mailers are sent out in batches to spread costs over a period of time. Let us further assume that these are sent out in batches of 1,000. The first question someone would ask is how to divide the list of names into these batches. If the average expectation of return is 10%, then would it not make a lot of sense to just send one batch of mails to those prospects that make up this 10% and be done with the campaign? Clearly this would save a lot of time and money and the net profit would jump to $19,000!

Can we identify all of these 10 percenters? While this is clearly unrealistic, we can use our classification techniques to *rank* or *score* prospects by their *likelihood* to respond to the mailers. Predictive analytics is after all about converting future uncertainties into usable probabilities (Taylor, 2011). Then we can use our predictive method to order these probabilities and send out our mailers to only those who score above a particular threshold (say 85% chance of response).

Finally, some techniques may be better suited to this problem than others. How do we compare the different available methods by their performance? Will logistic regression capture these top 10 percenters better than support vector machines? What are the different metrics we can use to select the best performing methods? These are some of the things we will discuss in this chapter in more detail.

8.1 CONFUSION MATRIX (OR TRUTH TABLE)

Classification performance is best described by an aptly named tool called the confusion matrix. Understanding the confusion matrix requires becoming familiar with several definitions. But before introducing the definitions, we must look at a basic confusion matrix for a binary or binomial classification where there can be two classes (say, Y or N). The accuracy of classification of a specific example can be viewed one of four possible ways:

- The predicted class is Y, and the actual class is also Y → this is a "True Positive" or TP
- The predicted class is Y, and the actual class is N → this is a "False Positive" or FP
- The predicted class is N, and the actual class is Y → this is a "False Negative" or FN
- The predicted class is N, and the actual class is also N → this is a "True Negative" or TN

A basic confusion matrix is traditionally arranged as a 2 x 2 matrix as shown in Table 8.1. The predicted classes are arranged horizontally in rows and the actual classes are arranged vertically in columns, although sometimes this order is reversed (Kohavi & Provost, 1998). (Note: We will follow the convention used by RapidMiner and lay out the predicted classes row-wise as shown in Table 8.1.) A quick way to examine this matrix or a "truth table" as it is also called is to scan the diagonal from top left to bottom right. An ideal classification performance would only have entries along this main diagonal and the off-diagonal elements would be zero.

These four cases will now be used to introduce several commonly used terms for understanding and explaining classification performance. As mentioned earlier, a perfect classifier will have no entries for FP and FN (i.e., the number of FP = number of FN = 0).

Sensitivity is the ability of a classifier to select all the cases that *need* to be selected. A perfect classifier will select all the actual Y's and will not miss any actual Y's. In other words it will have no false negatives. In reality, any classifier will miss some true Y's and thus have some false negatives. Sensitivity is expressed as a ratio

Table 8.1 Confusion Matrix

		Actual Class(Observation)	
		Y	**N**
Predicted Class (Expectation)	Y	**TP** (true positive) Correct result	**FP** (false positive) Unexpected result
	N	**FN** (false negative) Missing result	**TN** (true negative) Correct absence of result

(or percentage) calculated as follows: $TP/(TP + FN)$. However, sensitivity alone is not sufficient to evaluate a classifier. In situations such as credit card fraud, where rates are typically around 0.1%, an ordinary classifier may be able to show sensitivity of 99.9% by picking nearly all the cases as legitimate transactions or TP. We also need the ability to detect illegitimate or fraudulent transactions, the TNs. This is where the next measure, specificity, which ignores TPs, comes in.

Specificity is the ability of a classifier to reject all the cases that *need* to be rejected. A perfect classifier will reject all the actual N's and will not deliver any unexpected results. In other words, it will have no false positives. In reality, any classifier will select some cases that need to be rejected and thus have some false positives. Specificity is expressed as a ratio (or percentage) calculated as follows: $TN/(TN+FP)$.

Relevance is a term that is easy to understand in a document search and retrieval scenario. Suppose you run a search for a specific term and that search returns 100 documents. Of these, let us say only 70 were useful because they were *relevant* to your search. Furthermore, the search actually missed out on an additional 40 documents that could have been actually useful to you. With this context, we can define additional terms.

Precision is defined as the proportion of cases found that were actually relevant. For the above example, this number was 70 and thus the precision is 70/100 or 70%. The 70 documents were TP, whereas the remaining 30 were FP. Therefore precision is $TP/(TP+FP)$.

Recall is defined as the proportion of the relevant cases that were actually found among all the relevant cases. Again with the above example, only 70 of the total 110 (= 70 found + 40 missed) relevant cases were actually found, thus giving a recall of 70/110 = 63.63%. You can see that recall is the same as sensitivity, because recall is also given by $TP/(TP+FN)$.

Accuracy is defined as the ability of the classifier to select all cases that need to be selected and reject all cases that need to be rejected. For a classifier with 100% accuracy, this would imply that $FN = FP = 0$. Note that in the document search example, we have not indicated the TN, as this could be really large. Accuracy is given by $(TP+TN)/(TP+FP+TN+FN)$.

Finally, *error* is simply the complement of accuracy, measured by (1 – accuracy).

Table 8.2 Evaluation Measures

Term	Definition	Calculation
Sensitivity	Ability to select what needs to be selected	TP/(TP+FN)
Specificity	Ability to reject what needs to be rejected	TN/(TN+FP)
Precision	Proportion of cases found that were relevant	TP/(TP+FP)
Recall	Proportion of all relevant cases that were found	TP/(TP+FN)
Accuracy	Aggregate measure of classifier performance	(TP+TN)/(TP+TN+FP+FN)

Table 8.2 summarizes all the major definitions. Fortunately, the analyst does not need to memorize these equations because their calculations are always automated in any tool of choice. However, it is important to have a good fundamental understanding of these terms.

8.2 RECEIVER OPERATOR CHARACTERISTIC (ROC) CURVES AND AREA UNDER THE CURVE (AUC)

Measures like accuracy or precision are essentially aggregate in nature, in the sense that they provide the average performance of the classifier on the data set. A classifier can have a very high accuracy on a data set, but have very poor class recall and precision. Clearly, a model to detect fraud is no good if its ability to detect TP for the fraud = yes class (and thereby its class recall) is low. It is therefore quite useful to look at measures that compare different metrics to see if there is a situation for a trade-off: for example, can we sacrifice a little overall accuracy to gain a lot more improvement in class recall? One can examine a model's rate of detecting TPs and contrast it with its ability to detect FPs. The receiver operator characteristic (ROC) curves meet this need and were originally developed in the field of signal detection (Green, 1966). A ROC curve is created by plotting the fraction of true positives (TP rate) versus the fraction of false positives (FP rate). When we generate a table of such values, we can plot the FP rate on the horizontal axis and the TP rate (same as sensitivity or recall) on the vertical axis. The FP can also be expressed as (1 − specificity) or TN rate.

Consider a classifier that could predict if a website visitor is likely to click on a banner ad: the model would be most likely built using historic click-through rates based on pages visited, time spent on certain pages, and other characteristics of site visitors. In order to evaluate the performance of this model on test data, we can generate a table such as the one shown in Table 8.3.

The first column "Actual Class" consists of the actual class for a particular example (in this case a website visitor, who has clicked on the banner ad). The next column, "Predicted Class" is the model prediction and the third column, "Confidence of response" is the confidence of this prediction. In order to create a ROC

Table 8.3 Classifier Performance Data Needed for Building an ROC Curve

Actual Class	Predicted Class	Confidence of "response"	Type?	Number of TP	Number of FP	Fraction of FP	Fraction of TP
response	response	0.902	TP	1	0	0	0.167
response	response	0.896	TP	2	0	0	0.333
response	response	0.834	TP	3	0	0	0.500
response	response	0.741	TP	4	0	0	0.667
no response	response	0.686	FP	4	1	0.25	0.667
response	response	0.616	TP	5	1	0.25	0.833
response	response	0.609	TP	6	1	0.25	1
no response	response	0.576	FP	6	2	0.5	1
no response	response	0.542	FP	6	3	0.75	1
no response	response	0.530	FP	6	4	1	1
no response	no response	0.440	TN	6	4	1	1
no response	no response	0.428	TN	6	4	1	1
no response	no response	0.393	TN	6	4	1	1
no response	no response	0.313	TN	6	4	1	1
no response	no response	0.298	TN	6	4	1	1
no response	no response	0.260	TN	6	4	1	1
no response	no response	0.248	TN	6	4	1	1
no response	no response	0.247	TN	6	4	1	1
no response	no response	0.241	TN	6	4	1	1
no response	no response	0.116	TN	6	4	1	1

chart, we need to sort the predicted data in decreasing order of this confidence level, which has been done in this case. Comparing columns Actual class and Predicted class, we can identify the type of prediction: for instance, spreadsheet rows 2 through 5 are all true positives (TP) and row 6 is the first instance of a false positive (FP). As observed in columns "Number of TP" and "Number of FP", we can keep a running count of the TPs and FPs and also calculate the fraction of TPs and FPs, which are shown in columns "Fraction of TP" and "Fraction of FP".

Observing the "Number of TP" and "Number of FP" columns, we see that the model has discovered a total of 6 TPs and 4 FPs (the remaining 10 examples are all TNs). We also see that the model has identified nearly 67% of all the TPs before it fails and hits its first FP (row 6 above). Finally all TPs have been identified when Fraction of TP = 1) before the next FP was run into. If we were to now plot Fraction of FP (False Positive Rate) versus Fraction of TP (True Positive Rate), then we would see a ROC chart similar to the one shown in Figure 8.1. Clearly an ideal classifier would have an accuracy of 100% (and thus would have

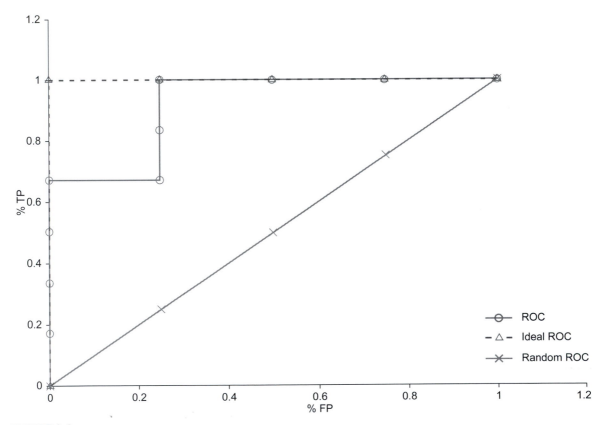

FIGURE 8.1

Comparing ROC curve for the example shown in Table 8.3 to random and ideal classifiers.

identified 100% of all TPs). Thus the ROC for an ideal classifier would look like the thick curve shown in Figure 8.1. Finally a very ordinary or random classifier (which has only a 50% accuracy) would possibly find one FP for every TP and thus look like the 45-degree line shown.

As the number of test examples becomes larger, the ROC curve will become smoother: the random classifier will simply look like a straight line drawn between the points (0,0) and (1,1)— the stair steps become very small. The area under this curve is basically the area of a right triangle (with side 1 unit and height 1 unit), which is 0.5. This quantity is termed *area under the curve* (AUC). AUC for the ideal classifier is 1.0. Thus the performance of a classifier can also be quantified by its AUC: obviously any AUC higher than 0.5 is better than random and the closer it is to 1.0, the better the performance. A common rule of thumb is to select those classifiers that not only have a ROC curve that is closest to ideal, but also an AUC higher than 0.8. Typical uses for AUC and ROC curves are to compare the performance of different classification algorithms for the same dataset.

8.3 LIFT CURVES

Lift curves or lift charts were first deployed in direct marketing where the problem was to identify if a particular prospect was worth calling or sending an advertisement by mail. We mentioned in the use case at the beginning of this chapter that with a predictive model, one can *score* a list of prospects by their propensity to respond to an ad campaign. When we sort the prospects by this score (by the decreasing order of their propensity to respond), we now end up with a mechanism to systematically select the most valuable prospects right at the beginning and thus maximize our return. Thus, rather than mailing out the ads to a random group of prospects, we can now send our ads to the first batch of "most likely responders," followed by the next batch and so on.

Without classification, the "most likely responders" are distributed randomly throughout the data set. Let us suppose we have a data set of 200 prospects and it contains a total of 40 responders or TPs. If we break up the data set into, say, 10 equal sized batches (called deciles), the likelihood of finding TPs in each batch is also 20%, that is, four samples in each decile will be TPs. However, when we use a predictive model to classify our prospects, a good model will tend to pull these "most likely responders" into the top few deciles. Thus we might find in our simple example that the first two deciles will have all 40 TPs and the remaining eight deciles have none.

Lift charts were developed to demonstrate this in a graphical way (Rud, 2000). The focus is again on the true positives and thus it can be argued that they indicate the sensitivity of the model unlike ROC curves, which can show the relation between sensitivity and specificity.

The basis for building lift charts is the following: *randomly selecting x% of the data (for prospects to call) would yield x% of targets (to call or not)*. Lift is the improvement over this random selection that a predictive model can potentially yield because of its scoring or ranking ability. For example in our earlier data from Table 8.3, there are a total of 6 TPs out of 20 test cases. If we were to take the *unscored* data and randomly select 25% of the examples, we could expect 25% of them to be TPs (or 25% of 6 = 1.5). However, scoring and reordering the data set by confidence will improve this. As can be seen in Table 8.4, the first 25% or quartile of scored (reordered) data now contains four TPs. This translates to a "lift" of 4/1.5 = 2.67. Similarly the second quartile of the unscored data can be expected to contain 50% (or three) of the TPs. As seen in Table 8.4, the scored 50% data contains all six TPs, giving a lift of 6/3 = 2.00.

The steps to build lift charts are as follows:

1. Generate scores for all the data points (prospects) in the test set using the trained model.
2. Rank the prospects by decreasing score or confidence of "response."
3. Count the TPs in the first 25% (quartile) of the data set, and then the first 50% (add the next quartile) and so on; see columns "Cumulative TP" and "Quartile" in Table 8.4.
4. *Gain* at a given quartile level is the ratio of the cumulative number of TPs in that quartile to the total number of TPs in the entire data set (six in the above example). The 1st quartile gain is therefore 4/6 or 67%, the 2nd quartile gain is 6/6 or 100%, and so on.
5. *Lift* is the ratio of gain to the random expectation at a given quartile level. Remember that random expectation at the xth quartile is x%. In the above example, the random expectation is to find 25% of 6 = 1.5 TPs in the 1st quartile, 50% or 3 TPs in the 2nd quartile, and so on. The corresponding 1st quartile lift is therefore 4/1.5 = 2.667, the 2nd quartile lift is 6/3 = 2.00, and so on.

The corresponding curves for the simple example are shown in Figure 8.2. Typically lift charts are created on deciles not quartiles. We chose quartiles because they helped to illustrate the concept using the small 20-sample test data set. However the logic remains the same for deciles or any other groupings as well.

8.4 EVALUATING THE PREDICTIONS: IMPLEMENTATION

We will use a built-in data set in RapidMiner to demonstrate how all the three classification performances (confusion matrix, ROC/AUC and lift/gain charts) are evaluated. The process shown in Figure 8.3 uses the *Generate Direct Mailing Data* operator to create a 10,000 record data set. The objective of the modeling (Naïve Bayes used here) is to predict whether a person is likely to respond to a

Table 8.4 Scoring Predictions and Sorting by Confidences is the Basis for Generating Lift Curves

Actual Class	Predicted Class	Confidence of "response"	Type?	Cumulative TP	Cumulative FP	Quartile	Gain	Lift
response	response	0.902	TP	1	0	1st	67%	2.666667
response	response	0.896	TP	2	0	1st		
response	response	0.834	TP	3	0	1st		
response	response	0.741	TP	4	0	1st		
no response	response	0.686	FP	4	1	1st		
response	response	0.616	TP	5	1	2nd	100%	2
response	response	0.609	TP	6	1	2nd		
no response	response	0.576	FP	6	2	2nd		
no response	response	0.542	FP	6	3	2nd		
no response	response	0.530	FP	6	4	2nd		
no response	no response	0.440	TN	6	4	3rd	100%	1.333333
no response	no response	0.428	TN	6	4	3rd		
no response	no response	0.393	TN	6	4	3rd		
no response	no response	0.313	TN	6	4	3rd		
no response	no response	0.298	TN	6	4	3rd		
no response	no response	0.260	TN	6	4	4th	100%	1
no response	no response	0.248	TN	6	4	4th		
no response	no response	0.247	TN	6	4	4th		
no response	no response	0.241	TN	6	4	4th		
no response	no response	0.116	TN	6	4	4th		

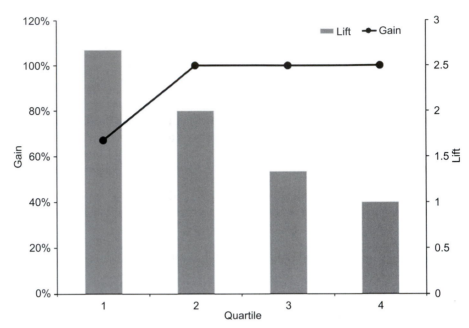

FIGURE 8.2

Lift and gain curves.

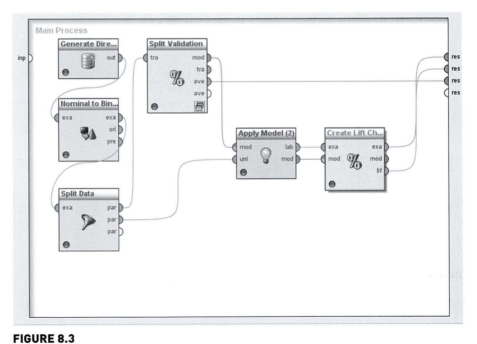

FIGURE 8.3

Process setup to demonstrate typical classification performance metrics.

direct mailing campaign or not based on demographic attributes (age, lifestyle, earnings, type of car, family status, and sports affinity).

Step 1: Data Preparation
Create a data set with 10,000 examples using the *Generate Direct Mailing Data* operator by setting a local random seed (default = 1992) to ensure repeatability. Convert the label attribute from polynomial (nominal) to binominal using the appropriate operator as shown. This enables us to select specific binominal classification performance measures.

Split data into two partitions: an 80% partition (8,000 examples) for model building and validation and a 20% partition for testing. An important point of note is that data partitioning is not an exact science and this ratio can change depending upon the data.

Connect the 80% output (upper output port) from the *Split Data* operator to the *Split Validation* operator. Select a relative split with a ratio of 0.7 (70% for training) and shuffled sampling.

Step 2: Modeling Operator and Parameters
Insert the *naïve Bayes* operator in the Training panel of the *Split Validation* operator and the usual *Apply Model* operator in the Testing panel. Add a *Performance (Binomial Classification)* operator. Select the following options in the *performance* operator: accuracy, false positive, false negative, true positive, true negative, sensitivity, specificity, and AUC.

Step 3: Evaluation
Add another *Apply Model* operator outside the *Split Validation* operator and deliver the model to its "mod" input port while connecting the 2,000 example data partition from Step 3 to the "unl" port. Add a *Create Lift Chart* operator with the following options selected: target class = response, binning type = frequency, and number of bins = 10. Note the port connections as shown in Figure 8.3.

Step 4: Execution and Interpretation
When the above process is run, we will generate the confusion matrix and ROC curve for the validation sample (30% of the original 80% = 2400 examples) whereas we will generate a lift curve for the test sample (2,000 examples). There is no reason why we cannot add another *Performance (Binomial Classification)* operator for the test sample or create a lift chart for the validation examples. (The reader should try this as an exercise —how will you deliver the output from the *Create Lift Chart* operator when it is inserted inside the *Split Validation* operator?)

	true no response	true response	class precision
pred. no response	1231	146	89.40%
pred. response	394	629	61.49%
class recall	75.75%	81.16%	

FIGURE 8.4

Confusion matrix for validation set of direct marketing data set.

The confusion matrix shown in Figure 8.4 is used to calculate several common metrics using the definitions from Table 8.1. Compare them with the Rapid-Miner outputs to verify your understanding.

TP = 629, TN = 1231, FP = 394, FN = 146

Term	Definition	Calculation
Sensitivity	TP/(TP+FN)	629/(629+146) = 81.16%
Specificity	TN/(TN+FP)	1231/(1231+394) = 75.75%
Precision	TP/(TP+FP)	629/(629+394) = 61.5%
Recall	TP/(TP+FN)	629/(629+146) = 81.16%
Accuracy	(TP+TN)/(TP+TN+FP+FN)	(629+1231)/ (629+1231+394+146) = 77.5%

Note that RapidMiner makes a distinction between the two classes while calculating precision and recall. For example, in order to calculate a *class* recall for "no response," the *positive* class becomes "no response" and the corresponding TP is 1231 and corresponding FN is 394. Therefore a class recall for "no response" is 1231/(1231+394) = 75.75% whereas our calculation above assumed that "response" was the positive class. Class recall is an important metric to keep in mind when dealing with highly unbalanced data. Data is considered unbalanced if the proportion of the two classes is skewed. When models are trained on unbalanced data, the resulting class recalls also tend to be skewed. For example, in a data set where there are only 2% responses, the resulting model can have a very high recall for "no responses" but a very low class recall for "responses." This skew is not seen in the overall model accuracy and using this model on unseen data may result in severe misclassifications.

The solution for this problem is to either balance the training data so that we end up with a more or less equal proportion of classes or to insert penalties or costs on misclassifications using the *Metacost* operator as discussed in Chapter 5

AUC: 0.876 (positive class: response)

ROC   — ROC (Thresholds)

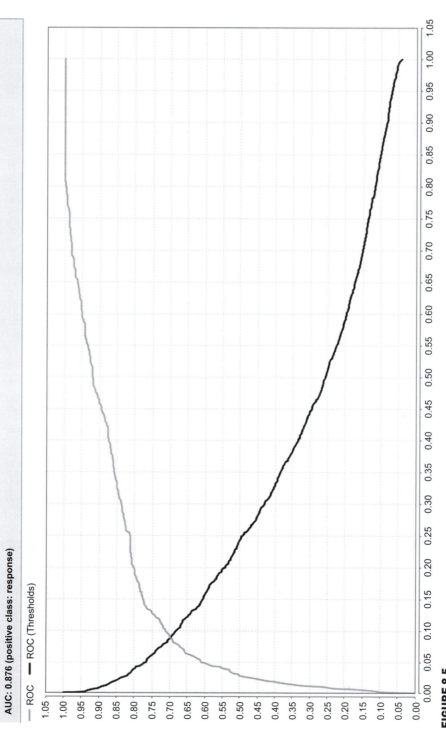

FIGURE 8.5

ROC curve and AUC.

Regression Methods. Data balancing is explained in more detail in Chapter 13 Getting Started with RapidMiner.

The AUC is shown along with the ROC curve in Figure 8.5. As mentioned earlier, AUC values close to 1 are indicative of a good model. The ROC captures the sorted confidences of a prediction. As long as the prediction is correct for the examples the curve takes one step up (increased TP). If the prediction is wrong the curve takes one step to the right (increased FP). RapidMiner can show two additional AUCs called "optimistic" and "pessimistic." The differences between the optimistic and pessimistic curves occur when there are examples with the same confidence, but the predictions are sometimes false and sometimes true. The optimistic curve shows the possibility that the correct predictions are chosen first so the curve goes steeper upwards. The pessimistic curve shows the possibility that the wrong predictions are chosen first so the curve increases more gradually.

Finally, RapidMiner's lift chart outputs do not directly indicate the lift values as we demonstrated with the simple example earlier. In step 5 of our process, we selected 10 bins for our chart and thus each bin will have 200 examples (a decile). Recall that to create a lift chart we need to sort all the predictions by the confidence of the positive class ("response"), which is shown in Figure 8.6.

The first bar in the lift chart shown in Figure 8.7 corresponds to the first bin of 200 examples after the sorting. The bar tells us that there are 181 TP in this bin (you can see from the table in Figure 8.6 that the very second example, Row No. 1973, is an FP). From our confusion matrix earlier, we know that there are 629 TPs in this example set. A random classifier would have identified 10% of these or 62.9 TPs in the first 200 examples. Therefore the lift for the first decile is 181/62.9 = 2.87. Similarly the lift for the first two deciles is (181+167)/(2*62.9) = 2.76 and so on. Also, the first decile contains 181/629 = 28.8% of the TPs, the first two deciles contain (181+167)/629 = 55.3% of the TPs, and so on. This is shown in the cumulative (percent) gains curve on the right hand y-axis of the lift chart output.

As described earlier, a good classifier will accumulate all the TPs in the first few deciles and will have very few FPs at the top of the heap. This will result in a gain curve that quickly rises to the 100% level within the first few deciles.

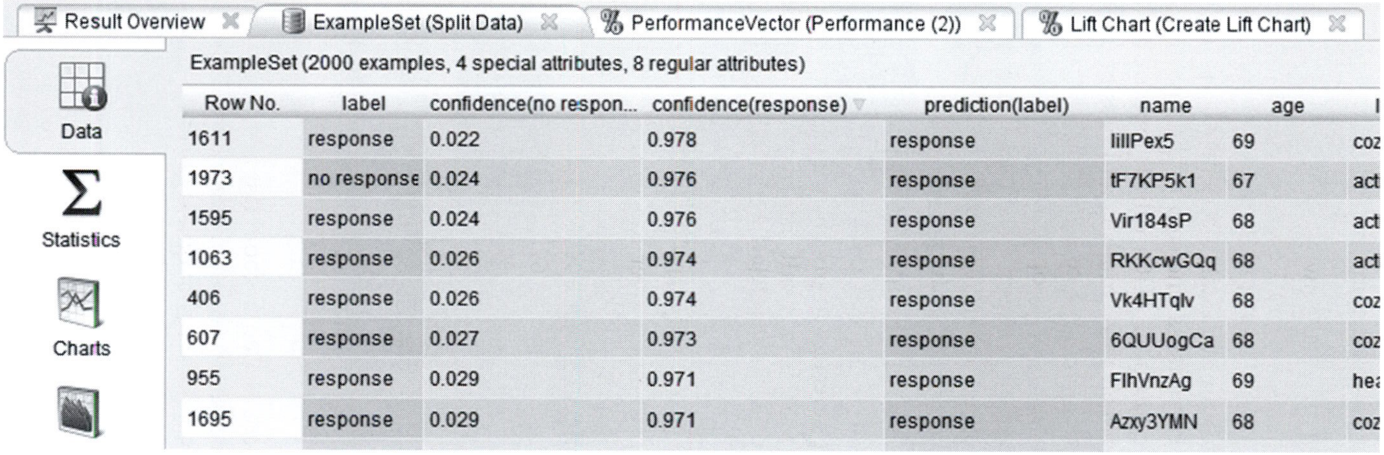

Row No.	label	confidence(no respon...	confidence(response) ▽	prediction(label)	name	age	l
1611	response	0.022	0.978	response	IiiIPex5	69	co2
1973	no response	0.024	0.976	response	tF7KP5k1	67	act
1595	response	0.024	0.976	response	Vir184sP	68	act
1063	response	0.026	0.974	response	RKKcwGQq	68	act
406	response	0.026	0.974	response	Vk4HTqIv	68	co2
607	response	0.027	0.973	response	6QUUogCa	68	co2
955	response	0.029	0.971	response	FlhVnzAg	69	hei
1695	response	0.029	0.971	response	Azxy3YMN	68	co2

ExampleSet (2000 examples, 4 special attributes, 8 regular attributes)

Result Overview | ExampleSet (Split Data) | PerformanceVector (Performance (2)) | Lift Chart (Create Lift Chart)

Data

Statistics

Charts

FIGURE 8.6

Table of scored responses used to build the lift chart.

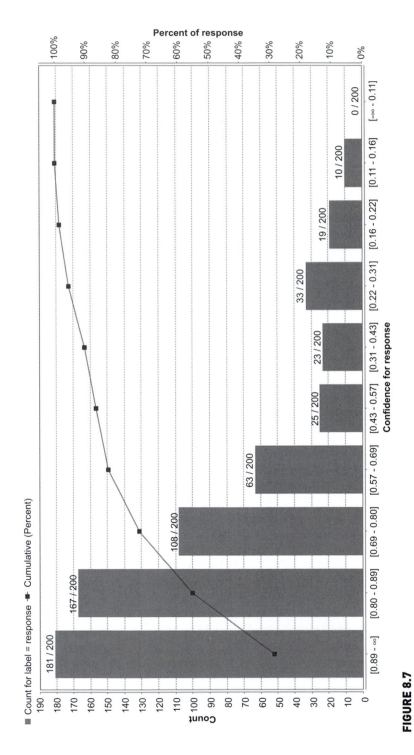

FIGURE 8.7

Lift chart generated by RapidMiner.

CONCLUSION

This chapter covered the basic performance evaluation tools that are typically used in classification methods. We started out by describing the basic elements of a confusion matrix and explored in detail concepts that are important to understanding it, such as sensitivity, specificity, and accuracy. We then described the receiver operator characteristic (ROC) curve, which had its origins in signal detection theory and has now been adopted for data mining, along with the equally useful aggregate metric of area under the curve (AUC). Finally, we described two very useful tools that had their origins in direct marketing applications: lift and gain charts. We discussed how to build these curves in general and how they can be constructed using RapidMiner. In summary, these tools are some of the most commonly used metrics for evaluating predictive models and developing skill and confidence in using these is a prerequisite to developing data mining expertise.

One key to developing good predictive models is to know when to use which measures. As discussed earlier, relying on a single measure like accuracy can be misleading. For highly unbalanced data sets, we rely on several measures such as class recall and specificity in addition to accuracy. ROC curves are frequently used to compare several algorithms side by side. Additionally, just as there are an infinite number of triangular shapes that have the same area, AUC should not be used alone to judge a model—AUC and ROCs should be used in conjunction to rate a model's performance. Finally, lift and gain charts are most commonly used for scoring applications where we need to rank-order the examples in a data set by their propensity to belong to a particular category.

REFERENCES

Berry, M. A. (1999). *Mastering Data Mining: The Art and Science of Customer Relationship Managemen*. New York: John Wiley and Sons.

Black, K. (2008). *Business Statistics for Contemporary Decision Making*. New York: John Wiley and Sons.

Green, D. S. (1966). *Signal Detection Theory and Psychophysics*. New York: John Wiley and Sons.

Kohavi, R., & Provost, F., (Editors) (1998). Glossary of Terms. *Machine Learning 30*, 271–274.

Rud, O. (2000). *Data Mining Cookbook: Modeling Data for Marketing, Risk and Customer Relationship Management*. New York: John Wiley and Sons.

Taylor, J. (2011, October 13). *Decision Management Systems: A Practical Guide to Using Business Rules and Predictive Analytics*. IBM Press.

CHAPTER 9

Text Mining

In this chapter we will learn how to extract patterns and discover new knowledge by applying many of the techniques we have learned so far, not on ordered data, but on unstructured natural language. This constitutes the vast and fast growing area of text and web mining. For all the techniques described up to this point, a cleaned and organized table consisting of rows and columns of data was fed as input to an algorithm. The output from the algorithm was a model that could then be used to predict outcomes from a new data set or to find patterns in data. But how do we apply the same techniques to extract patterns and predict outcomes when the input data looks like normal written communication or worse? This might seem baffling at first, but as we shall see in this chapter, there are ways of presenting text data to the algorithms that process "normal" data.

We start out with a brief historical introduction to the field of text mining to establish some context. In the following section, we will describe techniques that can convert common text into a semi-structured format that we, and the algorithms we have introduced so far, can recognize. Finally we will introduce the toolkit that is available in RapidMiner to do this conversion and apply it in two case studies: one involving an unsupervised (clustering) model and another involving a supervised (SVM) model. We will close the chapter with some key considerations to keep in mind while implementing text mining.

Text mining is the new frontier of predictive analytics and data mining. Eric Siegel in his book *Predictive Analytics* (Siegel, 2013) provides an interesting analogy: if all the data in the world was equivalent to the water on earth, then textual data is like the ocean, making up a majority of the volume. Text analytics is driven by the need to process natural human language, but unlike numeric or categorical data, natural language does not exist in a "structured" format consisting of rows (of examples) and columns (of attributes). Text mining is therefore the domain of unstructured data mining.

Some of the first applications of text mining came about when people were trying to organize documents (Cutting, 1992). Hearst (Hearst, June 20-26, 1999)

IT IS NLP, MY DEAR WATSON!

Perhaps the most famous application of text mining is IBM's Watson program, which performed spectacularly when competing against humans on the nightly game show Jeopardy! How does Watson use text mining? Watson has instant access to hundreds of millions of structured and unstructured documents, including the full content of Wikipedia entries.

When a Jeopardy! question is transcribed to Watson, it searches for and identifies candidate documents that score a very close match to the words of the question. The search and comparison methods it uses are similar to those used by search engines, and include many of the techniques, such as n-grams and stemming, which we discuss in this chapter. Once it identifies candidate documents, it again uses other text mining (also known as natural language processing or NLP) methods to rank them. For example, if the answer is, REGARDING THIS DEVICE, ARCHIMEDES SAID, "GIVE ME A PLACE TO STAND ON, AND I WILL MOVE THE EARTH, a Watson search for this sentence

in its databases might reveal among its candidate documents several with the term "lever." Watson might insert the word "lever" inside the answer text and rerun a new search to see if there are other documents with the new combination of terms. If the search result has many matches to the terms in the sentence—as it most likely would in this case—a high score is assigned to the inserted term.

If a broad and non-domain-focused program like Watson, which relies heavily on text mining and NLP, can answer open-ended quiz show questions with nearly 100% accuracy, one can imagine how successful specialized NLP tools would be. In fact IBM has successfully deployed a Watson-type program to help in decision making at health care centers (Upbin, 2013).

Text mining also finds applications in numerous business activities such as email spam filtering, consumer sentiment analysis, and patent mining to name a few. We will explore a couple of these in this chapter.

recognized that text analysis does not require artificial intelligence but "…a mixture of computationally-driven and user-guided analysis," which is at the heart of the supervised models used in predictive analytics that we have discussed so far.

People in the data warehousing and business intelligence domains can appreciate text mining in a slightly different context. Here, the objective is not so much discovering new trends or patterns, but cleaning data stored in business databases. For example, when people make manual entries into a customer relationship management (CRM) software, there is a lot of scope for typographic errors: a salesperson's name may be spelled "Osterman" in several instances (which is perhaps the correct spelling) and "Ostrerman" in a few instances, which is a misspelling. Text mining could be used in such situations to identify the "right" spelling and suggest it to the entry operator to ensure that data consistency is maintained. Similar application logic could be used in identifying and streamlining call center service data (McKnight, 2005).

Text mining, more than any other technique within data mining, fits the "mining" metaphor. Traditionally, mining refers to the process of separating dirt from valuable metal and in the case of text mining we attempt to separate valuable keywords from a mass of other words (or relevant documents from a sea of documents) and use them to identify meaningful patterns or make predictions.

9.1 HOW TEXT MINING WORKS

The fundamental step in text mining involves converting text into semi-structured data. Once you convert the unstructured text into semi-structured data, there is nothing to stop you from applying any of the analytics techniques to classify, cluster, and predict. The unstructured text needs to be converted into a semi-structured dataset so that you can find patterns and even better, train models to detect patterns in new and unseen text. The chart in Figure 9.1 identifies the main steps in this process at a high level.

We will now examine each of the main processes in detail and introduce some terminology and concepts that are necessary. But before we describe these processes, we need to define a few core ideas that will be essential.

9.1.1 Term Frequency–Inverse Document Frequency (TF–IDF)

Consider a web search problem where the user types in some keywords and the search engine extracts all the documents (essentially, web pages) that contain

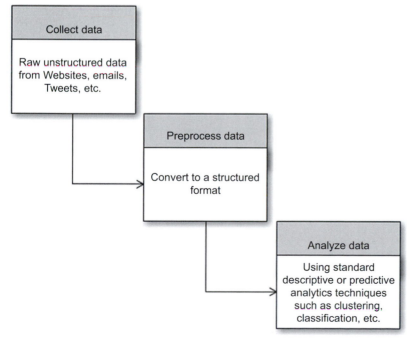

FIGURE 9.1
A high-level process for text mining.

these keywords. How does the search engine know which web pages to serve up? In addition to using network rank or page rank, the search engine also runs some form of text mining to identify the most relevant web pages. Suppose for example the user types in the following keywords: "RapidMiner books that describe text mining." In this case, the search engines run on the following basic logic:

1. Give a high weightage to those keywords that are relatively "rare."
2. Give a high weightage to those webpages that contain a large number of instances of the "rare" keywords.

In the above context, what is a "rare" keyword? Clearly, English words like "that," "books," "describe," and "text" possibly appear in a large number of web pages, whereas "RapidMiner" and "mining" may appear in a relatively smaller number of web pages. (A quick web search returned 382 million results for the word "books," whereas only 74,000 results were returned for "RapidMiner" at the time of this writing.) Therefore, these rarer keywords would receive a higher rating to begin with according to logic 1 above. Next, among all those pages that contain the rare keywords, only those pages that contain the largest number of instances of the rare keywords are likely to be the most relevant for the user and will receive high weightage according to logic 2 above. Thus the highest-weighted web pages are the ones for which the *product* of these two weights is the highest. Therefore, only those pages that not only contain the rare keywords, but have a high number of instances of the rare keywords should appear at the top of the search results.

The technique of calculating this weighting is called *TF–IDF*, which stands for Term Frequency–Inverse Document Frequency.

Calculating TF is very easy: it is simply the ratio of the number of times a keyword appears in a given document, $\mathbf{n_k}$ (where k is the keyword), to the total number of terms in the document, $\mathbf{n}$:

$$\text{TF} = \mathbf{n_k}/\mathbf{n} \tag{9.1}$$

Considering the above example, a common English word such as "that" will have a fairly high TF score and a word such as "RapidMiner" will have a much lower TF score.

IDF is defined as follows:

$$\text{IDF} = \log_2 (\mathbf{N}/\mathbf{N_k}) \tag{9.2}$$

where $\mathbf{N}$ is the number of documents under consideration (in a search engine context, $\mathbf{N}$ is the number of *ALL* the indexed webpages). For most text mining problems, $\mathbf{N}$ is the number of documents that we are trying to mine, and $\mathbf{N_k}$ is the number of documents thatcontain the keyword, k. Again, a word such as "that" would arguably appear in every document and thus the ratio (N/N_k) would be close to 1, and the IDF score would be close to zero for "that." However, a word like "RapidMiner" would possibly appear in a relatively fewer number of documents and so the ratio (N/N_k) would be much greater than 1. Thus the IDF score would be high for this less common keyword.

Finally, TF–IDF is expressed as the simple product as shown below:

$$TF - IDF = n_k/n * \log_2 (N/N_k) \tag{9.3}$$

Going back to the above example, when we multiply the high TF for "that" by its corresponding very low IDF, we will get a very low (or zero) TF–IDF whereas when we multiply the low TF for "RapidMiner" by its corresponding fairly high IDF, we would get a relatively higher TF–IDF.

Typically, TF–IDF scores for every word in the set of documents is calculated in the preprocessing step of the three-step process described earlier. Performing this calculation will help in applying any of the standard data mining techniques that we discussed so far in this book. In the following sections we will describe additional concepts that are commonly employed in text mining.

9.1.2 Terminology

Consider the following two sentences: "This is a book on data mining" and "This book describes data mining and text mining using RapidMiner.. Let us suppose our objective is to perform a comparison between them, or a "similarity mapping." For our purpose, each sentence is one unit of text that needs to be analyzed.

These two sentences could be embedded in an email message or in two separate webpages or in two different text files or could be two sentences in the same text file. In the text mining context, each sentence is considered a distinct *document*. Furthermore, in the simplest case, words are separated by a special character: a blank space. Each word is called a *token*, and the process of discretizing words within a document is called *tokenization*. For our purpose here, each sentence can be considered a separate document, although what is considered an individual document may depend upon the context. For now, a document here is simply a sequential collection of tokens.

Document 1	This is a book on data mining.
Document 2	This book describes data mining and text mining using RapidMiner.

We can impose some form of structure on this raw data by creating a matrix where the columns consist of all the tokens found in the two documents and the cells of the matrix are the counts of the number of times a token appears, as shown in Table 9.1.

Each token is now an attribute in standard data mining parlance and each document is an example. We therefore have a structured *example set*, to use standard terminology. Basically, unstructured raw data is now transformed into a format that is recognized, not only by the human users as a data table, but more importantly by all the machine learning algorithms which require such tables for training. This table is called a *document vector* or *term document matrix* (*TDM*) and is the cornerstone of the preprocessing required for text mining. Suppose we add a third statement, "RapidMiner is offered as an open source software program." This new document will increase the number of rows of our matrix by one (Document 3); however it increases the number of columns by seven (seven new words or tokens were introduced). This results in zeroes being recorded in nine other columns for row 3. As we add more new statements that have very little in common, we will end up with a very sparse matrix.

Note that we could have also chosen to use the term frequencies for each token instead of simply counting the number of occurrences and it would still be a sparse matrix. We can get TF by dividing each row of Table 9.1 by number of words in the row (document). This is shown in Table 9.2.[1]

Similarly, we could have also chosen to use the TF–IDF scores for each term to create the document vector. This is also shown in Figure 9.2.

One thing to notice in the two sample text documents above was the occurrence of common words such as "a," "this," "and," and other similar terms. Clearly in larger documents we would expect a larger number of such terms that do not really convey specific meaning. Most grammatical necessities such as articles, conjunctions, prepositions, and pronouns may need to be filtered before we perform additional analysis. Such terms are called *stopwords* and usually include most articles, conjunctions, pronouns, and prepositions. *Stopword filtering* is usually the second step that follows immediately after *tokenization*. Notice that our document vector has a significantly reduced size after applying standard English stopword filtering (see Figure 9.3).

In addition to filtering standard stopwords, we may also need to filter out some specific terms. For example, in analyzing text documents that pertain to the automotive industry, we may want to filter away terms that are common to this

---

[1]RapidMiner does a "double normalization" while calculating the TF scores. For example, in the case of Document 1, the TF score for the term "data" would be $(0.1428)/\sqrt{(0.1428^2 + 0.1428^2 + \dots + 0.1428^2)}$ = $(0.1428)/\sqrt{7*0.1428^2}$ = 0.3779 and so on for the other terms. This change in TF score calculation is reflected in the TF–IDF score. The double normalization makes it easy to apply algorithms such as SVM.

Table 9.1 Building a Matrix of Terms from Unstructured Raw Text

	this	is	a	book	on	data	mining	describes	text	rapidminer	and	using
Document 1	1	1	1	1	1	1	1	0	0	0	0	0
Document 2	1	0	0	1	0	1	2	1	1	1	1	1

Table 9.2 Using Term Frequencies Instead of Term Counts in a TDM

	this	is	a	book	on	data	mining	describes	text	rapidminer	and	Using
Docu-ment 1	$1/7 =$ 0.1428	0.1428	0.1428	0.1428	0.1428	0.1428	0.1428	0	0	0	0	0
Docu-ment 2	$1/10 =$ 0.1	0	0	0.1	0	0.1	0.2	0.1	0.1	0.1	0.1	0.1

ExampleSet (2 examples, 0 special attributes, 12 regular attributes)

Row No.	RapidMiner	This	a	and	book	data	describes	is	mining	on	text	using
1	0	0	0.577	0	0	0	0	0.577	0	0.577	0	0
2	0.447	0	0	0.447	0	0	0.447	0	0	0	0.447	0.447

FIGURE 9.2

Calculating TF–IDF scores for the sample TDM.

Row No.	RapidMiner	book	data	describes	mining	text	using
1	0	1	1	0	1	0	0
2	1	1	1	1	2	1	1

FIGURE 9.3

Stopword filtering reduces the size of the TDM significantly.

industry such as "car," "automobile," "vehicle," and so on. This is generally achieved by creating a separate dictionary where we define these context-specific terms and then apply *term filtering* to remove them from our data. (*Lexical substitution* is the process of finding an alternative for a word in the context of a clause and is used to align all the terms to the same term based upon the field or subject which is being analyzed—this is especially important in areas with specific jargon, for example, in clinical settings.)

We may encounter words such as "recognized," "recognizable," or "recognition" in different usages, but contextually they may all imply the same meaning. For example, "Einstein is a *well-recognized* name in physics" or "The physicist went by the easily *recognizable* name of Einstein" or "Few other physicists have the kind of name *recognition* that Einstein has." The so-called root of all these highlighted words is "recognize." By reducing terms in a document to their basic stems, we can simplify the conversion of unstructured text to structured data because we now only take into account the occurrence of the root terms. This process is called *stemming*. The most common stemming technique for text mining in English is the Porter method (Porter, 1980). Porter stemming works on a bunch of rules where the basic idea is to remove and/or replace the suffix of words. For example, one rule would be "Replace all terms which end in 'ies' by 'y,'" such as replacing the term "anomal*ies*" with "anomol*y*". Similarly, another rule would be to stem all terms ending in "s" by removing the "s," as in "algorithm*s*" to "algorithm." While the Porter stemmer is very efficient, it can make mistakes that could prove costly. For example, "arms" and "army" would both be stemmed to "arm," which would result in somewhat different contextual meaning. There are other stemmers available; which one you choose is usually guided by experience in your domain. Stemming is usually the next process step following term filtering. (A word of caution: stemming is completely dependent upon the human language being processed as well as the period of the language being processed.

Row...	label	RapidMiner	book	book_data	book_descr...	data	data_mining	describes	describes_data	mining	mining_text	mining_usi...	text_0	text_mining	using	using_RapidMiner
1	text1	0	0.447	0.447	0	0.447	0.447	0	0	0.447	0	0	0	0	0	0
2	text2	0.243	0.243	0	0.243	0.243	0.243	0.243	0.243	0.485	0.243	0.243	0.243	0.243	0.243	0.243

FIGURE 9.4

Meaningful n-grams show higher TF–IDF scores.

Table 9.3 A Typical Sequence of Preprocessing Steps to Use in Text Mining

Step	Action	Result
1	Tokenize	Convert each word or term in a document into a distinct attribute
2	Stopword removal	Remove highly common grammatical tokens/words
3	Filtering	Remove other very common tokens
4	Stemming	Trim each token to its most essential minimum
5	n-grams	Combine commonly occurring token pairs or tuples (more than 2)

Historical usage varies so widely that comparing text across generations—Shakespeare to present-day literature for instance—can raise concerns.)

There are families of words in the spoken and written language that typically go together. For example, the word "Good" is usually followed by either "Morning," "Afternoon," "Evening," "Night," or in Australia, "Day." Grouping such terms, called *n-grams*, and analyzing them statistically can present new insights. Search engines use word n-gram models for a variety of applications, such as automatic translation, identifying speech patterns, checking misspelling, entity detection, information extraction, among many different use cases. Google has processed more than a trillion words (1,024,908,267,229 words back as far back as 2006) of running text and has published the counts for all 1,176,470,663 five-word sequences that appear at least 40 times (Franz, 2006). While most text mining applications do not require 5-grams, bigrams and trigrams are quite useful. The final preprocessing step typically involves forming these n-grams and storing them in our document vector. Also, most algorithms providing n-grams become computationally expensive and the results become huge so in practice the amount of "n" will vary based upon the size of the documents and the corpus.

Figure 9.4 shows a TF-based document vector for bigrams (n = 2) from our examples and as you can see, terms like "data mining" and "text mining" and "using RapidMiner" can be quite meaningful in this context. Table 9.3 summarizes a typical sequence of preprocessing steps that will convert unstructured data into a semi-structured format.

Usually there is a preprocessing step before tokenization such as removing special characters, changing the case (upcasing and downcasing), or sometimes even performing a simple spell check beforehand. Data quality in text mining is just as important as in other areas.

9.2 IMPLEMENTING TEXT MINING WITH CLUSTERING AND CLASSIFICATION

We have introduced a few essential concepts that would be needed for a basic text mining project. In the following sections, we will examine two case studies that apply text mining. In the first example, we will take several documents (web pages) and group keywords found in them into similar *clusters*. In the second example, we will attempt to perform a *blog gender classification*. We start with several blogs (documents) written by men and women authors, to be used as training data. Using the article keywords as features, we will train several classification models, including a couple of SVMs, to recognize stylistic characteristics of authors and classify new unseen blogs as belonging to one of the two author classes (male or female).

9.2.1 Case Study 1: Keyword Clustering

In this first example, we will introduce some of the web mining features of RapidMiner and then create a clustering model with keyword data mined from a website. The objective of this case is to scan several pages from a given website and identify the most frequent words within these pages that also serve to characterize each page, and then to identify the most frequent words using a clustering model. This simple example can be easily extended to a more comprehensive document-clustering problem where we would use the most common words occurring in a document as flags to group multiple documents. The predictive objective of this exercise is to then use the process to identify any random webpage and determine if the page pertains to one of the two categories which the model has been trained to identify.

The site (http://www.detroitperforms.org) we are looking into is hosted by a public television station and is meant to be used as a platform for reaching out to members of the local community who are interested in the arts and culture. The site serves as a medium for the station to not only engage with community members, but also to eventually aid in targeted marketing campaigns meant to attract donors to public broadcasting. The site has pages for several related categories: Music, Dance, Theatre, Film, and so on. Each of these pages contains articles and events related to that category. Our goal is to characterize each page on the site and identify the top keywords that appear on each page. To that end, we will crawl each category page, extract the content, and convert the information into a structured document vector consisting of keywords. Finally, we will run a k-medoids clustering process to sort the keywords and rank them. Medoid clustering is similar to the k-means clustering described in Chapter 7. A "medoid" is the most centrally located object in a cluster (Park, 2009). K-medoids are less susceptible to noise and outliers when compared to k-means. This is because k-medoids tries to minimize dissimilarities rather than Euclidean distances, which is what k-means does.

Before we begin webpage clustering in RapidMiner, you need to make sure that the web mining and text mining extensions are installed. *(This is easily done by going to Help → Updates and Extensions on the main menu bar.)* RapidMiner provides three different ways to crawl and get content from websites. The *Crawl Web* operator will allow setting up of simple crawling rules and based on these rules will store the crawled pages in a directory for further processing. The *Get Page* operator retrieves a single page and stores the content as an example set. The *Get Pages* operator works similarly, but can access multiple pages identified by their URLs contained in an input file. We will use the *Get Pages* operator in this example. Both of the *Get Page(s)* operators allow the choosing of either the GET or POST HTTP request methods for retrieving content.[2]

Step 1: Gather Unstructured Data

The first step in this process is to create an input text file containing a list of URLs to be scanned by the *Get Pages* operator. This is specified in the *Read CSV* (renamed in the process shown in Figure 9.6a to *Read URL List*) operator, which initiates the whole process. The text file consists of three lines: a header line that is needed for the link attribute parameter for Get Pages and two lines containing the two URLs that we are going to crawl, as shown in Figure 9.5 below.[3] The first URL is the "Dance" category page and the second one is the "Film" category page on the website. Save the text file as "pages.txt" as shown in the figure.

The output from the *Get Pages* operator consists of an example set that will contain two main attributes: the URL and extracted HTML content. Additionally it also adds some metadata attributes that are not needed in this example,

FIGURE 9.5
Creating a URL read list.

---

[2]For more information on the differences between the two methods, and when to use which type of request, refer to the tutorials on www.w3schools.com.

[3]Be aware that websites may frequently change their structure or content or be taken down altogether. The results shown here for this example were obtained when the website listed was crawled at the time of writing. Your results may differ depending upon when the process is executed.

such as content length (characters), date, and so on. We can filter out these extra attributes using the *Select Attributes* operator.

Step 2: Data Preparation

Next, connect the output from this to a *Process Documents from Data* operator. This is a nested operator, which means this operator contains an inner subprocess where all the preprocessing takes place. The first step in this preprocessing is removing all the HTML tags and only preserving the actual content. This is enabled by the *Extract Content* operator. Put this operator inside the *Process Documents from Data* operator and connect the different operators as shown in Figures 9.6a and 9.6b. Refer to Table 9.3 from earlier to see which operators to use. The inset shows the operators inside the nested *Process Documents from Data* operator. In this case, we will need to use the word occurrences for the clustering. So you need to select Term Occurrences for the vector creation parameter option when configuring the *Process Documents from Data* operator.

Step 3: Apply Clustering (Descriptive Analytics) Technique

The output from the *Process Documents from Data* operator consists of (1) a word list and (2) a document vector or TDM. The word list is not needed for clustering, however the document vector is. Recall that the difference between the two is that in the document vector, each word is considered an attribute and each row or example is a separate document (in this case the web pages crawled). The values in the cells of the document vector can of course be word occurrences, word frequencies, or TF–IDF scores, but as noted in step 2, in this case the cells will have word occurrences. The output from the *Process Documents from Data* operator is filtered further to remove attributes that are less than 5 (that is all words that occur less than five times in *both* documents). Notice that RapidMiner will only remove those attributes (words) which occur less than five times in *both* documents—for example the word "dance" appears only two times in the Film category, but is the most common word in the Dance; it is not and should not be removed! Finally this cleaned output is fed into a k-medoids clustering operator, which is configured as shown in Figure 9.6c.

Upon running the process, RapidMiner will crawl the two URLs listed and execute the different operations to finally generate two clusters. To view these clustering outputs, you can select either the Centroid Table or Centroid Plot views in the Cluster Model (Clustering) results tab, which will clearly show the top keywords from each of the two pages crawled. In Figure 9.7, we see the top few keywords that characterize each cluster. One can then use this model to identify if the content of any random page would belong to either one of the categories.

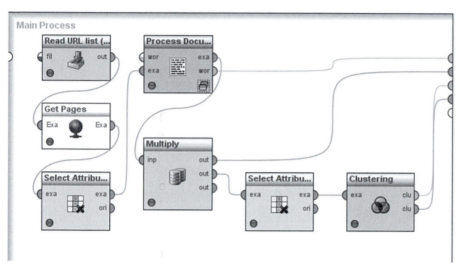

FIGURE 9.6a
Overall process of creating keyword clustering from websites.

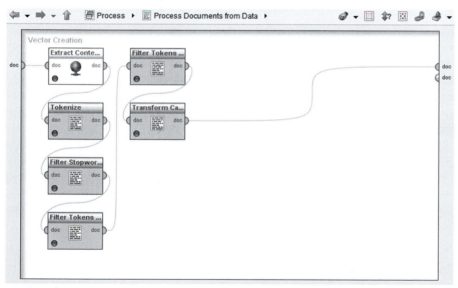

FIGURE 9.6b
Configuring the nested preprocessing operator: Process Documents from Data.

9.2.2 Case Study 2: Predicting the gender of blog authors
The objective of this case study is to attempt to predicting the gender of blog authors based on the content of the blog.

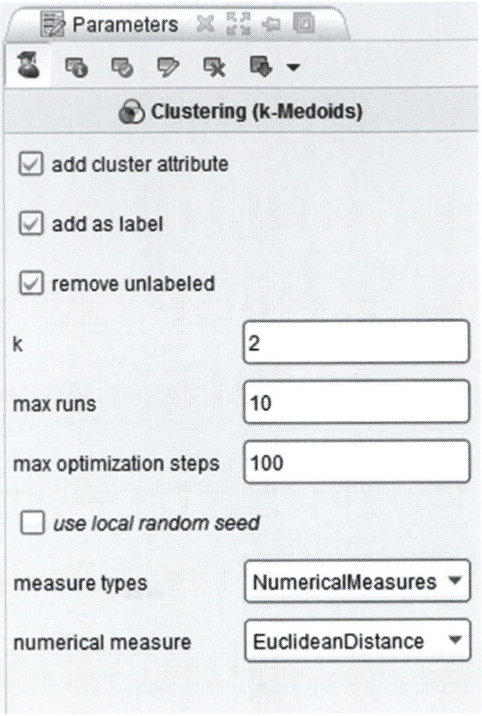

FIGURE 9.6c
Configuring the k-medoids operator.

Step 1: Gather Unstructured Data

The data set for this case study[4] consists of more than 3,000 individual blog entries (articles) by men and women from around the world (Mukherjee, 2010). The data is organized into a single spreadsheet consisting of 3,227 rows and two columns as shown in the sample in Table 9.4. The first column is the actual blog content and the second column is the author's gender, which has been labeled.

For the purpose of this case study, we will split the raw data into two halves: the first 50% of the data is treated as training data with known labels and the remaining 50% is set aside to verify the performance of the training algorithm.

---

[4]A compressed version of this data can be downloaded from the *Opinion Mining, Sentiment Analysis and Opinion Spam Detection* website (http://www.cs.uic.edu/~liub/FBS/sentiment-analysis.html). The data set is called *Blog Author Gender Classification dataset associated with the paper (Mukherjee and Liu, EMNLP-2010)*. This site is maintained by Prof. Bing Liu of the University of Illinois at Chicago. This site contains a lot of relevant information related to text mining and sentiment analysis, in addition to several other useful data sets.

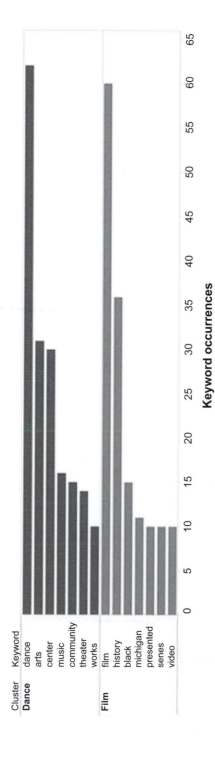

FIGURE 9.7

Results of the website keyword clustering process.

Table 9.4 Raw Data for the Blog Classification Study

BLOG	GENDER
This game was a blast. You (as Drake) start the game waking up in a train that is dangling over the side of a cliff. You have to climb up the train car, which is slowly teetering off the edge of the cliff, ready to plummet miles down into a snowy abyss. From the snowy beginning there are flashbacks to what led Drake to this predicament. The story unfolds in a very cinematic manner, and the scenes in between levels, while a bit clichéd by Hollywood standards, are still just as good if not better than your average brainless Mel Gibson or Bruce Willis action movie. In fact, the cheese is part of the fun and I would venture to say it's intentional.	M
My mother was a contrarian, she was. For instance, she always wore orange on St. Patrick's Day, something that I of course did not understand at the time, nor, come to think of it do I understand today. Protestants wear orange in Ireland, not here, but I'm pretty sure my mother had nothing against the Catholics, so why did she do it? Maybe it had to do with the myth about Patrick driving the snakes, a.k.a. pagans, out of Ireland. Or maybe it was something political. I have no idea and since my mother is long gone from this earth, I guess I'll never know.	F
LaLicious Sugar Soufflé body scrub has a devoted following and I now understand why. I received a sample of this body scrub in Tahitian Flower and after one shower with this tub of sugary goodness, I was hooked. The lush scent is deliciously intoxicating and it ended up inspiring compliments and extended sniffing from both loved ones and strangers alike. Furthermore, this scrub packs one heck of a punch when it comes to pampering dry skin. In fact, LaLicious promises that this body scrub is so rich that it will eliminate the need for applying your post-shower lotion. This claim is true — if you follow the directions.	F
Stopped by the post office this morning to pick up a package on my way to the lab. I thought it would be as good a time as any to clean up my desk and at the very least make it appear that I am more organized than I really am (seriously, it's a mess). It's pretty nice here on the weekends, it's quiet, there's less worry of disturbing undergrad classes if I do any experiments in the daytime.	M
Anyway, it turns out the t-shirt I ordered from Concrete Rocket arrived! Here's how the design looks: See here's the thing: Men have their neat little boxes through which they compartmentalize their lives. Relationship over? Oh, I'll just close that box. It's not that easy for women.	F
Our relationships are not just a section of our lives–they run through the entire fabric, a hot pink thread which adds to the mosaic composing who we are. Take out a relationship and you grab that thread and pull. Have you ever pulled a thread on a knit sweater? That's what it's like. The whole garment gets scrunched and disfigured just because that one piece was removed. And then you have to pull it back apart, smooth it out, fill in the gaps. See here's the thing: men have their neat little boxes through which they compartmentalize their lives. Relationship over? Oh, I'll just close that box. It's not that easy for women.	
I had pretty bad vision since I was in 3rd grade. About 5 years ago, after watching many people around me get Lasik, I decided to take the plunge. Because this was an elective surgery that in rare cases, could cause damage to my eyes, I decided to find the absolute best doctor for the job. I chose Dr Coleman Kraff and he was amazing to watch. Very confident, poised, fast, and focused…. well like a laser.	M

Then there's my work life. I had an incredible review from my boss 2 weeks ago, and have been slowly adding more and more to my occupational plate as opportunities have been presenting themselves. I'm now going to be the head coach for 7th/8th grade girls' volleyball in the fall. I'm working at the Harlem School of the Arts this summer, just two mornings a week, but they've tentatively asked me if I'd be interested in working their Saturday program during the school year. I have three new piano students for the fall – kids who are my students at school and will now also be my private piano students. I had my first lesson today with one of them, and it was incredible. **F**

We had problems in the past with contacts due to dryness and the hassle of always taking them out when I sleep. With Acuvue Oasys soft contact lenses I've had more comfort then ever. The dryness is gone. I can wear them longer. I can even sleep in them and not have to take them out every night. I just put in drops when I wake up and I'm good for the day. It's an ideal product for someone who is always on the go and has no energy to do anything but go to bed in the evening. At an affordable price you can't beat them, especially when you use up a new box less often. **F**

This camcorder is really good for the price and it has an easy button for people who are not good with camcoders. There is also a touch screen in the camcorder ang you can turn the screen so you can see yourself. It also has a built in lens cover and you don't have to worry about losing it. **M**

At the time Debbie and I moved to Rapid City our family started to grow by one boy and four girls. I'd like to introduce You to my "little kids". On the top row starting left to right, my son Brian and my daughter Leslie. On the bottom row; left-to-right, my youngest daughter Shelley, my eldest daughter Christy and my next eldest daughter Suzanne. **M**

They are all adults and they all live in Rapid City.

Ideally, the process for buying a laptop would involve a single question: "Which laptop should I buy?" The answer would then spring forth from the heavens or your favorite technology Web site. Unfortunately, finding the right laptop for your budget and needs involves answering not one but a series of questions. Fear not, laptop buyer, we know which questions to ask, the answers to those questions, along with the current market trends and where laptops are headed. **M**

Ok, so how stinkin' cute IS this bunny?? I saw an adorable Easter sign at Hobby Lobby a few weeks ago and thought it would make a great card. I can't find the adapter that allows me to download photos from my camera phone, so I can't show you the inspiration piece. But it was an Easter bunny peeking over the top of an Easter egg. **F**

Slept until 11am. Time change seems to have no effect. In fact filled my tires with air and went for a bike ride around the complex like 5 times. Legs were hurting so stopped and came inside. Time change no effect as of yet but being cautious. Feeling pretty up and positive. Need to get gas for car and then run a few errands. Laundry is going to wait again. Goal for next week is to complete all of it. It is at least in a semi organized piles and ready to be washed. Need to find a laundry shop to complete. Also need to register for IML volunteer and start working on getting taxes filed and the $5,000.00 medical bill from last hospitalization. That is approximate including Doctors which I have yet to receive. Funny they are charging me over $3,000 for the CPAP, that is the price of a new machine. I plan on fighting that charge to see what happens. Will be using health advocate to see what, if anything can be done. Last night did not sleep right away so created contracts for my support system alerting them if what they should be on the look out for and what actions to take if they see me doing those actions. **M**

Continued

Table 9.4 Raw Data for the Blog Classification Study—Cont'd

BLOG	GENDER
We celebrated St. Patty's Day with Ethan, Carys, and Molly and..... a dinner made 'o green! We had green pancakes with shamrock-shaped whip cream on top, green vanilla yogurt (green food coloring and I were special friends today) topped with green sprinkles, and honey dew. For dessert, we had a magically delicious treat I referred to as Pots o' Gold - halved orange peels filled with "gold" (yellow jello squares) and garnished with gold coins (chocolate Easter candy)! As for beverages, we had Sprite in clear cups with green Sprite ice cubes to color our drinks. It really was so much fun to get into the spirit of St. Patty's Day.	F
I'm so excited about the gorgeous weather we've been having lately. I feel like spring has crept up early, quickly and unexpectedly this year. But maybe that's just because I was prepared for it to be especially late in coming up here in Sudbury. I'm not getting my hopes up though that it's here to stay, because we'll likely have some more winter before it's gone for good.	F
I own a 9 1/2 year old German Shepherd mix. We believe his father was a black lab with chow mix. His mother was a full-blooded German Shepherd. Fred is a great dog. He weighs 110 lbs. So you can't ever pick him up and his meds cost a fortune, but he's worth every time. I watch a lot of Court TV and I feel much more secure having Fred in the house with me!He's settled down a lot over the years. He used to be much more high strung and jumped on people, etc. Now he just barks a lot. He's definitely the alpha dog of our family.	F
Yesterday we had dense fog, heavy rain last night and fog again this morning. It is supposed to transition (whatever happened to just saying "change"?) to rain beginning around ten this morning. And yes, today is the day we load carts onto the Bookmobile, unload them, reload them, unload them, reload them – all day long. This will be my first experience dealing with that in the rain. I understand that we have some flimsy tarps to put over the carts, but the word is that they are not all that helpful. At least it is supposed to get up to about 53 (11.6 C).	M
Apparently if the rain we are getting this weekend were snow, it would be about three feet deep. It is also pretty windy. Therefore the streets are awash with dead umbrellas rolling like tumbleweed across streets and frightening the dogs. The corpses are flung every which way including upside down. A few are neatly disposed of in garbage receptacles. Others look positively dangerous.	F

While developing models involving large amounts of data, which is common with unstructured text analysis, it is a good practice to divide the process into several distinct processes and store the intermediate data, models, and results from each process for recall at a later stage. RapidMiner facilitates this by providing special operators called *Store* and *Retrieve*. The *Store* operator stores an IO Object in the data repository and *Retrieve* reads an object from the data repository. The use of these operators is introduced in the following sections.

Step 2: Data Preparation

Once the data is downloaded and uncompressed, it yields a single MS Excel file, which can then be imported into the RapidMiner database using the *Read Excel* operator. The raw data consists of 290 examples that do not have a label and one example that has no blog content but has a label! This needs to be cleaned up. It is easier to delete this entry in the raw data—simply delete the row (#1523) in the spreadsheet that contains this missing entry and save the file before reading it into RapidMiner. Also make sure that the *Read Excel* operator is configured to recognize the data type in the first column as "text" and not polynominal (default) as shown in Figure 9.8. Connect the output from *Read Excel* to a *Filter Examples* operator, where will then remove the entries with missing labels. (If you are so inclined, you may want to store these entries with missing labels for use as testing samples—you can accomplish this with another *Filter Examples*, but by checking *Invert Filter* box and then storing the output. In this case however, we will simply discard examples with missing labels.) We can now separate the cleaned data with a 50/50 split using a *Split Data* operator. Save the latter 50% testing data (1,468 samples) to a new file with a *Write Excel* operator and pass the remaining 50% training portion to a *Process Documents from Data* operator.

This, as we now know, is a nested operator where all the preprocessing happens. Recall that this is where the conversion of unstructured data into a structured format will take place. Connect the different operators within as shown in Figure 9.9a. The only point to note here is that you will need a *Filter Stopword (Dictionary)* operator to remove any "nbsp" (" " is used to represent a nonbreaking space) terms that may have slipped into the content. Create a simple text file with this keyword inside it and let RapidMiner know that this dictionary exists by properly configuring the operator. To configure the *Process Documents from Data* operator, use the options as shown in Figure 9.9b.

The output from the process for step 2 consists of the document vector and a word list. While the word list may not be of immediate use in the subsequent steps, it is a good idea to store this along with the very important document vector. The final process is shown in Figure 9.9c.

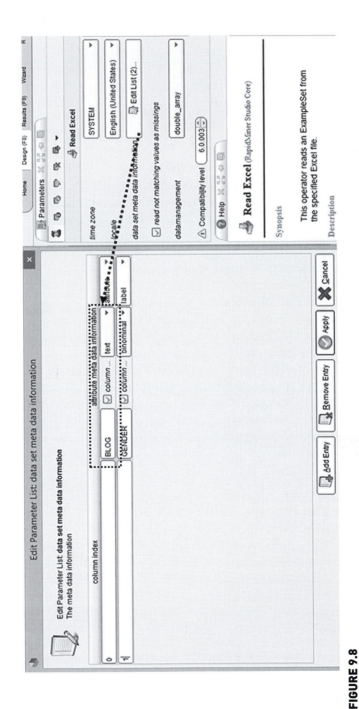

FIGURE 9.8

Properly configuring the Read Excel operator to accept text (not polynomial).

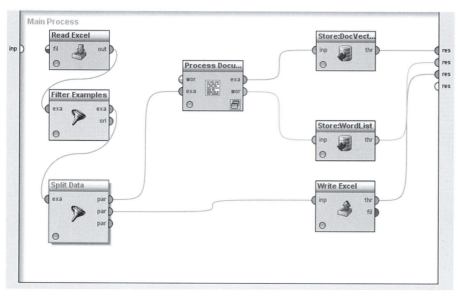

FIGURE 9.9a
Preprocessing text data using the Process Documents from Data operator.

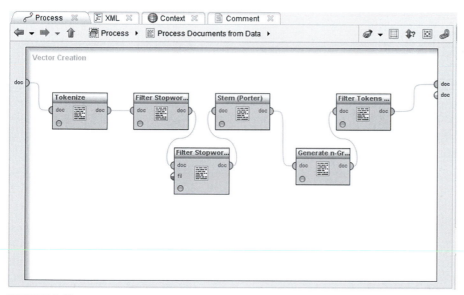

FIGURE 9.9b
Configuring the preprocessing operator.

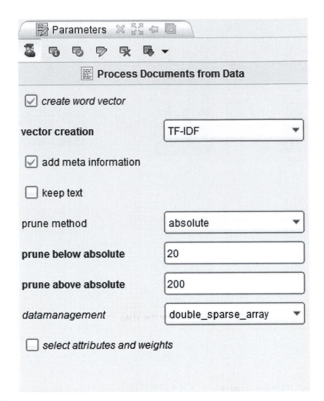

FIGURE 9.9c
Overall process for blog gender classification.

Step 3.1: Identify Key Features

The document vector that is the result of the process in step 2 is a structured table consisting of 2,055 rows—one for every blog entry in the training set—and 2,815 attributes or columns—each token within an article that meets the filtering and stemming criteria defined by operators inside *Process Documents* is converted into an attribute. Training learning algorithms using 2,815 features or variables is clearly an onerous task. The right approach is to further filter these attributes by using feature selection methods.

We will employ two feature selection methods using the *Weight by Information Gain* and *Weight by SVM* operators that are available. *Weight by Information Gain* (more details in Chapter 12 Feature Selection on this operator) will rank a feature or attribute by its relevance to the label attribute (in this case, gender) based on the information gain ratio and assigns weights to them accordingly. *Weight by SVM* will set the coefficients of the SV hyperplane as attribute weights. Once we rank them using these techniques, we can select only a handful of attributes (for example, the top 20) to build our models. Doing so will result in a reasonable reduction in modeling costs.

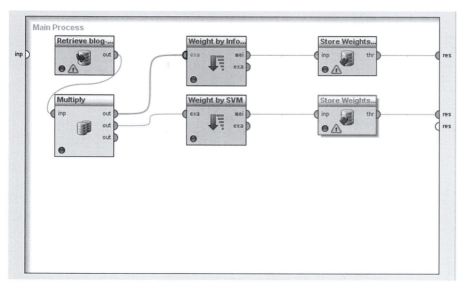

FIGURE 9.10
Using feature selection methods to filter attributes from the TDM.

The results of this intermediate process will generate two weight tables, one corresponding to each feature selection method. We start the process by retrieving the document vector saved in step 2 and then end the process by storing the weight tables for use in step 3.2 (see Figure 9.10).

In the paper by Mukherjee and Liu (Mukherjee, 2010) from which this data set comes, they demonstrate the use of several other feature selection methods, including a novel one developed by the authors that is shown to yield a much higher prediction accuracy than the stock algorithms (such as the ones we demonstrate here).

Step 3.2: Build Predictive Models

Once we have the document vector and attribute weights, we can experiment using several different machine learning algorithms to understand which give the best accuracy. The process illustrated in Figures 9.11a and b will generate the models and store them (along with the corresponding performance results) for later application. This is one of the key strengths of RapidMiner: once we have built up the necessary data for predictive modeling, switching back and forth between various algorithms requires nothing more than dragging and dropping the needed operators and making the connections. As seen in Figure 9.11b, we have five different algorithms nested inside the *X-Validation* operator and can conveniently switch back and forth as needed. Table 9.5 shows that the *LibSVM(linear)* and *W-Logistic* operators (Available through Weka extension for RapidMiner. Go to Help > Updates and Extensions) seem to give the best

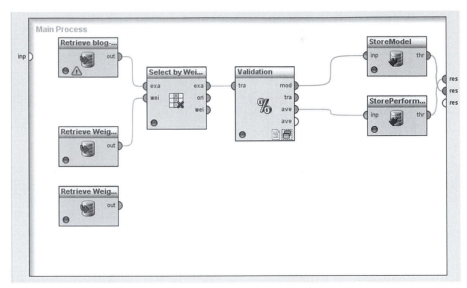

FIGURE 9.11a
Training and testing predictive models for blog gender classification.

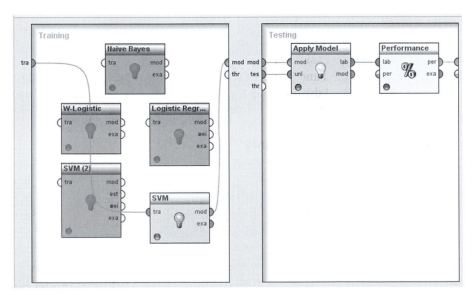

FIGURE 9.11b
Switching between several algorithms.

Table 9.5 Comparing the Performance of Different Training Algorithms for Blog Gender Classification

Algorithm	Class Recall (M)	Class Recall (F)	Accuracy
LibSVM (linear)	87	53	72
W-Logistic	85	58	73
Naïve Bayes	86	55	72
SVM (polynomial)	82	42	63

performance. Keep in mind that these accuracies are still not the highest and are in line with the performances reported by Mukherjee and Liu in their paper for generic algorithms.

To improve upon these, we may need to further optimize the best performers so far by nesting the entire validation process within an optimization operator. This is described in the chapter 13, in the section on optimization.

Step 4.1: Prepare Test Data for Model Application

Going back to the original 50% of the "unseen" data that was saved for testing purposes, we can actually evaluate the real-world performance of the best algorithm in classifying blogs by author gender. However, keep in mind that we cannot use the raw data that we set aside as is (what would happen if you did?). We need to also convert this raw test data into a document vector first. In other words, we need to repeat the step 2 process (without the filtering and split data operators) on the 50% of data that was set aside for testing. The *Process Documents from Data* operator can be simply copied and pasted from the process in step 2. (Alternatively, we could have preprocessed the entire dataset before splitting!) The document vector is stored for use in the next step. This process is illustrated in Figure 9.12.

Step 4.2: Applying the Trained Models to Testing Data

This is where the rubber hits the road! The last step will take any of the saved models created in step 3.2 and the newly created document vector from step 4.1 and apply the model on this test data. The process is shown below in Figures 9.13a and b. One useful operator to add is the *Set Role* operator, which will be used to indicate to RapidMiner the label variable. Doing so will allow us to sort the results from the Apply Model by "Correct Predictions" and "Wrong Predictions" using the View Filter in the Results perspective as shown here.

When you run this process you will find that the LibSVM (linear) model can correctly predict only 828 of the 1,468 examples, which translates to a poor 56% accuracy! The other models fare worse. Clearly the model and the process are in need of optimization and further refinement. Using RapidMiner's

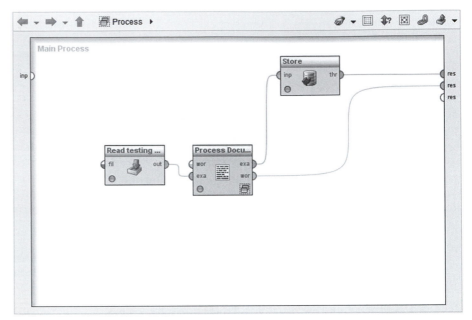

FIGURE 9.12
Preparing the "unseen" data for model deployment.

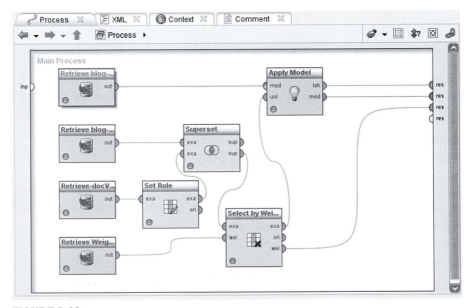

FIGURE 9.13a
Applying the models built in step 3 on the unseen data.

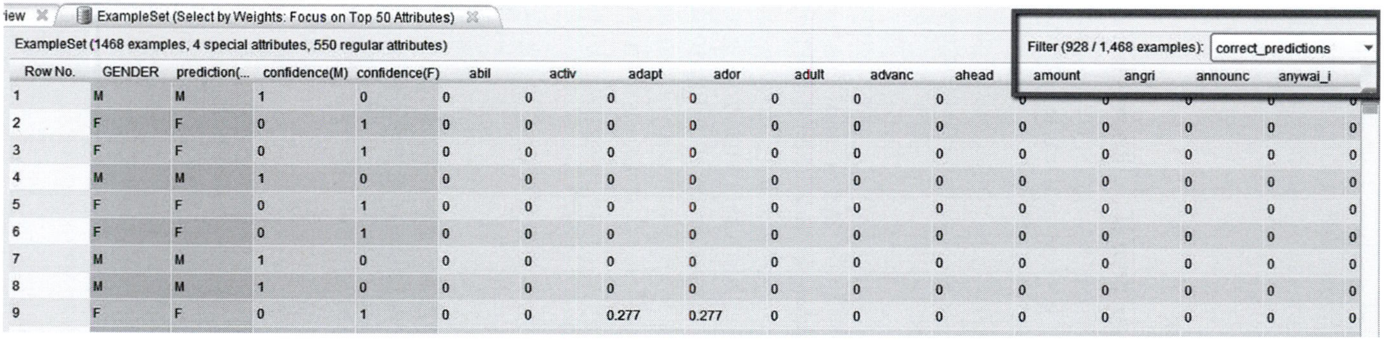

ExampleSet (1468 examples, 4 special attributes, 550 regular attributes)

Row No.	GENDER	prediction(...	confidence(M)	confidence(F)	abl	activ	adapt	ador	adult	advanc	ahead	amount	angri	announc	anywal_i
1	M	M	1	0	0	0	0	0	0	0	0	0	0	0	0
2	F	F	0	1	0	0	0	0	0	0	0	0	0	0	0
3	F	F	0	1	0	0	0	0	0	0	0	0	0	0	0
4	M	M	1	0	0	0	0	0	0	0	0	0	0	0	0
5	F	F	0	1	0	0	0	0	0	0	0	0	0	0	0
6	F	F	0	1	0	0	0	0	0	0	0	0	0	0	0
7	M	M	1	0	0	0	0	0	0	0	0	0	0	0	0
8	M	M	1	0	0	0	0	0	0	0	0	0	0	0	0
9	F	F	0	1	0	0	0.277	0.277	0	0	0	0	0	0	0

Filter (928 / 1,468 examples): correct_predictions

FIGURE 9.13b

The results view.

built-in optimization operators, one can easily improve upon this baseline accuracy. A discussion about how to use the optimization operators in general is provided in Chapter 13 Getting Started with RapidMiner. The truly adventurous can implement the Mukherjee and Liu algorithm for feature selection in RapidMiner based on the instructions given in their paper!

CONCLUSION

Unstructured data, of which text data is a major portion, appears to be doubling in volume every three years (Mayer-Schonberger, 2013). The ability to automatically process and mine information from such digital data will become an important skill in the future. These techniques can be used to classify and predict just as the other techniques throughout the book, except we are now working on text documents and even voice recordings that have been transcribed to text.

In this chapter we explained how unstructured data can be mined using any of the available algorithms presented in this book. The key to being able to apply these techniques is to convert the unstructured data into a semi-structured format. We introduced a high-level three-step process that will enable this. We discussed some key tools for transforming unstructured data, such as tokenization, stemming, n-gramming, and stopword removal. We then discussed how concepts such as TF–IDF will allow us to make the final transformation of a corpus of text to a matrix of numbers, which can be worked upon by the standard machine learning algorithms. Finally, we presented a couple of real-world examples, which will allow you to explore the exciting world of text mining using RapidMiner.

REFERENCES

Cutting, D. K. (1992). Scatter/gather: A cluster-based approach to browsing large document collections. *Proceedings of the 15th Annual International ACM SIGIR Conference on Research and Development in Information Retrieval*, 318–329 Copenhagen.

Franz, A. A. (2006, August 3). *All our N-gram are Belong to You*. Retrieved November 1, 2013, from Research Blog, http://googleresearch.blogspot.com/2006/08/all-our-n-gram-are-belong-to-you.html.

Hearst, M. (June 20–26, 1999). *Untangling Text Data MiningProceedings of Association for Computational Linguistics, 37th Annual Meeting 1999*. University of Maryland.

International Monetary Fund (n.d.). Retrieved from http://www.imf.org/external/pubs/ft/weo/2012/02/weodata/index.aspx.

Mayer-Schonberger, V. A. (2013). *Big Data: A Revolution That Will Transform How We Live, Work and Think*. London: John Murray and Co.

McKnight, W. (2005, January 1). *Text Data Mining in Business Intelligence*. Retrieved November 1, 2013, from Information Management, http://www.information-management.com/issues/20050101/1016487-1.html#Login.

Park, H. S., Jun, C. H. (2009). A simple and fast algorithm for K-medoids clustering. *Expert Systems with Applications*. 36(2), 3336–3341.

Porter, M. F. (1980). An algorithm for suffix stripping. *Program*. 14(3), 130–137.

Mukherjee, A. L. (2010). Improving Gender Classification of Blog Authors. *Proceedings of Conference on Empirical Methods in Natural Language Processing (EMNLP-10)* Cambridge, MA.

Siegel, E. (2013). *Predictive Analytics: The Power to Predict Who Will Click, Buy, Lie or Die*. Hoboken, NJ: John Wiley and Sons.

Upbin, B. (2013, February 8). IBM's Watson gets its first piece of business in Healthcare. *Forbes*.

CHAPTER 10

Time Series Forecasting

Time series forecasting is one of the oldest known predictive analytics techniques. Strictly speaking, it has existed and been in widespread use even before the term "predictive analytics" was ever coined!

Up to this point in this book, supervised model building was about collecting data from several different attributes of a system and using these to fit a "function" to predict the desired quantity or target variable. For example, if the "system" was a housing market, the attributes may have been the price of a house, its square footage, number of bedrooms, number of floors, age, and so on. A multiple linear regression model or a neural network model could be built to predict the price (target) variable given the other (predictor) variables. Similarly, purchasing managers may use data from several different commodity prices that influence the final price of a product to "model" the cost of the product. The common thread among these predictive models is that predictors or independent variables that potentially influence a target (price or product cost) are used to predict that target variable. The objective in time series forecasting is slightly different: use historical information about a particular quantity to make forecasts about value of the *same quantity* in the future. In general, there are two important differences between time series analysis and other supervised predictive models.

First, in time series analysis we are concerned with forecasting a specific variable, given that we know how this variable has changed over time in the past. In all other predictive models discussed so far, the time component of the data was either ignored or was not available. Such data are known as *cross-sectional data* (Figure 10.1).

Second, we may not be interested in (or might not even have) data for other attributes that could potentially influence the target variable. In other words, independent or *predictor* variables are not strictly *necessary* for univariate time series forecasting (but are strongly recommended for multivariate time series).

Such time series forecasting methods are called *data-driven* forecasting methods, where there is no difference between a predictor and a target. The predictor

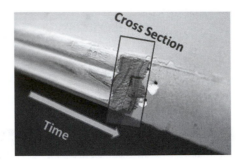

FIGURE 10.1

Cross-sectional data is a subset of time series data. *(Image modified from original sourced from Wikimedia Commons. Creative Commons Attribution.)*

is also the target variable. Techniques such as time series averaging or smoothing are considered data-driven approaches to time series forecasting.

However, there is also another class of time series forecasting techniques that are known as *model-driven* forecasting methods. Model-driven techniques are similar to "conventional" predictive models, which have independent and dependent variables, but with a twist: the independent variable is now time. The simplest of such methods is of course a linear regression model of the form

$$y(t) = a + b * t \tag{10.1}$$

where y(t) is the value of the target variable at time t. Given a training set, we estimate the values of coefficients a and b to forecast future y values. Model-driven techniques can get pretty complicated in the selection of the type of function. Commonly used functions are exponential, polynomial, and power law functions. Most people are familiar with the trend line function in spreadsheet programs, which offer several different function choices. In a nutshell, a model-driven time series forecast differs from a regular function-fitting predictive model in the choice of the independent variable.

A more sophisticated model-driven technique is based on the concept of autocorrelation. Autocorrelation refers to the fact that data from adjacent time periods may be correlated. The most well known among these techniques is ARIMA, which stands for *autoregressive integrated moving average*; this will be briefly covered in later sections. We will now describe the concepts of time series forecasting using data-driven and model-driven techniques.

Time series analysis can also be broadly classified into *descriptive* modeling, called time series analysis, and *predictive* modeling, called time series forecasting. Both of these rely on a technique called *decomposition*, where the data is split into a trend component, a seasonal component, and a noise component. The trend and seasonality are predictable (and are called systematic components) whereas the noise, by definition, is random (and is called the nonsystematic component). The discussions in this chapter focus only on time series forecasting techniques. For a complete description of time series decomposition, the reader is referred to books dedicated to time series analysis such as Hyndman (2014).

FORECASTING DEMAND OF A PRODUCT

A very common application of time series is in forecasting demand for a product. A manufacturing company makes anticorrosion wax tapes for use in gas and oil pipelines. The company makes more than a dozen varieties of wax tape products using a handful of assembly lines. The demand for these products varies depending upon several factors. For example, routine pipeline maintenance is typically done during warm weather seasons. So there could be a seasonal spike in the demand. Also over the last several years, growth in emerging economies has meant that the demand for their products also has been growing. Finally, any upcoming changes in pricing (which the company may announce ahead of time) may also trigger stockpiling by their customers, resulting in sudden jumps in demand. So, there can be both trend and seasonality factors (see Figure 10.2).

Their general manager needs to be able to predict demand for their products on a monthly, quarterly, and annual basis so that he can plan the production using their limited resources and his department's budget. He makes use of time series forecasting models to predict the potential demand for each of their product lines. By studying the seasonal patterns and growth trends, he can better prepare their production lines. For example, studying seasonality in the sales for the #2 wax tape, which is heavily used in cold climates, reveals that March and April are the months with the highest number of orders placed as customers buy them ahead of the maintenance seasons starting in the summer months. So the plant manager can dedicate most of their production lines to manufacturing the #2 tape during these months. This insight would not be known unless a time series analysis was performed.

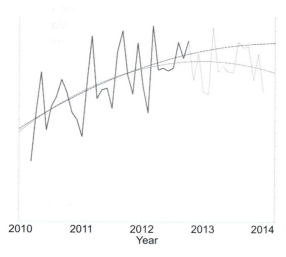

FIGURE 10.2

A time series analysis can reveal trends and seasonal patterns.

10.1 DATA-DRIVEN APPROACHES

It is helpful to start out with a basic notation system for time series in order to understand the different methodologies. The following measures are important:

- **Time periods:** t = 1, 2, 3, …, n . Time periods can be seconds, days, weeks, months, or years depending on the problem.
- **Data series corresponding to each time period above:** $y_1, y_2, y_3, … y_n$.
- **Forecasts:** F_{n+h} → forecast for the hth time period following n. Usually h = 1, the next time period following the last data point. However h can be greater than 1. "h" is called the *horizon*.
- **Forecast errors:** $e_t = y_t - F_t$ for any given time, t.

In order to explain the different methods, we will use a simple time series data function, Y(t). Y is the value of the time series at any time t. The data represents the value of Y over a 36-month period. (Data and accompanying models are available from the companion site www.LearnPredictiveAnalytics.com) As you can see in Figure 10.3, Y(t) can be imagined to be made up of a periodic (or seasonal) component and a random (noise) component. Additionally, Y(t) may have a small (in this case, upward) linear trend as well. Furthermore, the time periods are constant. However, for some data the period may be variable. In such cases, we assume that an interpolation scheme is applied to obtain equally spaced (in time) data points.

10.1.1 Naïve Forecast

Probably the simplest forecasting "model." Here we simply assume that F_{n+1}, the forecast for the next period in the series, is given by the last data point of the series, y_n:

$$F_{n+1} \left(= y_{n+1} \right) = y_n \tag{10.2}$$

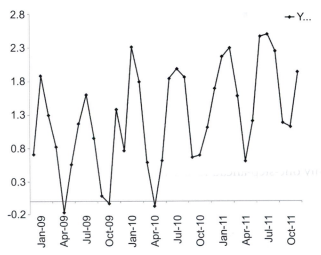

FIGURE 10.3

A simple time series, Y(t).

10.1.2 Simple Average

Moving up a level, we could compute the next data point as an average of all the data points in the series. In other words, this model calculates the forecasted value, F_{n+1}, as

$$F_{n+1} = \text{AVERAGE}(y_n, y_{n-1}, y_{n-2}, \ldots, y_1) \qquad (10.3)$$

Suppose we have monthly data from January to December and we want to predict the next January (n + 1) value, we simply average the values from January (n = 1) to December (n = 12).

10.1.3 Moving Average

The obvious problem with a simple average is figuring out how many points to use in the average calculation. As the data grows (as n increases), should we still use all the n time periods to compute the next forecast? To overcome this problem, we can select a window of the last "k" periods to calculate the average, and as the actual data grows over time, we always take the last k samples to average, i.e., n, n – 1, ..., n – k + 1. In other words, the window for averaging keeps moving forward and thus returns a moving average. Suppose in our simple example that the window k = 3; then to predict the January data, we take a three-month average using the last three months. When the actual data from January comes in, the February value is forecasted using January (n), December (n – 1) and November (n – 3 + 1 or n – 2). This model will result in problems when there is seasonality in data (for example, in December for retail or in January for healthcare insurance), which can skew the average.

10.1.4 Weighted Moving Average

For some cases, the most recent value could have more influence than some of the earlier values. Most exponential growth occurs due to this simple effect. The forecast for the next period is given by the model

$$F_{n+1} = (a * y_n + b * y_n - 1 + c * y_n - 2) / (a + b + c) \qquad (10.4)$$

where typically a > b > c. Figure 10.4 compares the forecast results for the simple time series introduced earlier. Note that all of the above methods are able to make only one-step-ahead forecasts due to the nature of their formulation. The coefficients a, b, and c may be arbitrary, but are usually based on some previous knowledge of the time series.

Next we will consider exponential smoothing, which is a slightly different form of weighted moving averages.

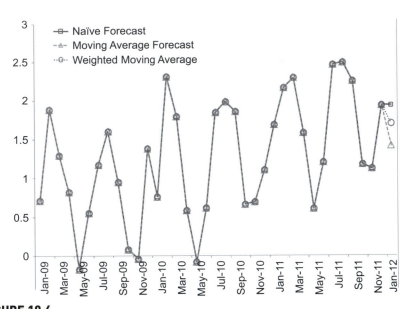

FIGURE 10.4
Comparing one-step-ahead forecasts for basic data-driven methods.

10.1.5 Exponential Smoothing

What would happen if we use the previously forecasted value for a given period to predict the value for the next period? Going back to our monthly example, if we wanted to make the February forecast using not only the actual January value but also the previously *forecasted* January value, the new forecast would have "learned" the data a little better. This is the concept behind basic exponential smoothing (Brown, 1956):

$$F_{n+1} = \alpha * y_n + (1 - \alpha) * F_n \tag{10.5}$$

α is generally between 0 and 1. If α is close to 1, then the previously forecasted value of the last period has less weight than the actual value of the last period and vice versa. Note that $\alpha = 1$ returns the naïve forecast of Equation 10.2. As seen in the charts in Figure 10.5, using a higher α results in putting more weight on actual values and the resulting curve is closer to the actual curve, but using a lower α results in putting more emphasis on previously forecasted value and results in a smoother but less accurate fit. Typical values for α range from 0.2 to 0.4 in practice.

This simple exponential smoothing is the basis for a number of very common data-driven forecasting methods. The above model has only one parameter, α, and can help to smooth the data in a time series so that it is easy to extrapolate and make forecasts. But if you examine Equation 10.5, you see that you cannot make forecasts more than one-step ahead, because to make a forecast for step $(n + 1)$, we need data for the previous step, n. It is not possible to make forecasts

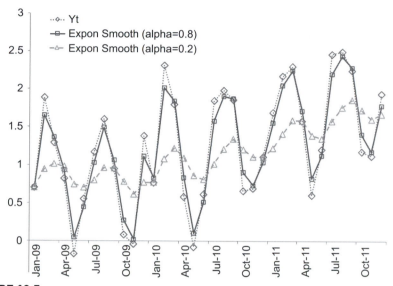

FIGURE 10.5
Exponential smoothing with different α levels.

several steps ahead, i.e., $(n + h)$, using the three methods described above (where we have simply assumed that $F_{n+h} = F_{n+1}$). Here "h" is called the "horizon." This obviously has limited utility. For making longer horizon forecasts, that is where $h \gg 1$, we need to also consider trend and seasonality information and the simple exponential smoothing methods quickly become more complicated. An overview of advanced exponential smoothing is described in the next few sections.

A time series is made up of what is known as nonstationary data. "Nonstationary" means that the series typically demonstrates a trend and a seasonal pattern in addition to "normal" fluctuations (Hyndman, 2014). As mentioned earlier, most time series can be decomposed into the following components: *trend, seasonality,* and *random noise* (see Figure 10.6). To be able to capture trend and seasonality, we need more sophisticated techniques than the ones described so far. The good news is that there are many well-established data-driven methods that can help accomplish this. Once we capture trend and seasonality, we can forecast the value at any time in the future, not just one step ahead values. We will give a bird's eye view of the common ones to introduce them.

10.1.6 Holt's Two-Parameter Exponential Smoothing

Anyone who has used a spreadsheet for creating trend lines on scatterplots intuitively knows what a trend means. A trend is an averaged long-term tendency of a time series. The simplified exponential smoothing model described

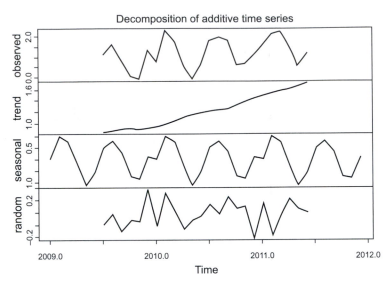

FIGURE 10.6

A typical decomposition of a time series.

earlier is not very effective at capturing trends. An extension of this technique called Holt's two-parameter exponential smoothing is needed to accomplish this.

Recall that exponential smoothing Equation (10.5) simply calculates the *average value* of the time series at n + 1. If the series also has a trend, then an average slope of the series needs to be estimated as well. This is what Holt's two-parameter smoothing does by means of another parameter, β. A smoothing equation similar to Equation 10.5 is constructed for the average trend at n + 1. With two parameters, α and β, any time series with a trend can be modeled and therefore forecasted. The forecast can be expressed as a sum of these two components, average value or "level" of the series, L_n, and trend, T_n, recursively as follows:

$$F_{n+1} = L_n + T_n \tag{10.6}$$

where, $L_n = \alpha * y_n + (1 - \alpha) * (L_{n-1} + T_{n-1})$ and $T_n = \beta * (L_n - L_{n-1}) + (1 - \beta) * T_{n-1}$

10.1.7 Holt-Winters' Three-Parameter Exponential Smoothing

When a time series contains seasonality in addition to a trend, we will need yet another parameter, γ, to estimate the seasonal component of the time series (Winters, 1960). The estimates for value (or level) are now adjusted by a seasonal index, which is computed with a third equation that includesγ. For mathematical details of all these algorithms, the reader is referred to one of the many texts dedicated to time series forecasting (Shmueli, 2011; Hyndman, 2014; Box, 2008).

10.2 MODEL-DRIVEN FORECASTING METHODS

Model-driven approaches to time series forecasting will overcome the one-step-ahead limitation of some of the data-driven methods. As mentioned at the beginning of the chapter, in model-driven methods, time is the predictor or independent variable and the time series value is the dependent variable. Model-based methods are generally preferable when the time series appears to have a "global" pattern. The idea is that the model parameters will be able to capture these patterns and thus enable us to make predictions for any step ahead in the future under the assumption that this pattern is going to repeat. For a time series with local patterns instead of a global pattern, using the model-driven approach requires specifying how and when the patterns change, which is difficult. For such a series, data-driven approaches work best because these methods usually rely on extrapolating the most recent local pattern as we saw earlier.

Figure 10.7 shows two time series: Figure 10.7a shows annual monsoon precipitation in Southwest India averaged over a five-year period (Krishnakumar, 2009). Figure 10.7b shows the adjusted month-end closing prices of the SPDR S&P 500 (SPY) Index over another five-year period. Clearly a model-driven forecasting method would work very well for the rainfall series. However the financial time series shows no clear start or end for any patterns. It is preferable to use data-driven methods to attempt to forecast this second series.

10.2.1 Linear Regression

The simplest of the model-driven approaches for analyzing a time series is using linear regression. As mentioned in the introduction to the chapter, we assume the time period is the independent variable and attempt to predict the time series value using this. For the simple 36-month dataset we have used so far, the chart in Figure 10.8a shows a linear regression fit created using a standard spreadsheet. As you can see, the linear regression model is able to capture the long-term tendency of the series, but it does a very poor job of fitting the data. This is reflected in the R^2 value shown as well.

10.2.2 Polynomial Regression

We can attempt to improve this using a more "sophisticated" polynomial fit. Polynomial regression is similar to linear regression except that higher-degree functions of the independent variable are used (squares and cubes). As seen in Figure 10.8b, it is difficult to argue that the cubic polynomial does a

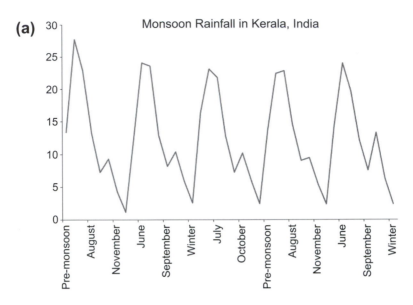

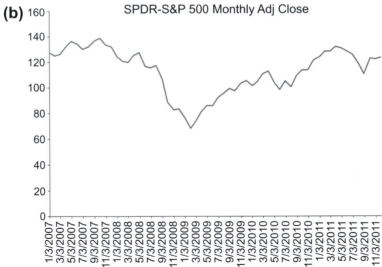

FIGURE 10.7

Illustration of when to use (a) model-driven and (b) data-driven time series forecasting.

significantly better job. However in either of these cases, we are not limited to a one-step-ahead forecast of the simple smoothing (data-driven) methods.

10.2.3 Linear Regression with Seasonality

But one can significantly improve upon the fit with linear regression by simply accounting for seasonality. This is done by introducing dummy variables for each month of the series, which trigger to 1 or 0 as seen in the table in

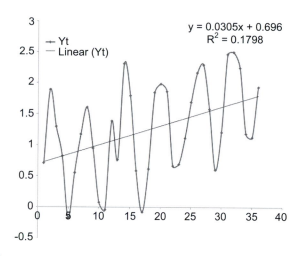

FIGURE 10.8a

Simple linear regression model.

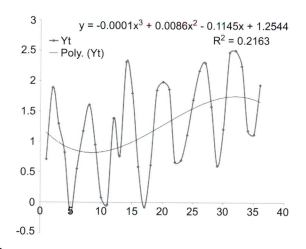

FIGURE 10.8b

Polynomial regression model.

Table 10.1. Just this very trivial addition to the predictors of the linear regression model can yield a surprisingly good fit as seen in Figure 10.9. Although the model equation may appear very complicated, in reality it is just a linear regression model in 13 variables: the time period and 12 dummy variables for each month of a year. The time-independent variable captures the trend and the 12 dummy variables capture seasonality. This regression equation can be used for predicting any future value beyond $n + 1$, and thus has significantly more utility than the corresponding simpler counterparts in the data-driven side.

Table 10.1 Seasonality Modeled via Linear Regression and the Accompanying Fit

Month	t	Dummy_1	Dummy_2	Dummy_3	Dummy_4	Dummy_5	Dummy_6	Dummy_7	Dummy_8	Dummy_9	Dummy_10	Dummy_11	Dummy_12	Yt
Jan	1	1	0	0	0	0	0	0	0	0	0	0	0	0.709
Feb	2	0	1	0	0	0	0	0	0	0	0	0	0	1.886
Mar	3	0	0	1	0	0	0	0	0	0	0	0	0	1.293
Apr	4	0	0	0	1	0	0	0	0	0	0	0	0	0.822
May	5	0	0	0	0	1	0	0	0	0	0	0	0	-0.173
Jun	6	0	0	0	0	0	1	0	0	0	0	0	0	0.552
Jul	7	0	0	0	0	0	0	1	0	0	0	0	0	1.169
Aug	8	0	0	0	0	0	0	0	1	0	0	0	0	1.604
Sep	9	0	0	0	0	0	0	0	0	1	0	0	0	0.949
Oct	10	0	0	0	0	0	0	0	0	0	1	0	0	0.08
Nov	11	0	0	0	0	0	0	0	0	0	0	1	0	-0.04
Dec	12	0	0	0	0	0	0	0	0	0	0	0	1	1.381

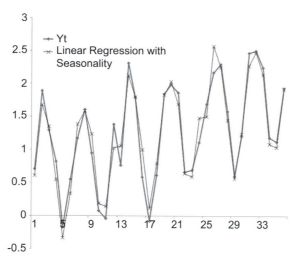

FIGURE 10.9

Seasonality modeled via linear regression and the accompanying fit.

There is of course no reason to use linear regression alone to capture both trend and seasonality. More sophisticated models can easily be built using polynomial equations along with the sine and cosine function to model seasonality. They will achieve the same effect.

10.2.4 Autoregression Models and ARIMA

The second column of Table 10.2 shows the data for our simple time series. In the third column, we collect the values from month 6 to month 12 of year 1 (2010), and in the fourth column we collect values from month 13 to month 18. This new series of values is termed a "lag "series and we see that there is some correlation between them. In particular, values belonging to the same row are strongly correlated. For example, every fifth month (May 2010, Nov. 2010, and May 2011), the values drop below zero. This phenomenon is called autocorrelation and it can be used to our advantage. Autoregression methods are basically regression models applied on lag series where each lag series is a new predictor used to fit the dependent variable, which is still the original series value, Y_t. In addition to creating a lag series of actual values, we can also create a lag series involving forecast errors and use this as another predictor.

The ARIMA methodology originally developed by Box and Jenkins in the 1970s (Box, 1970) allows us to do this type of modeling. ARIMA is a complex technique and it requires a great deal of experience to produce good forecast results. Although RapidMiner does provide means to perform lagging operations, it does not provide a simple way to implement ARIMA. We refer the reader to the

Table 10.2 Concept of Autocorrelation

Month	Yt	Lag 6-1	Lag 6-2
Jan-09	0.709	1.169	0.761
Feb-09	1.886	1.604	2.312
Mar-09	1.293	0.949	1.795
Apr-09	0.822	0.08	0.586
May-09	-0.173	-0.04	-0.077
Jun-09	0.552	1.381	0.613
Jul-09	1.169		
Aug-09	1.604		
Sep-09	0.949		
Oct-09	0.08		
Nov-09	-0.04		
Dec-09	1.381		
Jan-10	0.761		
Feb-10	2.312		
Mar-10	1.795		
Apr-10	0.586		
May-10	-0.077		
Jun-10	0.613		

many online and offline resources on ARIMA for further information about its applications (see for example, Alnaa, 2011). In the next few sections we focus on using RapidMiner to perform time series analysis and forecasts.

10.2.5 How to Implement

RapidMiner's approach to time series is based on two main data transformation processes. The first is *windowing* to transform the time series data into a generic data set: this step will convert the last row of a window within the time series into a label or target variable. We apply any of the "learners" or algorithms to predict the target variable and thus predict the next time step in the series. A "typical" time series and its transformed structure (after windowing) is conceptually shown in Figure 10.10.

The parameters of the *Windowing* operator allow changing the size of the windows (shown as vertical boxes in dashed lines, on the left of figure 10.10), the overlap between consecutive windows (also known as step size), and the prediction horizon, which is used for forecasting. The prediction horizon controls which row in the raw data series ends up as the label variable in the transformed series. (For example, in the above example, the prediction

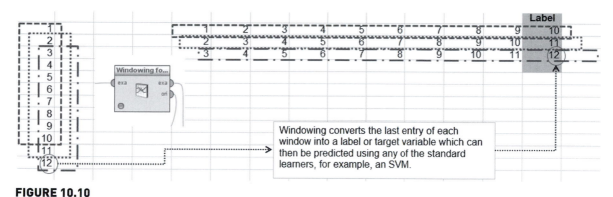

FIGURE 10.10

Concept of windowing transformation.

horizon is 0, the next section gives more details.) Thus series data are now converted into a generic cross-sectional data set that can be "predicted" with any of the available algorithms in RapidMiner.

The next main process required for running time series analyses using Rapid-Miner involves applying any of the available "learners" to "predict" the label variable shown in the gray box (see Figure 10.10). The example set (or raw data) for this learner is the "horizontal" data set shown above with the target or label variable in the box. Also, most of the *Performance* operators can be used to assess the fitness of the learning scheme to the data.

In this section, we will show how to set up a RapidMiner process to model the simple time series Y(t) described in Section 10.1. The data set could refer to historical monthly profits from a particular product, for example, from January 2009 to June 2010. The data was previously shown in Table 10.1 (column labeled Yt). Our objective in this exercise is to develop profitability forecasts for the next 12 months and also show some of the advantages of using machine learning algorithms for forecasting problems compared to conventional (averaging or smoothing type) forecasting algorithms. The process consists of the following three steps: (1) set up windowing; (2) train the model with several different algorithms; and (3) generate the forecasts.

Step 1: Set Up Windowing

The process window in Figure 10.11 shows the necessary operators for windowing. All time series will have a date column and this must be treated with special care. RapidMiner must be informed that one of the columns in the data set is a date and should be considered as an "id." This is accomplished by the *Set Role* operator. If you have multiple commodities in the input data, you may also want to Select Attributes that you want to forecast. In this case, we have only one series and strictly speaking we do not need this operator. However to

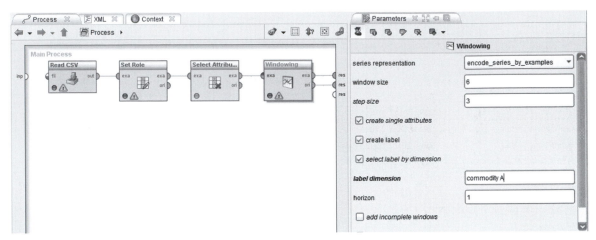

FIGURE 10.11
Applying windowing to raw time series data.

make the process generic we include it and select the column labeled "inputYt." The final operator is the *Windowing* operator. (You may need to install the Series extension, if you have not already. Go to Help -> Manage Extensions to verify.)

Additionally, you may want to use the *Filter Examples* operator to remove any attributes that have missing values. The main items to consider in Windowing are the following:

- **Window size:** Determines how many "attributes" are created for the cross-sectional data. Each row of the original time series within the window width will become a new attribute. In this example we choose w = 6.
- **Step size:** Determines how to advance the window. Let us use s = 1.
- **Horizon:** Determines how far out to make the forecast. If the window size is 6 and the horizon is 1, then the seventh row of the original time series becomes the first sample for the "label" variable. Let us use h = 1, as well.

Figure 10.12 shows the original data and the transformed output from the windowing process and describes the transformation details. The main point to keep in mind is that for the window selected and shown in the box the target or response variable value is the value from Jul 1, 2009. When training any algorithm using this data, the attributes labeled *inputYt-5* through *inputYt-0* form the independent variables. This is shown in the output of step 2 (Figure 10.13).

Date	inputYt
Jan 1, 2009	0.709
Feb 1, 2009	1.886
Mar 1, 2009	1.293
Apr 1, 2009	0.822
May 1, 2009	-0.173
Jun 1, 2009	0.552
Jul 1, 2009	1.169
Aug 1, 2009	1.604
Sep 1, 2009	0.949
Oct 1, 2009	0.080
Nov 1, 2009	-0.040
Dec 1, 2009	1.381
Jan 1, 2010	0.761

Date	label	inputYt-5	inputYt-4	inputYt-3	inputYt-2	inputYt-1	inputYt-0
Jun 1, 2009	1.169	0.709	1.886	1.293	0.822	-0.173	0.552
Jul 1, 2009	1.604	1.886	1.293	0.822	-0.173	0.552	1.169
Aug 1, 2009	0.949	1.293	0.822	-0.173	0.552	1.169	1.604
Sep 1, 2009	0.080	0.822	-0.173	0.552	1.169	1.604	0.949
Oct 1, 2009	-0.040	-0.173	0.552	1.169	1.604	0.949	0.080
Nov 1, 2009	1.381	0.552	1.169	1.604	0.949	0.080	-0.040
Dec 1, 2009	0.761	1.169	1.604	0.949	0.080	-0.040	1.381
Jan 1, 2010	2.312	1.604	0.949	0.080	-0.040	1.381	0.761
Feb 1, 2010	1.795	0.949	0.080	-0.040	1.381	0.761	2.312
Mar 1, 2010	0.586	0.080	-0.040	1.381	0.761	2.312	1.795
Apr 1, 2010	-0.077	-0.040	1.381	0.761	2.312	1.795	0.586
May 1, 2010	0.613	1.381	0.761	2.312	1.795	0.586	-0.077

Window size = 6
Step size = 1
Horizon = 1

Using data from 6 rows (Jan 2009 – Jun 2009) of the window, a learner can be trained to predict the label which is the value of the time series in the next time step (Jul 2009) and so on.

FIGURE 10.12
Output of windowing transformation.

Step 2: Train the Model

Once the windowing is done, then the real power of predictive analytics algorithms may be brought to bear on a time series analysis. This is where the advantage of using RapidMiner comes into play. Now that the time series is encoded and transformed into a cross-sectional data set, we can use any of the available machine learning algorithms such as regression, neural networks, or support vector machines, for example, to generate predictions. In this case we use linear regression to fit the "dependent" variable called label, given the "independent" variables $inputYt-5$ through $inputYt-0$.

Once the model fitting is done, the next step is to start the forecasting process. Note that given this configuration of window size and horizon, we can now only make the forecast for the next step. In the example, the last row of the transformed data set corresponds to Nov. 1, 2011. The independent variables are values from June through November 2011 and the target or label variable is from December 2011. But we can use the regression equation and the values from the Nov. 1, 2011 row to generate the forecast for January 2012. All we need to do is insert the values from July–December into the regression equation to generate the January 2012 forecast. This is just the $(n + 1)$th forecast and all the sophisticated windowing with equation fitting accomplishes nothing more than what the simple smoothing algorithms described in

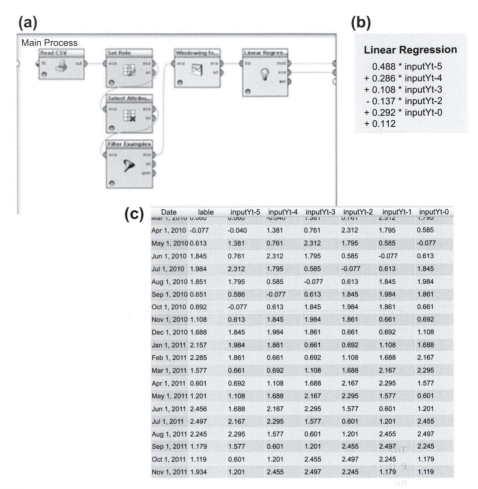

FIGURE 10.13

Using the process shown (a), the "label" variable is fitted using the six dependent variables via linear regression (b). Note that the label for any given row is the *inputYt-0* for the next row (c).

Section 10.1 could have done! At this point, extending this to provide future values beyond (n + 1) might have become apparent to the reader. Next, we need to generate a new row of data that would run from August–January to predict February using the regression equation. We have all the (actual) data from August to December and the predicted value for January at our disposal. Once we have the predicted February value, there is nothing stopping us from using the actual data from September–December plus predicted January and February values to forecast March.

Actually accomplishing this using RapidMiner is easier said than done. We need to break this up into *two separate parts*. First, you take the last forecasted

Prediction	Attribute-6	Attribute-5	Attribute-4	Attribute-3	Attribute-2	Attribute-1
v7*	v1	v2	v3	v4	v5	v6
v8*	v2	v3	v4	v5	v6	v7*
v9*	v3	v4	v5	v6	v7*	v8*
...	...	...	...	...	...	...

$(n+1)^{th}$ forecast: without looping this is the last value that windowing can predict.

Row No.	Date	prediction(label)	inputYt-5	inputYt-4	inputYt-3	inputYt-2	inputYt-1	inputYt-0
1	Nov 1, 2011	1.694	1.201	2.466	2.497	2.245	1.179	1.119
2	Dec 1, 2011	2.597	2.466	2.497	2.245	1.179	1.119	1.694
3	Jan 1, 2012	2.693	2.497	2.245	1.179	1.119	1.694	2.597
4	Feb 1, 2012	2.196	2.245	1.179	1.119	1.694	2.597	2.693
5	Mar 1, 2012	1.457	1.179	1.119	1.694	2.597	2.693	2.196
6	Apr 1, 2012	1.457	1.119	1.694	2.597	2.693	2.196	1.457
7	May 1, 2012	2.087	1.694	2.597	2.693	2.196	1.457	1.457
8	Jun 1, 2012	2.784	2.597	2.693	2.196	1.457	1.457	2.087
9	Jul 1, 2012 1	2.807	2.693	2.196	1.457	1.457	2.087	2.784
10	Aug 1, 2012	2.265	2.196	1.457	1.457	2.087	2.784	2.807
11	Sep 1, 2012	1.720	1.457	1.457	2.087	2.784	2.807	2.265
12	Oct 1, 2012	1.816	1.457	2.087	2.784	2.807	2.265	1.720
13	Nov 1, 2012	2.433	2.087	2.784	2.807	2.265	1.720	1.816
14	Dec 1, 2012	2.974	2.784	2.807	2.265	1.720	1.816	2.433
15	Jan 1, 2013	2.911	2.807	2.265	1.720	1.816	2.433	2.974

Looping allows forecasting to march ahead.

FIGURE 10.14

Using Loop function in the windowing process allows forecasting more than 1-step ahead.

row (in this case, December 2011), drop the current value of *inputYt-5* (current value is 1.201), rename *inputYt-4* to *inputYt-5*, rename *inputYt-3* to *inputYt-4*, rename *inputYt-2* to *inputYt-3*, rename *inputYt-1* to *inputYt-2*, rename *inputYt-0* to *inputYt-1*, and finally rename predicted *label* (current value is 1.934) to *inputYt-0*. With this new row of data, you can then apply the regression model to predict the next date in the series: January 2012. Next, you need to put this entire process inside a *Loop* operator that will allow you to repeatedly run these steps for as many future periods as you need.

The results of this process are illustrated in Figure 10.14 and the implementation is described in detail in step 3.

Step 3: Generate the Forecasts

The outer level process for the first part is shown in Figure 10.15. We can add another *Windowing* operator, which will transform input and allow us to collect the last forecasted row and feed it to an inner level Loop process (Figure 10.16). The *Loop* operator will contain all the mechanisms for accomplishing the renaming and, of course, to perform looping. Set the *iterations* in

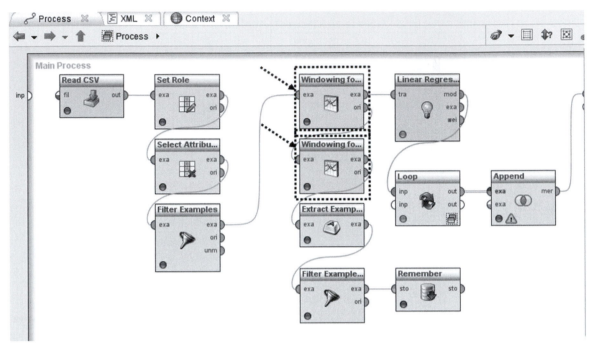

FIGURE 10.15

Outer process for generating forecasts. Two Windowing operators (arrows) are needed: one to train the model (upper) and another to feed the trained model (lower).

the *Loop* operator to the number of future months to forecast (horizon). In our case, this is defined by a variable called *futureMonths* whose value can be changed by the user before process execution. It is also possible to capture the Loop counts in a macro if you click the *set iteration macro* check box. A *macro* in RapidMiner is nothing but a variable that can be called by other operators in the process. When *set iteration macro* is checked and a name is provided in the *macro name* box, a variable will be created with that name whose value will be updated each time, one loop is completed. An initial value for this macro is set by the *macro start value* option. Loops may be terminated by specifying a *timeout*, which is enabled by checking the *limit time* box. A macro variable can be used by any other operator by using the format %{macro name} in place of a numeric value.

But before we start the looping, we need to store the last forecasted row in a separate data structure. This is accomplished by the macro titled *Extract Example Set*. The *Filter Example* operator simply deletes all rows of the transformed data set except the last forecasted row. Finally the *Remember* operator stores this in memory and allows us to "recall" the stored value once inside the loop.

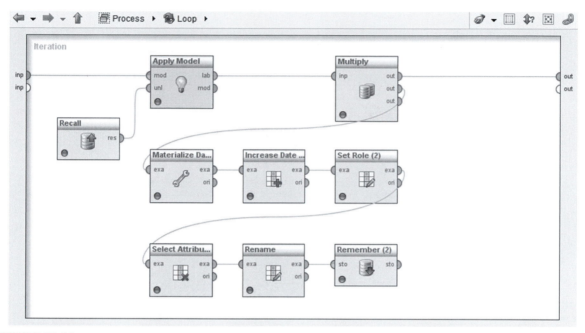

FIGURE 10.16
Inner level loop process for generating forecasts.

The loop parameter *iterations* will determine the number of times the inner process is repeated. During each iteration, the model is applied on the last forecasted row, and bookkeeping operations are performed to prepare application of the model to forecast the next month. This includes incrementing the month (date) by one, changing the role of the predicted label to that of a regular attribute, and finally renaming all the attributes as discussed in the last part of step 2. The newly renamed data is stored and then recalled before the next iteration begins.

The output of our process is shown in Figure 10.17 as an overlay on top of the actual data. (The tabular form of the results was already shown in Figure 10.14.) As seen, the simple linear regression model seems to adequately capture both the trend and seasonality of the underlying data. The real benefit of using RapidMiner for time series forecasting lies in being able to quickly change the modeling scheme. We can quickly swap out the *Linear Regression* operator of step 2 to a *Support Vector Machine* operator and test its performance without having to do any other programming or process modification. Ultimately, the user can select the best performing modeler with very little extra effort.

An important point about any time series forecasting is that one should not place too much emphasis on "point" forecasts. A complex quantity like a stock

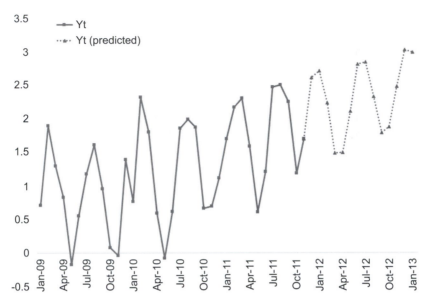

FIGURE 10.17

Output of the forecasting process.

price or sales demand for a manufactured good is influenced by too many factors and to claim that any forecasting will predict the exact value of a stock two days in advance or the exact value of demand three months in advance is unrealistic. However, what is far more valuable is the fact that recent undulations in the price or demand can be effectively captured and predicted. This is where RapidMiner excels by allowing us to swap modeling techniques and experiment.

CONCLUSION

In this chapter we have given a high level overview of the field of time series modeling. We started out by illustrating the key differences between predictive models for time series and predictive models for cross-sectional data. We then discussed the two main classes of time series forecasting approaches and showed how RapidMiner uses what may best be termed a "hybrid" approach. We finally demonstrated how to implement a real-world time series modeling and forecasting problem entirely using RapidMiner.

Univariate time series forecasting treats prediction as essentially a single-variable problem, whereas multivariate time series may use many time-concurred series for prediction. If you have a series of points spaced over time, conventional forecasting uses smoothing and averaging to "predict" where the next few points will likely be. However, for complex systems such as the economy or stock market, point forecasts are unreliable because these systems are functions of hundreds if not thousands of variables. What is more valuable or useful is the ability to predict trends, rather than point forecasts. We can predict trends with greater confidence and reliability (i.e., Are the quantities going to trend up or down?), rather than the values or levels of these quantities. For this reason, using different modeling schemes such as artificial neural networks or support vector machines or even polynomial regression can sometimes give highly accurate trend forecasts. With conventional forecasting available in the R extension, we have the option of using a variety of smoothing functions and modeling techniques such as ARIMA.

If you do have a time series that is not highly volatile (and therefore more predictable), conventional time series forecasting can help you understand the underlying structure of the variability better. In such cases, trends or seasonal components have a stronger signature than the random component. R does a very good job of taking any time series and breaking it up into these components. If your time series project involves decomposing data into trends and seasonality, then using the R extension in RapidMiner may be the best way to go.

REFERENCES

Alnaa, S. A. (2011). ARIMA approach to predicting inflation in Ghana. *Journal of Economics and International Finance*, 3(5), 328–336.

Box, G. A. (1970). *Time Series Analysis: Forecasting and Control*. San Francisco: Holding Day.

Box, G. J. (2008). *Time Series Analysis: Forecasting and Control*. Wiley Series in Probability and Statistics.

Brown, R. G. (1956). *Exponential Smoothing for Predicting Demand*. Cambridge, MA: Arthur D. Little.

Gardener, E. (1986). Exponential Smoothing: The state of the art. *J. Forecasting*, 4(1), 1–28.

Hyndman, R. A. (2014). *Forecasting: Principles and Practice*. Otexts.org.

Krishnakumar, K. P. (2009). Rainfall trends in the twentieth century over Kerala, India. *Atmospheric Environment*, 43(11), 1940–1944.

Shmueli, G. (2011). *Practical Time Series Forecasting: A hands on guide*. statistics.com.

Winters, P. (1960). Forecasting Sales by Exponentially Weighted Moving Averages. *Management Science*, 6(3), 324–342.

CHAPTER 11

Anomaly Detection

Anomaly detection is the process of finding outliers in the data set. Outliers are the data objects that stand out amongst other data objects and do not conform to the expected behavior in a data set. Anomaly detection algorithms have broad applications in business, scientific, and security domains where isolating and acting on the results of outlier detection is critical. For identification of anomalies, algorithms discussed in previous chapters such as classification, regression, and clustering can be used. If the training data set has objects with known anomalous outcomes, then any of the supervised data mining algorithms can be used for anomaly detection. In addition to supervised algorithms, there are specialized (unsupervised) algorithms whose whole purpose is to detect outliers without use of a labeled training data set. In the context of unsupervised anomaly detection, algorithms can either measure distance from other data points or density around the neighborhood of the data point. We can even leverage clustering techniques for anomaly detection. The outlier usually forms a separate cluster from other clusters because they are far away from other data points. We will be revisiting some of the techniques discussed in previous chapters in the context of outlier detection. Before discussing the algorithms, we need to define the term outlier or anomaly and understand why such data points occur in the data set.

11.1 ANOMALY DETECTION CONCEPTS

An outlier is a data object that is markedly different from the other objects in the data set. Hence an outlier is always defined in the context of other objects in the data set. A high-income individual may be an outlier in a middle-class neighborhood data set, but not in the membership of a luxury vehicle ownership data set. By nature of occurrence, outliers are also rare and hence they stand out amongst other data points. For example, the majority of computer network traffic is legitimate and the one malicious network attack would be the outlier.

11.1.1 Causes of Outliers

Outliers in the data set can originate from either error in the data or from valid inherent variability in the data. It is important to understand the provenance of the outliers because it will guide what action, if any, should be performed on the identified outliers. However, pinpointing exactly what caused an outlier is a tedious task and in many cases it is impossible to find the causes of outliers in the data set. Here are some of the most common reasons why an outlier occurs in the data set:

- **Data errors:** Outliers may be part of the data set because of measurement errors, human errors, or data collection errors. For example, in a data set of human heights, a reading such as 1.70 centimeters is obviously an error and most likely was entered wrongly in the system. These data points are often ignored because they affect the conclusion of the data mining task. Outlier detection here is used as a preprocessing step in algorithms such as regression and neural networks. Data errors due to human mistake could be either intentional introduction of error or unintentional error due to data entry error or significant bias.

- **Normal variance in the data:** In a normal distribution, 99.7% of data points lie within three standard deviations from the mean. In other terms, 0.26% or 1 in 370 data points lie outside three standard deviations from the mean. By definition, they don't occur frequently and are a part of legitimate data. An individual earning a billion dollars in a year or someone who is more than 7 feet tall falls under the category of outlier in an income data set and human height data set respectively. These outliers skew some of the descriptive statistics like the mean of the data set. Regardless, they are legitimate data points in the data set.

- **Data from other distribution classes:** The number of daily page views for a customer-facing website from a user IP address usually range from one to a few dozens. However, it is not unusual to find a few IP addresses making calls for hundreds of thousands page views in a day. This outlier could be an automated program from a computer (also called a bot) making the calls to scrape the content of the site or access one of the utilities of the site, either legitimately or maliciously. Even though they are an outlier, it is quite "normal" for bots registering thousands of page view calls to a website. All bot traffic falls under distribution of a different class—"traffic from programs" other than traffic from regular browsers that fall under the human user class.

- **Distributional assumptions:** Outlier data points can originate from incorrect assumptions made on the data or distribution. For example, if the data measured is usage of a library in a school, then during term exams there will be an outlier because of surge in usage of the library. Similarly, there will be a surge in retail sales during the day after Thanksgiving in the United States. An outlier in this case is expected, and doesn't represent the data point of a typical measure.

Understanding why outliers occur will help to determine what action to perform after outlier detection. In a few applications, the objective is to isolate and act on the outlier as we see in credit card transaction fraud monitoring. In this case, credit card transactions exhibiting different behavior from most normal transactions (such as high frequency, high amounts, or very large geographic separation between points of consecutive transactions) need to be isolated, alerted and credit card customer needs to be contacted immediately to verify the authenticity of the transaction. In other cases, we would need to filter out outliers because they may skew the final outcome. Here outlier detection is used as a preprocessing technique for other data mining or analytical tasks. For example, we may want to eliminate ultra-high-income earners to generalize a country's income patterns. Here outliers are legitimate data points, but we intentionally disregard them to generalize conclusions.

DETECTING CLICK FRAUD IN ONLINE ADVERTISING

The rise in online advertising has underwritten many successful Internet business models and enterprises. Online advertisements make free Internet services like web searches, news content, social networks, mobile application, and many other services viable. One of the key challenges in online advertisements is mitigating *click frauds*. Click fraud is a process where an automated program or a person imitates the action of a normal user clicking on an online advertisement, with the malicious intent of defrauding the advertiser, publisher, or advertisement network. Click fraud could be performed by contracting parties or third parties, like competitors trying to deplete advertisement budgets or to tarnish the reputation of the sites. Click fraud distorts the economics of advertising and poses a major challenge for all parties involved in online advertising (Haddadi, 2010). Detecting, eliminating, or discounting click fraud makes the entire marketplace trustworthy and even provides competitive advantage for all the parties.

Detecting click frauds takes advantage of the fact that fraudulent traffic exhibits an atypical web browsing pattern when compared with typical clickstream data. Fraudulent traffic often does not follow a logical sequence of actions and contains repetitive actions that would differentiate from other regular traffic (Sadagopan & Li, 2008). For example, most of the fraudulent traffic exhibits either one or many of following characteristics: they have very high click depth (number of web pages accessed deep in the website); the time between each click would be very low; a single session would have a high number of clicks on advertisements as compared with normal user; the originating IP address would be different from the target market of the advertisement; there would be very little time spent on advertiser's target website; etc. It is not one trait that differentiates fraudulent traffic from regular traffic, but the *combination* of the traits. Detecting click fraud is an ongoing and evolving process. Increasingly the click fraud perpetuators are getting sophisticated in imitating the characteristics of a normal web browsing user. Hence, click fraud cannot be fully eliminated; however it can be contained by constantly developing new algorithms to identify fraudulent traffic.

To detect click fraud outliers, first we need to prepare clickstream data in such a way that detection using data mining is easier. A relational column-row data set can be prepared with each visit occupying each row and the columns being traits like click depth, time between each clicks, advertisement clicks, total time spent in target website, etc. This multidimensional data set can be used for outlier detection using data mining. Clickstream traits or attributes need to be carefully considered, evaluated, transformed, and added in the data set. In multidimensional data space, the fraudulent traffic (data point) is distant from other visit records because of their attributes, such as number of ad clicks in a session. A regular visit usually has one or two ad clicks in a session, while a fraudulent visit would have dozens of ad clicks. Similarly, other attributes can help in identifying the outlier more precisely. Outlier detection algorithms reviewed in this chapter assign an outlier score (fraud score) for all the clickstream data points and the records with a higher score are predicted to be outliers.

11.1.2 Anomaly Detection Techniques

Humans are innately equipped to focus on outliers. The news we hear every day is mainly hinged on outlier events. Our interest around knowing who is the fastest, who earns the most, and who wins the most medals or scores the most goals is in part due to our increased attention to outliers. If the data is in one dimension like taxable income for individuals, we can identify outliers by a simple sorting function. Visualizing data by scatter, histogram, and box-whisker charts can help to identify outliers in the case of single attribute data sets as well. More advanced techniques would be fitting the data to a distribution model and using data mining techniques to detect outliers.

Outlier Detection Using Statistical Methods

Outliers in the data can be identified by creating a statistical distribution model of the data and identifying the data points that don't fit into the model or data points that occupy the ends of distribution tails. The underlying distribution of many practical data sets falls into the Gaussian (normal) distribution. The parameters for building a normal distribution (i.e., mean and standard deviation) can be estimated from the data set and the normal distribution curve can be created like the one shown in Figure 11.1.

Outliers can be detected based on where the data points fall in the standard normal distribution curve. A threshold for classifying an outlier can be specified, say three standard deviations from the mean. Any data point that is more than three standard deviations is identified as an outlier. Identifying outliers using this method considers only one attribute or dimension at a time. More advanced statistical techniques takes multiple dimensions into account and calculate the *Mahalanobis distance* instead of standard deviations from mean in a univariate distribution. Mahalanobis distance is the multivariate generalization of finding how many standard deviations away a point is from the mean of the multivariate distribution. Outlier detection using statistics provides a simple framework for building a distribution model and detection based on the variance of the data point from the mean. A limitation in using the distribution model to find outliers is that in many cases the distribution of the data set is not previously known. Even if the distribution is known, the actual data doesn't always fit the model.

Outlier Detection Using Data Mining

Outliers exhibit a certain set of characteristics that can be exploited to find them. Following are classes of techniques developed to identity outliers by using their unique characteristics (Tan et al., 2005). Each of these techniques has multiple parameters and hence a data point labeled as an outlier in one algorithm may not be an outlier to another. Hence it is prudent to rely on multiple algorithms before labeling the outliers.

- **Distance based:** By nature, outliers are different from other data objects in the data set. In multidimensional Cartesian space they are distant from other data points, as shown in Figure 11.2. If we measure average distance of the nearest N neighbors, the outliers will have a higher value than other normal data points. Distance-based algorithms utilize this property to identify outliers in the data.
- **Density based:** The density of a data point in a neighborhood is inversely related to the distance to its neighbors. Outliers occupy low-density areas while the regular data points often congregate in high-density areas. This is derived from the fact that the relative occurrence of an outlier is low compared with the frequency of normal data points.
- **Distribution based:** Outliers are the data points that have a low probability of occurrence and they occupy the tail ends of the

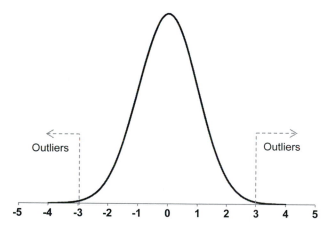

FIGURE 11.1
Standard normal distribution and outliers.

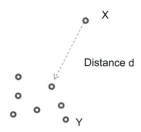

FIGURE 11.2
Distance-based outlier

distribution curve. So, if we try to fit the data set in a statistical distribution, these anomalous data points will stand out and hence can be identified. A simple normal distribution can be used to model the data set by calculating the mean and standard deviation.

■ **Clustering:** Outliers by definition are not similar to normal data points in a data set. They are rare data points far away from regular data points and generally do not form a tight cluster. Since most of the clustering algorithms have a minimum threshold of data points to form a cluster, the outliers are the lone data points that are not clustered. Even if outliers form a separate cluster, they are far away from other clusters.

■ **Classification techniques:** Nearly all classification techniques can be used to identify outliers, if previously known classified data is available. In classification techniques for detecting outliers, we need to have a known test data set where one of the class labels should be called "Outlier". The outlier detection classification model that is built based on the test data set can predict whether the unknown data is an outlier or not. The challenge in using a classification model is the availability of previously labeled data. Outlier data may be difficult to source because they are rare. This can be partially solved by stratified sampling where the outlier records are oversampled against normal records.

We have discussed supervised classification methods in previous chapters and we will discuss unsupervised outlier detection methods in the following sections. We will focus mainly on the distance and density based detection techniques in the following sections.

11.2 DISTANCE-BASED OUTLIER DETECTION

Distance or proximity-based outlier detection is one of the most fundamental algorithms for anomaly detection and it relies on the fact that outliers are distant from other data points. The proximity measures can be simple Euclidean distance for real values and cosine or Jaccard similarity measures for binary and categorical values. For the purpose of the discussion, let's consider a data set with numeric attributes and Euclidean distance as the proximity measure. Figure 11.3 shows a two-dimensional scatterplot of a sample data set. Outliers are the data points marked as grey and visually we can identify that they are away from groups of data. However, when working with multidimensional data with more attributes, visual techniques shows it's limitation very quickly.

11.2.1 How it Works

The fundamental concept of distance-based outlier detection is assigning a *distance score* for all the data points in the data set. The distance score should reflect how far a data point is separated from other data points. We have reviewed a similar concept in the k-nearest neighbor (k-NN) classification

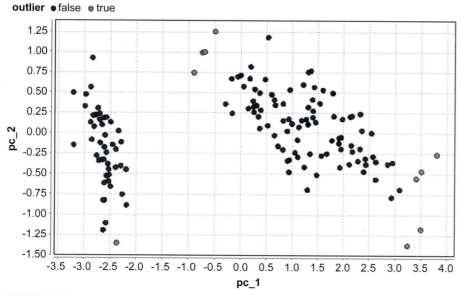

outlier • false • true

FIGURE 11.3
Data set with outliers

technique in Chapter 4 Classification. We can assign a distance score for each data object that is the distance to the kth-nearest data object. For example, we can assign a distance score for every data object that is the distance to the third-nearest data object. If the data object is an outlier, then it is far away from other data objects; hence the distance score for the outlier will be higher than for a normal data object. If we sort the data objects by distance score, then the objects with the highest scores are potentially outlier(s). As with k-NN classification or any algorithm that uses distance measures, it is important to normalize the numeric attributes, so an attribute with a higher absolute scale, such as income, does not dominate attributes with a lower scale, such as credit score.

In distance-based outlier detection, there is a significant effect based on the value of k, as in the k-NN classification technique. If the value of k = 1, then two outliers next to each other but far away from other data points are not identified as outliers. On the other hand, if the value of k is large, then a group of normal data points which form a cohesive cluster will be mislabeled as outliers, if the number of data points is less than k and the cluster is far away from other data points. With a defined value of k, once the distance scores have been calculated, we can specify a distance threshold to identify outliers or pick the top n objects with maximum distances, depending on the application and the nature of the data set. Figure 11.4 shows the results of two different outlier-detection algorithms based on distance for the Iris data set. Figure 11.4a shows the outlier detection with k = 1 and Figure 11.4b shows the detection of the same data set with k = 5.

11.2.2 How to Implement

Commercial data mining tools offer specific outlier detection algorithms and solutions as part of the package either in modeling or data cleansing sections. In RapidMiner, unsupervised outlier detection operator can be found in Data Transformation > Data Cleansing > Outlier Detection > Detect Outlier Distance. The example set we use in this process is the Iris data set with four numerical attributes and 150 examples.

Step 1: Data Preparation

Even though all four attributes of the Iris data set measure the same quantity (length) and are measured on the same scale (centimeters), a normalization step is included as a matter of best practice for techniques that involve distance calculation. The *Normalize* operator can be found in Data Transformation > Value modification > Numerical. The attributes are converted to a uniform scale of mean 0 and standard deviation 1 using Z-transformation.

For the purposes of this demonstration, a two-dimensional scatterplot with two attributes will be helpful to visualize outliers. However, the Iris data set has four attributes. To aid in this visualization objective, we will reduce four numerical attributes to two attributes (principal components) using the *principal component analysis (PCA)* operator. Please note the use of the *PCA* operator is optional and not required for outlier detection. The results of the outlier detection with or without *PCA* in most cases will be unchanged. But visualization of the results will be easy with two-dimensional scatterplots. *PCA* will be discussed in detail in Chapter 12

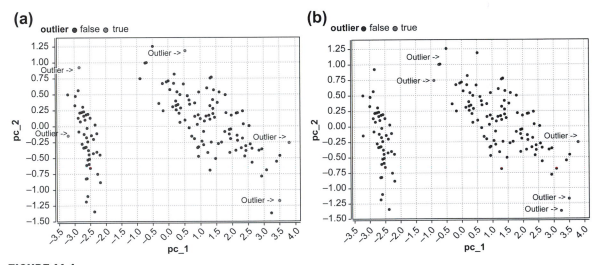

FIGURE 11.4

Top five outliers of Iris data set when (a) k = 1, (b) k = 5.

Feature Selection. In this process we have specified a variance threshold for the *PCA* operator of 0.95. Any principal component that has a variance threshold more than 0.95 is removed from the result set. The outcome of the *PCA* operator has two principal components.

Step 2: Detect Outlier Operator

The *Detect Outlier (Distances)* operator has a data input port and outputs data with an appended attribute called *outlier*. The value of the output outlier attribute is either true or false. The *Detect Outlier (Distances)* operator has three parameters that can be configured by the user.

- **Number of neighbors:** This is the value of k in the algorithm. The default value is 10. If the value is made lower, the process finds smaller outlier clusters with less data points.
- **Number of outliers:** The individual outlier score is not visible to the users. Instead the algorithm finds the data points with the highest outlier scores. The number of data points to be found can be configured using this parameter.
- **Distance function:** As in the k-NN algorithm, we have to specify the distance measurement function. Commonly used functions are Euclidian and cosine (for document vectors).

In this example we make k = 1, number of outlier = 10, and set the distance function to Euclidian. The output of this operator is the example set with an appended outlier attribute. Figure 11.5 provides the RapidMiner process with data extraction, PCA dimensional reduction, and outlier detection operators. The process can now be saved and executed.

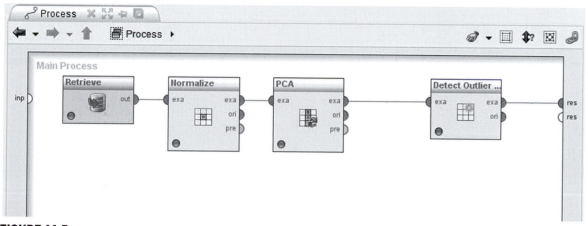

FIGURE 11.5

Process to detect outlier based on distance.

Step 3: Execution and Interpretation

The result data set can be sorted by outlier attribute, which has either a true or false value. Since we have specified 10 outliers in the parameter of the *Detect outlier* operator, that number of outliers can be found in the result set. An efficient way of exploring the outliers is to look at the scatterplot in the Chart view of results set. The X- and Y-axes can be specified as the principal components and the color as the outlier attribute. The output scatterplot shows the outlier data points along with all the normal data points as shown in Figure 11.6.

Distance-based outlier detection is a simple algorithm that is easy to implement and widely used when the problem involves many numeric variables. The execution becomes expensive when the data set involves a high number of attributes and records, because the algorithm needs to calculate distances with other data points in high-dimensional space.

11.3 DENSITY-BASED OUTLIER DETECTION

Outliers, by definition, occur less frequently compared to normal data points. This means that in the data space outliers occupy low-density areas and normal data points occupy high-density areas. Density is a count of data points in a normalized unit space and is inversely proportional to the distances between

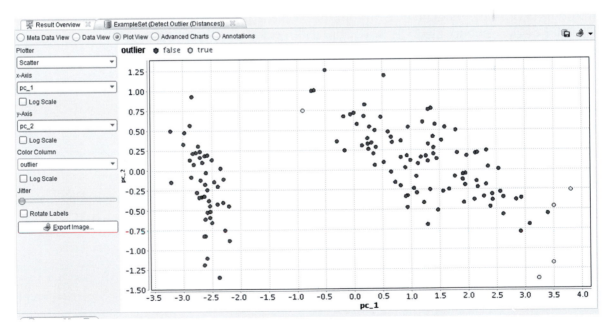

FIGURE 11.6

Outlier detection output

data points. The objective of a density-based outlier algorithm is to identify those data points from low-density areas. There are a few different implementations to assign an outlier score for the data points. We can find the inverse of average distance of all k neighbors. The distance between data points and density are inversely proportional. We can also calculate neighborhood density by calculating the number of data points from a normalized unit distance. The approach for density-based outliers is similar to the approach discussed for density-based clustering and for the k-NN classification algorithm.

11.3.1 How it Works

Since distance is the inverse of density, we can explain the approach of a density-based outlier with two parameters, distance (d) and proportion of data points (p). A point X is considered an outlier if at least p fraction of points lies more than d distance from the point (Knorr & Ng, 1998). Figure 11.7 provides a visual illustration of outlier detection. By the above definition, the point X occupies a low-density area. The parameter p is specified as a high value, above 95%. One of the key issues in this implementation is specifying distance d. It is important to normalize the attributes so that the distance makes sense, particularly when attributes involve different measures and units. If the distance d is specified too low, then more outliers will be detected, which means normal points have the risk of being labeled as outliers and vice versa.

11.3.2 How to Implement

The RapidMiner process for outlier detection based on density is very similar to outlier detection by distance, which was reviewed in the previous section. The process developed for previous distance-based outliers can be used, but we will replace the *Detect Outlier (Distances)* operator with the *Detect Outlier (Densities)* operator.

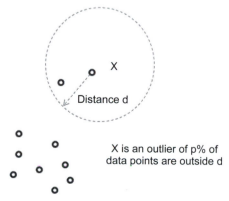

FIGURE 11.7
Outlier detection based on distance and propensity.

Step 1: Data Preparation

Data preparation will condition the data so the *Detect Outlier (Distances)* operator returns meaningful results. As with the outlier detection by distance technique, we will be using the Iris data set with normalization and the *PCA* operator so that we reduce the number of attributes to two for easy visualization.

Step 2: Detect Outlier Operator

The *Detect Outlier (Densities)* operator can be found in Data Transformation > Data Cleansing > Outlier Detection > and has three parameters:

- **Distance (d):** Threshold distance used to find outliers. For this example, we specify the distance as 1.
- **Proportion (p):** Proportion of data points outside of radius d of a point, beyond which the point is considered an outlier. For this example, the value we are specifying is 95%.
- **Distance measurement:** A measurement parameter like Euclidean, cosine, or squared distance. The default value is Euclidean.

Any data point that has more than 95% of other data points beyond distance d is considered an outlier. Figure 11.8 shows the RapidMiner process with the *Normalization, PCA* and *Detect Outlier* operators. The process can be saved and executed.

Step 3: Execution and Interpretation

The process adds an outlier attribute to the example set, which can be used for visualization using a scatterplot as shown in Figure 11.9. The outlier attribute is Boolean and indicates whether the data point is predicted to be an outlier

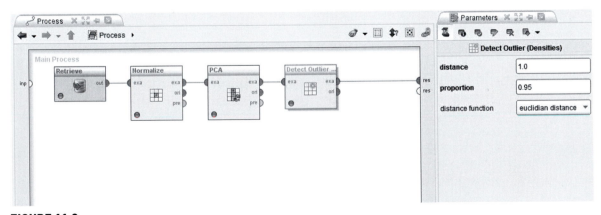

FIGURE 11.8

Process to detect outlier based on density.

or not. In the scatterplot, we can find a few data points marked as outliers. The parameters d and p of the *Detect Outlier* operator can be tuned to find the desired level of outlier detection.

Density-based outlier detection is closely related to distance-based outlier approaches and hence the same pros and cons apply. As with distance-based outlier detection, the main drawback is this approach doesn't work with varying densities. The next approach, local outlier factor (LOF) is designed for such data sets. Specifying the parameter distance (d) and proportion (p) is going to be challenging, particularly when the characteristics of the data are not previously known.

11.4 LOCAL OUTLIER FACTOR

The local outlier factor (LOF) technique is a variation of density-based outlier detection, and addresses one of its key limitations, detecting the outliers in varying density. Varying density is a problem in most of simple density-based methods, including DBSCAN clustering (see Chapter 7 Clustering). The LOF technique was proposed in the paper *LOF: Identifying Density-Based Local Outliers* (Breunig et al., 2000). LOF takes into account the density of the data point and the *density of the neighborhood* of the data point as well. A key feature of the LOF technique is that the outlier score takes into account the relative density of the data point. Once the outlier scores for data points are calculated, the data points can be sorted to find the outliers in the data set. The core of LOF lies in calculation of

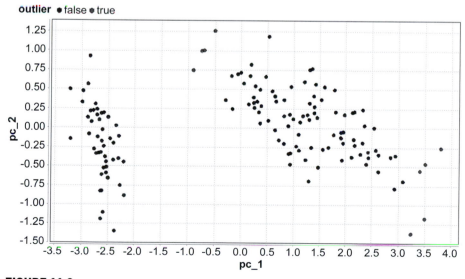

FIGURE 11.9

Output of density-based outlier detection.

the relative density. The relative density of a data point x with k neighbors is given by Equation 11.1:

$$\text{Relative density of } X = \frac{\text{density of X}}{\text{average density of all data points in the neighborhood}}$$

(11.1)

where the density of x is the inverse of average distance for the nearest k data points. The same parameter k also forms the locality of the neighborhood. By comparing the density of the data point and density of all the data points in the neighborhood, we can determine if the density of the data point is lower than the density of the neighborhood. This scenario indicates the presence of an outlier.

11.4.1 How to Implement

An LOF-based data mining process is similar to the other outlier process explained in RapidMiner. The *Direct Outlier (LOF)* operator is available in Data Transformation > Data Cleansing > Outlier Detection. The output of the *LOF* operator contains the example set along with a numeric outlier score. The LOF algorithm does not explicitly label a data point as an outlier; instead the score is exposed to the user. This score can be used to visualize a comparison to a threshold, above which the data point is considered an outlier. Having the raw score means that the data mining practitioner can "tune" the detection criteria, without having to rerun the scoring process, by changing the threshold for comparison.

Step 1: Data Preparation

Similar to the distance- and density-based outlier detection processes, the data set have to be normalized using *Normalize* operator. The *PCA* operator is used to reduce the four-dimensional Iris data set to two dimensions, so that the output can be visualized easily.

Step 2: Detect Outlier Operator

The *LOF* operator has a minimal points (*MinPts*) lower bound and upper bound as parameters. The minimal points lower bound is the value of k, the neighborhood number. The LOF algorithm also takes into account a *MinPts* upper bound to provide more stable results (Breunig et al., 2000). Figure 11.10 shows the RapidMiner process.

Step 3: Results Interpretation

After using the *Detect Outlier* operator, the outlier score is appended to the result data set. Figure 11.11 shows the result set with outlier score represented as the color of the data point. In the results window, we can use the outlier score to color the data points. The scatterplot indicates that points closer to blue spectrum are predicted to be regular data points and points closer to the

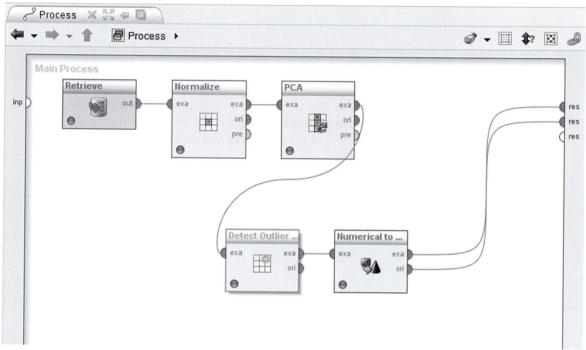

FIGURE 11.10

RapidMiner process for LOF outlier detection.

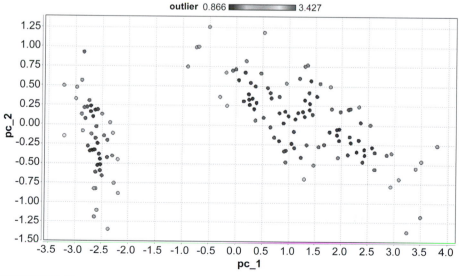

FIGURE 11.11

Output of LOF outlier detection

red spectrum are predicted to be outliers. If an additional Boolean flag indicating whether a data point is an outlier or not is needed, a *Numeric to Binominal* operator can be added to the result data set. The *Numeric to Binominal* operator converts the numeric outlier score to a binominal true or false based on the threshold specification in the parameter of the operator and to the score output from the *LOF* operator.

CONCLUSION

In addition to the three data mining techniques discussed for outlier detection, the RapidMiner Anomaly *Detection extension* (RapidMiner Extension: Anomaly Detection, 2014) offers more algorithms to identify outliers. Rapid Miner extensions can be installed by accessing Help > Updates and Extensions.

In theory, any classification algorithm can be used for outlier detection, if a previously classified data set is available. A generalized classification model tries to predict outliers the same way it predicts the class label of the data point. However, there is one key issue in using classification models. Since the probability of occurrence of an outlier is really low, say less than 0.1%, the model can just "predict" the class as "regular" for all the data points and still be 99.9% accurate! This method clearly does not work for outlier detection, since the *recall measure* (see Chapter 8 Model Evaluation for details about recall) is 0%. In many practical applications like detecting network intrusion or fraud prevention in high-volume transaction networks, the cost of not detecting an outlier is very high. The model can even have an acceptable level of false alarms, i.e., labeling a regular data point as an outlier. Therefore, special care and preparation is often needed to improve the detection of the outliers.

Stratified sampling methods can be used to increase the frequency of occurrence of outlier records in the training set and reduce the relative occurrence of regular data points. In a similar approach, the occurrence of outlier and regular records can be sampled with replacement so that there are an equal number of records in both classes. Stratified sampling boosts the number of outlier records in the test data set with respect to regular records in an attempt to increase both the accuracy and recall of outlier detection. In any case, it's important to know the biases in any algorithm that might be used to detect outliers and to specially prepare the training data set in order to make the resulting model effective. In practical applications, outlier detection models need to be updated frequently as the characteristics of an outlier changes over the time, and hence the relationship between outliers and normal records changes as well. In constant real time data streams, outlier detection creates additional challenges because of the dynamic distribution of the data and dynamic relationships in the data (Sadik & Gruenwald, 2013). Outlier detection remains one of the most profound applications of data mining that impacts the majority of population through financial transaction monitoring, fraud prevention, and early identification of anomalous activity in the context of security.

REFERENCES

Breunig, M. M., Kriegel, H., Ng, R. T., & Sander, J. (2000). LOF : Identifying Density-Based Local Outliers. *Proceedings of the ACM SIGMOD 2000 International Conference On Management of Data*, 1–12.

Haddadi, H. (2010). Fighting Online Click-Fraud Using Bluff Ads. *ACM SIGCOMM Computer Communication Review, 40*(2), 21–25.

Knorr, E. M., & Ng, R. T. (1998). *Algorithms for Mining Distance-Based Outliers in Large Datasets*. New York, USA: Proceedings of the 24th VLDB Conference. pp. 392–403.

RapidMiner Extension: Anomaly Detection (2014). German Research Center for Artificial Intelligence, DFKI GmbH. Retrieved from http://madm.dfki.de/rapidminer/anomalydetection.

Sadagopan, N., & Li, J. (2008). Characterizing typical and atypical user sessions in clickstreams. *Proceeding of the 17th International Conference on World Wide Web - WWW '08, 885*. http://dx.doi.org/10.1145/1367497.1367617.

Sadik, S., & Gruenwald, L. (2013). Research Issues in Outlier Detection for Data Streams. *ACM SIGKDD Explorations Newsletter, 15*(1), 33–40.

Tan, P.-N., Steinbach, M., & Kumar, V. (2005). Anomaly Detection. In *Introduction to Data Mining* (pp. 651–676). Boston, MA: Addison Wesley.

CHAPTER 12

Feature Selection

In this chapter we will focus on an important component of data set preparation for predictive analytics: feature selection. An overused rubric in data mining circles is that 80% of the analysis effort is spent on data cleaning and preparation and only 20% is typically spent on modeling. In light of this it may seem strange that this book has devoted more than a dozen chapters to modeling techniques and only a couple to data preparation! However, data cleansing and preparation are things that are better learned through experience and not so much from a book. That said, it is essential to be conversant with the many techniques that are available for these important early process steps. We are not going to be focusing on data cleaning in this chapter, which was partially covered in Chapter 2 Data Mining Process but on reducing a data set to its essential characteristics or features. This process goes by various terms: feature selection, dimension reduction, variable screening, key parameter identification, attribute weighting. (Technically, there is a subtle difference between dimension reduction and feature selection. Dimension reduction methods—such as principal component analysis, discussed in Section 12.2—combine or merge actual attributes in order to reduce the number of attributes of a raw data set. Feature selection methods work more like filters that eliminate some attributes.)

We start out with a brief introduction to feature selection and the need for this preprocessing step. There are fundamentally two types of feature selection processes: filter type and wrapper type. Filter approaches work by selecting only those attributes that rank among the top in meeting certain stated criteria (Blum, 1997; Yu, 2003). Wrapper approaches work by iteratively selecting, via a feedback loop, only those attributes that improve the performance of an algorithm. (Kohavi, 1997) Among the filter-type methods, we can classify further based on the data types: numeric versus nominal. The most common wrapper-type methods are the ones associated with multiple regression: stepwise regression, forward selection, and backward elimination. We will explore a few numeric filter-type methods: principal component analysis (PCA), which is strictly speaking a dimension reduction method; information gain–based filtering; and one categorical filter-type method: chi-square-based filtering. We will briefly discuss, using a RapidMiner implementation, the two wrapper-type methods.

12.1 CLASSIFYING FEATURE SELECTION METHODS

MOTIVATION FOR FEATURE SELECTION

Feature selection in predictive analytics refers to the process of identifying the few most important variables or attributes that are essential in a model for an accurate prediction. In today's world of big data and high speed computing, one might be forgiven for asking, why bother? What is the reason to filter any attributes when the computing horsepower exists? For example, some argue that it is redundant trying to "fit" a model to data; rather we should simply use a fast brute-force approach to sift through data to identify meaningful *correlations* and make decisions based on this (Bollier, 2010).

However models are still useful for many reasons. Models can improve decision making and help advance knowledge. Blindly relying on correlations to predict future states also has flaws. The now classic "My TiVo thinks I'm gay" example (Zaslow, 2002) illustrated how the TiVo recommendation engine, which works on *large data* and correlations, resulted in a humorous mismatch for a customer. As long we need to use models, feature selection will be an important step in the process. Feature selection serves a couple of purposes: it optimizes the performance of the data mining algorithm and it makes it easier for the analyst to interpret the outcome of the modeling. It does this by reducing the number of attributes or features that we must contend with.

There are two powerful technical motivations for incorporating feature selection in the data mining process. Firstly, a data set may contain highly correlated attributes, such as the number of items sold and the revenue earned by the sales of the item. We are typically not gaining any new information by including both of these attributes. Additionally, in the case of multiple regression–type models, if two or more of the independent variables (or predictors) are correlated, then the estimates of coefficients in a regression model tend to be unstable or counter intuitive. This is the *multicollinearity* discussed in Section 5.1. In the case of algorithms like naïve Bayesian classifiers, the attributes need to be independent of each other. Further, the speed of algorithms is typically a function of the number of attributes. So by using only one among the correlated attributes we improve the performance.

Secondly, a data set may also contain redundant information that does not directly impact the predictions: as an extreme example, a customer ID number has no bearing on the amount of revenue earned from the customer. Such attributes may be filtered out by the analyst before the modeling process may begin. However, not all attribute relationships are that clearly known in advance. In such cases, we must resort to computational methods to detect and eliminate attributes that add no new information. The key here is to include attributes that have a strong correlation with the predicted or dependent variable.

So, to summarize, feature selection is needed to *remove* independent variables that may be strongly correlated to one another, and to make sure we *keep* independent variables that may be strongly correlated to the predicted or dependent variable.

We may apply feature selection methods before we start the modeling process and filter out unimportant attributes or we may apply feature selection methods iteratively within the flow of the data mining process. Depending upon the logic, we have two feature selection schemes: filter schemes or wrapper schemes. The filter scheme does not require any learning algorithm, whereas the wrapper type is optimized for a particular learning algorithm. In other words, the filter scheme can be considered "unsupervised" and the wrapper scheme can be considered a "supervised" feature selection method. The filter model is commonly used in the following scenarios:

- When the number of features or attributes is really large
- When computational expense is a criterion

The chart in Figure 12.1 summarizes a high level taxonomy of feature selection methods, some of which we will explore in the following sections, as indicated. This is not meant to be a comprehensive taxonomy, but simply a useful depiction of the techniques commonly employed in data mining and described in this chapter.

12.2 PRINCIPAL COMPONENT ANALYSIS

We will start with a conceptual introduction to PCA before showing the mathematical basis behind the computation. We will then demonstrate how to apply PCA to a sample data set using RapidMiner.

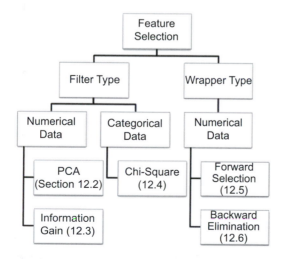

FIGURE 12.1

Taxonomy of common feature selection methods and the sections in this chapter that discuss them.

Let us assume that we have a dataset with m attributes (or variables). These could be for example, commodity prices, weekly sales figures, number of hours spent by assembly line workers, etc.; in short any business parameter that can have an impact on a performance that is captured by a label or target variable. The question that PCA helps us to answer fundamentally is this: Which of these m attributes explain a significant amount of variation contained within the data set? PCA essentially helps to apply an 80/20 rule: Can a small subset of attributes (the 20%) explain 80% or more of the variation in the data? This sort of variable screening or *feature selection* will make it easy to apply other predictive modeling techniques and also make the job of interpreting the results easier.

PCA captures the attributes that contain the greatest amount of variability in the data set. It does this by transforming the existing variables into a set of "principal components" or *new variables* that have the following properties (van der Maaten et al., 2009):

- They are uncorrelated with each other.
- They cumulatively contain/explain a large amount of variance within the data.
- They can be related back to the original variables via weightage factors.

The original variables with very low weightage factors in their principal components are effectively removed from the data set. The conceptual schematic in Figure 12.2 illustrates how PCA can help in reducing data dimensions with a hypothetical dataset of m variables.

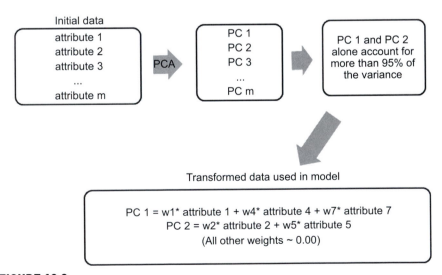

FIGURE 12.2

A conceptual framework illustrating the effectiveness of using PCA for feature selection. The final data set includes only PC1 and PC2.

12.2.1 How it Works

The key task is computing the principal components, z_m, which have the properties that were described just above. Consider the case of just two variables: v_1 and v_2. When the variables are visualized using a scatterplot, we would see something like the one shown in Figure 12.3.

As can be seen, v_1 and v_2 are correlated. But we could transform v_1 and v_2 into two new variables z_1 and z_2, which meet our guidelines for principal components, by a simple linear transformation. As seen in the chart, this amounts to plotting the points along two new axes: z_1 and z_2. Axis z_1 contains the maximum variability, and one can rightly conclude that z_1 explains a significant majority of the variation present in the data and is the first principal component. z_2, by virtue of being orthogonal to z_1, contains the next highest amount of variability. Between z_1 and z_2 we can account for (in this case of two variables) 100% of the total variability in the data. Furthermore, z_1 and z_2 are uncorrelated. As we increase the number of variables, v_m, we may find that only the first few principal components are sufficient to express all the data variances. The principal components, z_m, are expressed as a linear combination of the underlying variables, v_m:

$$z_m = \sum w_i{}^* x_i$$

(12.1)

When we extend this logic to more than two variables, the challenge is to find the transformed set of principal components using the original variables. This is easily accomplished by performing an *eigenvalue analysis* of the

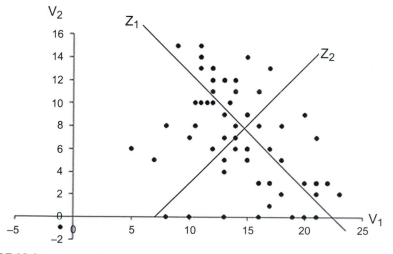

FIGURE 12.3
Transforming variables to a new basis is at the core of PCA.

covariance matrix of the original attributes.[1] The eigenvector associated with the largest eigenvalue is the first principal component; the eigenvector associated with the second largest eigenvalue is the second principal component and so on. The covariance explains how two variables vary with respect to their corresponding mean values—if both variables tend to stay on the same side of their respective means, the covariance would be positive, if not it would be negative. (In statistics, covariance is also used in the calculation of correlation coefficient.)

$$\text{Cov}_{ij} = E[V_iV_j] - E[V_i]E[V_j] \tag{12.2}$$

where expected value $E[v] = v_k\, P(v = v_k)$. For the eigenvalue analysis, a matrix of such covariances between all pairs of variables v_m is created. The reader is referred to standard textbooks on matrix methods or linear algebra for more details behind the eigenvalue analysis (Yu, 2003).

12.2.2 How to Implement

In this section, we will start with a publicly available data set[2] and use RapidMiner to perform the PCA. Furthermore, for illustrative reasons, we will work with nonstandardized or nonnormalized data. In the next part we will standardize the data and explain why it may be important sometimes to do so.

The data set includes information on ratings and nutritional information on 77 breakfast cereals. There are a total of 16 variables, including 13 numerical parameters (Table 12.1). The objective is to reduce this set of 13 numerical predictors to a much smaller list using PCA.

Step 1: Data Preparation

Remove the nonnumeric parameters "Cereal name," "Manufacturer," and "Type (hot or cold)," because PCA can only work with numeric attributes. These are columns A, B, and C. (In RapidMiner, we can convert these into ID attributes if needed for reference later. This can be done during the import of the data set into RapidMiner during the next step if needed; in this case we will simply remove these variables. The *Select Attributes* operator may also be used following the *Read Excel* operator to remove these variables.)

---

[1]Let **A** be an $n \times n$ matrix and **x** be an $n \times 1$ vector. Then the solution to the vector equation [A][x] = λ[x], where λ is a scalar number, involves finding those values of λ for which the above equation is satisfied. The values of λ are called *eigenvalues* and the corresponding solutions for **x** (**x** ≠ 0) are called *eigenvectors*.

[2]http://lib.stat.cmu.edu/DASL/Stories/HealthyBreakfast.html and http://lib.stat.cmu.edu/DASL/Datafiles/Cereals.html.

Table 12.1 Breakfast cereals data set for dimension reduction using PCA

name	mfr	type	calories	protein	fat	sodium	fiber	carbo	sugars	potass	vitamins	shelf	weight	cups	rating
100%_Bran	N	C	70	4	1	130	10	5	6	280	25	3	1	0.33	68.402973
100%_Natural_Bran	Q	C	120	3	5	15	2	8	8	135	0	3	1	1	33.983679
All-Bran	K	C	70	4	1	260	9	7	5	320	25	3	1	0.33	59.425505
All-Bran_with_Extra_Fiber	K	C	50	4	0	140	14	8	0	330	25	3	1	0.5	93.704912
Almond_Delight	R	C	110	2	2	200	1	14	8	-1	25	3	1	0.75	34.384843
Apple_Cinnamon_Cheerios	G	C	110	2	2	180	1.5	10.5	10	70	25	1	1	0.75	29.509541
Apple_Jacks	K	C	110	2	0	125	1	11	14	30	25	2	1	1	33.174094
Basic_4	G	C	130	3	2	210	2	18	8	100	25	3	1.33	0.75	37.038562

Read the Excel file into RapidMiner: this can be done using the standard *Read Excel* operator as described in earlier sections.

Step 2: PCA Operator

Type in the keyword "pca" in the operator search field and drag and drop the *Principal Component Analysis* operator into the main process window. Connect the output of Read Excel into the "Example set input" or "exa" port of the *PCA* operator.

The three available parameter settings for dimensionality reduction are *none, keep variance,* and *fixed number*. Here we use *keep variance* and leave the *variance threshold* at the default value of 0.95 or 95% (see Figure 12.4). The variance threshold selects only those attributes that collectively account for or explain 95% (or any other value set by user) of the total variance in the data. Connect all output ports from the *PCA* operator to the results ports.

Step 3: Execution and Interpretation

By running the analysis as configured above, RapidMiner will output several tabs in the results panel (Figure 12.5). By clicking on the PCA tab, we will see three PCA related tabs—Eigenvalues, Eigenvectors, and Cumulative Variance Plot.

Using Eigenvalues, we can obtain information about the contribution to the data variance coming from each principal component individually and cumulatively.

If, for example, our variance threshold is 95%, then PC 1, PC 2, and PC 3 are the only principal components that we need to consider because they are sufficient to explain nearly 97% of the variance. PC 1 contributes to a majority of this variance, at about 54%.

We can then "deep dive" into these three components and identify how they are linearly related to the actual or real parameters from the data set. At this point we consider only those real parameters that have significant weightage

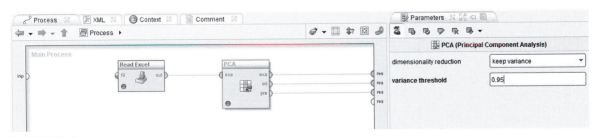

FIGURE 12.4

Configuring the PCA operator.

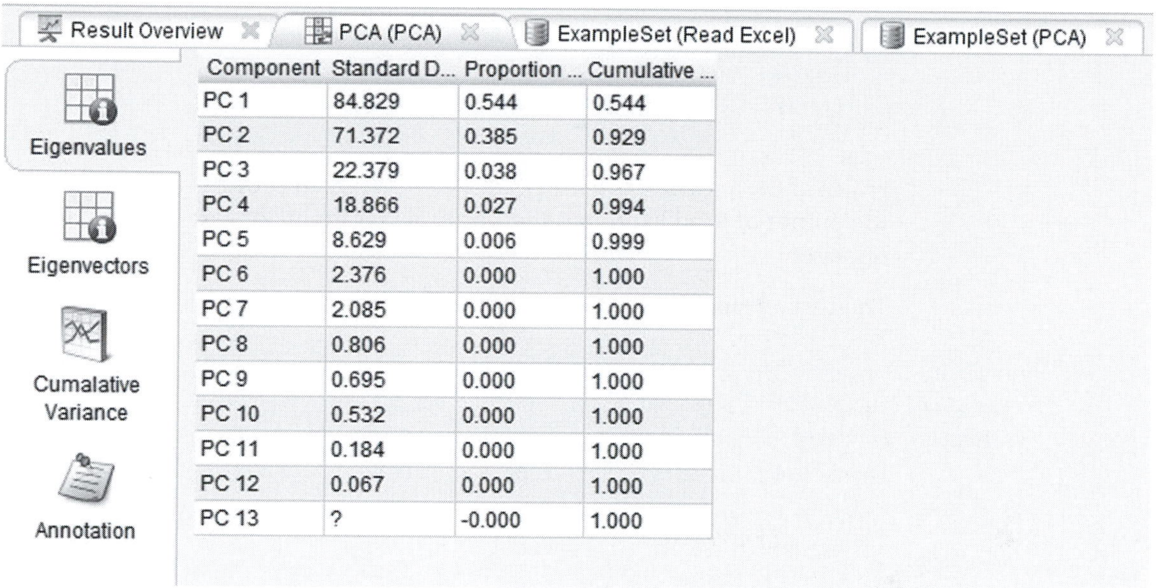
Result Overview
PCA (PCA)
ExampleSet (Read Excel)
ExampleSet (PCA)
Eigenvalues
Eigenvectors
Cumalative Variance
Annotation

Component	Standard D...	Proportion ...	Cumulative ...
PC 1	84.829	0.544	0.544
PC 2	71.372	0.385	0.929
PC 3	22.379	0.038	0.967
PC 4	18.866	0.027	0.994
PC 5	8.629	0.006	0.999
PC 6	2.376	0.000	1.000
PC 7	2.085	0.000	1.000
PC 8	0.806	0.000	1.000
PC 9	0.695	0.000	1.000
PC 10	0.532	0.000	1.000
PC 11	0.184	0.000	1.000
PC 12	0.067	0.000	1.000
PC 13	?	-0.000	1.000

FIGURE 12.5
Output from PCA.

contribution to the each of the first three PCs. These will ultimately form the subset of reduced parameters for further predictive modeling.

The key question is how do we select the real variables based on this information? RapidMiner allows us to sort the eigenvectors (weighting factors) for each PC and we can decide to choose the two to three highest (absolute) valued weighting factors for PCs 1 to 3. As seen from Figure 12.6, we have chosen the highlighted real attributes—calories, sodium, potassium, vitamins, and rating—to form the reduced data set. This selection was done by simply identifying the top three attributes from each principal component.[3]

For the above example, PCA reduces the number of attributes from 13 to 5, a more than 50% reduction in the number of attributes that any model would need to realistically consider. One can imagine the improvement in performance as we deal with the larger data sets that PCA enables. In practice, PCA is a very effective and widely used tool for dimension reduction, particularly when all attributes are numeric. It works for a variety of real-world applications, but it should not be blindly applied for variable screening. For most practical situations, domain knowledge should be used in addition to PCA

[3]More commonly, only the top three principal components are directly selected for building subsequent models. We took this route here to explain how PCA, which is a dimension reduction method, can be applied for feature selection.

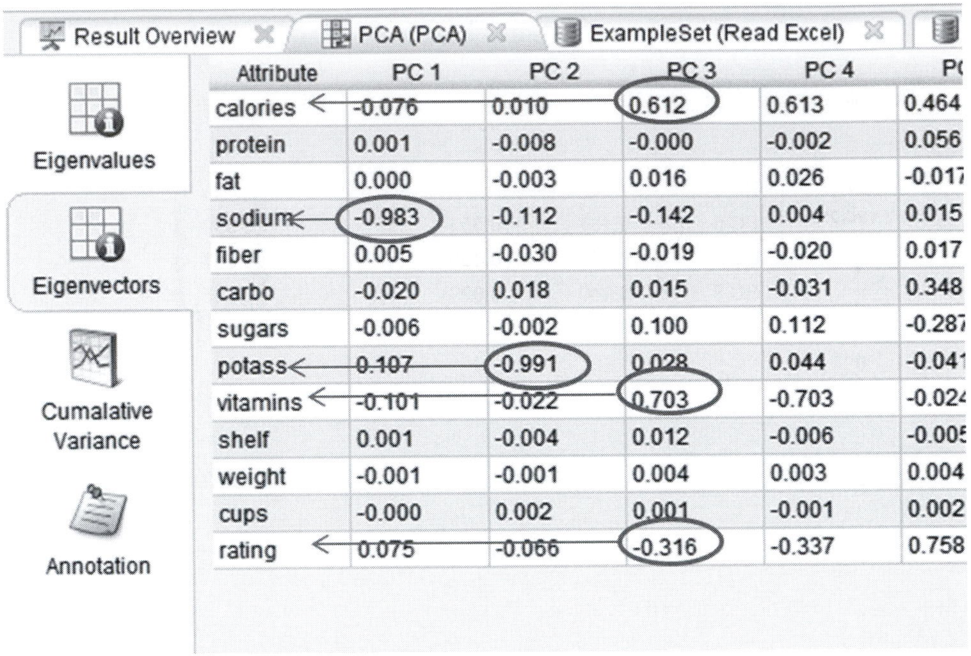

Attribute	PC 1	PC 2	PC 3	PC 4	PC
calories	-0.076	0.010	0.612	0.613	0.464
protein	0.001	-0.008	-0.000	-0.002	0.056
fat	0.000	-0.003	0.016	0.026	-0.017
sodium	-0.983	-0.112	-0.142	0.004	0.015
fiber	0.005	-0.030	-0.019	-0.020	0.017
carbo	-0.020	0.018	0.015	-0.031	0.348
sugars	-0.006	-0.002	0.100	0.112	-0.287
potass	0.107	-0.991	0.028	0.044	-0.041
vitamins	-0.101	-0.022	0.703	-0.703	-0.024
shelf	0.001	-0.004	0.012	-0.006	-0.005
weight	-0.001	-0.001	0.004	0.003	0.004
cups	-0.000	0.002	0.001	-0.001	0.002
rating	0.075	-0.066	-0.316	-0.337	0.758

FIGURE 12.6

Selecting the reduced set of attributes using the Eigenvectors tab from the PCA operator.

analysis before eliminating any of the variables. Here are some observations that explain some of the risks to consider while using PCA.

1. **The results of a PCA must be evaluated in the context of the data.**
   If the data is extremely noisy, then PCA may end up suggesting that the noisiest variables are the most significant because they account for most of the variation!
   An analogy would be the total sound energy in a rock concert. If the crowd noise drowns out some of the high-frequency vocals or notes, PCA might suggest that the most significant contribution to the total energy comes from the crowd—and it will be right! But this does not add any clear value if one is attempting to distinguish which musical instruments are influencing the harmonics, for example.

2. **Adding uncorrelated data does not always help. Neither does adding data that may be correlated, but irrelevant.**
   When we add more parameters to our data set, and if these parameters happen to be random noise, we are effectively led back to the same situation as the first point above. On the other hand, as analysts we also have to exercise caution and watch out for spurious correlations. As an extreme example, it may so happen that there is a correlation between the number of hours worked in a garment factory and

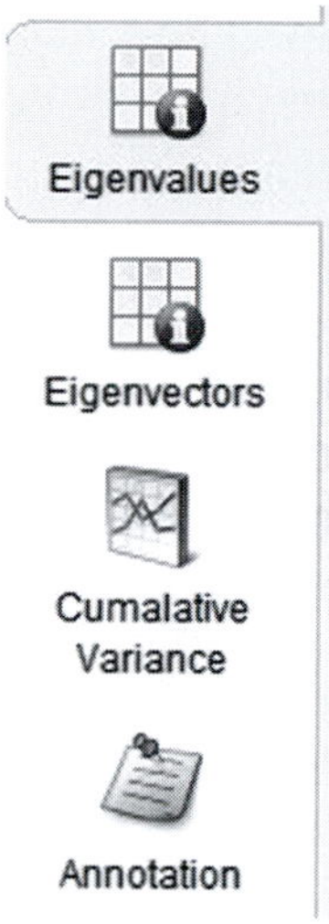

Component	Standard D...	Proportion of Variance	Cumulative Variance
PC 1	0.459	0.306	0.306
PC 2	0.392	0.224	0.530
PC 3	0.302	0.132	0.663
PC 4	0.287	0.120	0.782
PC 5	0.212	0.065	0.848
PC 6	0.187	0.051	0.898
PC 7	0.162	0.038	0.937
PC 8	0.140	0.029	0.965
PC 9	0.122	0.022	0.987
PC 10	0.067	0.006	0.993
PC 11	0.053	0.004	0.997
PC 12	0.043	0.003	1.000
PC 13	?	-0.000	1.000

Eigenvalues

Eigenvectors

Cumalative Variance

Annotation

FIGURE 12.7

Interpreting RapidMiner output for Principal Component Analysis.

pork prices (an unrelated commodity) within a certain period of time. Clearly this correlation is probably pure coincidence. Such correlations again can muddy the results of a PCA. Care must be taken to winnow the data set to include variables that make business sense and are not subjected to many random fluctuations before applying a technique like tPCA.

3. **PCA is very sensitive to scaling effects in the data**.

If we examine the data in the above example closely, we will see that the top attributes that PCA helped identify as the most important ones also have the widest range (and standard deviation) in their values. For example, potassium ranges from –1 to 330 and sodium ranges from 1 to 320. Comparatively, most of the other factors range in the single or low double digits. As expected, these factors dominate PCA results because they contribute to the maximum variance in the data. What if there was another factor such as sales volume, which would potentially range in the millions (of dollars or boxes), were to be considered for a modeling exercise? Clearly it would mask the effects of any other attribute.

To minimize scaling effects, we can range normalize the data (using for example, the *Normalize* operator). When we apply this data transformation, all attributes are reduced to a range between 0 and 1 and scale effects will not matter anymore. But what happens to the PCA results?

As Figure 12.7 shows, we now need eight PCs to account for the same 95% total variance. As an exercise, you can use the eigenvectors to filter out the attributes that are included in these eight PCs and you will find that (applying the top three rule for each PC as before), you have not eliminated any of the attributes!

This brings us to the next section on feature selection methods that are not scale sensitive and also work with nonnumerical datasets, which were two of the limitations with PCA.

12.3 INFORMATION THEORY–BASED FILTERING FOR NUMERIC DATA

In Chapter 4 we encountered the concepts of information gain and gain ratio. Recall that both of these methods involve comparing the *information exchanged* between a given attribute and the target or label attribute (Peng et al., 2005). As we discussed in Section 12.1, the key to feature selection is to include attributes that have a strong correlation with the predicted or dependent variable. With these techniques, we can rank attributes based on the amount of information gain and then select only those that meet or exceed some (arbitrarily) chosen threshold or simply select the top k (again, arbitrarily chosen) features.

Let us revisit the golf example we discussed first in Chapter 4. The data is presented here again for convenience in Figure 12.8a. When we apply the information gain calculation methodology that was discussed in Chapter 4 to compute information gain for all attributes (see Table 4.2), we will arrive at the feature ranking in Figure 12.8b in terms of their respective "influence" on the target variable "Play." This can be easily done using the *Weight by Information Gain* operator in RapidMiner. The output looks almost identical to the one shown in Table 4.2, except for the slight differences in the information gain values for Temperature and Humidity. The reason is that for that data set, we had converted the temperature and humidity into nominal values before computing the gains. In this case, we use the numeric attributes as they are. So it is important to pay attention to the discretization of the attributes before filtering. Use of information gain feature selection is also restricted to cases where the label is nominal. For fully numeric datasets, where the label variable is also numeric, PCA or correlation-based filtering methods are commonly used.

Figure 12.9 describes a process that uses the sample Golf data set available in RapidMiner. The various steps in the process convert numeric attributes, Temperature and Humidity, into nominal ones. In the final step, we apply the *Weight by Information Gain* operator to both the original data and

(a) ExampleSet (14 examples, 2 special attributes, 4 regular attributes)

Row No.	id	Play	Outlook	Temperature	Humidity	Wind
1	1	no	sunny	85	85	false
2	2	no	sunny	80	90	true
3	3	yes	overcast	83	78	false
4	4	yes	rain	70	96	false
5	5	yes	rain	68	80	false
6	6	no	rain	65	70	true
7	7	yes	overcast	64	65	true
8	8	no	sunny	72	95	false
9	9	yes	sunny	69	70	false
10	10	yes	rain	75	80	false
11	11	yes	sunny	75	70	true
12	12	yes	overcast	72	90	true
13	13	yes	overcast	81	75	false
14	14	no	rain	71	80	true

FIGURE 12.8a
Revisiting the golf example for feature selection.

(b)

attribute	
Outlook	0.247
Temperature	0.113
Humidity	0.102
Wind	0.048

FIGURE 12.8b
Results of information gain–based feature selection.

converted data set in order to show the difference between the gain computed using different data types. The main point to observe is that the gain computation depends not only upon the data types, but also how the nominal data is discretized. For example, we get slightly different gain values (see Table 12.2) if we divide Humidity into three bands (high, medium, and low) as opposed to only two bands (high and low). The reader can test these variants very easily using the process described. In conclusion, we select the top-ranked attributes. In this case, they would be Outlook and Temperature if we choose the nondiscretized version, and Outlook and Humidity in the discretized version.

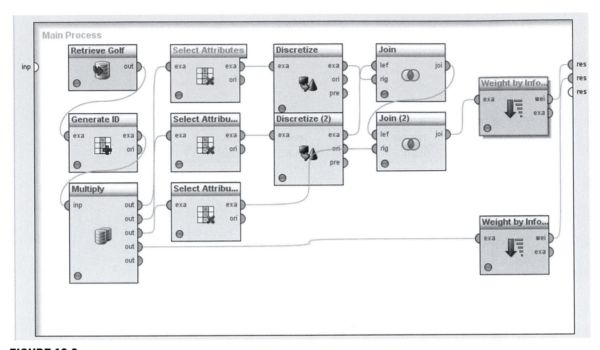

FIGURE 12.9
Process to discretize the numeric Golf data set before running information gain–based feature selection.

Table 12.2 Results of Information Gain Feature Selection

Attribute	Info Gain Weight (Not Discretized)	Info Gain Weight (Discretized)
Outlook	0.247	0.247
Temperature	0.113	0.029
Humidity	0.102	0.104
Wind	0.048	0.048

12.4 CHI-SQUARE-BASED FILTERING FOR CATEGORICAL DATA

In many cases our data sets may consist of only categorical (or nominal) attributes. In this case, what is a good way to distinguish between high influence attributes and low or no influence attributes?

A classic example of this scenario is the gender selection bias. Suppose we have data about the purchase of a big-ticket item like a car or a house. Can we verify the influence of gender on purchase decisions? Are men or women the primary decision makers when it comes to purchasing big-ticket items? For example, is gender a factor in color preference of a car? Here attribute 1 would be gender

id	Play	Humidity	Temperature	Outlook	Wind
1	no	High	hot	sunny	false
2	no	High	hot	sunny	true
3	yes	Normal	hot	overcast	false
4	yes	High	mild	rain	false
5	yes	Normal	cool	rain	false
6	no	Normal	cool	rain	true
7	yes	Normal	cool	overcast	true
8	no	High	mild	sunny	false
9	yes	Normal	cool	sunny	false
10	yes	Normal	mild	rain	false
11	yes	Normal	mild	sunny	true
12	yes	High	mild	overcast	true
13	yes	Normal	hot	overcast	false
14	no	Normal	mild	rain	true

FIGURE 12.10

Converting the golf example set into nominal values for chi-square feature selection.

and attribute 2 would be the color. A chi-square test would reveal if there is indeed a relationship between these two attributes. If we have several attributes and wish to rank the relative influence of each of these on the target attribute, we can still use the chi-square statistic.

Let us go back to the golf example in Figure 12.10—this time we have converted all numeric attributes into nominal ones. Chi-square analysis involves *counting* occurrences (of number of sunny days or windy days) and *comparing* these variables to the target variable based on the frequencies of occurrences. The chi-square test checks if the frequencies of occurrences across any pair of attributes, such as Outlook = overcast and Play = yes, are correlated. In other words, for the given Outlook type, overcast, what is the probability that Play = yes (existence of a strong correlation)? The multiplication law of probabilities states that if event A happening is independent of event B, then the probabilities of A and B happening together is simply $p_A * p_B$. The next step is to convert this joint probability into an "expected frequency," which is given by $p_A * p_B * N$, where N is the sum of all occurrences in the data set.

For *each* attribute, a table of observed frequencies, such as the one shown in Table 12.3, is built. This is called a *contingency table*. The last column and row (the margins) are simply the sums in the corresponding rows or columns as you can verify. Using the contingency table, a corresponding *expected frequency table* can be built using the expected frequency definition ($p_A * p_B * N$) from which the chi-square statistic is then computed by comparing the difference between the observed frequency and expected frequency for *each* attribute. The expected frequency table for *Outlook* is shown in Table 12.4.

The expected frequency for the event [Play = no and Outlook= sunny] is calculated using our expected frequency formula as (5/14 * 5/14 *14) =1.785 and is entered in the first cell as shown. Similarly, the other expected frequencies are calculated. The formula for the chi-square statistic is the summation of the square of the differences between observed and expected frequencies, as given in Equation 12.2:

$$\chi^2 = \sum \sum (f_o - f_e)^2 / f_e \tag{12.2}$$

where f_o is the observed frequency and f_e is the expected frequency. The test of independence between any two parameters is done by checking if the observed chi-square is less than a critical value that depends upon the confidence level chosen by the user (Black, 2007). In this case of feature weighting, we simply gather all the observed chi-square values and use them to rank the attributes. The ranking of attributes for our golf example is generated using the process described in Figure 12.11 and is shown in the table of observed chi-square values in Figure 12.12. Just like in information gain feature selection, most of the operators shown in the process are simply transforming the data into nominal values to generate it in the form shown in Figure 12.10.

Compare the output of the chi-square ranking to the information gain–based ranking (for the nominalized or discretized attributes) and you will see that the ranking is identical.

Table 12.3 Contingency Table of Observed Frequencies for Outlook and the Label Attribute, Play

Outlook =	sunny	overcast	rain	Total
Play = no	3	0	2	5
Play = yes	2	4	3	9
Total	5	4	5	14

Table 12.4 Expected Frequency Table

Outlook =	sunny	overcast	rain	Total
Play = no	1.785714	1.428571	1.785714	5
Play = yes	3.214286	2.571429	3.214286	9
Total	5	4	5	14

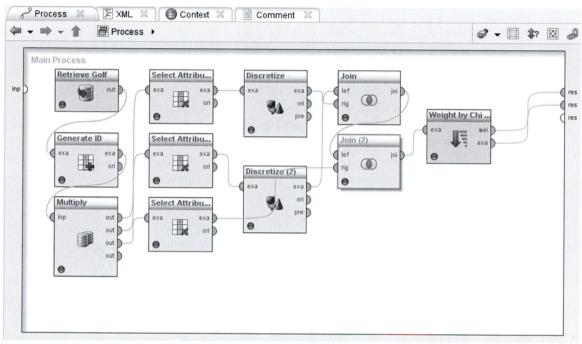

FIGURE 12.11
Process to rank attributes of the Golf data set by the chi-square statistic.

attribute	
Outlook	3.547
Humidity	1.998
Wind	0.933
Temperature	0.570

FIGURE 12.12
Results of the attribute weighting by the chi-square method.

Note that the "Normalize weights" option is sometimes also used, which is a range normalization onto the interval 0 to 1.

12.5 WRAPPER-TYPE FEATURE SELECTION

In this section of the chapter we will briefly introduce wrapper scheme feature reduction methods by using a linear regression example. As explained earlier, the wrapper approach iteratively chooses features to add or to remove from the current attribute pool based on whether the newly added or removed attribute improves the accuracy.

Table 12.5 All Possible Regression Models with Three Attributes

Model	Independent Variables Used
1	v1 alone
2	v2 alone
3	v3 alone
4	v1 and v2 only
5	v1 and v3 only
6	v2 and v3 only
7	v1, v2, and v3 all together

Wrapper-type methods originated from the need to reduce the number of attributes that are needed to build a high-quality regression model. A very thorough way to build regression models is something called the "all possible regressions" search procedure. For example, with thre attributes, *v1*, *v2*, and *v3*, we could build the different regression models in Table 12.5.

In general, if a data set contains k different attributes, then conducting all possible regression searches implies that we build $2^k - 1$ separate regression models and pick the one that has the best performance. Clearly this is impractical.

A better way, from a computational resource consumption point of view, to do this search would be to start with one variable, say v1, and build a baseline model. Then add a second variable, say v2, and build a new model to compare with the baseline. If the performance of the new model, for example, the R^2 (see Chapter 5), is better than that of the baseline, we make this model the new baseline, add a third variable, v3, and proceed in a similar fashion. If however, the addition of the second attribute, v2, did not improve the model significantly (over some arbitrarily prescribed level of improvement in performance), then we pick a new attribute v3, and build a new model that includes v1 and v3. If this model is better than the model that included v1 and v2, we proceed to the next step, where we will consider a next attribute v4, and build a model that includes v1, v3, and v4. In this way, we step forward selecting attributes one by one until we achieve a desired level of model performance. This process is called *forward selection*.[4]

A reverse of this process is where we start our baseline model with all the attributes, v1, v2, …, vk and for the first iteration, remove one of the variables, vj, and construct a new model. However, how do we select which vj to remove?

---

[4]Forward selection is considered a "greedy" approach, and does not necessarily yield the globally optimum solution.

Here, it is typical to start with a variable that has the lowest t-stat value, as you will see in the following case study.[5] If the new model is better than the baseline, it becomes the new baseline and the search continues to remove variables with the lowest t-stat values until some stopping criterion is met (usually if the model performance is not significantly improved over the previous iteration). This process is called *backward elimination*.

As you can see, the variable selection process wraps around the modeling procedure, hence the name for these classes of feature selection. We will now examine a case study, using data from the Boston Housing[6] model first introduced in Chapter 5, to demonstrate how to implement the backward elimination method using RapidMiner. You may recall that the data consists of 13 predictors and 1 response variable. The predictors include physical characteristics of the house (such as number of rooms, age, tax, and location) and neighborhood features (school, industries, zoning), among others. The response variable is the median value (MEDV) of the house in thousands of dollars. These 13 independent attributes are considered to be predictors for the target or label attribute. The snapshot of the data table is shown again in Table 12.6 for continuity.

12.5.1 Backward Elimination to Reduce the Data Set

Our goal here is to build a high-quality multiple regression model that includes as few attributes as possible, without compromising the predictive ability of the model.

The logic used by RapidMiner for applying these techniques is not "linear," but a nested logic. The graphic in Figure 12.13 explains how this nesting was used in setting up the training and testing of the *Linear Regression* operator for the analysis we did in Chapter 5 on the Boston Housing data. The arrow indicates that the training and testing process was nested within the *Split Validation* operator.

In order to apply a wrapper-style feature selection method such as backward elimination, we need to tuck the training and testing process inside another subprocess, a learning process. The learning process is now nested inside the *Backward Elimination* operator. We therefore now have double nesting as schematically shown in Figure 12.13. Next, Figure 12.14 shows how to configure the *Backward Elimination* operator in RapidMiner. Double clicking on the *Backward Elimination* operator opens up the learning process ,which can now accept the *Split Validation* operator we have used many times.

---

[5]RapidMiner typically tries removing attributes one after the other. Vice versa for forward selection: first it tries out all models having just one attribute. It selects the best, then adds another variable, again trying out every option.
[6]We use the dataset described and presented here: http://archive.ics.uci.edu/ml/datasets/Housing.

Table 12.6 Sample view of the Boston Housing data set

CRIM	ZN	INDUS	CHAS	NOX	RM	AGE	DIS	RAD	TAX	PTRATIO	B	LSTAT	MEDV
0.00632	18	2.31	0	0.538	6.575	65.2	4.09	1	296	15.3	396.9	4.98	24
0.02731	0	7.07	0	0.469	6.421	78.9	4.9671	2	242	17.8	396.9	9.14	21.6
0.02729	0	7.07	0	0.469	7.185	61.1	4.9671	2	242	17.8	392.83	4.03	34.7
0.03237	0	2.18	0	0.458	6.998	45.8	6.0622	3	222	18.7	394.63	2.94	33.4
0.06905	0	2.18	0	0.458	7.147	54.2	6.0622	3	222	18.7	396.9	5.33	36.2
0.02985	0	2.18	0	0.458	6.43	58.7	6.0622	3	222	18.7	394.12	5.21	28.7
0.08829	12.5	7.87	0	0.524	6.012	66.6	5.5605	5	311	15.2	395.6	12.43	22.9
0.14455	12.5	7.87	0	0.524	6.172	96.1	5.9505	5	311	15.2	396.9	19.15	27.1

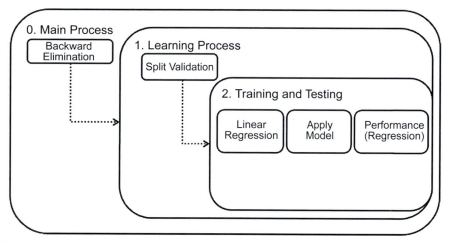

FIGURE 12.13

Wrapper function logic used by RapidMiner.

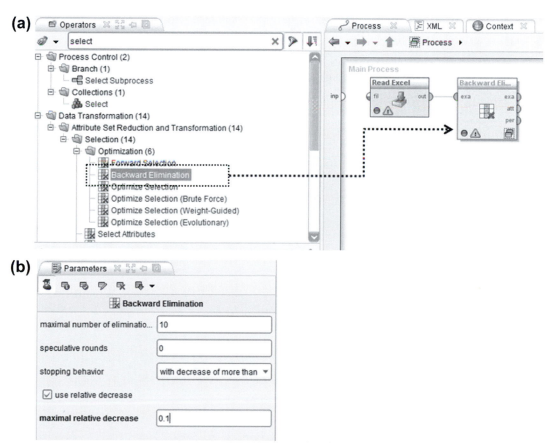

FIGURE 12.14

Configuring the Backward Elimination operator. a) Selecting the Backward Elimination nested operator and b) configuring the parameters.

The *Backward Elimination* operator can now be filled in with the *Split Validation* operator and all the other operators and connections required to build a regression model. The process of setting these up is exactly the same as discussed in Chapter 5 and hence is not repeated here. Now let us look at the configuration of the *Backward Elimination* operator. Here we can specify several parameters to enable feature selection. The most important one is the "stopping behavior." Our choices are "with decrease," "with decrease of more than," and "with significant decrease." The first choice is very parsimonious—a decrease from one iteration to the next will stop the process. But if we pick the second choice, we have to now indicate a "maximal relative decrease." In this example, we have indicated a 10% decrease. Finally, the third choice is very stringent and requires achieving some desired statistical significance by allowing you to specify an alpha level. But we have not said by how much the performance parameter should decrease yet! This is specified "deep inside" the nesting: all the way at the *Performance* operator that was selected in the Testing window of the *Split Validation* operator. In this example, the performance criterion was "squared correlation." For a complete description of all the other *Backward Elimination* parameters, the RapidMiner help can be consulted.

There is one more step that may be helpful to complete before running this model. Simply connecting the *Backward Elimination* operator ports to the output will not show us the final regression model equation. To be able to see that, we need to connect the "exa" port of the *Backward Elimination* operator to another *Linear Regression* operator in the main process. The output of this operator will contain the model, which can be examined in the Results perspective. The top level of the final process is shown in Figure 12.15.

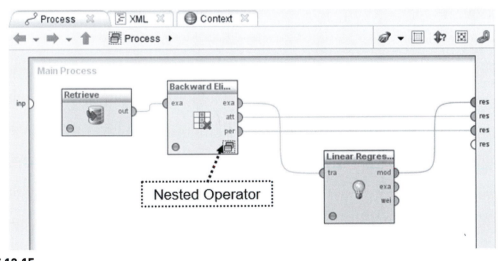

FIGURE 12.15
Final setup of the backward elimination wrapper process.

12.5.2 What Variables have been Eliminated by Backward Elimination?

Comparing the two regression equations (Figure 12.16a below and in Chapter 5, see Figure 5.6a) we can see that nine attributes have been eliminated. Perhaps the 10% decrease was too aggressive. As it happens, the R^2 for the final model with only three attributes was only 0.678. If we were to change the stopping criterion to a 5% decrease, we will end up with an R^2 of 0.812 and now have 8 of the 13 original attributes (Figure 12.16b). You can also see that the regression coefficients for the two models are different as well. The final judgment on what is the right criterion and its level can only be made with experience with the data set and of course, good domain knowledge.

Each iteration using a regression model either removes or introduces a variable, which improves model performance. The iterations stop when a preset stopping criterion or no change in performance criterion (such as adjusted R^2

(a) LinearRegression

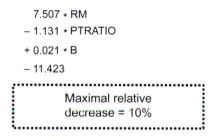

```
      7.507 * RM
    - 1.131 * PTRATIO
    + 0.021 * B
    - 11.423
```

> Maximal relative
> decrease = 10%

FIGURE 12.16a

Aggressive feature selection.

(b) LinearRegression

```
    - 0.060 * CRIM
    + 2.647 * CHAS
    + 4.453 * RM
    - 0.597 * DIS
    - 0.875 * PTRATIO
    + 0.010 * B
    - 0.583 * LSTAT
    + 16.698
```

> Maximal relative
> decrease = 5%

FIGURE 12.16b

A more permissive feature selection with backward elimination.

or RMS error) is reached. The inherent advantage of wrapper-type methods are that multicollinearity issues are automatically handled. However, you get no prior knowledge about the actual relationship between the variables. Applying forward selection is very similar and is left as an exercise for the reader.

CONCLUSION

This chapter covered the basics of a very important part of the overall data mining paradigm: feature selection or dimension reduction. A central hypothesis among all the feature selection methods is that good feature selection results in attributes or features that are highly correlated with the class, yet uncorrelated with each other (Hall, 1999). We presented a high-level classification of feature selection techniques and explored each of them in some detail. As stated at the beginning of this chapter, dimension reduction is best understood with real practice. To this end, we recommend readers apply all the techniques described in the chapter on all the data sets provided. We saw that the same technique can yield quite different results based on the selection of analysis parameters. This is where data visualization can play an important role. Sometimes, examining a correlation plot between the various attributes, like in a scatterplot matrix, can provide valuable clues about which attributes are likely redundant and which ones can be strong predictors of the label variable. While there is usually no substitute for domain knowledge, sometimes data is simply too large or mechanisms are unknown. This is where feature selection can actually help.

REFERENCES

Black, K. (2007). *Business Statistics*. New York: John Wiley and Sons.

Blum, A. L., & Langley, P. (1997). Selection of relevant features and examples in machine learning. *Artificial Intelligence*, 97(1–2), 245–271.

Bollier, D. (2010). *The promise and perils of big data*. Washington D.C: The Aspen Institute.

Hall, M. A. (1999). *Correlation based feature selection for machine learning*. New Zealand: Ph.D. Thesis, University of Waikato.

Kohavi, R., & John, G. H. (1997). Wrappers for feature subset selection. *Artificial Intelligence*, 97(1–2), 273–324.

Peng, H., Long, F., & Ding, C. (2005). Feature Selection Based on Mutual Information: Criteria of Max-Dependency, Max-Relevance and Min-Redundancy. *IEEE Transactions on Pattern Analysis and Machine Intelligence*, 27(8).

van der Maaten, L.J.P., Postma, E.O., & van den Herik, H.J. (2009). Dimensionality Reduction: A Comparative Review. *Tilburg University Technical Report*. TiCC-TR, 2009–005.

Yu, L., & Liu, H. (2003). Feature selection for high dimensional data: A fast correlation based filter solution. *Proceedings of the Twentieth International Conference on Machine Learning (ICML-2003)*. Washington DC.

Zaslow, J. (2002). Oh No! My TiVo thinks I'm gay. *Wall Street Journal* 4 December.

CHAPTER 13

Getting Started with RapidMiner

If you have never attempted any analysis using RapidMiner, this chapter would be the best place to start. In this chapter we will turn our attention from data mining processes to the actual tool set that we need to use to accomplish data mining. Our goal for this chapter is to get rid of any trepidation you may have about using the tool if this entire field of analytics is totally new to you. If you have done some data mining with RapidMiner but gotten frustrated because you got stuck somewhere during your process of self-learning using this very powerful set of tools, this chapter should hopefully get you "unstuck."

RapidMiner is an open source data mining platform developed and maintained by RapidMiner Inc. The software was previously known as YALE (Yet Another Learning Environment) and was developed at the University of Dortmund in Germany (Mierswa, 2006).

RapidMiner Studio is the GUI-based software where data mining and predictive analytics *workflows* can be built and deployed. Some of the advanced features are offered at a premium. In this chapter we will review some of the common functionalities and terminologies of the RapidMiner Studio platform. Even though we are zoning in on one specific data mining tool, the approach, process, and terms are very similar to other commercial and open source Data Mining tools.

We start out with a brief introduction to the RapidMiner Studio GUI to set the stage. The first step in any data analytics exercise is of course to bring the data to the tool, and this is what we will cover next. Once the data is imported, you may want to actually visualize the data and if necessary select subsets or transform the data. We cover basic visualization, followed by selecting data by subsets. We will provide an overview of the fundamental data scaling and transformation tools and explain data sampling and missing value handling tools. We will then present some advanced capabilities of RapidMiner such as process design and optimization.

13.1 USER INTERFACE AND TERMINOLOGY

13.1.1 Introducing the RapidMiner Graphical User Interface

We start by assuming that you have already downloaded and installed the software on your computer.[1] The current version at the time of this writing is version 6.0. Once you launch RapidMiner, you will see the screen in Figure 13.1. (The News section will only be seen if you are connected to the Internet.)

We will only introduce two of the main sections highlighted in the figure above, as the rest are self-explanatory.

Perspectives: The RapidMiner GUI offers three main perspectives. The Home or Welcome perspective, shown by the little home icon (version 5.3: indicated by the "i" icon) is what you see when you first launch the program. The Design perspective (version 5.3: indicated by a notepad and pencil icon) is where you create and design all the data mining processes and can be thought of as the canvas where you will create all your data mining programs and logic. This can also be thought of as a workbench. The Results perspective (indicated in 5.3 also by the chart icon) is where all the recently executed analysis results are available. You will be switching back and forth between the Design and Results perspective several times during a session. Version 6 also adds a wizard-style functionality that allows starting from predefined processes for applications such as direct marketing, predictive maintenance, customer churn modeling, and sentiment analysis.

Views: When you enter a given perspective, there will be several display elements available. For example, in the Design perspective, you have a tab for all the available operators, your stored processes, help for the operators, and so on. These "views" can be rearranged, resized, and removed or added to a given perspective. The controls for doing any of these are shown right on the top of each view tab.

First-time users sometimes accidentally "delete" some of the views. The easiest way to bring back a view is to use the main menu item View→Show View and the select the view that you lost.

13.1.2 RapidMiner Terminology

There are a handful of terms that one must be comfortable with to develop proficiency in using RapidMiner. These are explained with the help of Figure 13.2.

---

[1]Head over to http://rapidminer.com/download-rapidminer/ if you have not done so yet.

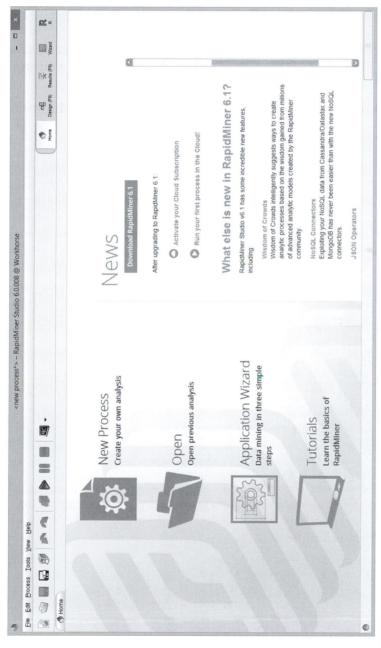

FIGURE 13.1
Launch view of RapidMiner 6.0.

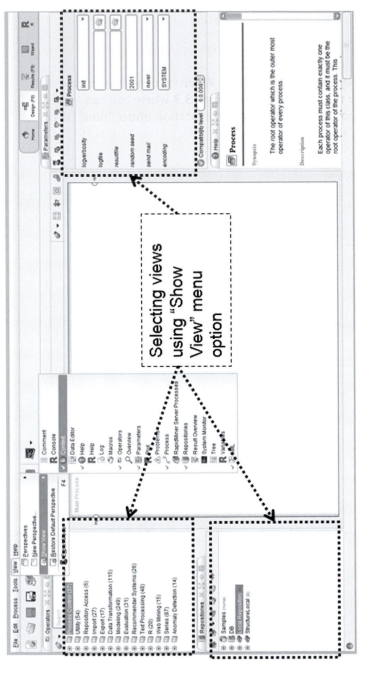

FIGURE 13.2

Activating different views inside RapidMiner.

Repository: A *repository* is a folder-like structure inside RapidMiner where users can organize their data, processes, and models. Your repository is thus a central place for all your data and analysis processes. When you launch Rapid-Miner for the first time, you will be given an option to set up your New Local Repository (Figure 13.3). If for some reason you did not do this correctly, you can always fix this by clicking on the New Repository icon (the one with a green "+" mark) in the Repositories view panel. When you click that icon, you will get a dialog box like the one shown in Figure 13.3 where you can specify the name of your repository under "Alias" and its location under "Root Direc-tory." By default, a standard location automatically selected by the software is checked, which can be unchecked if you want to specify a different location.

Within this repository, you can organize folders and subfolders to store your data, processes, results and models. The advantage of storing data sets to be analyzed in the repository is that metadata describing those data sets is stored alongside. This metadata is propagated through the process as you build it. Metadata is basically data about your data, and contains information such as the number of rows and columns, types of data within each column, miss-ing values if any, and statistical information (mean, standard deviation, and so on).

Attributes and examples: A *data set* or data table is a collection of columns and rows of data. Each column represents a type of measurement. For example, in the classic Golf data set (Figure 13.4) that is used to explain many of the algorithms within this book, we have columns of data containing Temperature levels and Humidity levels. These are numeric *data types*. We also have a col-umn that identifies if a day was windy or not or if a day was sunny, overcast, or rainy. These columns are categorical or nominal data types. In all cases, these columns represent attributes of a given day that would influence whether golf is played or not. In RapidMiner terminology, columns of data such as these are called *attributes*. Other commonly used names for attributes are variables

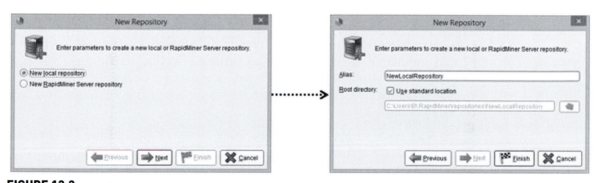

FIGURE 13.3
Setting up a repository on your local machine.

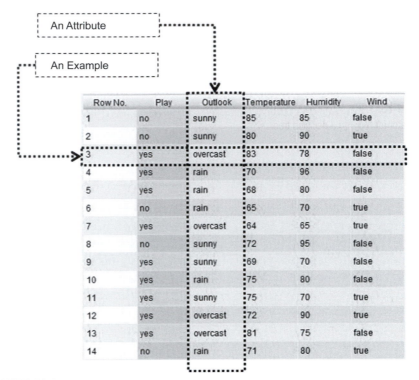

Row No.	Play	Outlook	Temperature	Humidity	Wind
1	no	sunny	85	85	false
2	no	sunny	80	90	true
3	yes	overcast	83	78	false
4	yes	rain	70	96	false
5	yes	rain	68	80	false
6	no	rain	65	70	true
7	yes	overcast	64	65	true
8	no	sunny	72	95	false
9	yes	sunny	69	70	false
10	yes	rain	75	80	false
11	yes	sunny	75	70	true
12	yes	overcast	72	90	true
13	yes	overcast	81	75	false
14	no	rain	71	80	true

FIGURE 13.4

RapidMiner terminology: attributes and examples.

or factors or features. One set of values for such attributes that form a row is called an *example* in RapidMiner terminology. Other commonly used names for examples are records, samples, or instances. An entire data set (rows of examples) is called an *example set* in RapidMiner.

Operator: An *operator* is an atomic piece of functionality (which in fact is a chunk of encapsulated code) performing a certain task. This data mining task can be any of the following: importing a data set into the Rapid-Miner repository, cleaning it by getting rid of spurious examples, reducing the number of attributes by using feature selection techniques, building predictive models, or scoring new data sets using models built earlier. Each task is handled by a chunk of code, which is packaged into an operator (see Figure 13.5).

Thus we have an operator for importing an Excel spreadsheet, an operator for replacing missing values, an operator for calculating information gain–based feature weighting, an operator for building a decision tree, and an operator for applying a model to new unseen data. Most of the time an operator requires some sort of input and delivers some sort of output (although

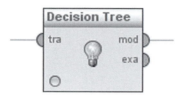

FIGURE 13.5
An operator for building a decision tree.

there are some operators that do not require an input). Adding an operator to a process adds a piece of functionality to the workflow. Essentially this amounts to inserting a chunk of code to a data mining program and thus operators are nothing but convenient visual mechanisms that will allow RapidMiner to be a GUI-driven application rather than a programming language like R or Python.

Process: A single operator by itself cannot perform data mining. All data mining and predictive analytics problem solving require a series of calculations and logical operations. There is typically a certain flow to these problems: import data, clean and prepare data, train a model to learn the data, validate the model and rank its performance, then finally apply the model to score new and unseen data. All of these steps can be accomplished by connecting a number of different operators, each uniquely customized for a specific task as we saw earlier. When we connect such a series of operators together to accomplish the desired data mining, we have built a *process* that can be applied in other contexts. A process that is created visually in RapidMiner is stored by RapidMiner as platform-independent XML code that can be exchanged between RapidMiner users (Figure 13.6). This allows different users in different locations and on different platforms to run *your* RapidMiner process on *their* data with minimal reconfiguration. All you need to do is send the XML code of your process to your colleague across the aisle (or across the globe). They can simply copy and paste the xml code in the XML tab in the Design perspective and switch back to the Process tab (or view) to see the process in its visual representation and run it to execute the defined functionality.

13.2 DATA IMPORTING AND EXPORTING TOOLS

RapidMiner offers at least 20 different operators or ways to connect to your data. The data can be stored in a flat file such as a comma-separated values (CSV) file or spreadsheet, the data can be stored in a database such as a Microsoft Access table, or it can be stored in other proprietary formats such as SAS or Stata or SPSS, etc. If your data is in a database, you need to have at least a basic understanding of databases, database connections and queries

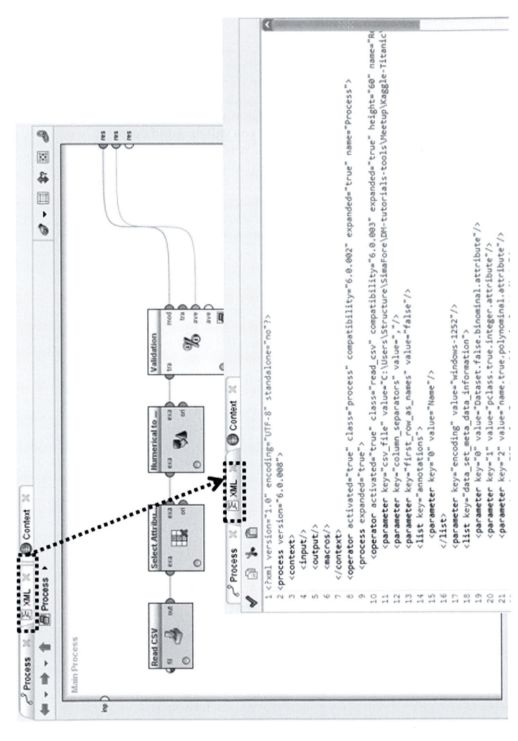

FIGURE 13.6

Every process is automatically translated to an XML document.

in order to use the operator properly. You may choose to simply connect to your data (which is stored in a specific location on disk) or you may choose to import the data set into your local RapidMiner repository itself so that it becomes available for any process within your repository and every time you open RapidMiner, this data set is available for retrieval. Either way, RapidMiner offers easy-to-follow wizards that will guide you through the steps. As you can see in Figure 13.7, when you choose to simply connect to data in a CSV file on disk using a *Read CSV* operator, you will drag and drop the operator to the main process window. Then you need to configure the *Read CSV* operator by clicking on the Import Configuration Wizard, which will lead you through a sequence of steps to read the data in.[2] The search box at the top of the operator window is also very useful—if one knows even part of the operator name then it's easy to find out if RapidMiner provides such an operator. For example, to see if there is an operator to handle CSV files, type "CSV" in the search field and both Read and Write will show up. Clear the search by hitting the red X. Using search is a quick way to navigate to the operators if you know some part of their name. Similarly try "principal" and you see the operator for principal component analysis even though you might not know where to look initially. Also, this search shows you the hierarchy of where the operators exist, which helps one learn where they are.

On the other hand, if you choose to import the data into your local Rapid-Miner repository, you can click on the green down arrow in the Repositories tab (as shown in Figure 13.7) and select Import CSV File. You will immediately be presented with the same five-step data import wizard. In either case, the data import wizard consists of the following steps:

1. Select the file on the disk that should be read or imported.
2. Specify how the file should be parsed and how the columns are delimited. If your data has a comma "," as the column separator in the configuration parameters, be sure to select it. By default, RapidMiner assumes that a ";" (semicolon) is the separator.
3. Annotate the attributes by indicating if the first row of your data set contains attribute names (which is usually the case). If you data set has first row names, then RapidMiner will automatically indicate this as "Name. If the first few rows of your data set has text or information, you will have to indicate that for each of the example rows. The available annotation choices are "Name," "Comment," and "Unit." See the example in Figure 13.8.

---

[2]For this and the next few sections we will use the data from the Indian Liver Patients data set available here: http://archive.ics.uci.edu/ml/machine-learning-databases/00225/.

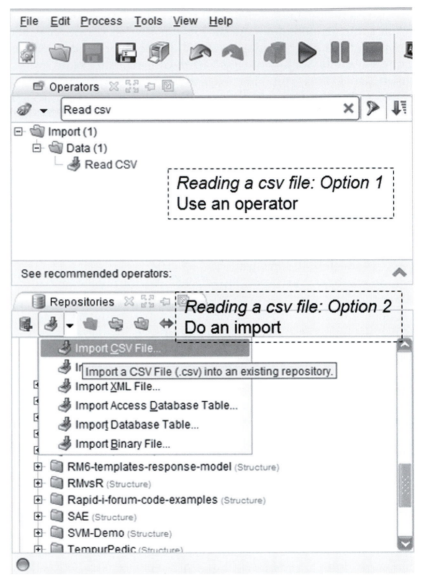

FIGURE 13.7
Steps to read in a comma-separated values (CSV) file.

4. In this step we can change the data type of any of the imported attributes and identify whether each column or attribute are "regular" attributes or special ones. By default, RapidMiner autodetects the data types in each column. However, sometimes we may need to override this and indicate if a particular column is of a different data type. The

Data import wizard - Step 3 of 5

This wizard guides you to import your data.
Step 3: In RapidMiner Studio, each attribute can be annotated. The most important annotation of an attribute is its name - a row with this annotation defines the names of the attributes. If your data does not contain attribute names, do not set this property. If further annotations are contained in the rows of your data file, you can assign them here.

Annotation	att1	att2	att3	att4	att5	att6	att7	att8	att9	att10	att11
Name	Age	Gender	Total Bilirubi	Direct Bilirut	Alkaline Pho	Alamine Ami	Aspartate An	Total Protien	Albumin	Albumin and	Disease (Y=
Comment	age of the re	gender of the	measured	measured	estimated	calculated	estimated	calculated	measuted	measured	estimated
-	years	***	mg	mg	***	mm	mm	mg	mg	mm	***
-	65	Female	0.7	0.1	187	16	18	6.8	3.3	0.9	1
Name	62	Male	10.9	5.5	699	64	100	7.5	3.2	0.74	1
Comment	62	Male	7.3	4.1	490	60	68	7	3.3	0.89	1
Unit	58	Male	1	0.4	182	14	20	6.8	3.4	1	1
.	72	Male	3.9	2	195	27	59	7.3	2.4	0.4	1
.	46	Male	1.8	0.7	208	19	14	7.6	4.4	1.3	1
.	26	Female	0.9	0.2	154	16	12	7	3.5	1	1
.	29	Female	0.9	0.3	202	14	11	6.7	3.6	1.1	1
.	17	Male	0.9	0.3	202	22	19	7.4	4.1	1.2	2
.	55	Male	0.7	0.2	290	53	58	6.8	3.4	1	1
.	57	Male	0.6	0.1	210	51	59	5.9	2.7	0.8	1
.	72	Male	2.7	1.3	260	31	56	7.4	3	0.6	1
.	64	Male	0.9	0.3	310	61	58	7	3.4	0.9	2
.	74	Female	1.1	0.4	214	22	30	8.1	4.1	1	1
.	61	Male	0.7	0.2	145	53	41	5.8	2.7	0.87	1
.	25	Male	0.6	0.1	183	91	53	5.5	2.3	0.7	2
.	38	Male	1.8	0.8	342	168	441	7.6	4.4	1.3	1
.	33	Male	1.6	0.5	165	15	23	7.3	3.5	0.92	2
.	40	Female	0.9	0.3	293	232	245	6.8	3.1	0.8	1
.	40	Female	0.9	0.3	293	232	245	6.8	3.1	0.8	1
.	51	Male	2.2	1	610	17	28	7.3	2.6	0.55	1
.	51	Male	2.9	1.3	482	22	34	7	2.4	0.5	1
.	62	Male	6.8	3	542	116	66	6.4	3.1	0.9	1
.	40	Male	1.9	1	231	16	55	4.3	1.6	0.6	1
.	63	Male	0.9	0.2	194	52	45	6	3.9	1.85	2

Previous   Next   Finish   Cancel

FIGURE 13.8
Properly annotating the data.

special attributes are columns that are used for identification (e.g., patient ID or employee ID or transaction ID) only or attributes that are to be predicted. These are called "label" attributes in RapidMiner terminology.

5. In this last step, if you are connecting to the data on disk using Read CSV, you simply hit Finish and you are done (Figure 13.9). If you are importing the data into a RapidMiner repository (using Import CSV File), you will be asked to specify the location in the repository for this.

When this process is finished, you should have either a properly connected data source on disk (for Read CSV) or a properly imported example set in your repository that you can use for any data mining process. Exporting

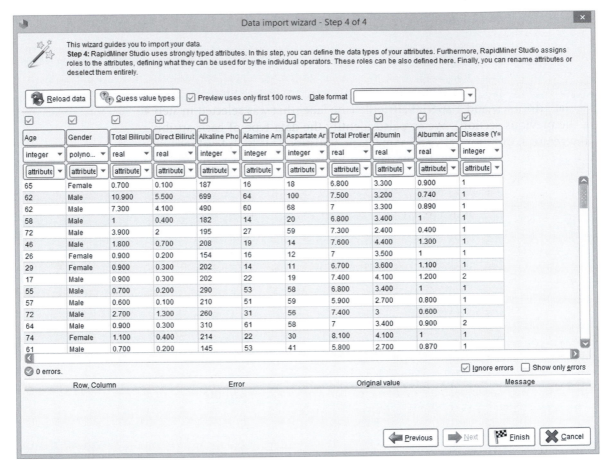

FIGURE 13.9
Finishing the data import.

data from RapidMiner is possible in a similar way using the *Write CSV* operator.

13.3 DATA VISUALIZATION TOOLS

Once you read a data set into RapidMiner, the next step is to explore the data set visually using a variety of tools. Before we jump into visualization, however, it is a good idea to check the metadata of the imported data to verify if we managed to get all the correct information. When the simple process described in Section 13.2 is run (be sure to connect the output of the read operator to the "res"ult connector of the process), we will get an output posted to the Results perspective of RapidMiner. You can see the data table to verify that indeed the data has been correctly imported under the *Data* tab on the left (see Figure 13.10).

By clicking on the Statistics tab (see Figure 13.11), we can examine the type, missing values, and basic statistics for all the imported data set attributes. Together the data and statistics tabs can tell us that there are 583 samples, 10 regular attributes, and 1 special attribute (the label that was selected in step 4 of the previous section). We can also identify the data type of each attribute (integer, real, or binomial), and some basic statistics. This high-level overview is a good way to ensure that your data set has been loaded correctly and you can now attempt to explore the data in more detail using the visualization tools described below.

There are a variety of visualization tools available for univariate (one attribute), bivariate (two attributes), and multivariate analysis. Select the Charts tab in the Results perspective to access any of the visualization tools or plotter. General details about visualization are available in Chapter 3 Data Exploration.

13.3.1 Univariate Plots
- **Histogram:** A density estimation for numeric plots and a counter for categorical ones.
- **Quartile (Box and Whisker):** Shows the mean value, median, standard deviation, some percentiles, and any outliers for each attribute.
- **Series (or Line):** Usually best used for time series data.

13.3.2 Bivariate Plots
All 2D and 3D charts show dependencies between tuples (pairs, triads) of variables.[3]

- **Scatter:** The simplest of all 2D charts, which shows how one variable changes with respect to another. RapidMiner allows the use of color; you can color the points to add a third dimension to the visualization.
- **Scatter Multiple:** Allows you to fix one axis to one variable while cycling through the other attributes.
- **Scatter Matrix:** Lets you look at all possible pairings between attributes. Color as usual adds a third dimension. Be careful with this plotter because as the number of attributes increase, rendering all the charts can slow down processing.

---

[3]A 2D plot can also depict three dimensions, for example using color. Bubble plots can even depict four dimensions! This categorization is done somewhat loosely.

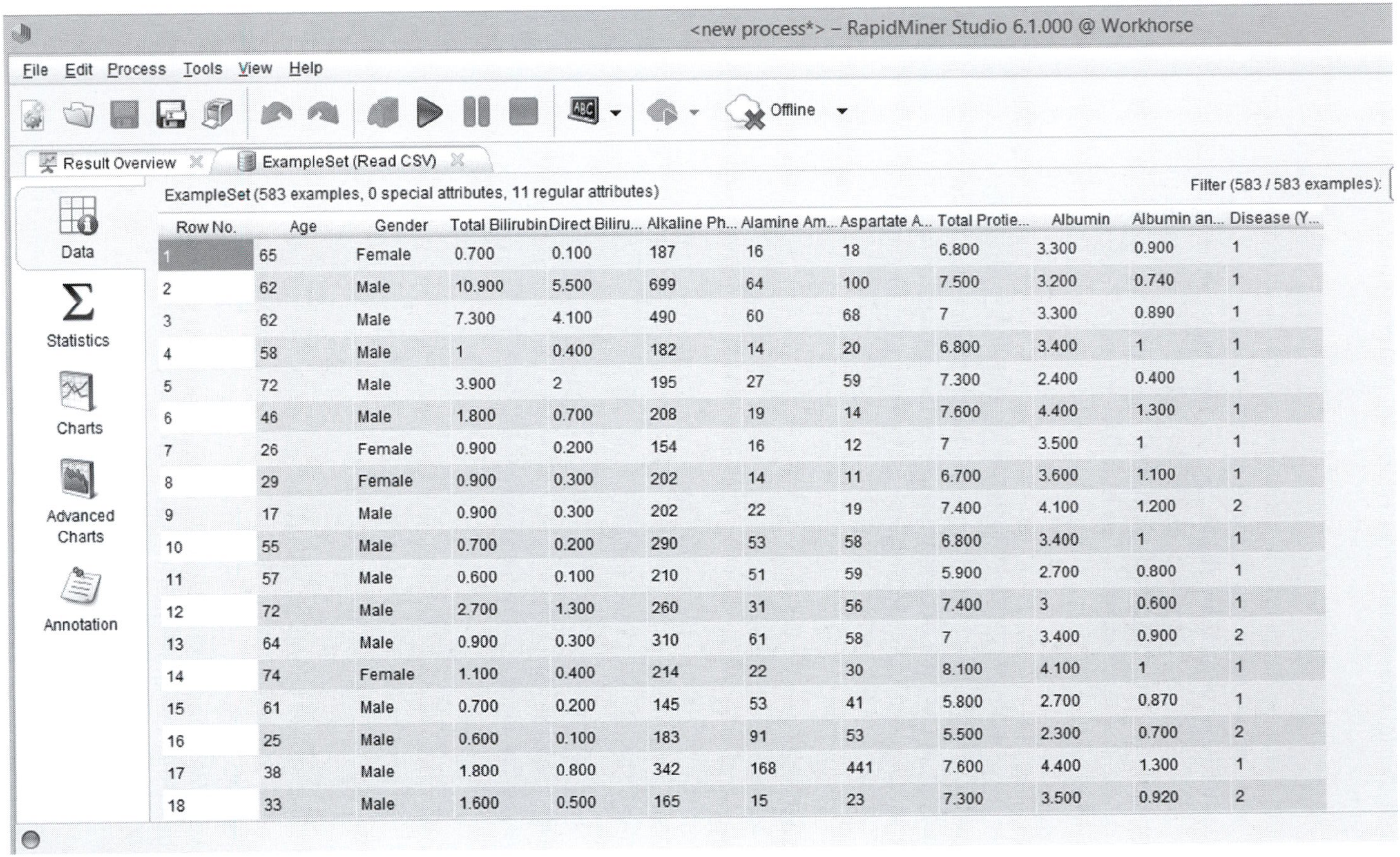

<new process*> – RapidMiner Studio 6.1.000 @ Workhorse
File Edit Process Tools View Help
Offline
Result Overview
ExampleSet (Read CSV)
Data
Statistics
Charts
Advanced Charts
Annotation
ExampleSet (583 examples, 0 special attributes, 11 regular attributes)
Filter (583 / 583 examples):

Row No.	Age	Gender	Total Bilirubin	Direct Biliru...	Alkaline Ph...	Alamine Am...	Aspartate A...	Total Protie...	Albumin	Albumin an...	Disease (Y...
1	65	Female	0.700	0.100	187	16	18	6.800	3.300	0.900	1
2	62	Male	10.900	5.500	699	64	100	7.500	3.200	0.740	1
3	62	Male	7.300	4.100	490	60	68	7	3.300	0.890	1
4	58	Male	1	0.400	182	14	20	6.800	3.400	1	1
5	72	Male	3.900	2	195	27	59	7.300	2.400	0.400	1
6	46	Male	1.800	0.700	208	19	14	7.600	4.400	1.300	1
7	26	Female	0.900	0.200	154	16	12	7	3.500	1	1
8	29	Female	0.900	0.300	202	14	11	6.700	3.600	1.100	1
9	17	Male	0.900	0.300	202	22	19	7.400	4.100	1.200	2
10	55	Male	0.700	0.200	290	53	58	6.800	3.400	1	1
11	57	Male	0.600	0.100	210	51	59	5.900	2.700	0.800	1
12	72	Male	2.700	1.300	260	31	56	7.400	3	0.600	1
13	64	Male	0.900	0.300	310	61	58	7	3.400	0.900	2
14	74	Female	1.100	0.400	214	22	30	8.100	4.100	1	1
15	61	Male	0.700	0.200	145	53	41	5.800	2.700	0.870	1
16	25	Male	0.600	0.100	183	91	53	5.500	2.300	0.700	2
17	38	Male	1.800	0.800	342	168	441	7.600	4.400	1.300	1
18	33	Male	1.600	0.500	165	15	23	7.300	3.500	0.920	2

FIGURE 13.10

Results perspective that is shown when the data import process is successful.

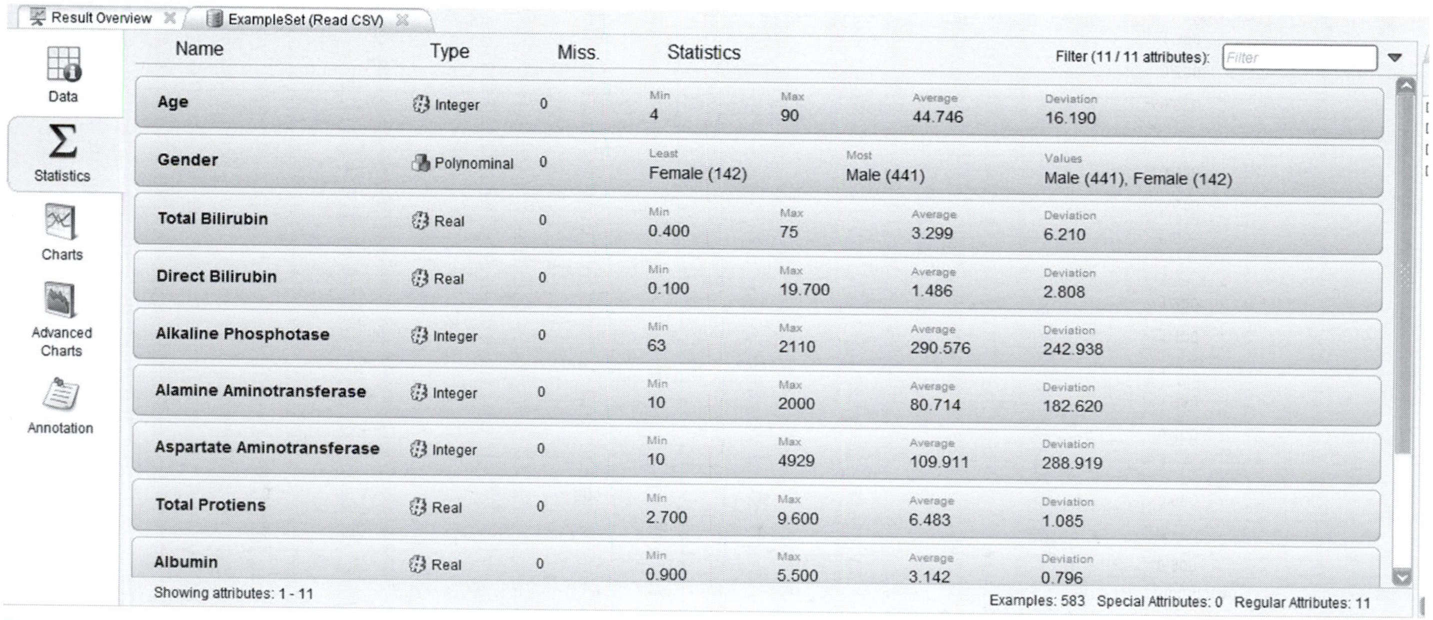

FIGURE 13.11

Metadata is visible under the Statistics tab.

- **Density:** Similar to a 2D scatter chart, except the background may be filled in with a color gradient corresponding to one of the attributes.
- **SOM:** Stands for a self-organizing map. It reduces the number of dimensions to two by applying transformations. Points that are "similar" along many attributes will be placed close together. It is basically a clustering visualization method. More details are in Chapter 8 on clustering. Note that SOM (and many of the parameterized reports) does not run automatically so if you switch to that report you will see a blank screen until the inputs are set and the in the case of SOM the "calculate" button is pushed.

13.3.3 Multivariate Plots

- **Parallel:** Uses one vertical axis for each attribute, thus there are as many vertical axes as there are attributes. Each row is displayed as a line in the chart. Local normalization is useful to understand the variance in each variable. However, a deviation plot works better for this.
- **Deviation:** Same as parallel, but displays mean values and standard deviations.
- **Scatter 3D:** Very similar to the scatter 2D chart but allows a three-dimensional visualization of three attributes (four, if you include the color of the points)
- **Surface:** A surface plot is a 3D version of an area plot where the background is filled in.

These are not the only available plotters. Some additional ones are not described here such as pie, bar, ring, block charts, etc. Generating any of the plots using the GUI is pretty much self-explanatory. The only words of caution are that when you have a large data set, generating some of the graphics intensive multivariate plots can be quite time consuming depending upon the available RAM and processor speed.

13.4 DATA TRANSFORMATION TOOLS

Many times the raw data is in a form that is not ideal for applying standard machine learning algorithms. For example, suppose you have categorical attributes such as gender, and you want to predict purchase amounts based on (among several other attributes) the gender. In this case you want to convert the categorical (or nominal) attributes into numeric ones by a process called "dichotomization." In the example above, we introduce two new variables called Gender=Male and Gender=Female, which can take (numeric) values of 0 or 1.

In other cases, you may have numeric data but your algorithm can only handle categorical or nominal attributes. A good example is where the label variable being numeric (such as the market price of a home in the Boston Housing example set discussed in Chapter 6 on regression) and you want to use logistic regression to predict if the price will be higher or lower than a certain threshold. Here we want to convert a numeric attribute into a binomial one.

In either of these cases, we may need to transform underlying data types into some other types. This activity is a very common data preparation step. The four most common data type conversion operators are the following:

- **Numerical to Binominal:** The *Numerical to Binominal* operator changes the type of numeric attributes to a binary type. Binominal attributes can have only two possible values: true or false. If the value of an attribute is between a specified minimal and maximal value, it becomes false; otherwise it is true. In the case of the market price example, our threshold market price is $30,000. Then all prices from $0 to $30,000 will be mapped to false and any price above $30,000 is mapped to true.
- **Nominal to Binominal:** Here if a nominal attribute with the name "Outlook" and possible nominal values "sunny," "overcast," and "rain'"is transformed, the result is a set of three binominal attributes, "Outlook = sunny," "Outlook = overcast," and "Outlook = rain" whose possible values can be true or false. Examples (or rows) of the original data set where the Outlook attribute had values equal to sunny, will, in the transformed example set, have the value of the attribute Outlook = sunny set to true, while the value of the Outlook = overcast and Outlook = rain attributes will be false.
- **Nominal to Numerical:** This works exactly like the *Nominal to Binominal* operator if you use the "Dummy coding" option, except that instead of true/false values, we will see 0/1 (binary values). If you use "unique integers" option, each of the nominal values will get assigned a unique integer from 0 and up. For example, if Outlook was sunny, then "sunny" gets replaced by the value 1, "rain" may get replaced by 2, and "overcast" may get replaced by 0.
- **Numerical to Polynominal:** Finally, this operator simply changes the type (and internal representation) of selected attributes, i.e., every new numeric value is considered to be another possible value for the polynominal attribute. In the golf example, the Temperature attribute has 12 unique values ranging from 64 to 85. Each value is considered a unique nominal value. As numeric attributes can have a huge number of different values even in a small range, converting such a numeric attribute to polynominal form will generate a huge number of possible values for the new attribute. A more sophisticated transformation method uses the discretization operator, which is discussed next.
- **Discretization:** When converting numeric attributes to polynominal, it is best to specify how to set up the discretization to avoid the previously

mentioned problem of generating a huge number of possible values—you do not want each numeric value to appear as an unique nominal one, but rather have them binned into some intervals. We can discretize the Temperature in the golf example by several methods: we can discretize using equal-sized bins with the *Discretize by Binning* operator. If we select two bins (default) we will have two equal ranges: [below 74.5] and [above 74.5], where 74.5 is the average value of 64 and 85. Based on the actual Temperature value, the example will be assigned into one of the two bins. We can instead specify the number of rows falling into each bin (*Discretize by Size* operator) rather than equal bin ranges. We can also discretize by bins of equal number of occurrences by choosing to *Discretize by Frequency*, for example. Probably the most useful option is to *Discretize by User Specification*. Here we can explicitly provide ranges for breaking down a continuous numeric attribute into several distinct categories or nominal values using the table shown in Figure 13.12a. The output of the operator performing that discretization is shown in Figure 13.12b.

Sometimes we may need to transform the structure of an example set or "rotate it" about one of the attributes, a process commonly known as "pivoting" or creating *pivot tables*. Here is a simple example of why we would need to do this operation. The table consists of three attributes: a customer ID, a product ID and a numeric measure called Consumer Price Index (CPI) (see Figure 13.13a). We see that this simple example has 10 unique customers and 2 unique product IDs. What we would like to do is to rearrange the data set so that we have two columns corresponding to the two product IDs and aggregate[4] or group the CPI data by customer IDs. This is because we would like to analyze data on the customer level, which means that each row has to represent one customer and all customer features have to be encoded as attribute values.

This is accomplished simply with the *Pivot* operator. We select "customer id" as the group attribute and "product id" as the index attribute as shown in Figure 13.13b. If you are familiar with Microsoft Excel's pivot tables, the group attribute parameter is similar to "row label" and the index attribute is akin to "column label." The result of the pivot operation is shown in Figure 13.13c.

A converse of the *Pivot* operator is the *De-pivot* operator, which reverses the process described above and may sometimes also be required during our data preparation steps. In general a *De-pivot* operator converts a pivot table into a relational structure.

---

[4]CAUTION: The *Pivot* operator does not aggregate! If the source data set contains combinations of product ID and customer ID occurring multiple times, you would have to aggregate before applying the *Pivot* operator in order to produce a data set containing only unique combinations first.

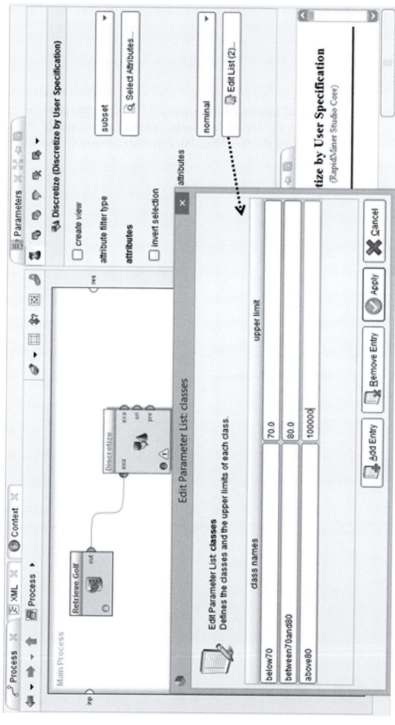

FIGURE 13.12a

Discretize operator.

ExampleSet (14 examples, 1 special attribute, 4 regular attributes)

Row No.	Play	Outlook	Temperature	Humidity	Wind
1	no	sunny	85	85	false
2	no	sunny	80	90	true
3	yes	overcast	83	78	false
4	yes	rain	70	96	false
5	yes	rain	68	80	false
6	no	rain	65	70	true
7	yes	overcast	64	65	true
8	no	sunny	72	95	false
9	yes	sunny	69	70	false
10	yes	rain	75	80	false
11	yes	sunny	75	70	true
12	yes	overcast	72	90	true
13	yes	overcast	81	75	false
14	no	rain	71	80	true

ExampleSet (14 examples, 1 special attribute, 4 regular attributes)

Row No.	Play	Temperature	Outlook	Humidity	Wind
1	no	above80	sunny	85	false
2	no	between70and80	sunny	90	true
3	yes	above80	overcast	78	false
4	yes	below70	rain	96	false
5	yes	below70	rain	80	false
6	no	below70	rain	70	true
7	yes	below70	overcast	65	true
8	no	between70and80	sunny	95	false
9	yes	below70	sunny	70	false
10	yes	between70and80	rain	80	false
11	yes	between70and80	sunny	70	true
12	yes	between70and80	overcast	90	true
13	yes	above80	overcast	75	false
14	no	between70and80	rain	80	true

FIGURE 13.12b

The output of the operation.

customer id	product id	CPI
c1	v1	0.97
c2	v1	0.86
c3	v1	missing
c4	v1	0.53
c5	v1	0.33
c7	v1	0.19
c9	v1	0.65
c10	v1	0.44
c1	v2	0.79
c2	v2	0.6
c3	v2	0.73
c4	v2	0.66
c5	v2	0.78
c6	v2	missing
c7	v2	missing
c8	v2	0.04
c9	v2	0.91
c10	v2	0.42

There are 2 missing entries corresponding to customer ids 6 and 8 for product id v1.

However the resulting pivot table will have 10x2=20 entries because there are 10 customers (c1:c10) and 2 products (v1,v2).

Note that missing values ("missing" in the CPI column) are different from missing entries!

FIGURE 13.13a

A simple data set to explain the pivot operation using RapidMiner.

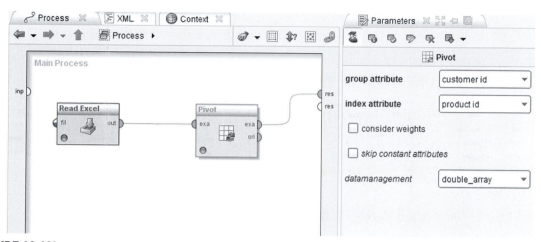

FIGURE 13.13b
Configuring the Pivot operator.

ExampleSet (10 examples, 0 special attributes, 3 regular attributes)

Row No.	customer id	CPI_v1	CPI_v2
1	c1	0.97	0.79
2	c10	0.44	0.42
3	c2	0.86	0.6
4	c3	missing	0.73
5	c4	0.53	0.66
6	c5	0.33	0.78
7	c6	?	missing
8	c7	0.19	missing
9	c8	?	0.04
10	c9	0.65	0.91

Column labels are prefixed by the name of the column label attribute

Missing entries from the original table become missing values

FIGURE 13.13c
Results of the pivot operation.

In addition to these operators, you may also need to use the *Append* operator to add examples to an existing data set. Appending an example set with new rows (examples) works as the name sounds—you end up attaching the new rows to the end of the example set. You have to make sure that the examples match the attributes exactly with the main data set. Also useful is the classic *Join* operator, which combines two example sets with the same observations units but different attributes. The *Join* operator offers the traditional inner, outer, and left and right join options. An explanation for joins is available in any of the books that deal with SQL programming as well as the RapidMiner help, which also provides example processes. We will not repeat them here.

Some of other common operators we have used in the various chapters of the book (and are explained there in context) are:

- Rename attributes
- Select attributes
- Filter examples
- Add attributes
- Attribute weighting

13.5 SAMPLING AND MISSING VALUE TOOLS

Data sampling might seem out of place in today's big data–charged environments. Why bother to sample when we can collect and analyze all the data we can? Sampling is a perhaps a vestige of the statistical era when data was costly to acquire and computational effort was costlier still. However there are many situations today with almost limitless computing capability, where "targeted" sampling is of use. A typical scenario is when building models on data where some class representations are very, very low. Consider the case of fraud prediction. Depending upon the industry, fraudulent examples range from less than 1% of all the data collected to about 2 to 3%. When we build classification models using such data, our models tend to be biased and would not be able to detect fraud in a majority of the cases with new unseen data, literally because they have not "learned" well enough!

Such situations call for "balancing" data sets where we need to *sample* our training data and increase the proportion of the minority class so that our models can be trained better. The plot in Figure 13.14 shows an example of imbalanced data: the "positive" class indicated by a circle is disproportionately higher than the "negative" class indicated by a cross.

Let us explore this using a simple example. The data set shown in the process in Figure 13.15 is available in RapidMiner's Samples repository and is called "Weighting." This is a balanced data set consisting of about 500 examples with the label variable consisting of roughly 50% "positive" and 50% "negative" classes. Thus it is a balanced data set. When we train a decision tree to classify this data, we get an overall accuracy of 84%. The main thing to note here is that the decision tree recall on both the classes is roughly the same: ~86% as seen in Figure 13.15.

We now introduce a subprocess called "Unbalance," which will resample the original data to introduce a skew: the resulting data set has more "positive" class examples than "negative" class examples. Specifically, we now have a data set with 92% belonging to the positive class (92% class recall) and 8% belonging

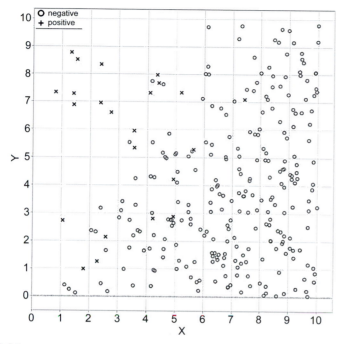

FIGURE 13.14

Snapshot of an imbalanced data set

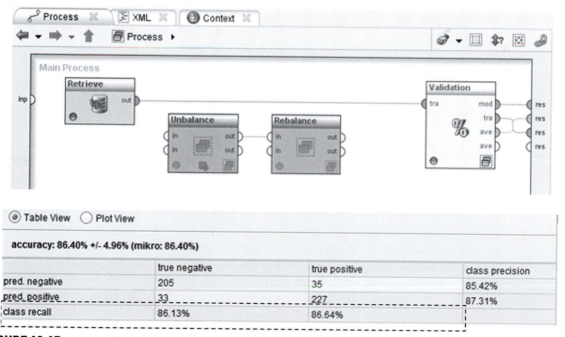

accuracy: 86.40% +/- 4.96% (mikro: 86.40%)

	true negative	true positive	class precision
pred. negative	205	35	85.42%
pred. positive	33	227	87.31%
class recall	86.13%	86.64%	

FIGURE 13.15

Performance of decision trees on well-balanced data.

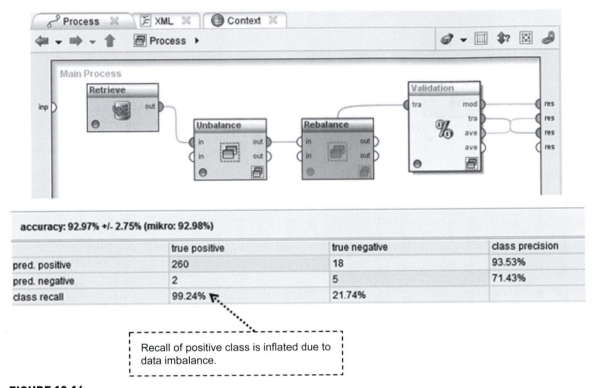

accuracy: 92.97% +/- 2.75% (mikro: 92.98%)

	true positive	true negative	class precision
pred. positive	260	18	93.53%
pred. negative	2	5	71.43%
class recall	99.24%	21.74%	

Recall of positive class is inflated due to data imbalance.

FIGURE 13.16
Unbalanced data and the resulting accuracy.

to negative class (8% class recall). The process and the results are shown in Figure 13.16. So how do we address this data imbalance?

There are several ways to fix this situation. The most commonly used method is to resample the data to restore the balance. This involves under-sampling the more frequent class—in our case, the "positive" class—and oversampling the less frequent "negative" class. The "rebalance" subprocess achieves this in our final RapidMiner process. As seen in Figure 13.17, the overall accuracy is now back to the level of the original balanced data. The decision tree also looks a little bit similar to the original, whereas for the unbalanced dataset it was reduced to a stub. An additional check to ensure that accuracy is not compromised by unbalanced data is to replace the accuracy by what is called "balanced accuracy." It is defined as the arithmetic mean of the class recall accuracies, which represent the accuracy obtained on positive and negative examples, respectively. If the decision tree performs equally well on either class, this term reduces to the standard accuracy (i.e., the number of correct predictions divided by the total number of predictions).

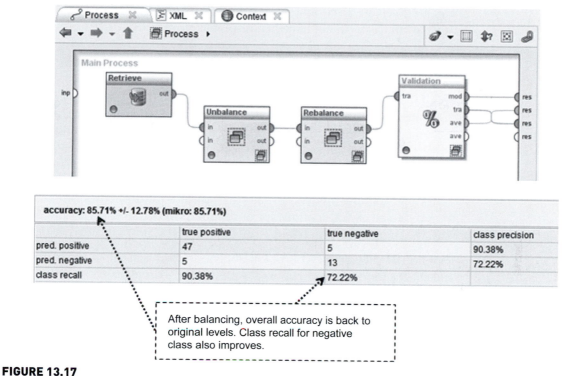

	true positive	true negative	class precision
pred. positive	47	5	90.38%
pred. negative	5	13	72.22%
class recall	90.38%	72.22%	

accuracy: 85.71% +/- 12.78% (mikro: 85.71%)

After balancing, overall accuracy is back to original levels. Class recall for negative class also improves.

FIGURE 13.17

Rebalanced data and resulting improvement in class recall.

There are several built-in RapidMiner processes to perform sampling: Sample, Sample (Bootstrapping), Sample (stratified), Sample (Model-Based), and Sample (Kennard-Stone). Specific details about these techniques are well described in the software help. We want to only remark on the Bootstrapping method here because it is a very common sampling technique. Bootstrapping works by sampling repeatedly within a base data set with replacement. So when you use this operator to generate new samples, you may see repeated or nonunique examples. You have the option of specifying an absolute sample size or a relative sample size and RapidMiner will randomly pick examples from your base data set with replacement to build a new bootstrapped example set.

We will close this section with a brief description of missing value handling options available in RapidMiner. The basic operator is called *Replace Missing Values*. This operator provides several alternative ways to replace missing values: minimum, maximum, average, zero, none, and a user-specified value. There is no median value option. Basically, all missing values in a given column (attribute) are replaced by whatever option is chosen. A better way to treat missing values is to use the *Impute Missing Values* operator. This operator changes the attribute with missing values to a label or target variable, and trains models to determine the relationship between this label variable and other attributes so that it may then be predicted.

13.6 OPTIMIZATION TOOLS[5]

Recall that in Chapter 5 on decision trees, we were presented with an opportunity to specify parameters to build a decision tree for the credit risk example (Section 4.1.2, step 3) but simply chose to use default values. Similar situations arose when building a support vector machine model (Section 4.6.3) or logistic regression model (Section 5.2.3), where also we chose to simply use the default model parameter values. When we run a model evaluation, the performance of the model is usually an indicator as to whether we chose the right parameter combinations for our model.[6] But what if we are not happy with the model accuracy (or its r-squared value)? Can we improve it? How?

RapidMiner provides several unique operators that will allow us to discover and choose the best combination of parameters for pretty much all of the available operators that need parameter specifications. The fundamental principle on which this works is the concept of a "nested" operator. We first encountered a nested operator in Section 4.1.2, step 2—the *Split Validation* operator. We also described another nested operator in Section 12.5 in the discussion on wrapper-style feature selection methods. The basic idea is to iteratively change the parameters for a learner until some stated performance criteria are met. The *Optimize* operator performs two tasks: determine what values to set for the selected parameters for each iteration, and determine when to stop the iterations. RapidMiner provides three basic methods to set parameter values: grid search, greedy search, and an evolutionary search (also known as genetic) method. We will not go deep into the workings of each method, but only do a high-level comparison between them and mention when each approach would be applicable.

To demonstrate the working of an optimization process, we will consider a very simple model: a polynomial function (Figure 13.18). Specifically, we have a function $y = f(x) = x^6 + x^3 - 7x^2 - 3x + 1$ and we wish to find the minimum value of y within a given domain of x. This is of course the simplest form of optimization—we want to select an interval of values for x where y is minimum. As seen in the functional plot, we see that for x in

---

[5]Readers may skip this section if completely new to RapidMiner, and return to it after developing some familiarity with the tool and data mining in general.

[6]Normally you can't judge from just one performance estimate whether you chose the right parameters. You'd have to see multiple performance values and their dependency on the parameter values to infer that you chose the right/optimal parameter values.

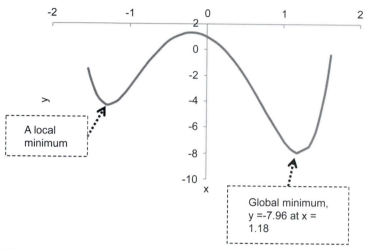

FIGURE 13.18

A simple polynomial function to demonstrate optimization.

[−1.5, 2], we have two minima: a local minimum of y = −4.33 @ x = −1.3 and a global minimum of y = −7.96 @ x = 1.18. We will show how to use RapidMiner to search for these minima using the *Optimize* operators. As mentioned before, the optimization happens in a nested operator, so we will describe what is placed inside the optimizer first before discussing the optimizer itself.

The nested process itself, also called the *inner* process, is very simple as seen in Figure 13.19a: *Generate Data* randomly generates values for "x" between an "upper bound" and a "lower bound" (see Figure 13.19b).

Generate Attributes will calculate "y" for each value of "x" in this interval. *Performance (Extract Performance)* will store the minimum value of "y" within each interval. This operator has to be configured as shown on the right of Figure 13.19a in order to ensure that the correct performance is optimized. In this case, we select "y" as the attribute that has to be minimized. The *Rename*, *Select Attributes*, and *Log* operators are plugged in to keep the process focused on only two variables and to track the progress of optimization.

This nested process can be inserted into any of the available *Optimize Parameters* operators. Let us describe how we do this with the *Optimize Parameters (Grid)* operator first. In this exercise, we are basically optimizing the interval [*lower bound, upper bound*] so that we achieve the objective of minimizing the function y = f(x). As we saw in the function plot, we wish to traverse the entire domain of "x" in small enough interval sizes so that we can catch the exact point at which "y" hits a global minimum.

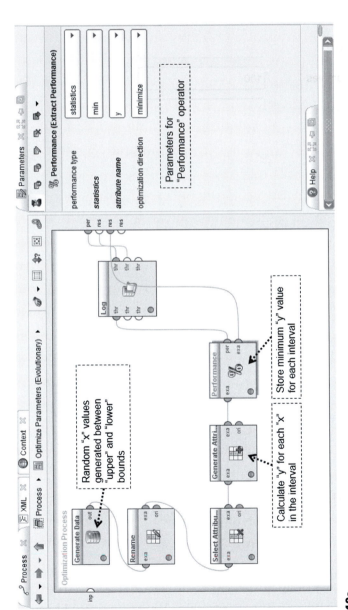

FIGURE 13.19a

The inner process that is nested inside an optimization loop.

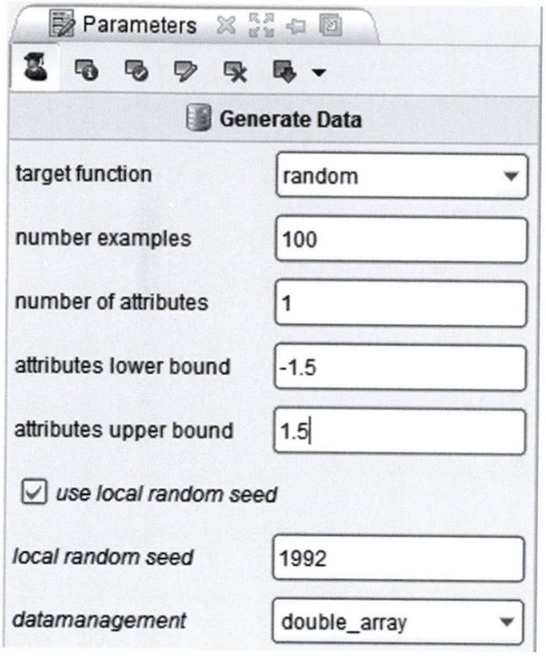

FIGURE 13.19b
Configuration of the generated data.

The grid search optimizer simply moves this interval window across the entire domain and stops the iterations after all the intervals are explored (Figure 13.20). Clearly it is an exhaustive but inefficient search method. To set this process up, we simply insert the inner process inside the outer *Optimize Parameters (Grid)* operator and select the *attributes upper bound* and *attributes lower bound* parameters from the *Generate Data* operator. To do this, we click on the *Edit Parameter Settings* option for the optimizer, select *Generate Data* under the *Operators* tab of the dialog box, and further select *attributes_upper_bound* and *attributes_lower_bound* under the *Parameters* tab (Figure 13.21).

We will need to provide ranges for the grid search for each of these parameters. In this case we set the lower bound to go from −1.5 to −1 and the upper bound to go from 0 to 1.5 in steps of 10. So the first interval (or window) will be x = [−1.5, 0], the second one will be [−1.45, 0] and so on until the last window, which will be [−1, 1.5] for a total of 121 iterations. The *Optimize Performance (Grid)* search will evaluate "y" for each of these windows, and store the minimum "y" in each iteration. The iterations will only stop after all 121 intervals are evaluated, but the final output will indicate the window that resulted in the smallest minimum "y." The plot in Figure 13.22 shows the progress of the iterations. Each point in the chart corresponds to the lowest value of y evaluated

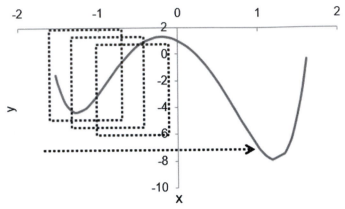

FIGURE 13.20
Searching for an optimum within a fixed window that slides across.

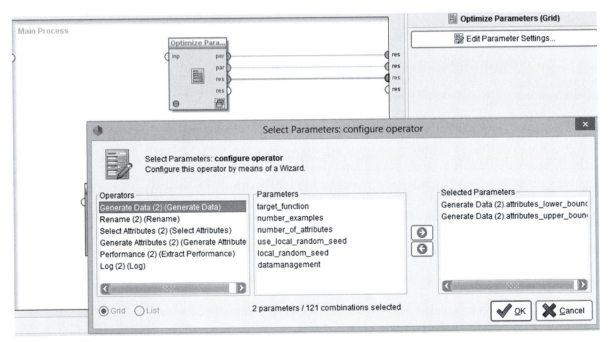

FIGURE 13.21
Configuring the grid search optimizer.

by the expression within a given interval. We find the local minimum of $y = -4.33$ @ $x = -1.3$ at the very first iteration. This corresponds to the window $[-1.5, 0]$. If the grid had not spanned the entire domain $[-1.5, 1.5]$, the optimizer would have reported the local minimum as the best performance. This is one of the main disadvantages of a grid search method.

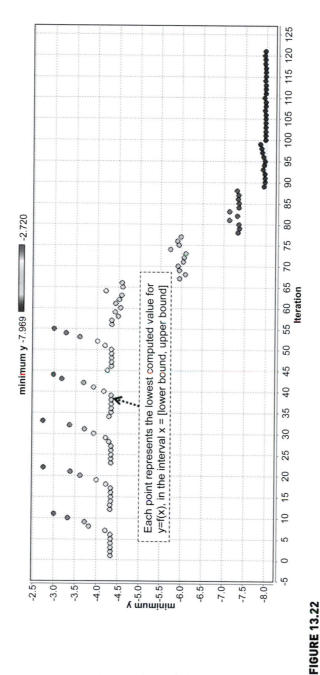

FIGURE 13.22

Progression of the grid search optimization.

The other disadvantage is the number of redundant iterations. Looking at the plot above, we see that the global minimum was reached by about the 90th iteration. In fact for iteration 90, $y_{minimum}$ = −7.962, whereas the final reported lowest $y_{minimum}$ was −7.969 (iteration 113), which is only about 0.09% better. Depending upon our tolerances, we could have terminated the computations earlier. But a grid search does not allow early terminations and we end up with nearly 30 extra iterations. Clearly as the number of optimization parameters increase, this ends up being a significant cost.

We next apply the *Optimize Parameters (Quadratic)* operator to our inner process. Quadratic search is based on a "greedy" search methodology. A greedy methodology is an optimization algorithm that makes a locally optimal decision at each step (Ahuja, 2000; Bahmani, 2013). While the decision may be locally optimal at the current step, it may not necessarily be the best for all future steps. k-nearest neighbor is one good example of a greedy algorithm. In theory, greedy algorithms will only yield local optima, but in special cases, they can also find globally optimal solutions. Greedy algorithms are best suited to find approximate solutions to difficult problems. This is because they are less computationally intense and tend to operate over a large data set quickly. Greedy algorithms are by nature typically biased toward coverage of large number of cases or a quick payback in the objective function.

In our case, the performance of the quadratic optimizer is marginally worse than a grid search requiring about 100 shots to hit the global minimum (compared to 90 for a grid), as seen in Figure 13.23. It also seems to suffer from some of the same problems we encountered in grid search.

We will finally employ the last available option: Optimize Parameters (Evolutionary). Evolutionary (or genetic) algorithms are often more appropriate than a grid search or a greedy search and lead to better results, This is because they cover a wider variety of the search space through mutation and can iterate onto good minima through cross-over of successful models based upon the success criteria. As we can see in the progress of iterations in Figure 13.24, we hit the global optimum without getting stuck initially at a local minimum—you can see that right from the first few iterations we have approached the neighborhood of the lowest point. The evolutionary method is particularly useful if we do not initially know the domain of the functions, unlike in this case where we did know. We see that it takes far fewer steps to get to the global minimum with a high degree of confidence—about 18 iterations as opposed to 90 or 100. Key concepts to understanding this algorithm are *mutation* and *cross-over*, both of which are possible to control using the RapidMiner GUI. More technical details of how the algorithm works are beyond the scope of this book and you can refer to some excellent resources listed at the end of this chapter (Weise, 2009).

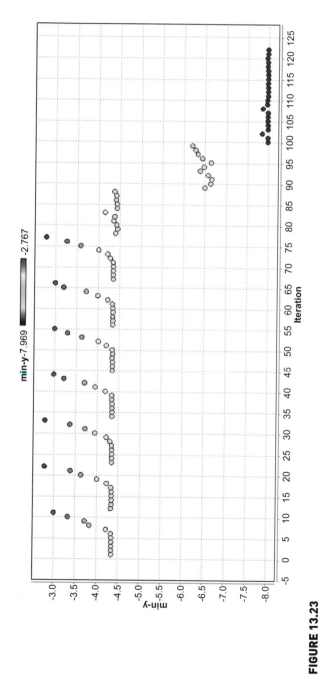

FIGURE 13.23

Progression of the quadratic greedy search optimization.

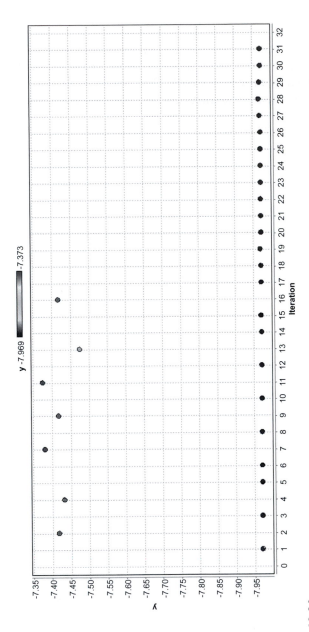

FIGURE 13.24
Progression of the genetic search optimization.

To summarize, there are three optimization algorithms available in Rapid-Miner all of which are nested operators. The best application of optimization is for the selection of modeling parameters, for example, split size, leaf size, or splitting criteria in a decision tree model. We build our machine learning process as usual and insert this process or "nest" it inside of the optimizer. By using the Edit Parameter Settings … control button, we can select the parameters of any of the inner process operators (for example a *Decision Tree* or *W-Logistic* or *SVM*) and define ranges to sweep. Grid search is an exhaustive search process for finding the right settings, but is expensive and cannot guarantee a global optimum. Evolutionary algorithms are very flexible and fast and are usually the best choice for optimizing machine learning models in RapidMiner.

CONCLUSION

As with other chapters in this book, the RapidMiner process explained and developed in this discussion can be accessed from the companion site of the book at www.LearnPredictiveAnalytics.com. The RapidMiner process (*.rmp files) can be downloaded to the computer and can be imported to RapidMiner from File > Import Process. The data files can be imported from File > Import Data.

This chapter provided a 30,000-foot view of the main tools that one would need to become familiar with in building predictive analytics models using RapidMiner. We started out by introducing the basic graphical user interface for the program. We then discussed options by which data can be brought into and exported out of RapidMiner. We provided an overview of the data visualization methods that are available within the tool, because quite naturally, the next step of any data mining process after ingesting the data is to understand in a descriptive sense the nature of the data. We then introduced tools that would allow us to transform and reshape the data by changing the type of the incoming data and restructuring them in different tabular forms to make subsequent analysis easier. We also introduced tools that would allow us to resample available data and account for any missing values. Once you are familiar with these essential data preparation options, you are in a position to apply any of the appropriate algorithms described in the earlier chapters for analysis. Finally, in Section 13.6 we introduced optimization operators that allow us to fine-tune our machine learning algorithms so that we can develop an optimized and good quality model to extract the insights we are looking for.

With this high-level overview, one can go back to any of the earlier chapters to learn about a specific technique and understand how to use RapidMiner to build models using that machine learning algorithm.

REFERENCES

Ahuja, R. O. (2000). A greedy genetic algorithm for quadratic assignment problem. *Computers and Operations Research*, 917–934.

Bahmani, S. R. (2013). Greedy Sparsity-Constrained Optimization. *Statistical Machine Learning*, 1–36.

Germano, T. (n.d.). Retrieved from http://davis.wpi.edu/~matt/courses/soms/.

International Monetary Fund (n.d.). Retrieved from http://www.imf.org/external/pubs/ft/weo/2012/02/weodata/index.aspx.

Mierswa, I. W. (2006). YALE: Rapid prototyping for complex data mining tasks. *Association for Computing Machinery – Knowledge Discovery in Databases*, 935–940.

Telecom, F. (n.d.). Retrieved from http://perso.rd.francetelecom.fr/lemaire/cours/Analyse-ExploratoireKohonen.pdf.

UC Irvine (n.d.). Data sets. Retrieved from http://archive.ics.uci.edu/ml/datasets.html.

UC Santa Barbara (n.d.). Retrieved from http://www.english.ucsb.edu/grad/student-pages/jdouglass/coursework/hyperliterature/soms/.

University of Pittsburg (n.d.). Retrieved from http://www.sis.pitt.edu/~ssyn/som/som.html.

Weise, T. (2009). Global Optimization Algorithms – Theory and Application. http://www.it-weise.de/.

Comparison of Data Mining Algorithms

Classification: Predicting a Categorical Target Variable

Algorithm	Description	Model	Input	Output	Pros	Cons	Use Cases
Decision Trees	Partitions the data into smaller subsets where each subset contains (mostly) responses of one class (either "yes" or "no")	A set of rules to partition a data set based on the values of the different predictors.	No restrictions on variable type for predictors.	The label cannot be numeric. It must be categorical.	Intuitive to explain to nontechnical business users. Normalizing predictors is not necessary.	Tends to overfit the data. Small changes in input data can yield substantially different trees. Selecting the right parameters can be challenging.	Marketing segmentation, fraud detection.
Rule Induction	Models the relationship between input and output by deducing simple IF/THEN rules from a data set.	A set of organized rules that contain an antecedent (inputs) and consequent (output class).	No restrictions. Accepts categorical, numeric, and binary inputs.	Prediction of target variable, which is categorical.	Model can be easily explained to business users. Easy to deploy in almost any tools and applications.	Divides the data set in rectilinear fashion.	Manufacturing, applications where description of model is necessary.
k-Nearest Neighbors	A lazy learner where no model is generalized. Any new unknown data point is compared against similar known data point in the training set.	Entire training data set is the model.	No restrictions. However, the distance calculations work better with numeric data. Data need to be normalized.	Prediction of target variable, which is categorical.	Requires very little time to build the model. Handles missing attributes in the unknown record gracefully. Works with nonlinear relationships.	The deployment runtime and storage requirements will be expensive. Arbitrary selection of value of k. No description of the model.	Image processing, applications where slower response time is acceptable.

Naïve Bayesian	Predicts the output class based on Bayes' theorem by calculating class conditional probability and prior probability.	A lookup table of probabilities and conditional probabilities for each attribute with an output class.	No restrictions. However, the probability calculation works better with categorical attributes	Prediction of probability for all class values, along with the winning class.	Time required to model and deploy is minimum. Great algorithm for benchmarking. Strong statistical foundation.	Training data set needs to be representative sample of population and needs to have complete combinations of input and output. Attributes need to be independent.	Spam detections, text mining.
Artificial Neural Networks	A computational and mathematical model inspired by the biological nervous system. The weights in the network learn to reduce the error between actual and prediction.	A network topology of layers and weights to process input data.	All attributes should be numeric.	Prediction of target (label) variable, which is categorical.	Good at modeling nonlinear relationships. Fast response time in deployment.	No easy way to explain the inner working of the model. Requires preprocessing data. Cannot handle missing attributes.	Image recognition, fraud detection, quick response time applications.

Continued

Classification: Predicting a Categorical Target Variable *Continued*

Algorithm	Description	Model	Input	Output	Pros	Cons	Use Cases
Support Vector Machines	Essentially a boundary detection algorithm that identifies/defines multidimensional boundaries separating data points belonging to different classes.	The model is a vector equation that allows us to classify new data points into different regions (classes).	All attributes should be numeric.	Prediction of target (label) variable, which can be categorical or numeric.	Very robust against overfitting. Small changes to input data do not affect boundary and thus do not yield different results. Good at handling nonlinear relationships.	Computational performance during training phase can be slow. This may be compounded by the effort needed to optimize parameter combinations.	Optical character recognition, fraud detection, modeling "black-swan" events.
Ensemble Models	Leverages wisdom of the crowd. Employs a number of independent models to make a prediction and aggregates the final prediction.	A meta-model with individual base models and a aggregator.	Superset of restrictions from the base model used.	Prediction for all class values with a winning class.	Reduces the generalization error.Takes different search space into consideration	Achieving model independence is tricky. Difficult to explain the inner working of the model.	Most of the practical classifiers are ensemble.

Regression: Predicting a Numeric Target Variable

Algorithm	Description	Model	Input	Output	Pros	Cons	Use Case
Linear Regression	The classical predictive model that expresses the relationship between inputs and an output parameter in the form of an equation.	The model consists of coefficients for each input predictor and their statistical significance. A bias (intercept) may be optional.	All attributes should be numeric.	The label may be numeric or binominal.	The workhorse of most predictive modeling techniques. Easy to use and explain to non-technical business users.	Cannot handle missing data. Categorical data are not directly usable, but require transformation into numeric.	Pretty much any scenario that requires predicting a continuous numeric value.
Logistic Regression	Technically, this is a classification method. But structurally it is similar to linear regression.	The model consists of coefficients for each input predictor that relate to the "logit." Transforming the logit into probabilities of occurrence (of each class) completes the model.	All attributes should be numeric.	The label may only be binominal.	One of the most common classification methods. Computationally efficient.	Cannot handle missing data. Not very intuitive when dealing with a large number of predictors.	Marketing scenarios (e.g., will click or not click), any general two-class problem.

Association Analysis: Unsupervised Process for Finding Relationships between Items

Algorithm	Description	Model	Input	Output	Pros	Cons	Use Case
FP Growth and Apriori	Measures the strength of co-occurrence between one item with another.	Finds simple, easy to understand rules like {Milk, Diaper} -> {Beer}	Trans-actions format with items in the columns and transactions in the rows.	List of relevant rules developed from the data set	Unsupervised approach with minimal user inputs. Easy to understand rules.	Requires prepro-cessing if input is of different format.	Recom-mendation engines, cross-selling, and content suggestions.

Clustering: An Unsupervised Process for Finding Meaningful Groups in Data

Algorithm	Description	Model	Input	Output	Pros	Cons	Use case
k-means	Data set is divided into k clusters by finding k centroids.	Algorithm find k centriods and all the data points are assigned to the nearest centriods, which form a cluster.	No restrictions. However, the distance calculations work better with numeric data. Data should be normalized.	Data set is appended by One of k cluster labels.	Simple to implement. Can be used for dimension reduction.	Specification of k is arbitrary and may not find natural clusters. Sensitive to outliers.	Customer segmentation, anomaly detection, applications where globular clustering is natural.
DBSCAN	Identifies clusters as a high-density area surrounded by low-density areas.	List of clusters and assigned data points. Default Cluster 0 contains noise points.	No restrictions. However, the distance calculations work better with numeric data. Data should be normalized.	Cluster labels based on identified clusters.	Finds the natural clusters of any shape. No need to mention number of clusters.	Specification of density parameters. A bridge between two clusters can merge the cluster. Can not cluster varying density data set.	Applications where clusters are nonglobular shapes and when the prior number of natural groupings is not known.
Self-Organizing Maps	A visual clustering technique with roots from neural networks and prototype clustering.	A two-dimensional lattice where similar data points are arranged next to each other.	No restrictions. However, the distance calculations work better with numeric data. Data should be normalized.	No explicit clusters identified. Similar data points occupy either the same cell or are placed next to each other in the neighborhood.	A visual way to explain the clusters. Reduces multidimensional data to two dimensions.	Number of centriods (topology) is specified by the user. Does not find natural clusters in the data.	Diverse applications including visual data exploration, content suggestions, and dimension reduction.

Anomaly Detection: Supervised and Unsupervised Techniques to Find Outliers in the Data

Algorithm	Description	Model	Input	Output	Pros	Cons	Use Case
Distance Based	Outlier identified based on distance if kth nearest neighbor.	All data points are assigned a distance score based on nearest neighbor.	Accepts both numeric and categorical attributes. Normalization is required since distance is calculated.	Every data point has a distance score. The higher the distance, the more likely the data point is an outlier.	Easy to implement. Works well with numeric attributes.	Specification of k is arbitrary.	Fraud detection, pre-processing technique.
Density Based	Outlier is identified based on data points in low-density regions.	All data points as assigned a density score based on the neighborhood.	Accepts both numeric and categorical attributes. Normalization is required since density is calculated.	Every data point has a density score. The lower the density, the more likely the data point is an outlier.	Easy to implement. Works well with numeric attributes.	Specification of distance parameter by the user. Inability to identify varying density regions.	Fraud detection, pre-processing technique.
Local outlier factor	Outlier is identified based on calculation of relative density in the neighborhood.	All data points as assigned a relative density score based on the neighborhood.	Accepts both numeric and categorical attributes. Normalization is required since density is calculated.	Every data point has a density score. The lower the relative density, the more likely the data point is an outlier	Can handle the varying density scenario.	Specification of distance parameter by the user.	Fraud detection, pre-processing technique.

Feature Selection: Selection of Most Important Attributes

Algorithm	Description	Model	Input	Output	Pros	Cons	Use Case
PCA (Filter Based)	PCA is in reality a dimension reduction method. It combines the most important attributes into a fewer number of transformed attributes.	N/A	Numerical attributes	Numerical attributes (reduced set). Does not really require a label.	Efficient way to extract predictors that are uncorrelated to each other. Helps to apply Pareto principle in identifying attributes with highest variance.	Very sensitive to scaling effects, i.e., requires normalization of attribute values before application. Focus on variance sometimes results in selecting noisy attributes.	Most numeric-valued data sets that require dimension reduction.
Info Gain (Filter Based)	Selecting attributes based on relevance to the target or label.	Similar to decision tree model.	No restrictions on variable type for predictors.	Data sets require a label. Can only be applied on data sets with nominal label.	Same as decision trees.	Same as decision trees.	Applications for feature selection where target variable is categorical or numeric.
Chi-Square (Filter Based)	Selecting attributes based on relevance to the target or label.	Uses the chi-square test of independence to relate predictors to label.	Categorical (poly-nominal) attributes	Data sets require a label. Can only be applied on data sets with a nominal label.	Very robust. A fast and efficient scheme to identify which categorical variables to select for a predictive model.	Sometimes difficult to interpret.	Applications for feature selection where all variables are categorical.

Continued

Feature Selection: Selection of Most Important Attributes *Continued*

Algorithm	Description	Model	Input	Output	Pros	Cons	Use Case
Forward Selection (Wrapper Based)	Selecting attributes based on relevance to the target or label.	Works in conjunction with modeling methods such as regression.	All attributes should be numeric.	The label may be numeric or binominal	Multicollinearity problems can be avoided. Speeds up the training phase of the modeling process	Once a variable is added to the set, it is never removed in subsequent iterations even if its influence on the target diminishes.	Data sets with a large number of input variables where feature selection is required.
Backward Elimination (Wrapper Based)	Selecting attributes based on relevance to the target or label.	Works in conjunction with modeling methods such as regression.	All attributes should be numeric.	The label may be numeric or binominal.	Multicollinearity problems can be avoided. Speeds up the training phase of the modeling process.	Need to begin with a full model, which can sometimes be computationally intensive.	Data sets with few input variables where feature selection is required.

Index

Note: Page numbers followed by "b", "f" and "t" indicate boxes, figures and tables respectively

About the Authors

Vijay Kotu

Vijay Kotu is Senior Director of Analytics at Yahoo. He leads the implementation of large-scale data and analytics systems to support the company's online business. He has practiced Analytics for over a decade with focus on business intelligence, data mining, web analytics, experimentation, information design, data warehousing, data engineering and developing analytical teams. Prior to joining Yahoo, he worked at Life Technologies and Adteractive where he led marketing analytics, created algorithms to optimize online purchasing behaviors, and developed data platforms to manage marketing campaigns. He is a member of the Association of Computing Machinery and is certified as a Six Sigma Black Belt by the American Society of Quality.

Bala Deshpande, PhD

Bala Deshpande is the founder of SimaFore, a custom analytics app development and consulting company. He has more than 20 years of experience in using analytical techniques in a wide range of application areas. His first exposure to predictive models and analytics was in the field of biomechanics, in identifying correlations and building multiple regression models. He began his career as an engineering consultant, following which he spent several years analyzing data from automobile crash tests and helping to build safer cars at Ford Motor Company. He is the co-chair of Predictive Analytics World–Manufacturing, an annual conference focused on promoting and evangelizing predictive analytics in the industry. He blogs regularly about data mining and predictive analytics for his company at www.simafore.com/blog. He holds a PhD in Bioengineering from Carnegie Mellon University and an MBA from the Ross School of Business (University of Michigan).